AF605846

Bluegrass Paradise

Bluegrass Paradise

Royal Spring and the Birth of Georgetown, Kentucky

GARY A. O'DELL

Scholarly publisher for the Commonwealth,
serving Bellarmine University, Berea College, Centre
College of Kentucky, Eastern Kentucky University,
The Filson Historical Society, Georgetown College,
Kentucky Historical Society, Kentucky State University,
Morehead State University, Murray State University,
Northern Kentucky University, Spalding University,
Transylvania University, University of Kentucky,
University of Louisville, University of Pikeville,
and Western Kentucky University.

Editorial and Sales Offices: The University Press of Kentucky
663 South Limestone Street, Lexington, Kentucky 40508–4008
www.kentuckypress.com

Library of Congress Cataloging-in-Publication Data

Names: O'Dell, Gary A., author.
Title: Bluegrass paradise : Royal Spring and the birth of Georgetown, Kentucky / Gary A. O'Dell.
Other titles: Royal Spring and the birth of Georgetown, Kentucky
Description: Lexington, Kentucky : University Press of Kentucky, [2023] | Includes bibliographical references and index.
Identifiers: LCCN 2022036151 | ISBN 9780813196718 (hardcover ; alk. paper) | ISBN 9780813196725 (pdf) | ISBN 9780813196732 (epub)
Subjects: LCSH: Water-supply—Kentucky—Georgetown—History. | Springs—Kentucky—Georgetown—History. | Royal Springs (Ky.)—History. | Georgetown (Ky.)—History.
Classification: LCC F459.G46 O34 2023 | DDC 976.9/425—dc23/eng/20221104
LC record available at https://lccn.loc.gov/2022036151

This book is printed on acid-free paper meeting
the requirements of the American National Standard
for Permanence in Paper for Printed Library Materials.

Manufactured in the United States of America

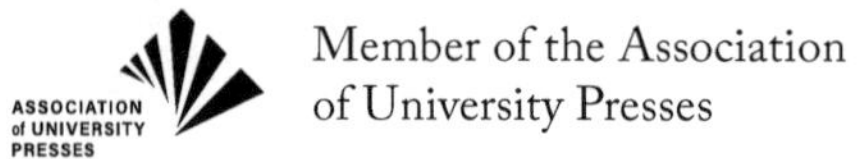

Contents

Preface vii
1. From Wilderness to City 1
2. The New Frontier 35
3. Bluegrass Paradise 60
4. A Goodly Land 74
5. The Land of Springs 101
6. Floyd's Spring 115
7. McClelland's Station 123
8. Serving God and Mammon 145
9. Clear Beautiful Spring Watter 155
10. Blue Grass Park and the Civil War 163
11. The Water Works 178
12. Who Owns Royal Spring? 187
13. Gulping Down Royal Spring Sewage 198
14. Protecting Royal Spring 219
15. A Dumping Ground Since Time Immemorial 234
16. Royal Spring Park 244
Acknowledgments 275
Notes 279
Index 329

Preface

This book is the product of a lifelong fascination with limestone springs and the history behind them. In the summer of 1966, when I was thirteen years old, my mother brought me to Lexington, Kentucky, to live. For a few months we occupied a rented house just off Dunkirk Drive in Cardinal Valley. The western part of Dunkirk ran along the edge of a thickly wooded valley, a tributary of Wolf Run Creek and an oasis of greenery surrounded by urban and suburban development. As a young teen, to me this represented a vast wilderness that required immediate exploration. Down into the valley I probed, a very young Daniel Boone, following narrow muddy trails until I came to a large stream of rushing water. Wading into the ankle-deep water for the sheer joy of it, I followed the creek upstream until I came to the source. To my delight, this proved to be a low cave opening, about three feet high and twenty wide, from which the water emerged. Many years later I learned that this was the historic Preston's Cave Spring, so-called for William Preston of Virginia for whom John Floyd had, in 1774, surveyed one thousand acres of prime Bluegrass land in which it was embedded. I knelt and peered into the cave, but was not persuaded to enter. I had no flashlight, the water appeared deeply pooled inside, and further investigation would require crawling or perhaps even swimming to unlock the secrets beyond the daylight.

A few days later, I carried my explorations further afield, discovering the railroad tracks that bordered the valley opposite Dunkirk Drive and following them eastward, blithely unconcerned with the signs that sternly forbade walking on the tracks. Reflecting on these youthful explorations many years later and with a greater appreciation for the history of the city in which I resided, I was impressed by the coincidental circumstances in which local historian George W. Ranck was struck and killed by a commuter train in August 1901 while walking on the L&N tracks that paralleled Town Branch a little to the north of Cardinal Valley. At the time, Ranck was attempting to resolve the question of just which spring, of the many in the region, had been the site where the future city of Lexington had received its name. According to historical documents, in early summer 1775 a group of surveyors and explorers were camped about a large spring when they received word of the opening engagement of the Revolutionary War, the Battle of Lexington in Massachusetts. They were inspired by this to designate their location in the wilderness by this name. Evidence was rather vague as to the precise spring where this had occurred, and so Ranck set out to resolve the controversy. At the time of his death, he had just visited the Ater Spring, which discharged into Town Branch, and was on his way to visit the Royle Spring, also located on Town Branch. The most direct route between the two springs was by way of the railroad, and, apparently deep in thought, Ranck did not hear the approaching train.[1]

I saw no trains that day, nor on subsequent excursions. I continued down the tracks, stepping from tie to tie. Off to the north were rows of industrial buildings. After little more than a half-mile, another woodland valley suddenly came into view, and so I eagerly descended into the greenery, making my way down a steep and slippery slope. This was a very unusual place, I soon discovered. Small valleys, in my experience, emptied into larger valleys. Once I reached the bottom, however, I saw there was no such outlet to this particular valley. The stream plunged down through a tangle of old truck tires and discarded rolls of wire fencing and disappeared underground. Above the sink point, the valley terminated in a wall of soil and rock that rose fifty feet above the stream back to the level of the railroad. To a geologist, this was a feature known as a blind valley, one that ends abruptly with a sinking stream.

I had no such knowledge at the time, of course, and could only marvel at the phenomenon as I turned upstream to follow the water. How wonderful, I thought, to find such an island of greenery in the middle of a city, a wild place empty of humanity that I imagined resembled the wilderness encountered by the pioneer explorers of Kentucky. The stream widened as I hiked eastward along the bank, dappled by sunlight through the branches overhead and often obscured by broad expanses of watercress flourishing in the cold water. Another surprise lay ahead, for after traveling about five hundred feet from the sink point, I came upon a low bluff, perhaps ten feet high, from which all the water emerged, boiling upward through rock rubble at the base. The tumbled ruins of an old rock fence paralleled the southern margin of the stream at this point, the first sign of civilization I had encountered. Where was all this water coming from, I wondered, and after a short pause to inspect this newly discovered spring, I pressed onward.

Little more than a hundred feet beyond the rocky spring, I found the water again, flowing placidly toward me in a relatively flat area to disappear beneath a bedrock ledge. Nearby was the foundation of some old building. A short walk upstream brought discovery of the point of origin for the water, a nearly circular pool some twenty feet across, blue-green in color and obviously very deep. Many years later, I learned that this location was the surveyors' camp of 1775 that had been sought, unsuccessfully and tragically, by George Ranck. Meticulous research by Carolyn M. Wooley, published in 1975 on the Lexington bicentennial anniversary, had gathered sufficient evidence to convince most historians that this "sinking spring," claimed by pioneer William McConnell, was the location where the future city had received its name. Recognition of the historic significance of this site, along with its potential for environmental education, would in time lead to acquisition of the property by Lexington and establishment as the popular McConnell Springs city park, an effort championed by my longtime friend James R. Rebmann.[2]

I returned to my "secret" valleys many times during my brief period of residence in Cardinal Valley. On one such occasion, I salvaged an old concrete mixing trough of steel, about five feet long and three wide, that had been thrown over the embankment into the second valley. I launched the sturdy little craft into the water, and happily poled it up and down the stream between the rocky spring and the final sink point. For this endeavor, I am proud to claim distinction as the founding (and only) member of the McConnell Springs Yacht Club.

This was my first encounter with the peculiar, cavernous type of landscape known as karst, and I was fascinated by the concept of a stream that could not seem to make up its mind whether to flow on the surface or travel underground. It was a pivotal moment in my young life, one that would help set my course forward. During the next year, I joined the National Speleological Society and the local chapter of that organization known as the Blue Grass Grotto, and from that time my life has largely focused on investigating caves and springs and the terrain in which they occur. It was not long before I discovered that my interests were not limited to explorations and scientific study of these phenomena, but expanded to include their social histories.

Karst terrains do not exist in isolation. They are platforms for human habitation. Moreover, such landscapes are not static but are dynamic, and landscape features appear and disappear over time, a process that is accelerated by human activity. What we might observe, on any given day, is but a snapshot in a continuous process of landscape evolution. Disciplines within the social sciences and the physical sciences are often considered antithetical by their practitioners, but this is an erroneous perception. History is capable of informing geology, and a grasp of landscape processes provides the context for the historical record. In working toward a common goal, the respective methods of the historian and the karst scientist can be complementary.

As local base level is lowered by deepening stream and river valleys, groundwater flow develops new pathways at lower elevations and older conduits are abandoned. Reduction of the land surface by weathering and erosion gradually diminishes the thickness of the carbonate rock overlying those conduits nearest the surface, weakening its structural integrity. During this process, cavern passages are breached through sinkhole subsidence, collapse, and the widening of valleys. Cave entrances appear and are buried, high-level springs diminish and dry up, and new springs appear lower in the topography. Ultimately, through the millennia, karst conduit systems develop in sequence and are destroyed as the rock in which they occur is removed by erosion, until the given carbonate rock unit is entirely eliminated.

The natural processes at work in a karst landscape are also influenced by human activity, often to considerable extent. This is particularly true in urban karst, where the landscape may be deliberately and profoundly altered as the community develops. Springs, once cherished as water supply sources, may be filled in or the flow diverted through storm drains so that the land may be used for other purposes. Sinkholes and cave entrances are covered to provide level land for development. In rural areas, springs tend to retain value as water sources for livestock and are thus usually preserved, though often modified with protective enclosures, retention basins, artificial channels, mill dams, and other structures intended to provide greater utility of the resource. Steep-sided sinkholes in the rural landscape are typically viewed as unusable land, since they cannot be farmed or grazed, and often end up as dump sites for farm and household waste or fill materials. Alterations made to springs and sinkholes may disturb the natural drainage, surface and subsurface, to such an extent that flow pathways in the conduit network are rerouted, breaking out as new springs in unpredictable locations or accelerating new sinkhole development through collapse or subsidence.

Caves and springs have played important roles in human history for millennia. Caves served as habitats and workshops for prehistoric peoples, and in Kentucky, as noted archaeologists Patty Jo Watson and Mary C. Kennedy concluded, Kentuckians of the Late Archaic period (prior to 1000 BCE) were exploring caves of the Mammoth Cave region mainly for sport. Somewhat later, Native Americans of the region excavated deposits of crystalline minerals such as gypsum, selenite, epsomite, and mirabilite in Mammoth and neighboring caves during the period from about 500 BCE to 300 CE. These minerals may have been used in making pigment base for paints used in rituals, employed as medicines, or traded outside the region. More recently, since colonial settlement, caves have been used as temporary shelters, as livestock pens, as natural refrigerators in which to store perishables such as milk and vegetables, and, during the early history of our nation, as sources of the mineral known as saltpeter, the primary ingredient used to make gunpowder. The enthusiasm of prehistoric people for cave exploration has carried into modern times, since today there are tens of thousands worldwide engaged in the activity for recreational or scientific purposes.[3]

Throughout human history, however, society has generally attached greater value to natural springs, as sources of water and power, than to caves. More than two thousand years ago, Aristotle noted the importance of water supply springs in city planning, and the mythology and religious practices of the Greeks and Romans were replete with examples of legendary and sacred springs. Major springs were landmarks in the wilderness of frontier America, focal points of networks of trails used by Native Americans and early pioneers. Mineral springs were of particular significance, the salt-encrusted earth on their margins attracting game animals and the waters, when boiled down in iron kettles, providing salt for the settlements. The distribution of springs was partly responsible for the pattern of settlement in pioneer Kentucky. Spring water was (and so remains, today) perceived as superior to any other water source. Early explorers and settlers were eager to claim land containing a significant spring, which became the sites of pioneer stations and communities. Lexington, Georgetown, Versailles, Lancaster, Harrodsburg, and many other cities and towns of the Bluegrass region owe their location to the presence of a spring during the settlement era that was considered sufficient for a community water supply.[4]

Large springs were also in high demand as industrial water sources, powering water wheels at mill dams and the machinery used to grind corn and wheat, and in the manufacture of various articles. The perceived superiority of spring water led to its use in manufacturing operations where water quality was an important factor in the finished product. This was particularly true for the distillation of whiskey; in 1810, Kentucky had more than two thousand individual distillers, many of whom, perhaps most, relied on spring water. Many distillers used this fact in their advertising, such as the famous James E. Pepper Distillery in Lexington. An 1891 advertisement for "Old Pepper" whiskey included the statement "all the water used is from the celebrated 'Wilson Spring' on our premises, which is the largest Natural Spring of Pure Limestone Water in Central Kentucky." Although the James E. Pepper Distillery was located along a surface stream, the owner chose to lease the water rights from a spring nearly a mile distant, and constructed a pipeline to bring the water to the distillery.[5]

Nearly every cave or spring of significance has a richly detailed history of human interaction; each has a story to tell. I developed a passion for uncovering the historical context, and began to compile information on caves, springs, and other karst features that I found to be of interest, focusing on Lexington and the Bluegrass area. I interviewed property owners, consulted local histories, read newspaper microfilms, and traced property transfers from the pioneer era to the present day, loading file folders with the products of my research.

My first view of Royal Spring, the largest in the Inner Bluegrass karst region, occurred in 1980 when I accompanied Larry Spangler to Georgetown to visit this famous spring. Larry was a graduate student in geology at the University of Kentucky, one of several such students working on similar projects under the direction of Dr. John Thrailkill. Larry's assigned research area encompassed northern Fayette and southern Scott counties, and his objective was to investigate the karst flow systems of the region, using dye traces to determine the extent and approximate boundaries of their watersheds. This is accomplished by introducing nontoxic dyes into sinkholes and other inlets and monitoring local springs for the presence of dye. Although I was not one of Thrailkill's graduate students, I had taken undergraduate courses from him in the early 1970s. He knew of my great interest in regional caves, and for many years afterward I performed minor tasks for him from time to time, such as investigating a reported sinkhole collapse or a regional cave in which he had an interest. Because of my local knowledge, Thrailkill thought it might be a good idea if Spangler and I became acquainted.

Larry and I quickly became good friends, a relationship that has persisted to the present day. I often accompanied him in the field as he pursued his investigation of the karst flow systems in his research area. Studies of this nature require a thorough inventory of all of the springs and sinkholes and other possible subsurface inlets. It can be very frustrating to a karst researcher to inject dye into a sinkhole and never find a trace of it because it discharged from a spring that had not been discovered during field reconnaissance. So, we hiked through the pastures and followed the streams in his study area, and Larry taught me about conducting dye tracing. Royal Spring was one of the systems that he was investigating, and so one day I came with him to Georgetown to see this unique spring. The size and volume of the spring, and the setting within the heart of the city, made a lasting impression on me.[6]

In the fall of 1991, I obtained a position as an environmental technologist in the Groundwater Branch of the Kentucky Division of Water in Frankfort, a position I held until 2001 when I resigned to join the faculty of Morehead State University. Royal Spring was a frequent topic of discussion among the geologists in my branch, since it was by this time one of the most thoroughly studied springs in Kentucky. It was also of importance because, as the primary source of water supply for the city of Georgetown, it was regulated by the state as a public water system. My primary responsibility was to maintain the division's groundwater database, which included information on water supply wells, on wells used for monitoring groundwater quality, and on the springs of Kentucky. My duties also allowed me plenty of time in the field. I received additional training in modern dye tracing methods, being mentored in this by Joseph A. Ray, who had in turn been taught by Dr. James Quinlan, chief geologist at Mammoth Cave National Park. I was also assigned the task of helping to set up the Kentucky Groundwater Monitoring Network. This was a very enjoyable task, since it involved traveling all across the state of Kentucky to speak with landowners about allowing their springs or wells to be sampled on a routine basis in order to assess local and regional groundwater quality.

It was during my time at the Division of Water that I began to put together the information I had been collecting on the karst features of the Lexington vicinity into a book manuscript. The book would be organized on the basis of karst systems, the components of which are sinking streams, sinkholes, caves, and springs. An individual karst flow system might contain several caves, representing branches or segments of the subsurface conduit network, whose waters discharge from a single or multiple springs. Understanding these systems is complicated by the fact that these are three-dimensional networks whose connections may vary according to flow conditions. During wet weather and high flow, water in the system may overflow though higher conduits into adjacent karst basins to activate springs that are normally dry. This was the geologic framework, which would be enhanced by detailed histories of the springs and caves within. These karst systems would each constitute chapters in the manuscript. It remains a work in progress, although nearly completed, some thirty years after I began the project.

I decided to include Royal Spring in the manuscript. Even though the spring is located in Scott County, the greater part of its recharge area, or watershed, lies in Fayette County. As I soon discovered, I had amassed so much geological and historical information about Royal Spring that, as I wrote, the account of this particular feature grew, and grew, and grew, to the point where it could no longer be framed as a chapter in a book since it was itself of book length. And so, this account of Royal Spring and the city it fostered came into existence as a separate entity. It has been a fascinating journey.

A rather significant proportion of the present work concerns the pioneer history of Kentucky. I believe this to be appropriate because McClelland's Station, the precursor to Georgetown, is often noted as being, along with Harrod's Fort, Fort Boonesborough, and Logan's Fort, among the most important early settlements of the region. It is no coincidence that this book both begins and ends with an examination of the city's pioneer heritage. Georgetown has long celebrated its origins, which coincided with the birth of the American nation, and this same historic tradition has great potential to provide significant economic benefits to the community in the future. Georgetown began as a seed planted in the fertile soil of the Inner Bluegrass, which grew to maturity watered by the ample flow of Royal Spring.

1

From Wilderness to City

This is the story of a spring that grew a city.

The city is Georgetown, located in Scott County among the gently rolling hills of the Inner Bluegrass karst region of central Kentucky. For nearly 250 years, a very large spring known as the Royal Spring has faithfully served the water needs of the community and was, in fact, the reason for its very existence. The spring is located in the western section of the city, not far from Main Street, and during Kentucky's pioneer era the locale was so inviting, so obviously perfect for habitation, that it hosted first an explorer's camp, then a temporary fortified settlement, and lastly the town that became the modern city. With a present-day population of more than 37,000 inhabitants, Georgetown is one of the largest cities in the Commonwealth of Kentucky, and much of the early growth and economic development of Georgetown can be attributed to the presence of this magnificent spring.

Before towns could exist, a wilderness had to be settled and tamed. The early settlers were confronted with an environment that, while bountiful in its gifts and holding the promise of future prosperity, could be unforgiving of the unprepared. In July 1774, a party of land surveyors exploring the Bluegrass region came across a copious spring of cold, clear water pouring out from beneath limestone ledges. It was the largest spring they had seen during their travels, so impressive that the explorers set up their camp beside it and the leader of the group, John Floyd,

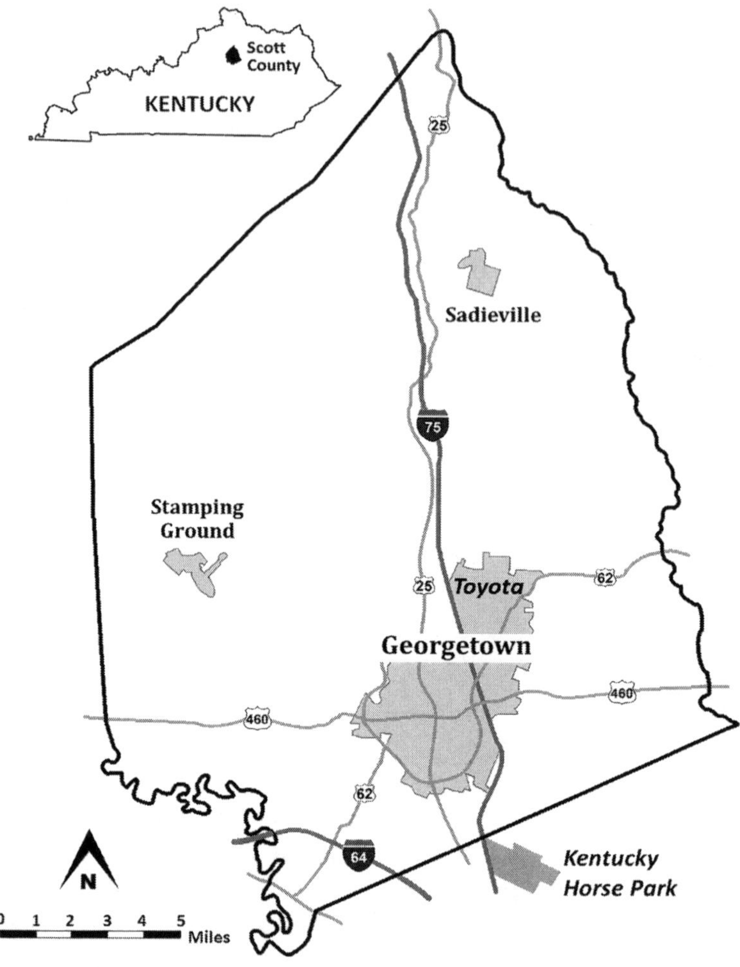

Present-day Scott County, Kentucky. The Toyota Motor Manufacturing Kentucky facility (TMMK) is located adjacent to the county seat, Georgetown. The facility has an enormous footprint, sprawling over more than 1,300 acres, and the automobile assembly plant here is one of the largest buildings in the world with 8.1 million square feet under one roof. Map by Gary O'Dell.

immediately surveyed and claimed the land surrounding the spring as his own. The presence of an abundantly flowing spring that could be used as a water supply source was one of the most important criteria used by Euro-American pioneers to select land for settlement. A year later, a fortified settlement, known as McClelland's Station, was established on the level ground above the discharge point of this "Royal" spring. The station did not survive for long, being abandoned in January 1777 following an Indian attack that killed the leader, John McClelland. This was a time, known as the "year of the bloody sevens," when raids by hostile Indians were so frequent that many other fledgling settlements were also abandoned, the residents retreating to the few substantial forts or fleeing the region entirely.

The Inner Bluegrass region was one of two focal points for early settlement west of the Appalachian Mountains, the other being the Nashville Basin, which possessed a very similar and equally appealing landscape. Prior to the settlement period, which took place in central Kentucky from about 1773 to 1796, Daniel Boone and a few other explorers and "long hunters" (so called for the duration of their trips) penetrated the trans-Appalachian wilderness, most entering through the Cumberland Gap in southeast Kentucky. These men brought back tales of their adventures and described the Inner Bluegrass as a land of fertile soils and abundant game, a virtual Eden. Their accounts generated considerable excitement in the eastern colonies, where the game had long since been hunted out and fertility of the soils depleted. A trickle at first, soon a steady stream of immigrants poured into Kentucky, bypassing the mountains and establishing precarious settlements in the Inner Bluegrass region. With few exceptions, it was not until all the best land of the region had been claimed that settlements were made peripheral to the Inner Bluegrass, expanding outward in more-or-less concentric circles.[1]

These hope-filled immigrants did not fully grasp the hardships they would face in the wilderness. After a long and grueling trip into central Kentucky, they would face isolation and loneliness, shortages of food and provisions, and the constant threat of Indian attack. A very durable myth asserts that Kentucky was never inhabited by Native Americans, but served only as a hunting territory and battleground for opposing tribes. Nothing could be further from the truth. For more than ten thousand years, Native Americans maintained a continuous presence in Kentucky, evidence of their occupation provided by numerous habitation sites and cultural artifacts. By 1760, however, native peoples abandoned all of their villages in the region, relocating beyond Kentucky's borders. The outmigration was a response by local tribes to unrelenting attacks on villages from southern Indians, such as the Catawba, and fears of reprisals from the English and their Indian allies during the French and Indian War. The Shawnee, Delaware, and Miami became concentrated in villages in the area that would become Ohio. To the south, Tennessee, Mississippi, and Alabama were populated by Cherokee and Chickasaw immigrants, and some tribes relocated to New York and the Great Lakes area. Most of these villages were multitribal, but generally referred to by the name of the dominant tribal group.[2]

Relocation of the tribal villages did not, however, mean that they intended to relinquish use and control of the land and resources south of the Ohio River. Kentucky remained an important hunting ground and source of the furs and deerskins that were necessary for trade. By the terms of the 1768 Treaty of Fort Stanwix, the powerful Iroquois of New York ceded their claim to the Kentucky lands and much of West Virginia to Great Britain. The Shawnee and Delaware, although present at the negotiations, were not signatories to the treaty and did not acknowledge Britain's ownership of the land. In the early 1770s, as the first land surveyors and settlers from the colonies began to filter into Kentucky, they encountered small Indian hunting parties who were outraged by this intrusion. Greatly angered as immigrants kept pushing into the region, the Indians responded by forming multitribal raiding parties, primarily Shawnee, that harassed the settlers. Since the villages from which raiding parties originated were often located at a considerable distance from central Kentucky, most raids were brief and tended to involve a limited number of warriors. During the Revolutionary War, raids involving larger forces were often led by British officers and sometimes included British troops.[3]

The early settlers quickly learned that, under the circumstances, a log cabin did not provide adequate security unless it was strongly fortified. In the spring of 1774, James Harrod led a group of thirty Pennsylvania men to the Inner Bluegrass. Following an old buffalo trail to a rich caneland on the Salt River in present-day Mercer County, on June 16 the men founded the first permanent settlement in Kentucky. They laid out the town, known initially as Harrod's Town, in a plat of half-acre "in-lots" and five-acre "out-lots," and built a half-dozen crude log cabins, ten feet square, on the lots. There was no chinking between the logs to seal them from the elements and low "crawl holes" for doors. The inhabitants made no attempt to fortify the town by a stockade or enclosure of log pickets, and this proved to be a significant error. Less than a month after their arrival, nine of Harrod's men were attacked by a band of twenty Shawnee Indians at a spring a few miles northwest of the town site. Three of the men were killed, and the others fled back to the town to report on the disastrous encounter. Their situation appeared more precarious than they had anticipated, and so Harrod and his men decided to abandon their fledgling community for the time being. They left on July 9 and headed to Powell's Valley, in east Tennessee, by way of Cumberland Gap. In March 1775, Harrod returned with a much larger company and, this time, directed his men to build a large, strong fort to provide a secure shelter.[4]

A similar situation characterized the settlement of both Boonesborough on the Kentucky River and St. Asaph's, near the site of present-day Stanford in Lincoln County. The Boonesborough settlement was intended to be the centerpiece of Richard Henderson's audacious Transylvania Colony scheme, and the first settlers arrived with Daniel Boone on the first day of April 1775. Henderson showed up on the 23rd, and within a few days directed a survey to lay out town lots, which were assigned to settlers by a drawing. Construction of a fort was considered essential to the community, but work on the structure was hindered by dissension as to the best location and reluctance of many settlers to divert time and labor from their own efforts to claim and clear land. A new arrival to Boonesborough in February 1776 noted an absence of "forting." Only a half-dozen cabins had been built at this time, scattered rather than in rows, and lacked pickets to fill in the gaps. After a stockade was erected, two of the four corner blockhouses were not built until 1778. The St. Asaph's settlement was established in the spring of 1775, a town laid out and cabins built, but the safety of the community was not secured until early 1777 when, in view of the heightened sense of danger in the country, Benjamin Logan began building Logan's Fort.[5]

From these examples—Harrod's Fort, Fort Boonesborough, and Logan's Fort—it is clear that the earliest settlers did not perceive an immediate threat of attack and felt free to begin laying out townsites. This perception changed, however, with the intensification of Indian raids from across the Ohio in 1776 and 1777.

On the Kentucky frontier, necessity dictated structures capable of being defended against a hostile force. The Virginia colonial, and later

Revolutionary, government had neither the resources nor the inclination to send troops across the mountains into Kentucky to build and garrison forts to protect the settlers. It was up to local leaders, able to command or persuade a sufficient labor force to erect substantial fortifications, and to individuals concerned with safeguarding their families, to solve the problem of secure housing. The defensive network that made possible the settlement of Kentucky evolved naturally, rather than as a strategic plan. The primary nodes in the network were the handful of public forts, large structures built through communal effort enclosing a number of cabins. These served as administrative centers and as staging points for a transient population of settlers. There were three of these public forts. Two of them were located in the southern part of the Inner Bluegrass region, Harrod's Fort and Fort Boonesborough; Logan's Fort was situated in the Outer Bluegrass, southwest of the others.

Most of the immigrants coming into the Bluegrass region, through Cumberland Gap, by way of Ohio River landings, or by ascending the Kentucky River, initially gravitated to one of the three public forts. Here they were able to reside for a time in relative safety, protected from Indian attack, while they oriented themselves as to conditions on the frontier. They could share their experiences with other new arrivals, and would learn much from conversations with community leaders and with the experienced frontiersmen who served as scouts and hunters. The fort provided a temporary base as new arrivals acclimatized and then set off to claim land for themselves and begin making improvements to secure that claim, building rough cabins and clearing land to raise corn. During years when attacks were frequent, many settlers opted to reside in the forts for months at a time, emerging only to plant crops and clear additional land. The overall pattern of relatively brief occupancy resulted in a rapid turnover of fort residents, with new pioneers arriving to take the places of those who had struck out on their own.[6]

The pioneers who moved out of the forts into the surrounding countryside selected land that they intended to have surveyed and to claim, according to the laws of Virginia in effect at the time. The lands were chosen on the basis of apparent soil fertility and the presence of a spring, which would be used as a water supply source. Many settlers undertook no more than the minimum improvements necessary to legally establish their claim, marking boundary trees, clearing enough land to plant a small crop of corn, and building a crude cabin. Many such cabins were little more than unroofed pens consisting of a few stacked logs, the gaps unchinked, and not really intended for occupation. More industrious settlers established homesteads on their land, known on the frontier as "stations." These stations differed from public forts by being privately held, occupied and controlled by a single family, or a group of related families and friends. All of the known stations in the Bluegrass region were located near a spring, these being perceived as possessing the highest quality potable water, with the stations usually situated on higher ground for the advantage in defense.[7]

Although stations were intended to be defensible habitations, the size of stations and the quality of their defenses varied considerably. By far, the majority of stations were simply barricadable cabins, either single or in clusters. Multiple cabins on a site might be protected by log pickets installed between cabins to provide a protective enclosure, but construction was generally less sturdy than that of the public forts. Stations could grow in size as additional structures were added to accommodate new residents, essentially becoming small forts. Stations such as Strode's Station in Clark County, Ruddle's Station in Harrison County, and McClelland's Station at Royal Spring in Scott County were all sizable fortified communities housing many families. Bryant's Station, near Lexington, was a stockaded station reportedly 600 feet long and either 150 or 250 feet wide (depending on the source), thus embracing at least two acres within the walls. This was significantly larger than, for example, Harrod's Fort, which formed a square 264 feet wide and contained 1.6 acres. Although some stations were thus as large or larger than the public forts, they were designated as stations because they were privately held.[8]

Founded at Royal Spring in the autumn of 1775, McClelland's was one of the earliest stations and one of the first to be enclosed with a stockade for protection. Although some lands had been surveyed and minor improvements made on claims, at this time there were only five other stations in all of Kentucky, in addition to the communities at Harrod's Fort, Boonesborough, and St. Asaph's. That year was relatively peaceful in Kentucky, an interval during which hostile Indian activity was largely absent, but an attack on the Leestown settlement at the mouth of Elkhorn Creek in April 1776 marked the onset of raiding parties of

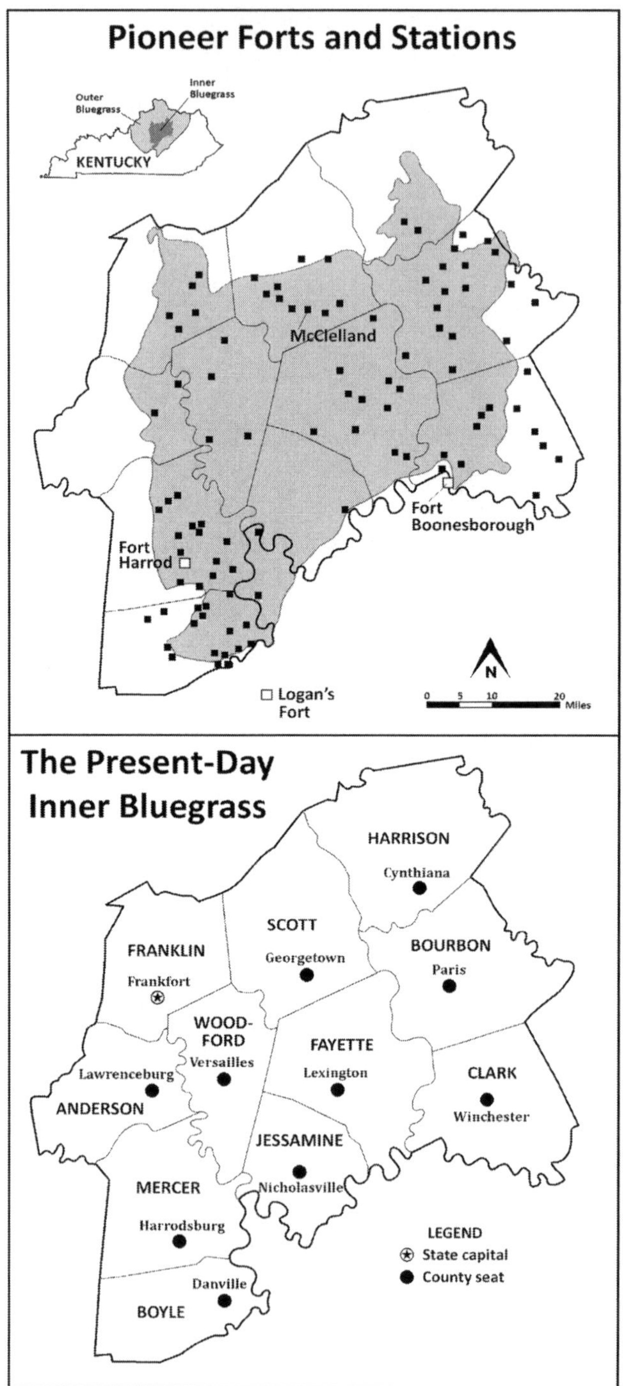

Top: Public forts and station settlements in the Inner Bluegrass Kentucky established between 1774–1796, for which locations could be determined. Adapted from Richard Ulack, Karl Raitz, and Gyula Pauer, *Atlas of Kentucky* (Lexington: Univ. Press of Kentucky, 1998), 60. *Bottom*: Present-day county seats of the Inner Bluegrass. Maps by Gary O'Dell.

increasing frequency. McClelland's Station was particularly vulnerable, being the only sizable station north of the Kentucky River and thus relatively isolated and exposed. In the last week of 1776, a party of Wyandots attacked McClelland's and killed the founder, John McClelland, prompting the inhabitants to abandon the station. Armed and encouraged by the British, Indian raiders intensified their forays into Kentucky in 1777, alarming the settlers to the point where many of the stations were abandoned. The region was virtually depopulated, most of the settlers leaving the country altogether for a time, others taking shelter in one of the public forts. All three of the public forts withstood major attacks by large numbers of Indians during this turbulent year.[9]

Despite continued conflict from 1777 to the end of the Revolutionary War in 1783, settlers kept pouring into the Bluegrass region in ever increasing numbers. By the end of the war, as Gwynn Henderson and David Pollack observed, "there were too many settlers, an estimated 12,000, and too many settlements, for native raiding parties to drive the colonists from Kentucky." Not even the Battle of Blue Licks on August 19, 1782, a shocking and demoralizing disaster in which a force of about 60 British rangers and 300 Indians ambushed and routed 182 Kentucky militiamen, killing 64, was sufficient to deter the immigrants for long. In response to this debacle, Kentuckians took the war into the Indians' territory, launching expeditions northward across the Ohio River to destroy villages and crops. The Battle of Fallen Timbers in northwestern Ohio on August 20, 1794, effectively ended the Indian wars in Kentucky and Ohio and opened up the Northwest for settlement. A combined force of Continental troops led by General Anthony Wayne and Kentucky militia commanded by General Charles Scott defeated a large confederation of Shawnee, Ottawa, and other allied Indians. The subsequent Treaty of Greenville and Jay's Treaty forced withdrawal of Native Americans from most of Ohio.[10]

The ad-hoc defensive network of public forts and fortified stations proved adequate to secure the frontier sufficiently to permit widespread settlement despite persistent Indian resistance. A preliminary model of frontier settlement was proposed by geographer John C. Hudson and further developed by Michael J. O'Brien, drawing on examples of the pioneer experience in the Inner Bluegrass and Missouri. The Bluegrass served as a source region for thousands of immigrants who came to

Missouri prior to the Civil War. The modified model envisioned three processes or stages of rural settlement. In the first stage, colonization, a population begins to move into a new territory. This process is followed by spread, spaces between the early settlements filling in as the established colonial population grows and overall settlement density increases. The spread phase ends when all of the agriculturally productive land has been acquired and the rural population approaches the carrying capacity of the environment. From this point, competition among farmers for one another's land appears, favoring the expansion of large farms at the expense of smaller ones.[11]

Archaeologist Nancy O'Malley linked the O'Brien model to chronological phases in the settlement of Kentucky, which took place as a series of pulses: Pre-Revolutionary (1773–1777), Revolutionary (1778–1782), Post-Revolutionary (1783–1785), and Post-Frontier (after 1785). The Pre-Revolutionary period represents O'Brien's colonization phase, during which settlers first began to survey land and to establish a few stations, such as McClelland's, along with public forts, such as Harrod's and Boonesborough, that provided secure refuges during the most precarious stage. Most of the stations established during the earliest period were small in size and crudely constructed, McClelland's being a notable exception to this tendency. The number of stations in the Inner Bluegrass region multiplied dramatically, to more than seventy, during the main pulse of the Revolutionary period, equivalent to the model's "spread" phase. Numerous settlements were made in nearly all of the counties of the region, the exceptions being Franklin and Woodford, where only a handful of stations were established because the land was considered less desirable and less well-connected by trails to the rest.[12]

After the close of the Revolutionary War, although the Indian threat was greatly reduced, nearly all of the best land had already been claimed, so that the Post-Revolutionary period marked the beginning of the competition phase described by O'Brien, which continued during the Post-Frontier period. About fifty new stations were established in the Inner Bluegrass during this phase, so that by the end of the Post-Frontier period the total number of station settlements in the region exceeded 150. Many of these newer stations were founded by immigrants who had previously claimed land but, apprehensive of Indian attack, waited until the threat subsided to make their settlements. Other new arrivals were forced to purchase land from speculators or from settlers already present in the region. With a greater sense of security now prevailing, many of the earlier stations were abandoned by their residents during this phase, torn down and the materials recycled to build larger, more comfortable domiciles and outbuildings. In general, stations were relatively short-lived features of the landscape, averaging about five years between construction and abandonment. The forts, no longer needed as refuges, were replaced as central places by the establishment of small towns as well as crossroads communities that served a rural farm population.[13]

Although McClelland's Station was abandoned in January 1777, Royal Spring was surrounded by some of the richest land to be found in Kentucky, the soil deep and fertile, and the site did not lie fallow for long. In 1787, the community of Georgetown was laid out beside the spring, which has ever since served the population as its primary water source. Soon after its founding, Georgetown grew to become one of the largest towns in central Kentucky. At the beginning of the nineteenth century there were eleven significant towns in the Inner Bluegrass region, these being the county seats of the modern era: Cynthiana (Harrison County), Danville (Boyle), Frankfort (Franklin), Georgetown (Scott), Harrodsburg (Mercer), Lancaster (Garrard), Lexington (Fayette), Nicholasville (Jessamine), Paris (Bourbon), Versailles (Woodford), and Winchester (Clark). All of these towns had been founded within the last quarter-century, and nearly half were less than a decade old. A twelfth county seat, Lawrenceburg (Anderson) was established later than these others and was not represented in the 1800 census. Initially named Lawrence, the town was laid out in 1818; when Anderson County was created in 1827, the name was changed to Lawrenceburg.[14]

In 1800, Georgetown was among the most populous of the new Bluegrass communities; inhabited by nearly 350 persons, free and enslaved. The town was exceeded in size only by Lexington (1,795 persons) and Frankfort, the state capital (578 persons). Georgetown even outstripped the Outer Bluegrass town of Louisville on the Ohio River, which was established in 1778 but had experienced little growth to this point in time. The size ranking of Georgetown relative to other towns of the Inner Bluegrass remained essentially unchanged until after the Civil War, the top two spots occupied by Lexington and Frankfort, respectively, and Georgetown in third or fourth place. For several decades after

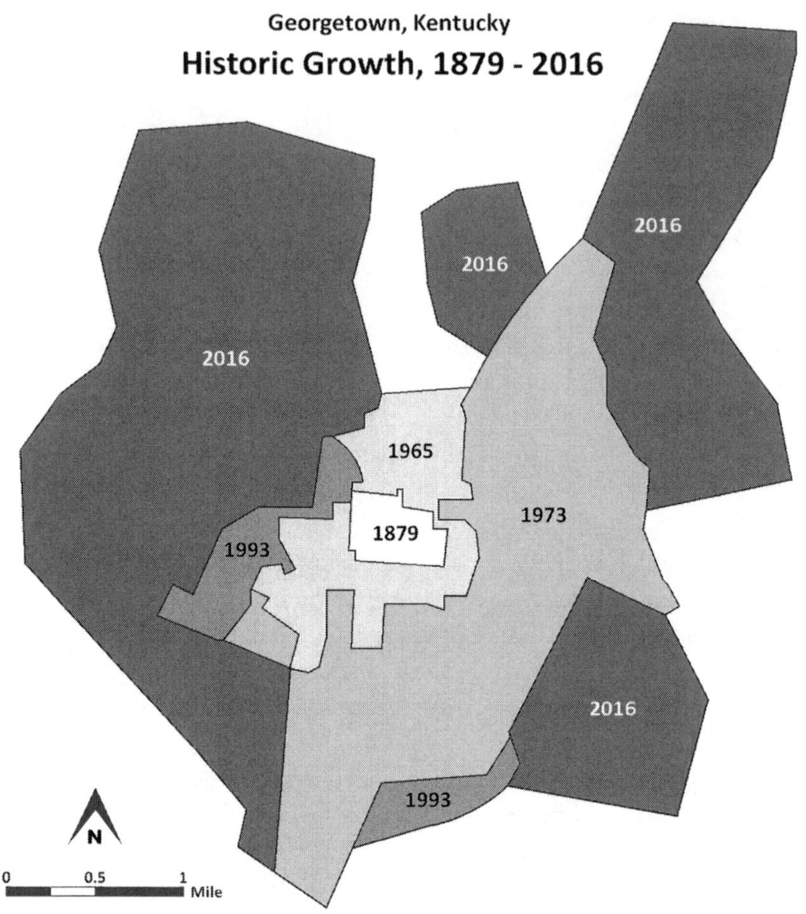

Growth of Georgetown. An agricultural community, Georgetown grew slowly for the first two hundred years of its existence but exploded in population and size following establishment of the Toyota assembly plant in 1986. Map by Gary O'Dell, adapted from Conrad Kickert and Ryan Geismar, *Core of Georgetown: Planmaking Workshop Fall 2016* (Cincinnati, Ohio: University of Cincinnati School of Planning, 2016).

the war, Georgetown slipped to near the bottom in population, possibly because strong support for the Confederacy among Scott County residents resulted in considerable loss of personal wealth and weak postwar growth compared to other communities. By 1900, however, the town rebounded strongly, and for the duration of the twentieth century it would seldom rank less than sixth place in population. Lastly, during the

1980s, the city received an enormous boost to its economic development with the establishment of the nearby Toyota automobile assembly plant that propelled community growth to a size beyond all other Bluegrass cities save Lexington, eclipsing even the state capital, Frankfort, in the twenty-first century.[15]

The explanation for Georgetown's early rise to prominence among Bluegrass communities appears to lie with a highly favorable site and situation. Geographers use these concepts to analyze the historical growth and development of settlements, since site and situational characteristics determine whether a settlement will grow to become a large city or remain no more than a small village. Site refers to the physical attributes of the place where a city originated and evolved, such as surface landforms, local geology, climate, vegetation, soil quality, defensibility, level land for building, availability of construction materials (wood and stone), water bodies, and availability of potable water. Factors such as these often determine the initial selection of a settlement location. Situational factors can be even more significant to the growth or decline of a city than are site characteristics. Situation refers to the location of a settlement relative to other settlements and surrounding regions, and is an indication of how well that place is connected to other places and resources. Cities that are centrally located at trade route junctions, being well-connected to markets and sources of raw materials, are more likely to prosper and grow than cities lacking such connections.[16]

Water is the lifeblood of a community, necessary for life itself and for economic development. The story of Georgetown is, in many ways, a story about water. Through history, water has always been one of the most important site and situational factors that influenced the location and prosperity of human settlements. Rivers and lakes provided a source of clean drinking water, and served as transportation routes linking cities together. From ancient times to the present day, with few exceptions the largest and most successful cities were those established along the banks of lakes and navigable rivers, in deltas or along coastlines. Many of the first settlements in North America were made at or near river mouths along the eastern coast, prompted both by an understandable hesitation to venture too far into the unknown wilderness and by the need to remain connected to the transatlantic supply line from the mother country. Other early settlements were made slightly inland all along the coast as ships followed the rivers to the point, known as the Fall Line, where the waters were no longer navigable because of rapids. This line of navigational obstacles, roughly parallel to the Atlantic coast, occurred where the durable crystalline rocks of the Piedmont contacted the softer, more erodible sedimentary rocks of the Coastal Plain, producing a nine hundred-mile-long transitional escarpment that ranges from imperceptible to more than one hundred feet high in some locations. On these rivers, settlements were founded just below the Fall Line in order to maintain the necessary supply line during their infancy. In time, these settlements grew to become modern cities, including Augusta, Georgia; Columbia, South Carolina; and Richmond, Virginia. At such locations, goods bound for upriver would have to be unloaded from ships below the Fall Line and either reloaded onto ships above the line or else transported overland, a process known as break-in-bulk.[17]

The floodplains of river cities provided fertile soils for crop production, and whereas inland cities could only rely on agriculture, foraging, and hunting for sustenance, cities on rivers, lakes, and seacoasts could obtain food from both the land and water environments to ensure a steady supply for growing populations. Locations along large water bodies also provided opportunities for waterborne commerce, linking local economies to global trade routes. Transport over water was more efficient than land transport because ships could haul much larger cargoes and travel faster. River cities were able to harness the flow of water to irrigate crops, and to provide power for mills and, more recently, hydroelectric generation. All these factors, and more, helped to favor the general growth and dominance of cities on water over landlocked cities. Most of the world's largest cities are located on rivers, and in Kentucky thirteen of the twenty largest cities in the state are so situated. The majority are along the Ohio River, including Louisville, the largest. Of the remaining seven cities, all but one was founded at a freshwater spring, and the single exception, Radcliff (a latecomer established in 1919), depends on groundwater furnished by the Hardin County Water District obtained from wells and a large spring.[18]

It might appear as given that the many Kentucky cities scattered along the Ohio River would obtain their potable water supply from the river, but this is not the case. Instead, Louisville and other river cities extract groundwater from well fields. Just as most of the Atlantic coastal cities draw their water from the granular aquifers of unconsolidated Coastal Plain sediments rather than from coastal rivers, so the Ohio River cities tap into similar aquifers of alluvial sediments along the river floodplain. Surface water flowing in the Ohio tends to be quite turbid with suspended sediments, and carries industrial and agricultural contaminants derived from upstream activity. Groundwater in the granular aquifers is derived from rainfall that infiltrates to the subsurface and is relatively clean compared to surface water. A long-standing historical perception of superior groundwater quality means that, given a choice, many communities prefer groundwater sources, such as wells and springs.

The widely held perception of natural groundwater purity is most pronounced in regard to freshwater springs, a belief that might be termed the "spring water mystique." This conviction dates to antiquity and derives from a poor understanding of the nature of groundwater flow, whether in karst terranes or other geologic settings. The assumption was that water from springs emerged from deep reservoirs within the earth, far below any potential surface contamination. Evidence of this perception can be found in many historic accounts. The late nineteenth-century debate over the possible establishment of a water works to serve the population of Lexington, Kentucky, provides numerous examples of a prevailing belief in vast, deeply set groundwater bodies that fed surface springs. The conventional wisdom was that such a large body of groundwater existed beneath the city, the source of the many springs in the region. During the summer of 1879, one gentleman proposed what must have seemed an eminently practical solution to achieve an inexhaustible supply:

> Let four holes, at right angles of a six foot square, be bored into the ground until they pierce the cavernous reservoir that everyone believes underlies Lexington. Let the holes be about four inches in diameter. As soon as water is reached let four pumps be set to work on those holes and test the supply of water. If found sufficient, the earth plug between the holes can be blown out and an orifice made for a stream of water large enough to supply Lexington.

The Wilson Spring (today known as one of the McConnell Springs), a large circular blue hole, was frequently proposed as a water source for the water works. An editorial stated, "All who have seen this wonderful spring agree that it is the outlet of a subterranean lake or river," an assertion that appeared regularly in print during the water works debate.[19]

Because most groundwater aquifers lie relatively close to the surface, rather than at great depth, and are thus subject to infiltration of surface contaminants, the assumption of purity is erroneous. About half of Kentucky's land surface is underlain by carbonate bedrock, limestone being the most widespread and significant of these rocks. As precipitation, being naturally mildly acidic, infiltrates through the soil and into the bedrock, joints and bedding planes are gradually enlarged by dissolution of the limestone, creating flow systems composed of conduit networks that ultimately discharge groundwater from springs. The resulting landscape, in which water moves from the surface to the subsurface by diffuse infiltration through the soil and directly by way of sinkholes and sinking streams, is known as karst, and in Kentucky includes the Inner Bluegrass karst region.[20]

Water supplies derived from karst aquifers are far more vulnerable to contamination than are those from granular aquifers, which are composed of unconsolidated sediments, such as sand and gravel. Groundwater percolates slowly through granular aquifers, and relatively effective filtration of particles, microorganisms and many chemical constituents occurs along with attenuation (die-off) of microorganisms. Many pathogenic organisms do not survive for lengthy periods outside a host body. Groundwater obtained from the granular aquifers of alluvial and coastal sediments thus provides a relatively safe drinking water supply.[21]

In contrast, groundwater flow systems in karst areas such as that of the Inner Bluegrass region are not only highly vulnerable to surface contamination but exhibit little filtration or attenuation of microorganisms. There are many potential sources of groundwater contamination, which can be described as point or nonpoint sources. Point sources release pollution into the environment from a single point or location, such from a chemical spill or a leaking sewer pipe. Nonpoint pollutants are those that originate from across broad areas rather than a specific identifiable source, such as fertilizer and pesticides applied to agricultural fields or suburban yards, or road salt on highways. Runoff from precipitation carries water bearing contaminants into streams and rivers, and into karst systems by way of diffuse infiltration and directly through sinkholes and sinking streams. As soils are relatively thin in most karst regions, only a minimal amount of contaminant removal occurs in the soil layer during diffuse infiltration. Biological or chemical contaminants carried into sinkholes or sinking streams swiftly enter karst conduits and travel through the system at nearly the same flow rates as water in surface streams, discharging from springs in virtually unaltered form.[22]

From the past through the present day, sinkholes have been used as receptacles for waste by persons unfamiliar with the nature of groundwater in karst or unconcerned by the potential health consequences of such disposal. On many occasions I have observed Inner Bluegrass sinkholes filled nearly to the brim with trash and garbage, including the carcasses of dead animals, empty pesticide containers, and fertilizer sacks. Some horse farms, after mucking out stalls, have routinely disposed of manure into sinkholes. Such contaminants are rapidly transported by groundwater flowing in karst conduits to nearby or distant springs that may be used to water livestock or as sources for human consumption.

Prior to the environmental awakening of the 1960s, the Earth's air, land, and water were thought to be sinks of infinite capacity for absorbing all of the waste products and pollutants generated by human activity. The concentrated population of cities, in which little provision was made for collection and treatment of waste until near the end of the nineteenth century, contributed to considerable local environmental degradation and exacerbated hazards to human health. Not until after mid-century did any American city construct sewers for removal of human waste, and not until after 1880 were sewerage systems constructed by most municipalities.[23]

Before the era of sewer construction, cities were reeking, filthy places. Used water and human waste were usually disposed of in cesspools and privy vaults, or sometimes simply thrown onto streets or in vacant lots. Cesspools and privy vaults were usually little more than holes in the ground, sometimes lined, from which wastes usually leached into the surrounding soil. Privies were built in the most convenient locations, often adjacent to wells, springs, and streams, and contaminated surface and groundwater through seepage and by overflow during heavy rains. For most of the nineteenth century, water works were constructed without provision for sewage removal. The greater quantities of water used as a result of connection to the public water system often overtaxed the capacity of the cesspools and vaults so that they overflowed onto the surface and contaminated local streams. A similar hazard was produced by most early sewerage systems, which were built as combined sanitary and storm-water systems due to construction expense and the wholly ineffective notion of sewage treatment through dilution.[24]

In the Bluegrass, for example, the primary city of Lexington built its water works system in 1885, but it was not until 1905 that a sewerage system began to be constructed, a process that took several decades to complete. Prior to this date, limited parts of the city were served by private sewer systems. In Georgetown, the water supply system was established in 1889, but nearly twenty years would pass before sewer construction was initiated. In both cases, sewer construction was prompted by the filthy condition of local streams and concerns about human health and epidemic disease. In the modern era, simultaneous provision of water carriage and sewerage became mandated for expansion of city services into new areas.[25]

The greater concern in the late nineteenth century with provision of clean water to citizens was closely tied to a growing realization of the relationship between contaminated water and epidemic disease. Waterborne diseases have been responsible for some of the most devastating pandemics in world history. Viruses, bacteria, and protozoans are all classes of pathogens transmitted by contaminated water. Polio, hepatitis A and E, and meningitis are among the waterborne viral pathogens; bacterial pathogens include cholera, typhoid, salmonella, shigella, and *E. coli* O157:H7; and protozoans include giardia and cryptosporidium.[26]

The connection between pathogenic microorganisms and disease was not understood until well after the American Civil War. Previously, sickness was attributed, variously, to malicious spirits; to being a punishment from God for sinful behavior; or to being a consequence of poor diet, gluttony, or intemperance. During the emerging sanitary movement of the early nineteenth century, more rational explanations were offered, in particular the related "filth" and "miasmatic" theories that dominated medical thinking through much of the century. The filth theory held that accumulations of decomposing waste, sewage, and other organic material in cellars, roadways, and ditches produced emanations of noxious gases, evident as foul stenches, and these "miasmas" of the air carried with them invisible infectious agents causing disease. The effects of epidemic disease were most pronounced in cities, where large numbers of people lived in close proximity, often in unsanitary conditions. People living in poverty were observed to be filthy and sick, and it was thereby assumed that their sickness was caused by filth. Medical authorities believed, not entirely without merit, that disease could be averted by sanitary measures, such as thorough cleansing of streets and yards. Although the existence of microorganisms was known, there was as yet no real understanding of the relationship between microorganisms and disease.[27]

Asiatic cholera was among the deadliest of waterborne diseases, and the study of cholera outbreaks played a major role leading to the connection between microorganisms and disease and to modern germ theory. The pathogen *Vibrio cholerae* is a particularly virulent organism that has been responsible for a great deal of human suffering and death during pandemics of an explosive nature. The disease is transmitted by consumption of food and water that has been contaminated by the fecal material of other cholera patients. During the nineteenth century, four cholera pandemics spread from south Asia to Europe and from there to North America, carried by infected passengers aboard ships docking at major ports, such as Quebec, New York, and New Orleans. From the ports, the disease was spread inland and up the rivers by travelers. Kentucky was scourged by cholera during 1832–1833, 1848–1854, 1866, and again in 1872–1873. At the first touch of the disease, city residents fled to the countryside and to other communities, carrying cholera with them across the commonwealth. The state had one of the highest cholera fatality rates in America.[28]

An important first step toward understanding how cholera and other waterborne diseases are transmitted was made during 1849–1854 by Dr. John Snow of London, England. Snow carried out an investigation of differential cholera mortality in thirty-two subdistricts of the city supplied with water from the Thames by two separate companies during the epidemic, and of an outbreak in the Golden Square district of Soho, where residents obtained water from a public pump on Broad Street. One of the most important tools in his analysis was the use of maps to plot the location of fatalities, and he soon realized that nearly all of the deaths in Golden Square had taken place within a short distance of the pump. This discovery led to his often-quoted advice to the Board of Governors that the pump handle should be removed to alleviate the disease. From his studies, Snow concluded that inhalation of atmospheric miasmas was not responsible for cholera and that the disease was only transmitted by ingesting the "morbid matter" specific to the disease. Although he did not propose that the "poison" of cholera was germs, he empirically demonstrated that the disease was a waterborne affliction. Working independently in Italy in 1854, Filippo Pacini was the first to observe cholera bacteria present in human feces under a microscope, and in 1884 Robert Koch was able to isolate *V. cholerae* from culture media.[29]

In Kentucky, although there had been plenty of circumstantial evidence during the 1833 and 1849 epidemics suggesting that contaminated water was responsible for cholera, the root cause and connection was still not understood. The *Covington Journal* came close to grasping the truth after the second epidemic when it observed that cholera did not seem to have been as severe in communities where most citizens obtained their drinking water from rainwater collection or from the Ohio River. When cholera once more afflicted the state in 1872–1873, Lexington remained relatively unaffected because most citizens had changed their drinking water source from wells to concrete-lined cisterns supplied by rainwater, protected from seeping contamination. Presented with this evidence, by the fall of 1873 most physicians in Kentucky were convinced that cholera was spread by contaminated water. Before the end of the century, the work of John Snow, Louis Pasteur, Joseph Lister, and Robert Koch led to a widespread acceptance of the germ theory of disease.[30]

Lexington was not the only Inner Bluegrass community to have changed its source of water supply since the settlement era. Every town in the region was founded at the location of a spring believed irrevocably pure in quality and sufficient to supply the needs of a community, but this perception proved shortsighted. In nearly every case, although the original settlement spring proved adequate to serve the needs of a few hundred inhabitants, population growth soon forced citizens to seek out additional or alternate water sources. Continued growth, prior to the establishment of centralized public water systems beginning in the late nineteenth century, resulted in a plethora of water supply sources for many communities. Supply and sanitary considerations, however, promoted a gradual evolution of favored source types.

The development of Lexington's water supply from the pioneer era to the present day may be considered as fairly typical for the region, representing a transition from groundwater sources to surface water. The city was founded in 1779 at a significant spring on the bank of a minor stream called Town Branch, the so-called "middle fork" of Elkhorn Creek. This was designated the "Public Spring" and was the initial primary water source for the settlement. As the population grew and demand increased, efforts were made to increase the flow of the spring. A resolution of the town trustees in December 1782 called for "every freeholder of Lexington, living on the north side of the branch, [to] meet on the 2nd day of January next at the Springs to assist in availing the same." Martin Wymore, an early resident, observed that they "dug that in farther, and more, and it got stronger, as they went farther into the bank." There were a number of lesser springs along Town Branch within the boundaries of the community that were used; one located near the schoolhouse became the second public water supply source. The citizens also set about digging at all of the wet-weather seeps. These efforts were successful, as "the seeps . . . gradually opened, and new springs broke out."[31]

By 1810 much of the town's water supply was obtained from wells, although some springs continued to be used. During the next half-century, the use of groundwater declined generally so that by the time of the 1873 cholera epidemic most Lexington residents were collecting rainwater in privately owned concrete-lined cisterns that, coincidentally, protected their supply against waterborne disease. Despite being a safer source, seasonably variable rainfall collection proved unable to meet the demands of a growing city, and after a series of disastrous fires late in the century, there was considerable public agitation for a public water works. Many possible sources were proposed, including a number of large springs. The debate finally coalesced around two possible surface water sources: either construction of a large artificial reservoir or bringing water from the Kentucky River by pipeline. The reservoir proposal triumphed, and a dam was built during 1884 and 1885 on a tributary of Hickman Creek just southeast of the city. Within a few months a pumping and filtering plant was in operation, and over the next three decades three more reservoirs were added to the catchment system. Even these reservoirs would in time prove inadequate; following the severe drought of 1930, the city built the first of four pipelines to the Kentucky River.[32]

The Lexington experience was essentially duplicated at the smaller communities across the Inner Bluegrass. For pioneer communities, public springs served as assembly points drawing residents to the source to carry water away to their homes. Some persons may have used springs located on their own property. As the towns developed and population increased, springs were inadequate for the demand and wells were excavated for both public and private use. Following the series of cholera epidemics of the nineteenth century, groundwater was no longer trusted and rainwater collection supplanted most wells and springs. With continued growth, communities turned to surface water sources obtained from artificial reservoirs and from pipelines to major streams and rivers, sometimes building dams to create impoundments that provided a greater and more reliable supply.

Georgetown was the sole exception to this evolution. Although every other community established in the Inner Bluegrass during the settlement era initially depended on and ultimately abandoned its spring, no community in all of Kentucky had a spring quite like Royal Spring. Except during periods of exceptional drought, Royal Spring was perfectly capable of providing a supply of water able to support a population of at least ten thousand citizens. Although most other Kentucky communities eventually turned away from groundwater, Royal Spring was just too valuable a resource to abandon. Not everyone in the city used water from the spring. Some persons or businesses located more distant from the spring excavated wells for their greater convenience, and during the nineteenth century the city not only established a number of public cisterns for firefighting but also built a dam on Elkhorn Creek to serve as a backup water supply. Nevertheless, in the twenty-first century Georgetown is the only community in the entire commonwealth that still relies on the original settlement spring to supply its primary water needs.

Water supply for Inner Bluegrass communities thus initially evolved from one or a few mostly public groundwater sources to many and varied private sources, surface and groundwater. The number of community supply sources greatly contracted late in the nineteenth century when most began to rely on public or privately held water works to provide water, usually obtained from a single surface source and distributed to homes and businesses through a pipeline system.

Georgetown's water supply situation was complicated by the fact that the city did not hold title to the land above the spring and only possessed one-half of the width of the stream, on the east side, from the discharge point downstream. In 1895, the western half of the spring and branch was part of a former farm that would soon be cut up into housing tracts. A small tract of land immediately to the east of the springhead was granted by the city to the privately owned Water Supply Company, on which a water works and an ice-making plant were built. Controversy over control of the water source developed during the closing years of the century when, during a severe drought, the ice company continued to take water for making ice and the city desired to assert its rights to prevent this.

The ensuing litigation occupied nearly a decade and ultimately determined that the city of Georgetown was able to exert partial control over the source of its water supply. Water rights in the eastern United States are governed by riparian doctrine, a concept developed in this country during the antebellum period to replace the principles of "natural flow" and "prior appropriation" derived from English common law. Establishment of riparian rights law was largely a response to increasing industrialization and water demand of the era, and specifically to the proliferation of mill dams, whose impoundments often infringed on the property of other persons along the watercourse. The "natural flow" theory in English common law contained the seeds of riparian doctrine, allowing that the owner of land on the banks of a watercourse had exclusive rights to use the water any way he chose provided that use did not interfere with the natural flow and the equal rights of downstream owners. Prior appropriation, on the other hand, stated that primacy in the right to water belonged to the first person to make beneficial use of the water. Under English law, natural flow determined ownership and prior appropriation was used to resolve disputes between users. Under America riparian doctrine, each owner has the right to make *reasonable* use of the water. Western states, however, assign water rights on the basis of a modified version of prior appropriation, commonly expressed as "first in time, first in right."[33]

The rules of law were more difficult to apply to groundwater. Until advances in hydrogeology during the latter part of the twentieth century, there was considerable ignorance as to the nature of groundwater flow, long defined as "unknown and unascertainable." Accordingly, common law of groundwater was developed without a real understanding of the resource, and it was treated as separate from surface water even though both are part of a single hydrologic cycle. As legally defined at the beginning of the twentieth century, groundwater was divided into two categories. "Percolating groundwater" passed through the ground without a definite channel (as in the case of granular aquifers), and it was to this category that the body of groundwater law applied. Percolating waters were considered part of the land on which they occurred and "belong absolutely to the owner of the land, who may deal with them as he sees fit." The other category applied to subterranean waters that flowed in a distinct channel beneath the surface (as in karst systems), and these were governed by riparian doctrine. Owners of the land beneath which channeled groundwater flows had the same riparian rights as landowners for surface streams. The problem with this definition was that, until modern times, there was often no practical way to determine the subterranean course of waters discharging from a spring, or if the spring was even fed by water flowing in an underground channel. The legal presumption was that all groundwater was percolating, and for riparian doctrine to apply the existence and course of a permanent channel must be demonstrated.[34]

Riparian doctrine did, however, apply to the discharge point of a spring and the waters flowing downstream of the exit point, as in the case of Royal Spring. The owner or owners of a spring and the land adjacent to its watercourse had the usual rights of a riparian proprietor, along with the right to "improve and enlarge the spring by digging, cleaning out, curbing, and walling it up, or he may sell the water or grant the right to draw from the spring, subject to the rights of the [other] riparian owners." For a community water supply source, American law gave precedence to the "public good" in water usage through the potential use of eminent domain to acquire primary control of the source. According to one commentator, "The supply of water to a city or town for its proper municipal purposes and for the general use of its inhabitants is a 'public use' in aid of which the power of eminent domain may be exercised," provided just compensation was made in the taking.[35]

In the dispute between the city of Georgetown and the Water Supply Company, neither riparian doctrine nor eminent domain came into significant play. Instead, it would appear that the courts applied the concept of prior appropriation, although not explicitly stated as such. In rendering its verdict, the appeals court relied on the long historic tradition of water use by the city and its maintenance of the useful condition of the spring, as well as permits issued by the city to the water company for obtaining water from the spring. The court ruled that Georgetown was not the absolute owner of the entirety of the spring but that conditions expressed in the permit allowed the city to determine where withdrawals could be made.[36]

There can be little doubt that, as a site factor, Royal Spring played an important role in the early growth and development of Georgetown as an important Inner Bluegrass city. Settlement growth patterns that develop as a result of site and situational factors are addressed by central place theory. Developed by geographer Walter Christaller in the 1930s and subsequently modified by August Lösch, central place theory presents a model to explain the regular size, spacing, and functions of urban settlements as they might be distributed across a fertile agricultural region consisting of relatively level land. Cities that are market centers are known as central places and provide a variety of retail functions for the surrounding area. The largest, or higher-order cities, are surrounded by medium-sized cities, which in turn are surrounded by smaller cities and towns, and in like manner down to the lowest orders, villages and hamlets, of a spatially organized, nested hierarchy. The regularity in location of central places is accounted for by marketing principles; in contrast, transportation cities exhibit linear patterns developed along rail lines, coastlines, or major rivers. Regional examples of linear cities developed along river corridors include Charleston on the Kanawha River in West Virginia, and the Huntington-Ashland-Ironton complex spread out along the Ohio River in West Virginia-Kentucky-Ohio. Although Christaller's theory was based on his observations of settlements on the plains of southern Germany, it has over time proven relevant to describing urban patterns elsewhere in regions possessing similar characteristics and applies particularly well to the gently rolling, fertile agricultural plain of Kentucky's Bluegrass region.[37]

Central place functions, according to Leslie King, are any activities "carried on in the urban place that derives at least part of its support from people living in the rural areas around the place." Larger cities provide more goods and services than lower-order communities. Goods and services can also be categorized as low- or high-order. Low-order goods are less expensive commodities, such as groceries or newspapers, that must be purchased frequently; depending on the historical era, low-order services might include barbershops, bathhouses, inns, laundries, and post offices. Because such items and services are purchased regularly, perhaps daily, small businesses in lesser communities are able to persevere because most people prefer the convenience of shopping locally rather than making a trip into a city. This was especially true in the pre-automobile era, when even a short journey by horse or wagon became an all-day affair. In contrast, higher-order goods are more expensive specialty items, such as furniture, carriages (or automobiles), and fine jewelry that are purchased less often. Merchants who sell such items must locate in cities serving a large customer base located within the urban area and surrounding hinterland because small towns cannot support such businesses. This is also true for higher-order services, which can include hospitals, hotels, factories, and supermarkets.[38]

Central place theory endeavors to explain the economic relationships of cities with smaller communities. When combined with site and situational factors, the theory provides insight as to why cities exist in particular locations and the manner in which they serve the surrounding lower-order communities with specialty goods and services. For central and northern Kentucky, the highest order cities, or central places, would be Lexington, Louisville, and Cincinnati. In the Inner Bluegrass, the largest city, Lexington, is surrounded by smaller-order satellite cities, such as Frankfort, Georgetown, Paris, Winchester, Richmond, Nicholasville, and Versailles. These are spaced around Lexington at almost equidistant intervals from one another, at an average distance of fourteen miles from the larger city (Frankfort and Richmond being a little farther).

Lexington has served as the central place for the Bluegrass since shortly after its founding in 1779. In 1860, Lexington had a population of 9,321 residents. The seven surrounding communities, named above, had an average population of 1,536 persons, a ratio of 6:1 between the central place of the Bluegrass and its satellites. In 2020, although there was a greater variability in population among the satellite cities than in 1860, the population ratio had increased to 13:1 as a result of a higher growth rate for Lexington. As a second-order central place, Georgetown serves lower-order towns, including Sadieville (estimated 2020 population of 320) and Stamping Ground (population 780), along with a number of unincorporated villages, such as Delaplain, Great Crossing, and Minorsville. In 1980, prior to the Toyota-driven growth surge, the population ratio between Georgetown and its two primary satellite towns was about 27:1. By 2020, Georgetown had nearly seventy times the average population of these smaller communities.[39]

Given that site characteristics such as climate, soil, vegetation, etc. were more or less equivalent across the Inner Bluegrass, situational factors had a greater influence over the relative growth and development of townsites in the region. For more than forty years after settlement, such factors favored the growth of Lexington more than any other community in Kentucky and promoted the initial growth of Georgetown above most other towns of the Inner Bluegrass. Lexington is centrally located in the Inner Bluegrass, the region most desired by settlers for its fertile soils, and was the terminus for the two most important routes by which immigrants were funneled into the region, a branch of the Wilderness Trail leading from Boonesborough and the buffalo trace from the Limestone landing on the Ohio River. Although initially no more than rough horse trails, these routes guided tens of thousands of immigrants into the region during the settlement years. As the Bluegrass became more settled, the trails were soon improved to wagon roads. After the founding of Maysville at the Limestone landing in 1787, the road from the Ohio River to Lexington became generally known as the Maysville Road and was the single most important access route to the Bluegrass.[40]

Lexington was also possibly the most well-defended settlement during the pioneer era. From the original blockhouse erected in 1779, a substantial stockaded fort was quickly erected enclosing about two dozen cabins, and town lots were laid out in January of the following year. In 1781, noting that "the inhabitants of Fayette County have been so harassed this Spring by the Indians," Colonel John Todd directed construction of an even stouter fortification that would be "proof against Swivels and small Artillery which so terrify our people." The security offered by these preparations certainly would have been an inducement to potential residents. As Lexington grew, albeit slowly at first, it extended a network of roads outward in a radial pattern to connect with other towns, becoming the transportation nexus and commerce center of the state.[41]

At the beginning of the nineteenth century, Lexington residents were busily engaged in manufacturing and trade; as traveler Thomas

Chapman early observed, "I never saw a Town the size of Lexington, where there is more the appearance of trade and Business carrying on." Admiring visitors soon began to refer to this burgeoning commercial powerhouse as the "Philadelphia of Kentucky," even as the proliferation of cultural amenities, including the only western university, two newspapers, and a public library led to the designation of Lexington as the "Athens of the West." Lexington expanded to become the most important economic and cultural center of the trans-Appalachian country. Compared to the transformation of Lexington, as the author of an 1818 guidebook to the region observed, "nowhere in America has the almost instantaneous change, from an uncultivated waste to the elegances of civilization, been so striking." Without a doubt, it was one of the fastest-growing communities in the nation, such that in 1815 the *Niles Register* predicted it would become the greatest inland city in the western world.[42]

Lexington's regional dominance would soon be eclipsed by Louisville and Cincinnati, both cities on the Ohio River. The primary city of the Inner Bluegrass was landlocked, partly encircled by the Kentucky River at a distance of more than ten miles, and the watercourse that flowed through the community, Town Branch, was an insignificant stream that often dwindled to a trickle in the summer months. The site of Louisville was originally established in 1778 by George Rogers Clark as a staging point for expeditions into the Northwest Territory. Navigation of the Ohio at this location was seriously hindered by a series of limestone ledges that extended across the river, producing a zone of rapids known as the "Falls of the Ohio." The only navigational obstacle over the entire course of the river, these rapids rendered passage difficult at best and nearly impossible at low water. Because of this obstacle, the town necessarily became a break-in-bulk point (analogous to those of the eastern Fall Line), where goods were unloaded from vessels onto wagons, carted beyond the Falls, and reloaded onto water transport. Steamboat traffic was inaugurated on the Ohio in 1811, and by 1819 thirty-one vessels were plying the western waters, most between New Orleans and Louisville. After the Falls were bypassed by a canal excavated between 1825 and 1830, Louisville began its growth to a regional economic powerhouse. Cincinnati, established in 1788, experienced a similar growth surge, so that by 1850 the population of Louisville exceeded 43,000 and Cincinnati, 115,000, compared to just 8,200 for Lexington.[43]

Nevertheless, Lexington continued to dominate the economic landscape of the Inner Bluegrass, while Georgetown was among the leading regional cities prior to 1850, benefiting from some of the same factors that contributed to Lexington's early success. Georgetown also occupied a central location within the Inner Bluegrass, surrounded by country that, with a little effort, would become productive agricultural land. Georgetown, like Lexington, had a well-developed road network from an early date. Although not directly connected to either the Wilderness or Maysville Roads, before 1800 the city had some distinct connective advantages over other second-order regional communities. Georgetown was located on the road system halfway between Lexington and Frankfort, the latter chosen as the state capital in 1792 and the second-largest city of the region, and was also on the route between Lexington and Cincinnati.

Shortly after Georgetown was founded, the first wagon road out of the town was built to Great Crossings, about two-and-a-half miles west. This was extended another fifteen miles to Frankfort when, in 1793, the state legislature authorized construction of a road from Frankfort to northern Kentucky, connecting the capital to Cincinnati and facilitating commerce. Northward from Georgetown, the new Cincinnati road passed over Elijah Craig's mill dam on North Elkhorn Creek, just east of the Royal Spring branch, and followed a ridge crest that was the drainage divide between the Licking River watershed to the east and that of the Kentucky River to the west. This provided a great advantage in both road-building and travel, because for the sixty miles from Georgetown to the Ohio floodplain there were no significant streams to cross. Much of the route was laid out over the old buffalo trail that led from Big Bone Lick to the Lower Blue Licks, and became known as the Dry Ridge or Georgetown Road. A road from Lexington to Georgetown was also cut in 1793 to facilitate travel to Cincinnati.[44]

These early roads were made ten to twelve feet wide, the trees cut off close to the ground and the stumps rounded rather than removed, with a surface of natural soil. In winter they were nearly impassable. As historian J. Winston Coleman observed, "All roads were bad beyond belief and, according to the season, they choked with dust or held the traveler prisoner in quagmires." Some idea of traveling conditions on the wagon roads can be gleaned from the account of William Blane, who traveled from Maysville to Lexington in 1822:

> The road was beyond all comparison the worst I had ever seen. It was full of holes, and in many places nearly up to the horse's knees, in mud intermixed with large stones and pieces of rock, which seemed as if put there on purpose to annoy equestrians. . . . The road is a natural one, that is to say, it is a track left open and cleared, but which has never had a single cart load of gravel or stones thrown upon it. Add to this, a great many heavily laden wagons are obliged to travel over it, when carrying goods to Lexington. . . . My journey was impeded by several creeks and rivers of no inconsiderable depth. On coming to one of them after a fall of rain, the traveller is obliged either to halt or to swim, for in the whole distance between Maysville and Lexington, there are only two bridges.

Blane considered himself fortunate to be able to make thirty to thirty-five miles per day by horseback. These "natural roads," as they were called, were maintained rather haphazardly by court-appointed local labor, who were "notoriously inefficient and profoundly ill-equipped; they lacked training and informed direction in the most elementary forms of roadwork."[45]

Recognizing the difficulties of travel on such roads, during the second decade of the nineteenth century the Kentucky General Assembly authorized the incorporation of numerous turnpike companies to improve the condition of major thoroughfares. Maintenance was funded by erection of toll gates, at which tolls could be collected. In 1817, the legislature approved establishment of a company to make an "artificial road" from Maysville to Lexington, and a turnpike from Georgetown to Lexington in 1818. Early in the following year, noting that "the road leading from Georgetown to Cincinnati, through the counties of Scott, Pendleton, Boone, and Campbell, passes through a tract of country so thinly inhabited, that a large portion of it cannot be kept in repair," the legislature approved formation of a turnpike company to build a road, thirty feet wide, along this route. These "artificial" roads were laid out by professional engineers on routes "selected to minimize gradients by following a land surface excavated or filled to create a well-drained, elevated cross-section, often with a broken stone or macadam surface." Macadamized roads began to be built in Kentucky during the 1830s and 1840s, the term referring to a method in which the road bed is made of a layer of crushed stone of uniform size, thoroughly compacted and capped with smaller rock and rock dust. Roads of similar construction can be seen today as gravel roads throughout the rural areas of the state, termed "traffic-bound" in which a mixture of crushed limestone and limestone dust is compacted and hardened by traffic.[46]

Georgetown's developing road network linked the town to its rural environs, to other Bluegrass communities, and to the wider world accessible from the Ohio River. As Raitz and O'Malley observed, "Roads activated rural communities by fostering the ready movement of people and farm products to markets and linking farmsteads, meeting houses, mills, and other social and economic interaction nodes." Residents of the Inner Bluegrass began to engage in light industrial production as soon as the threat of Indian attack had lessened. Enterprising individuals built mills and mill dams to provide power on streams across the region, processing facilities that prepared resources of the land for human use. The products of these mills were mainly intended for local use rather than export; most were grist mills established to grind corn into meal. Although never a major industrial city, Lexington led the region in the variety, quantity, and value of manufactured products, but a flourishing early industrial base also developed in Georgetown.[47]

Two factors stimulated manufacturing in Georgetown shortly after the town was established: the presence of Royal Spring and the entrepreneurial zeal of the founder, Elijah Craig. The outflow from Royal Spring produced a large stream of water; the spring branch, along with North Elkhorn Creek (situated no more than a mile from the community), provided sites for a number of mill dams and mills. Elijah Craig, although a Baptist minister, promoted the rapid economic development of Georgetown by establishing a variety of manufacturing operations along both watercourses, and several other residents followed suit. By 1800, city mills were converting "grain into meal and flour, fiber and wool into textiles, and rags and fiber into paper." In addition, "Ropewalks were established to weave hempen fiber into ropes and bagging, and distilleries were constructed to convert products of orchard and field into whiskey. . . . Paper mills, carding and fulling mills, and hemp and rope factories were in operation and hatters, blacksmiths, cabinet makers, tanners, and blue-dyers were busy plying their trades.

Present-day downtown Georgetown historic district, looking west toward the valley of the Royal Spring branch. The courthouse tower is visible in center background. Photograph by Gary O'Dell.

Still others made spinning wheels, candles, bricks, nails, shoes, saddles, and harnesses." Just as the agricultural economy of Scott County was built on slave labor, enslaved persons were used in many Georgetown manufacturing operations, either owned outright by the proprietors or leased from other residents.[48]

Although the bulk of these products were for local markets, a busy export-import trade was also conducted. For example, the *Kentucky Gazette*, published in Lexington, was printed on paper made at Georgetown, and bulky corn crops could be converted into compact and valuable whiskey for export. Merchants traveled in groups, leading trains of packhorses loaded with items of local manufacture to market centers in the east and south, returning with imported and American-made products for the local trade. After 1805, the number of merchants and stores in Georgetown increased as Conestoga wagons began to transport larger loads over the road networks. Despite a thriving base of light industry and commerce, Georgetown remained essentially an agricultural community until the city's economic and social fabric was dramatically transformed late in the twentieth century.[49]

In December 1985, Georgetown residents were shocked by the announcement that Toyota Motor Manufacturing had committed to building an automobile assembly plant at a site in Scott County a few miles north of the city. Ground was broken in May 1986, and construction was completed in May 1988. Soon, 1989 model four-cylinder Camrys began rolling off the assembly line. The factory initially employed 4,300 workers, but today, after several expansions, the labor force has grown to more than 10,000.[50]

Georgetown has been radically transformed by the plant establishment. In the agreement made between the Commonwealth of Kentucky and the auto manufacturer, Toyota agreed to give priority to hiring workers from Kentucky, and 95 percent of the plant's employees are Kentuckians from all over the state. In the three decades since production came on line, the population of the city has tripled to more than 37,000 persons, making Georgetown the sixth-largest city in the state. The city and county infrastructure were accordingly placed under considerable strain in trying to cope with this unprecedented and sustained growth, resulting in a surge of housing and commercial construction, including many new subdivisions and a beltway around the southern half of the city. The community now features several "big box" stores that were lacking before Toyota came to Scott County, as well as a variety of strip stores and fast food chains.[51]

Although water to the Toyota plant was not taken from Royal Spring but provided by a dedicated line constructed by the Kentucky American Water Company of Lexington, rapid population growth began to stress the community's water supply. As a sole source, the spring was simply no longer up to the demand, and so city officials began, as so many other Kentucky communities had done generations before, to seek out other water sources that could carry the city and county into the future. The spring continues to be the city's primary water source and is at present capable of handling demand except during periods of low flow in dry weather. Provision for an emergency supply was made by construction of a pipeline from Frankfort, fifteen miles distant, during the early 1990s. Ensuring a future water supply capable of meeting the demands of Georgetown's continuing rapid growth rate remains of great concern to city planners and administrators.[52]

Over two and a half centuries as a community water supply, stewardship of the Royal Spring and its riparian corridor has been inconstant. For the first century after settlement, the spring and its environs served as a grassy common enjoyed by the citizenry, but in the latter part of the nineteenth century the site was transformed into an industrial wasteland and dumping ground for rubbish. Generations of artists, ignoring the blighted landscape surrounding the spring, were nevertheless inspired to render the springhead as a tranquil romantic setting, nature at its finest. Citizen concerns about its condition gave focus to sporadic, century-long efforts at remediation intended to transform the blighted landscape into a serene oasis for contemplation, recreation, and community activities, a sorely needed city green space and park. Today, the spring is regarded and protected as a priceless natural resource and an historic and cultural asset for Georgetown.

2

The New Frontier

In the autumn of 1775, when John McClelland and his family and friends established McClelland's Station at Royal Spring, they were well aware that they were committing an illegal act. More than a decade before, King George III had issued a total prohibition on any settlements west of the Appalachian Mountains, intending to forestall future conflicts between colonists and the Native Americans who viewed this land as their own. The McClelland party knew of the ban but chose to ignore it, reasoning that a prohibition on settlement could only be temporary and it would be prudent to establish their claims under the land laws of Virginia before other settlers arrived and vacant land became scarce. At this time, a few like-minded settlers and land surveyors were beginning to come into the wilderness of Virginia's Fincastle County. Created from Botetourt County just two years before, Fincastle was now the new western frontier of the colony. All of these adventurous souls had the same goal: to locate and claim large tracts of prime frontier land that could be transformed into homesteads, farms, and communities. Soon, the trickle would swell to a flood of thousands of immigrants; far to the east across the mountains, many residents of the thirteen colonies were desperate to acquire land of their own.

From a population of less than 30,000 in 1640, in little more than a century the colonies had increased to more than 2 million inhabitants by 1770, the result of natural growth, imported enslaved people, and the stream of European immigrants. The rapidly expanding population of the English colonies was confined to the east between the Atlantic Ocean and the Appalachian mountain wall. Stretching almost fifteen hundred miles from Canada nearly to the Gulf of Mexico, the Appalachians presented a formidable barrier to westward expansion of the English colonies in America. The continuity of the mountain system, the bewildering array of near-identical ridges, and the rough terrain and cloak of heavy forest and undergrowth held the settlers on the coastal plain and Piedmont. The rapidly expanding population generated increasing pressure to find a way through the highland region to allow settlement of the continental interior.[1]

Although the overall standard of living for American colonists was higher than that of commoners in England, in the years just before the Revolutionary War the number of persons living in relative poverty greatly increased. The recently concluded war against the French and Indians for control of the continent had left numerous widows and men incapacitated by debilitating wounds. Emigration from Europe surged after 1763, with poor newcomers crowding into coastal cities, depressing wages and swelling unemployment. Most of the colonial population was rural and agricultural, but in long-settled regions the growing population was hindered by the limited supply of available land. There was still plenty of unoccupied land in the colonies, but much of this was second-rate land unsuitable for agriculture, or marginal at best. Under these circumstances, young persons had few options, forced to either move to a city and work for wages or to rent farmland from others. Tenancy was relatively rare and temporary when land was abundant, but by the mid-eighteenth century more and more rural residents became trapped as lifelong tenant farmers, poor and getting poorer. In areas of better land, already claimed, many farmers suffered from declining yields and incomes in consequence of poor farming practices that reduced soil fertility. For such as these, the vast expanse of trans-Appalachian lands beckoned irresistibly.[2]

In addition to the poor and landless, there were other segments of colonial society who felt compelled to migrate westward. Restless souls such as Daniel Boone and the long hunters felt confined in the crowded eastern colonies, comfortable only in the wilderness; as the frontier moved west, so would they, ever seeking freedom from conventional society and culture. Others hoped to found utopian communities lacking distinctions based on class, wealth, or property, or to escape religious persecution. Such was the case for Elijah Craig, founder of Georgetown, and the members of his family, who left Virginia to seek a new life in Kentucky so that they might practice their religion unhindered. Although most immigrants possessed a vision of wealth to be obtained in the acquisition of free land, the "wealth" they sought was most often in the form of independence and an ideal life rather than financial gain. Regardless of other motivations, it was the hunger for land that drove most immigrants westward. Few, however, were able to realize their hopes of a family farm and independence, for their dreams were confounded by the manipulations of speculators. Taking advantage of complex and confusing land policies, wealthy men in the eastern colonies and in Europe were far more adept at navigating the legal intricacies necessary to acquire land, and by means both fair and foul were able to acquire huge blocks of the best land in eastern Kentucky and the Bluegrass.[3]

Despite the ardent desires of those in the thirteen colonies to build new and better lives in the Ohio Valley, the way west remained blocked for many years by hostile Native Americans and by policies of the British government, which, hesitant to encourage further conflict with the tribes, prohibited settlement west of the Appalachian Mountains. Following the Revolutionary War, such impediments to western expansion were removed, leaving only the formidable physical barrier of the mountains to hinder movement of thousands of eager settlers to Kentucky.[4]

Both the French and the British laid claim to the Ohio Valley before the beginning of the eighteenth century. France's claim was based on the explorations of Robert Cavalier, the Sieur de la Salle, who discovered the Ohio River in 1669. During further explorations in 1682–1683, la Salle led an expedition in canoes down to the mouth of the Mississippi River and claimed the entire river basin for France. In 1749, the governor of Canada commissioned Pierre Joseph Celoron De Blainville to journey down the Ohio and place engraved plates in various locations reasserting the French claim to the Ohio Valley. The boundaries of the British crown colony of Virginia, on the other hand, were extended westward by royal charter in 1609 to include all of the land in a four hundred-mile-wide swath "from sea to sea," or from the Atlantic coast to the Pacific Ocean. After King George revoked the Virginia Colony's charter in 1624, Virginians interpreted this as affecting "the government only and not the political existence of the colony within the original bounds, which remained intact, subject in its vacant lands to the eminent domain of the King." In the opinion of the Virginia government, Native American claims to the Ohio Valley were extinguished by the 1744 Treaty of Lancaster with the Six Nations of the Iroquois. Although the Iroquois were under the impression that they had sold only the Shenandoah Valley to the English, the Virginians chose to interpret the treaty provisions as indicating that the tribes had given up all claim on the lands within the 1609 chartered boundaries of the colony. This monumental difference of opinion was partly resolved by the new Treaty of Logstown in 1752, in which the Iroquois acknowledged English rights to the land southeast of the Ohio River. Other tribal groups, such as the Shawnee and Delaware, did not recognize the validity of this treaty.[5]

Access to the trans-Appalachian region was, however, a considerable problem due to physical and political barriers. Only at the northern and southern ends of the mountain ranges were there easy routes to the interior, but these passages could not be traversed by English colonists. In the north, the St. Lawrence River offered a direct water passage to the Great Lakes and the heart of the continent, but this was dominated by the French in Canada. Similarly, the Hudson River could be followed northward from the coast through New York to its junction with the Mohawk River. The broad Mohawk Valley, carved by glacial action during the last ice age, provided a westward passage between the Adirondacks and the northern Allegheny Plateau to Lake Ontario, but this again was French territory and the gateway was blocked by hostile tribes of the Iroquois confederacy. To the south in Georgia and Alabama, warlike Cherokee and Creek Indians blocked access to the interior around the termination of the Appalachian ranges.[6]

The western edge of the Piedmont was bordered by the Blue Ridge mountain section of the highlands. To the south, the mountains were more than fifty miles wide, lofty, massive, and apparently impenetrable, but they thinned out northward, pierced by a number of water gaps carved by rivers flowing to the Atlantic. These gaps allowed access to the Great Appalachian Valley, a prominent landscape feature west of and parallel to the Blue Ridge. The Great Valley was not a single valley, but

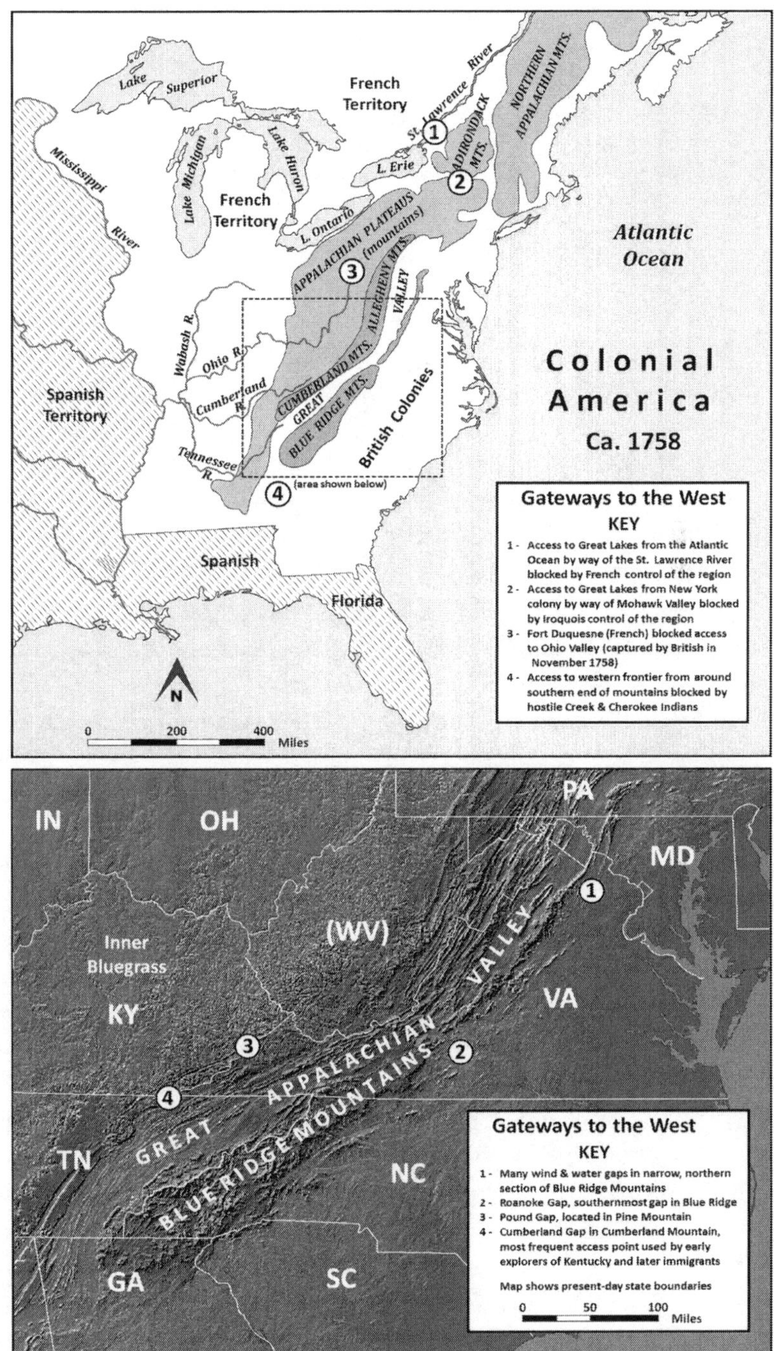

Gateways to the west. The Appalachian Mountain barrier allowed only a few access points to the western frontier, and prior to the conclusion of the French and Indian War most of these were inaccessible to potential settlers. The Treaty of Paris (1763) transferred lands formerly controlled by the French to Great Britain, but many routes were still very dangerous because of hostile Native Americans. Map by Gary O'Dell.

was instead formed by lateral branches of rivers that had cut gaps through the terrain. Traveling down the Great Valley was simply a matter of following the course of one branch southwest to its headwaters and then crossing over the moderate divide into the headwaters of the next tributary stream of an eastward-flowing river. The Great Valley allowed passage down the entire length of the highland region from Canada to Alabama.[7]

Routes through the valley were first traversed by prehistoric Native Americans. During colonial times, a major Indian pathway through the valley, known as the Great Indian Warpath, was an important trading and war trail between northern and southern tribes. By the 1730s, the Great Valley became open to settlement after treaty cessations and purchase of land from the powerful Six Nations of the Iroquois granted access through Pennsylvania. A road, known as the Great Wagon Road, was laid out from Philadelphia west to the Susquehanna Gap and then followed the old Indian Warpath south to Roanoke Gap in western Virginia. A later western branch, known as the Wilderness Road, followed another Indian trail that split off from the main road near Roanoke and went into east Tennessee. Some settlers climbed into the Blue Ridge Mountains and established homesteads, whereas others continued farther down the valley into northeastern Tennessee, where the frontier communities of the Clinch, Holston, and Powell River Valleys provided a staging ground for later penetration through Cumberland Gap into Kentucky.[8]

During the first half of the eighteenth century a handful of trappers, hunters, and explorers from the French and English colonies visited the lands west of the Appalachian mountain wall, but they left no published reports of their travels. The first descriptions of the Ohio Valley region were provided by two Anglo explorers, Dr. Thomas Walker (1715–1794) and Christopher Gist (1706–1759), both of whom came into the west in 1750 but from two different directions. Dr. Walker was one of the directors of the recently founded Loyal Company of Virginia, a land speculation corporation that received a grant from Virginia of 800,000 acres in what is now southeastern Kentucky and intended to profit by selling these lands to prospective settlers. Since this was unknown territory, the company sent Walker and five companions on a horseback expedition to explore and survey the region.[9]

Walker and his men departed from his home in present-day Albemarle County, Virginia, on March 6, 1750, and traveled southwest, crossing the Blue Ridge on the 14th at Buford's Gap, a wind gap in the mountains in Bedford County. The expedition traveled down the Great Valley and came into southeastern Kentucky on April 13 by way of a notch in the mountains, known today as Cumberland Gap. The gap was the only break in a high mountain ridge spanning more than a hundred miles, and the movements of large mammals such as deer and bison had produced a well-trampled trail used by Native Americans for thousands of years. The gap was well known to a handful of explorers and long hunters who had been visiting Kentucky for at least a decade prior to Walker's expedition. The Walker party spent several weeks exploring the land north and west of the Cumberland River before turning northward in mid-May. They discovered and crossed the Kentucky River in the vicinity of present-day Irvine, and came back to Virginia in late June.[10]

The Ohio Company was a competitor of the Loyal Company, organized to attract settlers to the region beyond the mountains known as the Ohio Country, and had been awarded a grant by the Crown of 500,000 acres for this purpose. Christopher Gist was a resident of the Yadkin River Valley area, in northwestern North Carolina; one of his near neighbors was Daniel Boone, who would later earn considerable fame on the Kentucky frontier. In 1750, Gist was employed by the Ohio Company to travel into the interior and select and survey lands for the company.[11]

Like Thomas Walker, Gist also kept a daily journal in which he recorded his travels and activities. On October 31, Gist set out from western Maryland, accompanied only by a young enslaved person. Traveling through western Pennsylvania and southern Ohio, Gist and his companion crossed the Ohio River on March 12, 1751, coming into Kentucky in the vicinity of Vanceburg, in Greenup County. They followed a southwestward course through the Inner Bluegrass, traversing the present counties of Harrison, Nicholas, Scott, and Franklin to the Kentucky River on March 16. Reaching the vicinity of the Falls of the Ohio (adjacent to present-day Louisville) on March 18, they were alarmed by increasing Indian sign in the vicinity and retreated from the area. Gist set out on a southeast course diagonally across Kentucky that took him back through the Bluegrass region, passing through present Woodford and Fayette counties on the 19th, and continued onward into eastern Kentucky. The explorer then followed the North Fork of the Kentucky River, crossing back into Virginia most likely by way of the Pound Gap through Pine Mountain. After seven months in the wilderness, Gist finally arrived back at his home on the Yadkin River on May 18, 1751. Gist's reports, like those of Walker, generated considerable excitement in the colonies. Beyond the mountains was a generous land ripe for settlement.[12]

The confluence of the Allegheny and Monongahela rivers, coming together to form the Ohio River in far western Pennsylvania, would in time become one of the primary launch points for settlement of the Ohio Valley. During the summer of 1753, the French began constructing a line of forts extending from the shore of Lake Erie in northwestern Pennsylvania down the Allegheny River to the Ohio to assert their possession of the Ohio Country. Young George Washington and Christopher Gist were sent by Governor Robert Dinwiddie of Virginia in November on a mission to demand that the French abandon the chain of forts and depart the region. Pausing at the Forks of the Ohio, the two men were greatly impressed by the strategic advantages offered by the confluence of the rivers. Continuing onward, they were received cordially by the French, who nevertheless denied the validity of English claims to the region. Returning to Virginia in haste, Washington reported to the governor and legislature of Virginia, who considered the French rejection of British demands to be a hostile act and prepared to drive the French from their frontier outposts.[13]

The Virginia government sent orders to William Trent, an employee of the Ohio Company then in the vicinity of the Forks building a trading post, to gather men and erect a fort at the strategic junction. The fortification was still incomplete on April 17, 1754, when a large flotilla of small boats came down the Allegheny and unloaded 600 French soldiers and eighteen artillery pieces about 150 yards from the fort. The French aimed their cannon at the flimsy structure and the commander, Claude-Pierre Pécaudy de Contrecœur, informed the occupants that they had one hour to surrender or they would be blown to pieces. There were less than fifty men inside the walls and many had no training as soldiers, being fur trappers, traders, and hunters who had volunteered to help raise the stockade. Greatly outnumbered, the occupants wisely chose to surrender, and were allowed to depart peaceably. The French tore down the partly built structure and constructed a larger fortification, naming it Fort Duquesne after the newly appointed governor-general of Canada.[14]

This was the opening move in the French and Indian War, the North American theater of a globe-spanning conflict between the French and English and their allies known as the Seven Years' War. Most of the subsequent American conflicts were waged along the Great Lakes and St. Lawrence River. The war went badly for the British in the early stages, and soon degenerated into a stalemate. Fort Duquesne and the line of French forts extending up the Allegheny River was a particularly vexing problem. General Edward Braddock led an expedition to capture the stronghold at the Forks of the Ohio in 1755 but failed disastrously, suffering the worst military defeat in British history to that point. In 1758, a successful venture against Fort Duquesne was led by General John Forbes, commanding British and colonial forces. The French fort was demolished and replaced by a larger structure named Fort Pitt. By cutting a road through the mountains to facilitate movement of his troops, Forbes opened the way from Philadelphia to the Ohio Valley. The French in North America were finally defeated after losing the fortress of Louisburg in Nova Scotia in 1758 and the cities of Quebec and Montreal in 1759 and 1760, respectively. By the terms of the Treaty of Paris on February 10, 1763, the French were forced to relinquish their land claims in North America east of the Mississippi River, including Canada. Spain, which sided with France in 1761, was forced to give up Florida and all land east of the Mississippi.[15]

Great Britain was now in nominal control of the entire Appalachian highland region in North America and the natural gateways to the lands beyond the mountains. In the Deep South, the Gulf coastal plain as far as Louisiana passed from Spanish hands to that of Britain; Cumberland Gap provided access to the Ohio Country from Virginia, North Carolina, and Tennessee; and Fort Pitt's strategic location at the Forks would allow waterborne access to the interior down the Ohio River. To the north, both the Mohawk Valley and the St. Lawrence River gave access to the Great Lakes and the lucrative fur trade. In theory, the way was now open into the mountains and the interior for settlement and exploitation of natural resources, but the trans-Appalachian region was occupied by Native Americans who were, understandably, unwilling to tolerate further encroachment by white settlers. The peace agreement signed by European nations at Paris in February 1763 did not ensure peace on the frontier.

The Seven Years' War was the most expensive war in British history, and its conclusion left the government saddled with an enormous debt and the citizens of Britain burdened with the very high taxes necessary to pay this debt. In North America, the continued threat from Native Americans angered by constant encroachment upon their lands meant that regiments raised for the war would still be needed for the security of the colonies and could not be demobilized or withdrawn; soldiers would still have to be supplied and paid. Above all else, the government did not want to fight another expensive war like the French and Indian War, and was determined to keep Indians and colonists separated.[16]

On October 17, 1763, the British government issued a major revision of its North American settlement policies, known as the Royal Proclamation of 1763, that would have far-reaching consequences. The proclamation drew a line along the crest of the Appalachian highlands from Florida to Quebec that created a huge "Indian Reserve" west of the mountains from which colonial settlement was banned. The line was defined by the eastern continental divide; all land with rivers that flowed into the Atlantic was reserved for the colonists, while all the land with rivers that flowed into the Mississippi River was reserved for Native Americans. British colonists were forbidden to trespass or settle on native lands, and colonial officials were forbidden to award grants in the reserve without royal approval, thus giving the Crown a monopoly on all future land purchases from American Indians. There could be no settlements, only trading posts.[17]

The proclamation line was not intended to be a permanent boundary, but a temporary measure that could gradually be extended to allow settlement to take place in an orderly, lawful manner. The boundary line would have the further effect of keeping the colonial population along the eastern seaboard, where they would easier to govern, tax, and regulate. Colonists who moved to the west would be out of reach of British tax collectors. The government would have to expend considerable resources to spread its offices and regulators to the interior or enormous sums of tax revenues would be lost. Equally compelling, colonists confined to the coastal region were more likely to engage in transatlantic trade with the mother country than settlers planted deep in the interior.[18]

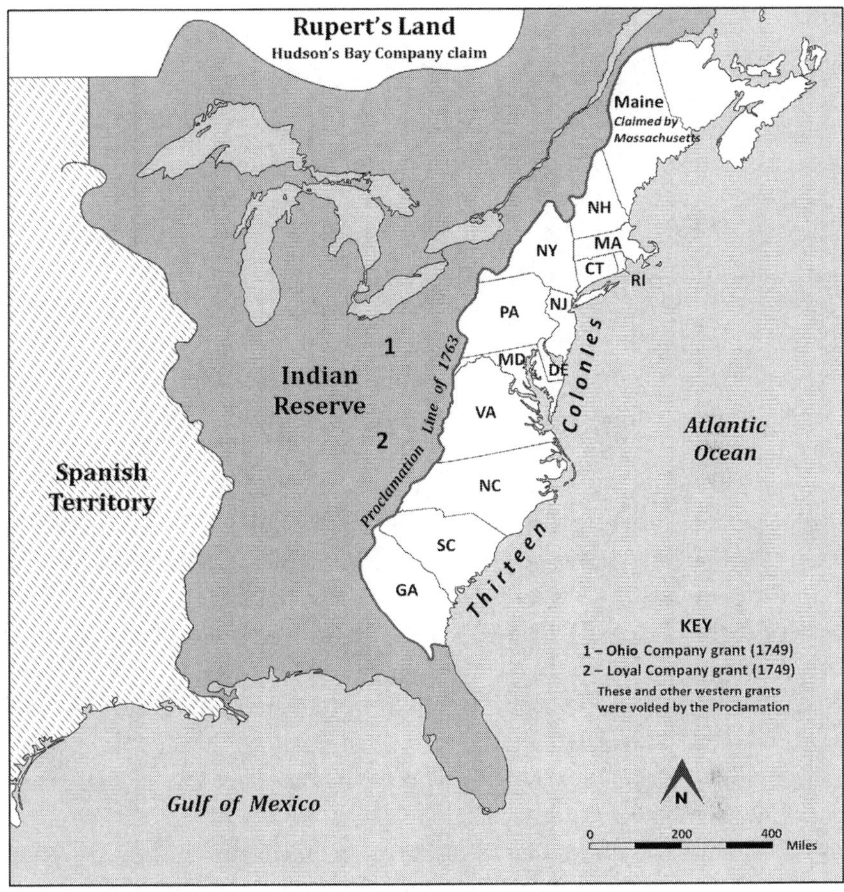

Proclamation line of 1763. Concerned over the expenses incurred by the colonial wars against Native Americans and their allies, King George III imposed a ban on western settlement with the Proclamation of 1763. The prohibition angered both speculators and potential settlers, and was generally ignored. Map by Gary O'Dell.

With the stroke of a pen, George III angered many in the colonies by abruptly terminating all westward expansion. The proclamation required that any persons who had already settled west of the mountains abandon their homes and return east. Many frontiersmen who had risked their lives in the recent war felt they had earned the right to settle in the lands over which they had fought. The hopes of land speculators were dashed—those who had anticipated gaining title to vast tracts of western lands at little or no cost from the Crown or colonial government and those, such as the Loyal Company and the Ohio Company, who had already obtained huge grants and expended considerable resources intending to attract settlers to the frontier. Colonists were also angered by the imposition of a number of new taxes, such as the Sugar Act (1764), Stamp Act (1765), and Townshend Acts (1767). The British government felt that it was only fair that the colonies should share in the burden of recouping the costs of the war, since the conflict in North America had been fought largely on their behalf. Resentment against these taxes and, to a lesser extent, the settlement restrictions, were important contributing factors that led to the Revolutionary War.[19]

The king's edict was by its nature unenforceable. By the time it was issued, there were already colonial settlements beyond the boundary line, in western Virginia, in Pennsylvania near Fort Pitt, and in New York. Military leaders at Fort Pitt and other frontier forts were aware of the proclamation but generally made only half-hearted efforts to comply with the prohibition on westward migration, periodically stopping some settlers as they headed west and forcibly removing others. The boundary was as porous as a sieve and generally ignored by settlers from the colonies, who flocked westward without fear of punishment. Prominent colonists joined with land speculators in Britain to lobby the British government, and as a result of these pressures sections of the proclamation line were adjusted westward.[20]

Despite the ban, settlers began to enter Kentucky in the final years leading up to the Revolutionary War, swelling to a flood during the conflict. By the end of the war, the risk of Indian attacks on travelers had greatly diminished, so that navigating the physical landscape provided the only real challenge to immigrants. An unending stream of prospective colonists converged on Fort Pitt and the small but growing community of Pittsburgh, the launching point from which thousands of settlers migrated west down the Ohio River to settle the Kentucky territory, and later into Ohio after the war. Increasing numbers of settlers also began to come into Kentucky through the other primary gateway, the Cumberland Gap. The Inner Bluegrass region was the focus of their hunger for land, of their dreams for independence and a better life. For most of these would-be homesteaders, however, the dream would remain out of reach, their ability to acquire fee-simple titles to frontier land being frustrated by the chaos of Virginia's land laws and the manipulations of nonresident speculators.

During the early eighteenth century, the burgeoning population of the Virginia colony expanded from the Tidewater region into the Piedmont and through the Blue Ridge into the Shenandoah Valley. Land on the frontier was never free for the taking, but citizens could claim unoccupied land though headrights, treasury rights, military warrants, or grants from the Crown or from the colonial governor and his Council of State. All of these methods were preserved, in one form or another, through the period of Kentucky settlement. Established by Virginia in 1618, headright, or importation, grants were initially intended to attract immigrants to the colony and were given to anyone willing to cross the Atlantic and pay for the transportation costs of laborers, indentured servants, or enslaved people. The person who financed the trip was allowed to survey and claim fifty acres of land for himself and for each immigrant transported. A 1705 act of Virginia's General Assembly allowed settlers to acquire uninhabited land on the western frontier through headright grants. A citizen could claim up to five hundred acres for himself, and if he possessed five or more servants or enslaved people upon whom the poll tax had been paid, was entitled to an additional headright quantity of two hundred acres for each such person, to a maximum of four thousand acres. Clear title to the tract or tracts could be obtained after paying certain fees to the state, registering a survey of the land on the books of the county surveyor, and improving the land within three years by "seating and planting"—that is, "building of one house of wood, after the usuall manner of building in this colony, being at least in length twelve foot, and in breadth, twelve foot, and clearing, planting and tending at least one acre of land."[21]

By means of treasury rights, citizens could also purchase vacant land from the colonial government—or after 1717, from the county surveyor—for a fee of six shillings for every fifty acres. Claimants secured their titles through the same process of "seating and planting" that was required for headright claims. Whereas most of the Virginia land titles during the seventeenth century were acquired through the headright system, during the eighteenth century treasury rights became the dominant system, and was reaffirmed in the form of treasury warrants in 1779 when Virginia revised and clarified the land laws. The "military right," encouraging or rewarding military service with a grant of frontier land, was established by the General Assembly in 1630 and further elaborated in 1701 as being necessary to the general welfare, "specifically that the dedication of a portion of the 'common stock' of land in consideration of the establishment of a military barrier . . . would inure to the protection of the community as a whole." The greatest number of military grants by the colonial government took place in consequence of the French and Indian War (1754–1763) and Dunmore's War against the Shawnee of the western frontier in 1774, and by the new American republic following the Revolutionary War, all of which allocated Kentucky lands to persons who served in these conflicts. During the French and Indian War, grants of frontier land were offered to encourage voluntary military service and as bounties for service performed. The quantity of land awarded varied according to rank, with field officers allocated as much as five thousand acres, two hundred acres to noncommissioned officers, and fifty acres to privates. The government's expectation was that soldiers who received such land would remain on the frontier afterward and thus help provide security in the future.[22]

During the early 1700s, speculators among the Virginia gentry, seeing opportunity in land-hungry immigrants, appropriated much of the land in the Piedmont and Shenandoah frontier region through enormous grants of tens and even hundreds of thousands of acres, receiving preferential treatment from the Virginia colonial government. These wealthy planters were the first to take up land in the region, some to establish large tobacco estates for themselves and their younger sons, others primarily interested in profits to be made by selling land to the settlers who would soon follow. "Virginia history," wrote Warren Hofstra, "had been the story of the engrossment of land in larger and larger quantities by a coterie of powerful men becoming more and more closely allied through intermarriage, inheritance, and political dominance in Williamsburg. They had always controlled land in their own interests and had spent much of the 1720s amassing huge tracts in Virginia's Piedmont to the east of the Blue Ridge." Many settlers were brought in by the grantees from the Tidewater, from Pennsylvania, or from Ireland to cultivate the land or to meet the obligations of their grants, which, beginning in 1730, required one family to be settled for every thousand acres allocated. Prospective settlers could occupy and improve unclaimed land on the frontier, but most found it far more convenient to purchase small farms from speculators than to locate and survey land and secure patents from the government at Williamsburg. At this point in Virginia settlement, as Richard L. Morton observed, speculators "made a profit on their land, but they did not profiteer."[23]

As the settlement of Virginia moved past the mountains to the frontier of Kentucky, the interest of speculators also advanced into the region. The plans of the Ohio and Loyal Companies, who had received grants totaling 1.3 million acres of western land, were disrupted by the French and Indian War and by the subsequent ban on western settlement by King George III, but they also had rivals. Among the earliest of the speculators, and certainly having the boldest vision, was Richard Henderson (1735–1785), a self-made lawyer and judge residing in the Yadkin Valley of North Carolina's Piedmont region, nearly in the shadow of the Blue Ridge Mountains. During the 1760s, Henderson began devising one of the most audacious land-grab schemes in American history, planning to coopt more than half of Kentucky through means that were patently illegal.[24]

To become familiar with the region, Henderson first secretly hired Daniel Boone and several other long hunters to explore the region beyond the mountains and south of the Ohio River. With their reports in hand, he formed the Louisa Company, later renamed the Transylvania Company, with nine wealthy men of North Carolina. As powerful as these men were within the colony, they lacked influence with the Crown. Accordingly, instead of seeking to obtain a royal grant, the proprietors of the company planned to bargain directly with the Cherokee to obtain the land they sought. After the Battle of Point Pleasant in October 1774, representatives for many of the Shawnee tribes agreed to a peace treaty with the colonies and gave up their claims to the land south of the Ohio River, leaving the Cherokee as the only major Indian power still contesting occupation of the region. Henderson began negotiating with the Cherokee for the purchase of an enormous tract of Kentucky land in the autumn of 1774. He was so confident of a successful conclusion to his efforts that, on Christmas day, he began circulating a broadside throughout North Carolina encouraging settlers to come to his lands in Kentucky though as yet he possessed none.[25]

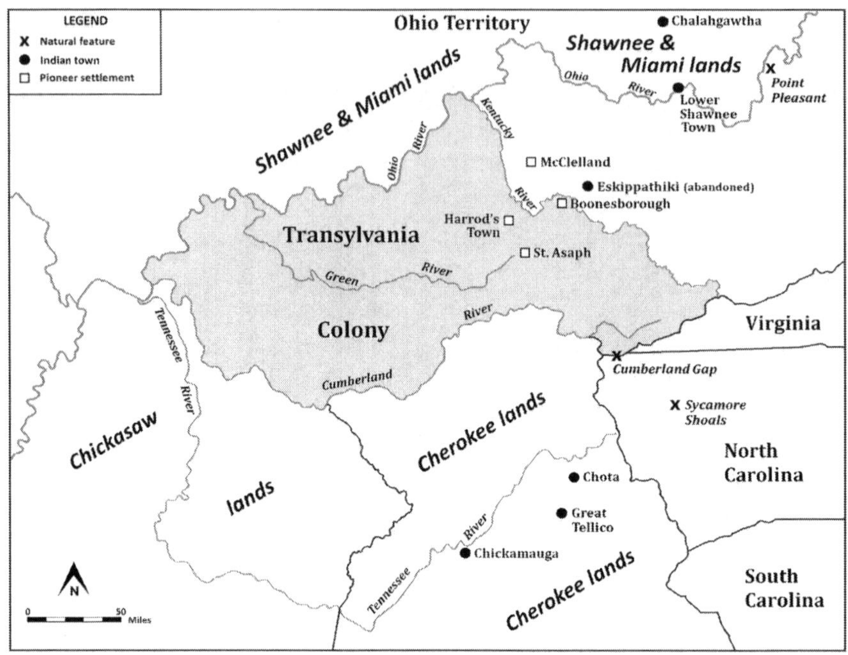

Transylvania Colony map. In 1775, Richard Henderson of North Carolina and his associates made a bold, if illegal, attempt to claim more than half of Kentucky by purchasing the land from the Cherokee. Map by Gary O'Dell.

In March 1775, Henderson met with an assembly of more than one thousand Cherokee at Sycamore Shoals, a stretch of rapids along the Watauga River in northeast Tennessee. Although many of the Cherokee present were opposed to ceding the land, on March 17 those in favor finalized a deal with Henderson. For "two thousand pounds of lawful money of Great Britain" and about £8,000 worth of trade goods, which were distributed among the Indians present, the Cherokee sold more than 17 million acres in Kentucky and northern Tennessee to the Transylvania Company. The deed conveyed all of the land encompassed by the Kentucky River on the east, the Ohio River to the north and west, and the Cumberland River to the south. The agreement also included an extra 200,000 acres around Cumberland Gap to secure passage to Henderson's new domain. Again, supremely confident in the outcome, a few days before the treaty was signed, Henderson sent Boone and thirty frontiersmen to cut a trail from Cumberland Gap to the Inner Bluegrass to establish his capital, Boonesborough.[26]

With this daring but risky gambit, Henderson bypassed the Crown and colonial authority, and outmaneuvered other speculators for a prize beyond measure. Reaction to his spectacular coup was immediate; men of wealth and power were outraged by this act, which was not only illegal but threatened their own speculative interests. Henderson's purchase not only violated the king's Proclamation of 1763 against western settlement but also trespassed on the frontier claims of Virginia and North Carolina and ignored the Crown's right of title to all undistributed lands. It also violated an act of the North Carolina General Assembly that prohibited any citizen from purchasing land from the Indians without specific permission from the government. The colonial governors of both Virginia and North Carolina, Lord Dunmore and Josiah Martin, issued statements condemning the Transylvania Company and threatening punitive action. In a subsequent letter to William Legge, the Earl of Dartmouth, Martin described Henderson and his associates as "an infamous Company of land Pyrates."[27]

Arriving at the newly established Boonesborough on May 20, 1775, three days later Henderson convened an ostentatious open-air assembly of his colonists and the House of Delegates for Transylvania beneath the shade of an enormous elm. Despite the appearance of democratic representation, however, the delegates had little real authority. Transylvania was essentially a proprietary colony, with executive power reserved to Henderson and the other partners rather than with an elected governor. Henderson alone had the right to appoint judges and all other civil and military officers, and his colonists were little more than vassals in a feudal barony, lacking even a clear title to the land granted to them but required to pay annual quit-rents of "two shillings sterling per hundred [acres]" in perpetuity.[28]

As ambitious as the Transylvania Colony scheme was, it was doomed from the start. Henderson's unconventional accomplishment managed to offend virtually everyone, high and low, both on the frontier and back in the eastern colonies. Pioneers such as James Harrod, who had previously made settlements south of the Kentucky River that now fell within the boundaries of the new colony, were angered by the notion of becoming vassals to some feudal overlord, and contested the validity

In spring 1775, Daniel Boone led a party of trail blazers cutting the Wilderness Trail through southeastern Kentucky, founding the capital of Richard Henderson's new Transylvania Colony, Boonesborough, in early April. The painting *Gateway to the West: Daniel Boone Leading the Settlers through Cumberland Gap, 1775* inaccurately depicts the composition of the party, which in reality contained only two women, an unnamed enslaved woman and Boone's adult daughter, Susannah Hays. Original 48 by 36 inches oil on canvas by David Wright, 2002. The painting was commissioned for the Cumberland Gap Historical National Park Visitor Center. Courtesy of the artist.

of Henderson's purchase from the Cherokee. Other early settlers were anxious as to whether their claims, made under Virginia law, would be recognized under Transylvania jurisdiction. The ultimate demise of the new colony came about largely as a result of an ill-conceived policy established by Henderson and his partners in which they refused to sell large tracts of Transylvania land to anyone who would not immediately settle the land. This eliminated purchases by absentee speculators. Secondary speculators were further discouraged by the higher prices charged by the proprietors for greater quantities of land, which would diminish resale profits. Henderson thus alienated many powerful men who had considerable influence in the Virginia assembly. By the fall of 1776,

Virginia had become an independent commonwealth in the new American nation, and it had no intention of giving up any of its territory to schemers such as Henderson. Over Henderson's objections, on December 7, 1776, Virginia created the new county of Kentucky, which effectively eliminated the Transylvania Colony and Henderson's fledgling empire. As compensation, Virginia granted Henderson and his company 200,000 acres of Kentucky land situated between the Ohio and Green rivers, and North Carolina followed suit with a similar grant in Tennessee. In November 1778, the state legislature officially voided the Transylvania purchase, to the great relief of most Kentucky settlers.[29]

The handful of Kentucky settlements made prior to the American declaration of independence, including Henderson's Boonesborough, Harrod's Fort, and McClelland's Station, had all been in violation of the king's proclamation, but the technical illegality of trans-Appalachian settlement did not deter land-hungry immigrants. Colonial authorities, recognizing the impossibility of thwarting all movement of westward-bound pioneers, generally did little to hinder them. Disdaining the mountains of eastern Kentucky, the immigrants pressed onward to central Kentucky and the Inner Bluegrass region, which by word of mouth and various narratives had achieved an almost mythical status as a paradisical land and thus became the favored destination.

Settlement prior to the Revolution proceeded in a rather haphazard manner, as settlers chose tracts of fertile Bluegrass land watered by cool, sparkling springs. They made improvements of varied quality to fulfill the "seating and planting" requirements of the old colonial law, marking the boundaries of their land with tomahawk slashes and initials on trees. In the summer of 1776, an irate John Floyd wrote to William Preston that "The Devel to pay here about land pray try to get something by the Convention with regards to selling those lands, or there'll be bloodshed soon. . . . Hundreds of wretches come down the Ohio & build pens or cabins, return to sell them; the people come down & settle on the lands they purchase; these same places are claimed by some one else, & then quarrels ensue." This was the case for McClelland's Station at Royal Spring, land which had been surveyed and claimed by Floyd in July 1774 and upon which John McClelland built his station, not knowing of Floyd's prior appropriation. This particular instance was settled amicably, although Floyd's initial reaction on learning of the infringement had been outrage. Similar circumstances doubtless occurred many times during the settlement period.[30]

In his letter to Preston, Floyd referred to the Virginia Conventions, a succession of assemblies that began meeting in 1774 as a replacement for the Virginia colonial government after the House of Burgesses was dissolved by Governor Dunmore on May 26. Fearful of being attacked by rebellious colonists, on June 8, 1775, Dunmore fled the capital of Williamsburg and took refuge aboard a warship on the York River. On May 15, 1776, the Convention declared independence from Britain and formed the Commonwealth of Virginia.[31]

In addition to the exigencies of forming a new government and defensive preparations, the Virginia Conventions and, later, the commonwealth's General Assembly had numerous pressing concerns to deal with—among them, handling the administration and allocation of former Crown lands on the frontier. There were many problems in this regard, old and new. Richard Henderson's controversial purchase of Kentucky land for his Transylvania Colony, transgressing upon Virginia's own claim, was a particular irritation, as was the problem of those settlers who felt their rights had been trampled on by the land company. There were unfinished land transactions based on colonial requirements, the need to generate revenue by land sales, and the need to stimulate military recruiting by bounty awards in the form of land grants. Virginia's leaders recognized the need for a new and better system to award land titles for past and present claims, but little was accomplished in this regard until 1778, when the General Assembly began to draft new legislation on the topic.[32]

On June 24, 1776, the Convention resolved that, in consequence of numerous petitions received from inhabitants of the western frontier, "all persons who are now actually settled on any unlocated or unappropriated lands in Virginia, to which there is no other just claim, shall have the preemption, or preference, in the grants of such lands." This reaffirmed the validity of claims under the old land law of 1705, and was further clarified by the General Assembly in October 1777, with legislation allowing that settlers upon vacant lands on the western waters were entitled to four hundred acres of land. The deliberations of 1778 resulted in two new land laws passed in May 1779. The first of these, intended to resolve conflicts under older systems, granted recognition of legal titles and claims made under the former colonial government, including those made under charter rights, headrights, treasury rights, and governor's military warrants. Legitimate settlers who had occupied land in Kentucky prior to January 1, 1778, were allowed to claim four hundred acres at their place of settlement. If they wished more land than this, claimants could obtain a pre-emption of up to one thousand acres of adjoining land if they had built a "house or hut," or made other improvements on this land. These "bona fide" settlers were defined as those who had "made a crop of corn in that country, or resided there at least one year since the time of their settlement." Settlers arriving after January 1, 1778, but prior to the passage of the land act were also allowed four hundred acres.[33]

This act also provided for the appointment of a number of commissioners who would travel to the frontier and set up ad-hoc courts to adjudicate land claims. The commissioners would determine which settlers had the earliest and most legitimate claims and validate these by issuing certificates for either four hundred (occupancy), one thousand (pre-emption), or fourteen hundred (combined) acres. The lands thus awarded were not free, but required a payment of ten shillings sterling per hundred acres as well as fees allocated to the clerk, county surveyor, and sheriff. For the Kentucky District, the surveyor's office was located near Harrodsburg, and the commissioners were William Fleming, James Barbour, Edmund Line, and Stephen Trigg. These officials held the first land court at St. Asaph's on October 13, 1779, and then traveled to the other major settlements, including Boonesborough, Harrodsburg, Bryant's Station, and Louisville. More than thirteen hundred claims were heard during the six months they were in session, and certificates were granted for over 1.3 million acres. Subsequently, an additional 2 million acres were soon entered on treasury warrants.[34]

The second act of May 1779 established a land office to govern the terms and manner of granting unappropriated land in the future. From this point forward, titles to unoccupied land in Kentucky could be obtained only through military grants or purchase of treasury warrants at a cost of £40 per one hundred acres (8 shillings per acre), a measure intended to help offset Virginia's Revolutionary War debts. Once a claimant had received their certificate and this had been conveyed to the land office, a warrant would be issued specifying the quantity of land and authorizing an official survey. Surveyors were to determine that boundaries were clearly marked and that the width of a parcel was to be at least one-third of its length, unless constrained by physical obstacles or by the land of previous claimants.[35]

Despite the best intentions of the framers, the result of the new land laws was largely to increase the amount of chaos that had characterized land acquisition in Kentucky ever since settlers began arriving on the frontier. Early settlers were generally able to secure their claims, but the new law proved unfortunate for immigrants arriving after passage of the acts. The new laws allowed plenty of leeway for unscrupulous or greedy individuals to secure large quantities of land at the expense of immigrants who faced the hardships of the wilderness and intended to settle the land themselves. The sale of treasury warrants offered the greatest opportunities for abuse of the system and encouraged speculation and concentration of land into the hands of a few wealthy and often nonresident individuals, because there was no limit upon the amount of land that could be purchased in this manner. These warrants were very attractive investments for great speculators, because the price of such warrants remained fixed while the value of Virginia currency depreciated rapidly during the settlement period. Within a few years, tens of millions of acres of land had passed into the hands of a few score men of wealth. One historian estimated that fully one-fourth of Kentucky was claimed by just twenty-one extensive speculators.[36]

Surveys of lands granted by treasury warrants began on May 1, 1780. So many warrants were sold that there simply was not enough land in the Bluegrass region to accommodate them all, resulting in numerous overlapping claims. This problem was further exacerbated by the fact that claims were being made in a wilderness with few landmarks and with competition, rather than cooperation, among land-seekers. Rough boundary marks or minimal improvements by others could be missed—or ignored—by claimants and surveyors, so it was little wonder that boundaries of many tracts infringed on those of prior claims. Entries presented to the commissioners were yet to be surveyed and often quite vague in describing the location of the land in question, and the commissioners had neither the means nor the time to engage in cross-checking for conflict with earlier claims. Ambiguous descriptions allowed dishonest claimants to relocate their surveys away from older, conflicting entries, onto the lands of another person having a newer entry—clearly an illegal act, but hard to prove in court.[37]

A large proportion of settlers sold or traded all or part of their claims shortly after receiving their certificates, many of which ended up in the hands of speculators. Legitimate settlers in particular reviled the corrupt "land jobbers," who, even though legally restricted as individuals to a single pre-emption, built numerous crude cabin "improvements" on vacant land and marked the boundaries with the initials of conniving friends, rather than their own. Certificates were subsequently issued in the names of these friends, who acted as fronts, and then were sold to new immigrants or to absentee speculators. Similar abuses also occurred; as Brandon Robison observed, "Many patentees never came to Kentucky, but promptly sold their patents to speculators or anyone else who would purchase them. Many names on the books are false, with imposters amassing huge estates through dozens of fictional aliases." The land laws stimulated inflation in land prices; newcomers, discovering that nearly all of the best land had been taken up, primarily by speculators, were forced to purchase land from title holders, at prices that sometimes were double that of state warrants. Many could not afford to buy tracts at inflated prices, and thus remained landless. As a consequence of the system and those who exploited it, most of the Bluegrass immigrants could not realize their dream of a family farm and independence.[38]

In 1792, the majority of Kentucky's residents inhabited the Bluegrass region, the oldest settled part. The tax books for the new state recorded 12,554 heads of households, yet two-thirds of the total, more than 8,000 households, possessed no land of their own. In the Bluegrass section, the concentration of landless households was even higher, nearly three-quarters of all residents. For three of the Bluegrass counties, Mason, Jefferson, and Bourbon, about 84 percent of households did not own any land. A high rate of landless occupancy also applied to Scott County, which was separated from Woodford County in that same year. Landless households in Woodford, and Scott by association, amounted to about 55 percent of the population in 1792, and remained fairly consistent over the next decade at about half of the county population. Fredrika Teute attributes widespread landlessness as being "a direct outgrowth of the big land grab that took place in Kentucky."[39]

As the pioneer settlement of Kentucky evolved, the earliest arrivals, such as those who came to the public forts or established stations such McClelland's, fared best, although many would subsequently sell their claims. Many of the successful settlers expanded their holdings over time, becoming more prosperous. Those who arrived after passage of the land laws did less well, often being unable to obtain land that was increasingly engrossed by speculators and far too costly for all but wealthy immigrants. Such persons, often impoverished to begin with, remained poor, forced to eke out a meager living on too-small holdings, to become illegal squatters on land not their own, to become town residents as indigents or common laborers, or to move with the frontier, as in the case of those numerous Kentuckians who relocated to Missouri.

In 1796, Moses Austin, a wealthy entrepreneur whose son, Stephen F. Austin, would lead the effort to colonize Texas on the basis of his father's Spanish grant, set out on a journey on horseback from Virginia through the western country to scout out possible sources of lead for his industrial enterprises. As he traveled from Cumberland Gap toward a well-known way station on the Cumberland River, Richard Ballinger's tavern, he was appalled by the wretched condition of so many of his fellow travelers as they followed the Wilderness Road toward Kentucky in hopeful anticipation. In his travel journal, he wrote: "I cannot omit Noticeing the many Distress.d families I pass.d in the Wilderness nor can any thing be more distressing to a man of feeling than to see woman and Children in the Month of Decemb.r Travelling a Wilderness Through Ice and Snow passing large rivers and Creeks with out Shoe or Stocking, and barely as maney raggs as covers their Nakedness, with out money or provisions except that the Wilderness affords. . . . to say they are poor is but faintly express'g there Situation."

Curious as to why so many would endure such hardships, Austin made inquiries among the immigrants he passed:

> Ask these Pilgrims what they expect when they git to Kentucky the Answer is Land. have you any. No, but I expect I can git it. have you any thing to pay for land, No. did you Ever see the Country. No but Every Body says its good land. can any thing be more Absurd than the Conduct of man, here is hundreds Travelling hundreds of Miles, they Know not for what Nor Whither, except its to Kentucky, passing land almost as good and easy obtained . . . but it will not do its not Kentucky its not the Promis.d land its not the goodly inheritance the Land of Milk and Honey.

> and when they arriv.d at this Heaven in Idea what do they find? A goodly land I will allow but to them forbiden Land. Exhausted and worn down with distress and disappointment they are at last Oblig.d to become hewers of wood and Drawers of water.

Austin's rather sour dismissal of immigrant expectations was, in fact, a sad reality, a fate that awaited all too many of the travelers who fully expected to find paradise in Kentucky.[40]

3

Bluegrass Paradise

By the beginning of the nineteenth century, nearly 200,000 persons had migrated from the East and from Europe to Kentucky, most settling within the Inner Bluegrass region. The Appalachian mountain barrier allowed only a few points of access to the western frontier, either by way of the Ohio River or through one of the few mountain passes. During the earliest years of settlement, few pioneers were hardy enough to risk the river route, where the threat of Indian ambush was a constant danger. River travel for large parties, requiring construction or purchase of a flatboat, could also be quite expensive, and so, although the land route was nearly as hazardous and the physical obstacles challenging, most early immigrants chose instead to make the long and difficult overland trek through Cumberland Gap into the region. After 1783, when the danger had lessened, most settlers bypassed the mountains and came down the Ohio River in canoes and flatboats, putting ashore at the mouth of Limestone Creek (site of present-day Maysville) or another of the river landings that served as thresholds to the Bluegrass. Travel through the western country was hazardous, but the lure of central Kentucky was so compelling that immigrants were eager to brave the hardships of travel and wilderness, certain that upon their arrival they would find the proverbial land of milk and honey.[1]

The first reports describing the fertile lands beyond the mountains came from contacts between whites (often traders at frontier outposts) and Native Americans who were familiar with the region, primarily the Iroquois, Shawnee, and Cherokee. Of these, the Iroquois provided the earliest information, being well-known to eastern colonists and having often raided into Kentucky, sometimes taking Shawnee captives. The Shawnee occupied villages in Kentucky for a brief period during the early to mid-eighteenth century, until conflict with other tribes and with Euro-Americans during the French and Indian War prompted their relocation north of the Ohio River. The Cherokee were the most numerous of the southern tribes, and their homeland during this period occupied a large part of the southeastern woodlands in western Virginia, southeastern Tennessee, western North and South Carolina, and northeastern Georgia. Cherokee traded extensively with other tribes and with colonists settling in the Great Valley. Such secondhand information was not very reliable, and often edged into the fantastical. In 1663, the Jesuit Hierosme Lalemant, obtaining information from the Iroquois about Kentucky, described garden-like lands along a "beautiful river" where "the climate is always temperate—a continual Spring and Autumn," the soils so fertile that corn grew to the height of trees with ears two feet long, and orchard-like forests consisting almost entirely of fruit trees were occupied by a variety of game animals and birds of all colors.[2]

More accurate reports based on firsthand observation began to filter into the eastern colonies by the middle of the eighteenth century as the Kentucky wilderness was penetrated by a handful of adventurous hunters, trappers, explorers, and traders to the Indians. These early accounts were mainly spread through word of mouth when the largely illiterate frontiersmen returned home and regaled their family and friends with colorful tales of their adventures in the land beyond the mountains. The same oral dissemination was also true for the accounts of the best-known of these early explorers, Dr. Thomas Walker and Christopher Gist, the former visiting southeastern Kentucky in 1750 and the latter entering the region in 1751. Although both men kept detailed journals of their travels, neither of these were published in America until late in the nineteenth century, long after the pioneer settlement of Kentucky. Walker's report was not published until 1888, and while Gist's travel diary was printed in London in 1776, few copies found their way to American shores.[3]

The respective employers of Walker and Gist, the Loyal and Ohio land companies, had a vested interest in controlling the information that was released about conditions in their grants. Because their primary purpose was the sale of land, the companies wished to portray the western frontier only in the most positive light while avoiding mention of hazards or any other negative aspects. The Loyal Company conducted an aggressive advertising campaign throughout the colonies, inviting settlers to purchase lands at £3 per hundred acres. Walker was the most active agent promoting land sales after his return from Kentucky, and he was in fact willing to share his notes with certain interested parties. Much of Walker's geographical and topographical information was obtained at an early date by mapmakers, although the resulting maps contained many inaccuracies. Information from Gist's journey also managed to percolate through the colonies. From the efforts of both men, both the Loyal and Ohio companies "performed a valuable service for the Crown and the colonists in acquainting them with the geography as well as with the flora and fauna of the trans-Appalachian west." Neither company fared particularly well, however, because of the vagaries in the locations of their respective grants, issues over colonial boundaries, and, of greatest import, the royal ban against western settlement issued in 1763.[4]

John Findlay is among the earliest identifiable explorers of the Kentucky wilderness. Through his friendship with and influence upon Daniel Boone, Findlay had a significant role in establishing the idea of Kentucky, and the Bluegrass in particular, as a new Eden. The garrulous Irishman possessed intimate knowledge of the region and persuaded Boone to accompany him on a journey into Kentucky during 1769. From firsthand observation of a verdant landscape filled with game, Boone was convinced, and he spread the word upon his return home. As the frontiersman gained fame, Boone's biographers elaborated on the theme of a paradisical Bluegrass, which circulated widely in the colonies and persuaded many to seek a new life in the western country.

John Findlay became familiar with the Inner Bluegrass when, in 1752, he established a trading post at the Shawnee village of Eskippakithiki in the Bluegrass region (present-day eastern Clark County) on behalf of his employer, George Croghan. One of Pennsylvania's leading fur traders, Croghan became highly successful by establishing trading posts in Native American villages, often far into the frontier. This had long been the French custom, as opposed to the British practice of establishing posts at a convenient location and requiring Indians to come to them for goods and supplies. During the autumn of 1752, Findlay came down the Ohio with four servants and a stock of trade goods in canoes, first putting in at the Falls of the Ohio. Finding no Indians there to trade with, he returned back upriver to northern Kentucky, where he met a party of friendly Shawnee, who invited him to come with them to their home at Eskippakithiki.[5]

With nearly a thousand inhabitants, at the time Eskippakithiki was the largest Native American settlement in Kentucky. Glad for the opportunity, Findlay took his canoes up the Kentucky River and Upper Howard's Creek to the village, where he built a stockaded house and commenced trading with the inhabitants—in competition with French traders already present. His post did not remain long, however, for in January 1753 a party of Ottawa Indians, hostile to English traders, took offense at Findlay's presence and attacked, killing three of his servants and confiscating all of his property. Findlay and his remaining servant fled through the woods back to Pennsylvania. With commencement of the French and Indian War in 1754, the inhabitants of Eskippakithiki abandoned their town to join with the Shawnee of Ohio's Scioto Valley.[6]

Findlay joined General Edward Braddock's ill-fated expedition against the French and Indians at Fort Duquesne, which departed from Fort Cumberland in western Maryland on May 10, 1755. Composed of about 1,350 red-coated Irish regulars and 500 colonials, the army's roster included many men well-known on the western frontier. George Washington, now promoted to lieutenant colonel, served on the general's staff as aide-de-camp. George Croghan, who had brought along a small contingent of Indian allies, served as guide and advisor on Native Americans of the region, as did Christopher Gist. Dr. Thomas Walker was also present, serving in the role of commissariat; he had spent the months prior to the army's departure securing tons of necessary supplies. These supplies were loaded into the 150 wagons that followed at the expedition's rear with the artillery, one of which was driven by Daniel Boone, then just twenty-one years old. These six men, so significant to frontier history, would escape with their lives from the debacle soon to follow.[7]

John Findlay was assigned to the cadre of wagon drivers, where he met Boone when the teamsters gathered around the cookfires at the end of a day's travel. Young Boone listened avidly to the older man's lavish praise of the beauty, fertility, and abundant game of the Bluegrass country, and determined to see this land for himself. Findlay told him that there was a notch in the Cumberland Mountains that would allow easy access to the interior along an old buffalo trace that had been used by the Indians for generations. Boone, in turn, most likely described his home in the Yadkin Valley of North Carolina, where Findlay would seek his new friend after the war. The Braddock campaign ended in disaster when, on July 9, the army was ambushed along the Monongahela River, just a few miles short of their destination, by a mixed force of French and Indian warriors sent out from Fort Duquesne. Out of nearly 1,500 men in the British command, strung out along a trail, 456 were killed, including Braddock, and 421 wounded. This was the worst military disaster in British history to that point in time. Braddock was an experienced and courageous soldier, but nothing in his career had prepared him for the uncertainties of wilderness warfare.[8]

During the winter of 1768–1769, Daniel Boone was pleasantly surprised to find at his door an acquaintance he had not seen in more than a dozen years. John Findlay, who was now operating as a peddler, came to the Yadkin Valley in search of his old friend and had been directed by the flatlanders to Boone's cabin on the headwaters of the Yadkin, in the foothills of the Brushy Mountains. Feeling cramped by the ever-increasing "civilization" of the Yadkin Valley, in recent years Boone had kept moving his family farther and farther up the valley. Findlay's glowing descriptions of the wonders of Kentucky had remained fixed in Boone's mind, and as the two men settled into a comfortable reunion, the talk turned naturally again to the western country. Boone told him of the unsuccessful trip he had made in 1767 with his brother Squire Boone and a friend, William Hill, to find Kentucky. Unable to locate the notch described by Findlay, Cumberland Gap, they had with difficulty crossed the mountains much farther north and come into a region (the Levisa Fork in eastern Kentucky) that was poor land, hilly and tangled with laurel thickets. Boone and his companions gave up hope of penetrating into Kentucky and returned home, not realizing that they had, in fact, entered Kentucky and that a few days' travel west would have brought them into the Bluegrass.[9]

Findlay wanted to go back to Kentucky again, but as he was getting older and was no expert woodsman, he needed a guide to help him find the mountain gap. Boone enthusiastically agreed to lead a party to find the route into Kentucky. Squire Boone, who was present during these conversations, was also glad to take part, and the two brothers had little

Daniel Boone's First View of Kentucky. Daniel Boone, at center, gazes out upon the fertile lands of the Bluegrass from a vantage point atop a large hill while John Findlay points outward. The presence of Findlay and the other men in this scene is debatable, as Boone's accounts of the event are contradictory. His autobiography in Filson (1784) states "we . . . saw with pleasure the beautiful level of Kentucky," but in 1812 he recalled, "I proceeded alone to the heights." This etching by Alfred Jones from an 1849 painting by William Tylee Ranney (1813–1857) appeared as the frontispiece for the *Bulletin of the American Art-Union* (May 1850).

trouble persuading three other local men to accompany them on an expedition "in quest of the country of Kentucke." The six men set out on the expedition to Kentucky on May 1, 1769, taking a course farther to the west than the Boone party of 1767. They crossed into the Great Valley and followed it southward to Martin's Station in Powell's Valley, at the time the westernmost settlement of Virginia. From here, following in the steps of Dr. Thomas Walker, they came across the trail leading through Cumberland Gap and entered Kentucky. Shortly after emerging from the Gap, the Boone party cut a new trail to the west and camped on a tributary of the Rockcastle River. From the camp, Daniel spotted a prominent hill (believed to be Pilot Knob in Powell County) and, believing that the bountiful lands described by Findlay must be near, climbed to the summit. From here, he had a fine view into the Bluegrass region and knew that his dream was about to become reality.[10]

Although the men in his party would come and go over the course of the ensuing year, some being new faces and others departing never to return, and in the end Boone found himself alone in the wilderness for some months, he managed to explore a great deal of Kentucky. He traveled extensively through the Bluegrass region, both Outer and Inner sections, and as far to the west as the Falls of the Ohio. His brother Squire Boone was his most steadfast companion. The apparently limitless quantity of game in the country was amazing to Boone, who hunted and feasted on deer, elk, bear, buffalo, and other denizens of the wild. The Boone brothers finally returned to the Upper Yadkin in May 1771, Daniel having spent two full years in the wilderness of Kentucky.[11]

In the years that followed, the reputation of the famous frontiersman continued to grow, but despite his many contributions in opening Kentucky to settlement, he was never to secure any lasting fortune. Constantly entangled in lawsuits over conflicting land claims, by 1799, landless and nearly destitute, he moved with his family to a sparsely populated region in what is now St. Charles County in Missouri, then part of Spanish Louisiana. When, in 1804, Missouri became part of the United States as a result of the Louisiana Purchase, Boone again was deprived of his land, which had been based on Spanish grants that were never properly secured. In 1812, now seventy-eight years old and plagued with debts, he sent a petition to the legislature of Kentucky asking that body to help him regain the Missouri lands he had lost. In this petition, which was ultimately successful, Boone recalled his first view of the Bluegrass from Pilot Knob: "[I] proceeded alone to the heights which overlook this terrestrial paradise, from whence [I] descended into those fertile plains, which are unequalled on our earth, and by the fairest claim to the description of the garden of God."[12]

Early explorers and settlers of Kentucky such as Boone frequently referred to the Inner Bluegrass as an earthly paradise, expressing this view in letters, journals, and by word of mouth. These accounts were received with great excitement east of the mountains. In his journal entry for July 1, 1774, explorer Thomas Hanson described the vicinity of Elkhorn Creek, near the future site of Georgetown: "All the land we passed over today is like a Paradise it is so good & beautiful." Writing to his friend

William Preston in 1775, John Brown Sr. of Virginia described the excitement about Kentucky, saying, "to hear people speak of it one Would think it was a new found Paradise." In that same year, Felix Walker of North Carolina set out from his home in Rutherford County with a group of friends, bound to explore the new frontier of Kentucky, "greatly renowned and highly spoken of as the best quality of land." Walker's party reached the Watauga River just in time to witness Richard Henderson negotiating his purchase of Kentucky land from the Cherokee, and continued on into central Kentucky with Daniel Boone and the trail blazers. As they entered the Bluegrass region, Walker recalled, "We felt ourselves as passengers through a wilderness just arrived at the fields of Elysium or at the garden where was no forbidden fruit." Even more extreme, perhaps, was the opinion of the Baptist preacher Lewis Craig, who came to Kentucky in 1781 ahead of his brother, Elijah Craig, founder of Georgetown. Searching for the right words to describe Heaven to his congregation, he paused, and then impulsively stated, "Heaven . . . is a mere Kentucky of a place!"[13]

Here was a land, these immigrants and visitors informed their friends and relatives, where the streams swarmed with fish, wild game of all sorts was plentiful, and the soils were of such fecundity that one scarcely need make an effort to be rewarded with bounteous crops far beyond anything that could be produced in the tired earth of the East. After crossing the Kentucky River into the Inner Bluegrass in early May 1790, the well-traveled Reverend Francis Asbury noted in his journal that, "as to the land, it is the richest body of fertile soil I have ever beheld." Harry Toulmin, a Baptist minister, came to Kentucky from England in 1793 and kept a detailed dairy of observations about his new country. According to a reliable source, he recorded, in the first-rate land near Lexington during wet or warm weather corn would grow as much as six to eight inches in a single day. Charles Scott, who came down the Ohio with George Rogers Clark in 1778, told his son Patrick of keeping watch in his cornfield on an island near the Falls of the Ohio, where he "thought he could hear the corn go tick, tick—it grew so fast." In 1796, David Meade, an emigrant from Williamsburg, Virginia, boasted that on his Jessamine County plantation "I have, in my view, more Corn growing, than all the crops which I made at Maycox put together for twenty Years would amount to." As the eminent Kentucky historian Thomas D. Clark observed, "The pioneers kept diaries and journals, and occasionally wrote letters back home to describe the new lands of Kentucky, but it was their words that filled the trails with immigrants."[14]

Many persons in the East and in Europe were already long predisposed to believe in the existence of a paradise in the West. The biblical Garden of Eden was traditionally placed at the edge of the world in Asia, which after the voyages of Columbus was thought possible to access from the west. Located at the limits of geographical knowledge, the Garden was portrayed as a region of extraordinary fertility, blessed with sparkling rivers and gushing springs, beautiful flowering and fruit-bearing trees, birds and wildlife of all description, with access guarded by a formidable barrier—mountains or sea—through which only the valiant soul may pass. Pioneer accounts of the Inner Bluegrass region of Kentucky aligned closely with this model in nearly all significant aspects, and so the region became the focus of the paradisical myth in the New World. Regardless of whether immigrants truly sought an actual earthly paradise in which to bask in God's bounty or understood the Bluegrass as a land whose characteristics resembled those of an Edenic ideal, individuals were caught up in a wild enthusiasm for the new land beyond the mountains. Land companies were quite willing to exploit this perception, and many individuals were seduced by the vision of a paradise in Kentucky and set out in haste for the frontier with little appreciation for the realities of wilderness settlement.[15]

The widespread perception of Kentucky as a second paradise on earth was strongly reinforced by published works such as John Filson's *Discovery, Settlement and Present State of Kentucke* (1784), which praised the bounty and beauty of the new land. Filson's book provided the first history of Kentucky, the first published map to focus on the region, and included a ghostwritten autobiography by Daniel Boone that propelled the intrepid frontiersman to international fame and the archetype of the American hero. The contributions of his book to Kentucky's reputation cannot be overstated; as Filson's biographer John Walton observed, "if there had been no Filson, Kentucky would not have been so favorably known on two continents."[16]

Well-educated and an accomplished surveyor, Filson came to Kentucky in late 1783 and was employed as a surveyor and school teacher in Lexington. Fascinated by the new land in which he now resided, he

Portrait of John Filson, oil on canvas, 29.25 by 24.5 inches, by Aurelius O. Revenaugh, circa 1885–1913. Courtesy of the Filson Historical Society. The painting was commissioned by Reuben T. Durrett, who founded the Filson Club in 1884, now the Filson Historical Society. The Revenaugh portrait and other likenesses of Filson are based on a crude pencil sketch in the flyleaf of an old book, allegedly a self-portrait, although there is no hard evidence that Filson was the artist.

began to write a book, traveling from station to station and gathering information from some of the most experienced and knowledgeable pioneers of the region. Completed manuscript in hand, Filson traveled to Wilmington, Delaware, in the summer of 1784 and placed it into the care of the printer James Adams with an order for fifteen hundred copies. The front matter of the book contained an endorsement by Daniel Boone, Levi Todd, and James Harrod, noting that they had carefully reviewed and revised the manuscript, and believed that it contained "as accurate a description of our country as we think can possibly be given." In the preface, Filson acknowledges the assistance of these men.[17]

Kentucke was a relatively short book of 118 pages. It began with an essay on the settlement history and geography of the region, with short chapters on boundaries, rivers, soil, climate, economic products, wildlife, population, natural wonders, and trade, very similar in character and organization to Thomas Jefferson's later *Notes on the State of Virginia* (1785). Following this was the thirty-three-page Boone autobiography, "from his own mouth," and an appendix concerning the Indian nations of the thirteen colonies. The book was a mixture of hyperbole and matter-of-fact information. Historians who have analyzed the content found Filson's descriptions to be generally accurate, although with some exaggerations and errors of fact. Willard R. Jillson, Kentucky state geologist for many years and eminent historian, carried out a line-by-line critique of Filson, and praised his "remarkable powers of observation" and ability to accomplish so much in such a short time. While making note of Filson's errors, he rated the account of the physical aspects of the Bluegrass and adjacent regions as "excellent," river and waterway descriptions "marvelously good," discussion of the procedure by which settlers took new lands in Kentucky as "crystal clear," and of the characteristics of Indian tribes of the western Appalachians as "good in all general respects, and in some particular details excellent." The reliability of Filson's information can be attributed to the experience and cooperation of the sources he drew upon, the prominent frontiersmen of Kentucky.[18]

The merits of Filson's book aside, it is clear that his motives for publishing were largely self-serving. Almost immediately on arriving in Kentucky, John Filson laid claim to more than twelve thousand acres near the Ohio River based on treasury warrants he had purchased. Filson's *Kentucke* was written not only to satisfy the author's literary ambitions but also with the purpose of attracting immigrants to the region, which would increase land values and thus the worth of his holdings. One biographer referred to the book as "a piece of promotional literature," and another historian described it as being essentially a "real-estate prospectus." The map that accompanied the text emphasized features of the landscape that would be of interest to potential immigrants and encourage settlement, showing the principal forts and stations, rivers, mountains, salt springs, "fine cane lands," major roads, towns, and mills. The map was drawn from pioneer accounts rather than surveys and was not very accurate, being severely compressed from east to west, so that Kentucky appeared to be as wide as it was high, from north to south. The Bluegrass region was rendered with the most attention to detail and accuracy.[19]

The theme of Kentucky as the promised land was woven throughout the text of Filson's book. This was "the most extraordinary country that the sun enlightens with his celestial beams." Here the cane grew to more than twelve feet high, the woods were filled with flowering trees, game animals and fowl were abundant but serpents few in number, the streams were filled with fish, the climate was the most favorable in North America, swampland was altogether absent, and the soils of astounding fertility, so that the best land was capable of producing more than a hundred bushels of corn per acre. The famous frontiersman Daniel Boone called Kentucky "a second paradise" in the narrative of his adventures. In his concluding remarks, Filson's hyperbole soared to new heights in extolling the virtues of this new Eden in the west:

> This fertile region, abounding with all the luxuries of nature, stored with all the principal materials for art and industry, inhabited by virtuous and ingenious citizens, must universally attract the attention of mankind. . . . In your country, like the land of promise, flowing with milk and honey, a land of brooks and water, of fountains and depths, that spring out of valleys and hills, a land of wheat and barley, and all kinds of fruits, you shall eat bread without scarceness, and not lack any thing in it; where you are neither chilled with the cold of capricorn, nor scorched with the burning heat of cancer; the mildness of your air so great, that you neither feel the effects of infectious fogs, nor pestilential vapors. Thus, your country, favoured with the smiles of heaven, will probably be inhabited by the first people the world ever knew.[20]

Filson planned to issue a second printing of his book, and even requested George Washington to provide an essay on the waterways favoring trade with Kentucky, which was declined. A second American edition did not materialize, but the book found a very receptive audience in Europe. A French translation was published in Paris in 1785, a German edition in 1790, and a London edition in 1793, greatly stimulating interest in the trans-Appalachian west and encouraging European immigration to the region. In the new American republic, Filson's *Kentucke* created a minor sensation, and well-thumbed copies were passed from hand to hand until they were dog-eared and tattered. Plagiarized editions were published by unscrupulous authors under their own names, without crediting Filson. Gilbert Imlay's *Topographical Description of the Western Territory of North America*, first published in 1792, drew heavily on Filson as a source, and in later editions reprinted Filson in its entirety, giving due credit. Every bit as sentimental in his writing style as Filson, Imlay continued the motif of Kentucky as an earthly paradise.[21]

John Filson received little profit from his seminal work on Kentucky, for he disappeared into the wilderness of southern Ohio in 1788 and his fate remains unknown to this day. The most likely possibility is that he was killed by Indians. Although his fame burned brightly during the settlement era of the late 1700s, during the ensuing century he vanished into obscurity, nearly forgotten for almost a hundred years until rediscovered by historians late in the nineteenth century.[22]

Filson promised immigrants that, on entering Kentucky, they would be returned to the Garden of Eden. This "Heaven in Idea," as sarcastically described by Moses Austin in 1796, sprang from the observations of the first explorers to carry word of these rich and fertile lands back to the colonies, reinforced over time by those who followed. The expectations of a promised land and wealth to be gained by convincing others of this notion prompted speculators to send out men like Thomas Walker and Christopher Gist to scout out the west and report on their findings. Surveyors, such as John Floyd, were tasked with charting the wilderness and establishing the first claims, and in their footsteps came hope-filled immigrants like the McClelland party to establish the initial settlements. Others came later and built communities, such as Lewis Craig, who came to Kentucky to escape religious persecution and helped establish the Baptist church in Kentucky, and his brother Elijah, who laid out Georgetown on the banks of Royal Spring branch.[23]

These immigrants had been persuaded by assurances of unbounded opportunity and personal liberty to be found in the trans-Appalachian west, and they came by the thousands to Kentucky. What they discovered on arrival was not the paradise of their dreams but, as Moses Austin acknowledged, "a goodly land" indeed.[24]

4

A Goodly Land

The Inner Bluegrass region was not the paradise envisioned by so many immigrants, but it was nevertheless a land that was rich in potential for those with the fortitude to withstand hardship, to reshape and domesticate a wilderness. Although John Filson and other visitors had exaggerated the qualities and benevolence of the country, they had not been all that far off the mark. This was indeed a land of great beauty, with numerous rivers and streams and cold, clear springs pouring from hillsides, a land of forest and woodlands and expanses of "fine cane." Here could be found game of all sorts to provide meat for the table: bison, elk, deer, bear, turkey, and grouse. Most important to the legions of would-be farmers who poured into central Kentucky, much of the region was cloaked by a deep, well-drained, and very fertile soil that would promote vigorous growth in any crop the climate could support. Soils are derived from the gradual disintegration of surface bedrock by physical and chemical processes mixed with the organic residue of decayed plants. The Inner Bluegrass was limestone country, and the slow weathering of limestone bedrock produced the rich silt loams characteristic of the region, as well as the gently rolling topography. This was the land that the immigrants found on their arrival, and how it came to be is a tale that spans nearly half a billion years.[1]

The Inner Bluegrass lies at the center of the greater Bluegrass region. Encompassing an area of about twenty-four hundred square miles, the Inner Bluegrass includes all or parts of twelve present-day counties: Anderson, Bourbon, Boyle, Clark, Fayette, Franklin, Garrard, Harrison, Jessamine, Mercer, Scott, and Woodford. The Bluegrass can be defined as a cultural region, based on similar social and economic characteristics of the population, or as a geomorphic region, based on physical characteristics of the landscape. The nature of the Bluegrass landscape is derived from the characteristics of the bedrock and the geologic processes that, over time, shaped the topography into its present form.[2]

Nearly half a billion years ago, from middle Cambrian to middle Ordovician time, Kentucky and most of the southern states were submerged beneath a shallow sea. The ancestral North American continent, known as Laurentia, was much smaller in size and located squarely astride the equator, slowly migrating northward. Sediments eroded from the land mass accumulated on the seafloor as deposits of sandstones and shales. In particular, the tropical conditions of this period fostered deposition of calcium carbonate precipitated from seawater, building thick beds of carbonate rocks, such as limestone. During the middle to late Ordovician (circa 460 million years ago), a volcanic island arc approaching from the east collided with Laurentia, generating a long mountain chain in the collision zone. This was the Taconic orogeny, or mountain-building event. Farther west, this same event warped the planetary crust to create an elongate upward northeast-southwest bulge framed by troughs on either side. The eastern trough, the Appalachian Basin, was gradually filled with sediments eroded from adjacent lands. In time, the former basin region would be uplifted and dissected by stream erosion to become the mountains of eastern Kentucky. The central bulge, known as the Cincinnati Arch, stretches from Tennessee through Kentucky into central Ohio. Two domed structures, nearly circular, are developed along the axis of the arch: the Jessamine Dome in central Kentucky and the Nashville Dome in central Tennessee, separated by a slight dip known as the Cumberland Saddle.[3]

These are structural features of the bedrock, and not apparent from the land surface except in bedrock exposures. Following the uplift that created the Cincinnati Arch, hundreds of millions of years of erosion planed off the domes to create the gently rolling landscape that is characteristic of both the Inner Bluegrass and the area around Nashville. This similarity in geologic history accounts for the topographic similarity of the two regions, both of which were once known as "the Bluegrass." Because the beds of the dome dip gently away from the center in all directions, erosional leveling exposed the oldest rocks in the center of the Jessamine Dome. These are surrounded by roughly concentric circles of progressively younger rocks in a fashion somewhat resembling a "bulls-eye" target pattern. Departing Lexington and traveling eastward along I-64, one is, in a sense, traveling through time, millions of years of bed-rock age with every milepost of the highway, so that by the time one reaches Ashland on the West Virginia border, the bedrock is younger by about 150 million years.

Thus, the oldest rocks to be found in Kentucky are those of the Inner Bluegrass region, the center of the Jessamine Dome, and consist almost entirely of a thick layer of Ordovician limestone, the Lexington limestone. This limestone is in large part responsible for the agricultural largess of the region, as it has weathered to produce deep residual soils of great fertility. Visiting the Bluegrass in 1795, the Baptist preacher David Barrow lavishly praised its quality: "I think sincerely that the great Creator has inbued [*sic*] it with every rich property in the greatest proportion that is to be found in the whole of North America, if not in the whole world." These dark brown silt loams have an unusually high phosphate content that favors livestock production, a contributing factor in development of the Thoroughbred industry here. Outward from the center of the Jessamine Dome, an area of shaley hills of upper Ordovician age surrounds the gently rolling lowland of the Inner Bluegrass. The Eden shale belt, ranging in width from one to thirty miles, has much steeper terrain and thinner, less fertile soils. The Outer Bluegrass region encircles the Eden hills, developed on limestone and shales and topographically similar to the Inner Bluegrass but a little hillier. Soils range from thick (over limestones) to thin (over shales), and in some areas are nearly as fertile as those of the Inner Bluegrass.[4]

Basil Duke, a native of Scott County who attended Georgetown College and served with Confederate calvary raider John Hunt Morgan during the Civil War, described the landscape of his Inner Bluegrass home in this manner: "The beauty of this country is much enhanced by its peculiar topography. It is neither hilly nor level but undulates in all directions in a succession of wide 'swells,' rising to no great height, the depression of the intervening ground being so gradual that it rarely gives the impression of a valley." Nathan Reid came to Kentucky in 1776 with John Floyd, who had discovered and claimed Royal Spring two years earlier, and resided at Boonesborough during that summer. Many years later, he described his adventures in pioneer Kentucky to his son, Nathan Reid Jr. "Our time was mostly spent in locating and surveying lands, or in hunting the buffalo and deer, of which there were vast herds. Sometimes we extended our excursions far into the country—and what a country it was at that day! It would be difficult for the most fertile imagination to draw an exaggerated picture of its then lovely appearance."[5]

The broad limestone lowland of the Inner Bluegrass is karst country. Nearly half of the land area of Kentucky is characterized as karst, including most of the Inner Bluegrass region in which Scott County is located and a vast area encircling the Outer Bluegrass from western Kentucky to the mountains of the east. This type of landscape develops as a result of the gradual dissolution of the bedrock by mildly acidic groundwater. The defining features of a karst landscape are sinkholes, sinking streams, and networks of enlarged conduits constituting groundwater flow systems. Carbon dioxide and water vapor combine in the atmosphere to form carbonic acid, H_2CO_3, which is carried to earth in solution in precipitation. This acid is present everywhere in the natural waters of the planet, and can also be found, for example, in carbonated soft drinks, the result of the combination of carbon dioxide with the water in the soda. At the surface, acidic rainfall infiltrates into the soil, absorbing additional carbon dioxide from the organic matter as it percolates downward and enhancing its acidity. Upon contacting limestone, the acidic water moves laterally along the soil-bedrock interface until it encounters vertical crevices and descends into the bedrock. Most of these fissures carry water downward without showing signs of this activity at the surface, providing diffuse inputs into a groundwater flow system. Some are gradually enlarged as the rock dissolves, the overlying soil gradually migrating downward to create an enlarging sinkhole. If the sinkhole is intercepted by a surface stream, this becomes a sinking stream that plunges directly into the groundwater flow system.[6]

Groundwater continues to move downward through fractures and crevices until it encounters a resistant rock layer, such as shale, becoming "perched" on the unit, and then flows laterally through bedrock partings, dissolving the bedrock to create a network of horizontal flow conduits.

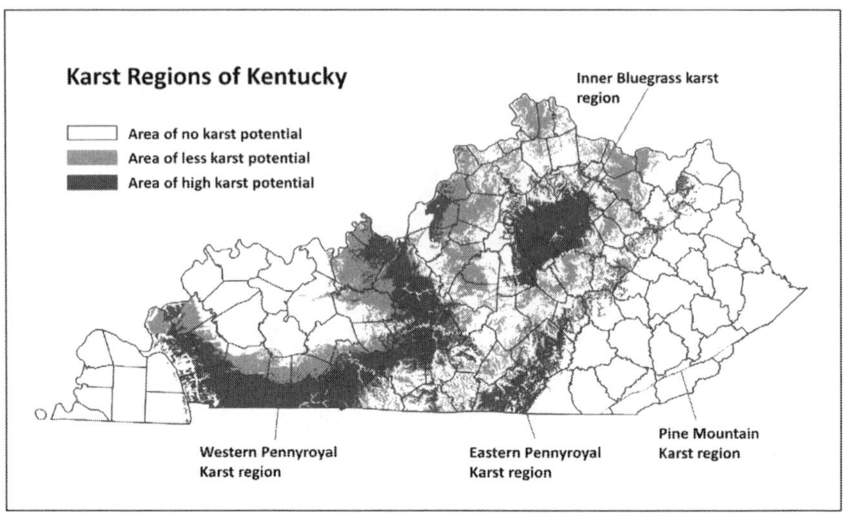

Karst areas in Kentucky. Carbonate rocks, mainly limestone, constitute nearly half of Kentucky's surface bedrock. Slow dissolution of the rock by percolation of naturally acidic precipitation produces a landscape known as karst, characterized by sinkholes, sinking streams, and caves. Courtesy of the Kentucky Geological Survey.

If the flow system has an external opening and conduits large enough for persons to traverse, this is termed a cave. Points where groundwater discharges to the surface are springs. These are of two basic types: gravity springs, which emerge from hillsides and flow down slope, and artesian springs, which are fed by water that rises from depth under pressure, often forming a circular pool. Springs that discharge at the level of the surface stream into which it flows are base-level springs. Royal Spring is a gravity spring of this type, flowing from the point of emergence to North Elkhorn Creek with only a modest gradient. Other springs may be perched by insoluble rocks, guided to discharge from hillsides well above local stream levels. These generally drain smaller areas and have a lower flow volume than base-level springs.[7]

Because much of the regional drainage is carried underground, surface streams are less abundant in the Inner Bluegrass than in non-karst areas of the state. Channels of smaller streams are often dry, especially in the summer months, their flow being diverted underground. The early explorers and settlers often made note of the scarcity of water.

James Nourse, traveling through northern Woodford County in late May 1775 observed, "We passed several dry branches but no running water." In the same year, David Barrow described the streams he saw in the Inner Bluegrass: "In the winter and wet seasons, their creeks which are numerous are flush sweetly gliding over rock bottoms and appear to be never failing: but in midsummer if the season should be dry, disappear for miles altogether, and then perhaps break out again, which subterranean passages giving vent to their springs." Two centuries later, geological research would show that this was an almost perfect description of the hydrological situation of Royal Spring.[8]

The most prominent watercourse of the Bluegrass is the Kentucky River, which originates in the mountains of eastern Kentucky and flows northwestward through central Kentucky to merge with the Ohio River in the northern part of the state. The Kentucky is an ancient river that has been flowing for more than 100 million years and, after departing the mountain region and passing into the plains of Bluegrass, exhibits broadly looping meanders characteristic of mature lowland river systems. The river is, however, deeply incised through the Inner Bluegrass, forming a gorge more than three hundred feet deep in places, as are tributaries as they approach the river. The incision of the Kentucky River was the result of increased channel erosion during the Pleistocene ice ages. Prior to this time, the Kentucky river flowed farther northward to join with the ancient Teays River; there was no Ohio River prior to glaciation. When the continental ice sheet buried most of the Teays River, the Ohio River came into existence along the margin of the ice sheet, and the Kentucky became a tributary of the new river system. Abandonment of its more distant junction with the Teays in favor of the Ohio shortened the course of the Kentucky River. The shortened path, in combination with a lowered sea level and the depression of the continental land mass north of Kentucky by the great ice sheets, increased the flow gradient and consequently the rate of erosion, entrenching the Kentucky into the landscape.[9]

Elkhorn Creek is the most significant tributary of the Kentucky River in central Kentucky, and in fact drains a larger area than some actual rivers in the state, such as the Dix River and the Red River. The watershed of this stream lies within four modern counties: Fayette, Franklin, Woodford, and Scott. They possess some of the most fertile land in the state. The Elkhorn forms from the junction of two branches, South and North Elkhorn creeks. South Elkhorn, spring-fed along much of its length, originates in southwest Lexington, in Fayette County, near the border with Jessamine County, and flows north and then west to join with the north branch. North Elkhorn begins just to the east of Lexington and flows north and then west, passing by Georgetown, to merge with South Elkhorn just east of Frankfort at the Forks of Elkhorn. From the Forks, the stream flows north to join with the Kentucky River fourteen river miles below Frankfort. Discovered and named in 1773 by surveyors Hancock Taylor and Robert and James McAfee, Elkhorn is a shallow stream with bars and rapids and is not navigable except by canoe. During the pioneer era the Elkhorn helped to funnel explorers and settlers into the region, and so it was that, in 1774, John Floyd followed first Elkhorn, then North Elkhorn until he came to Royal Spring.[10]

Most groundwater conduit systems in the Inner Bluegrass tend to be aligned with local fracture systems, exhibiting patterns that are commonly oriented northwest-southeast. Such systems may be marked by a line of sinkholes that feed into the system. In contrast to the massively bedded Mississippian limestones of the surrounding region, in which complex multi-level caves of considerable length have developed, the Ordovician-age limestone in this part of the state is thinly bedded and most of the caves are low, short, and wet. Mundy's Landing Cave in Woodford County, surveyed to a little more than 14,000 feet, is the longest cave in the Inner Bluegrass, followed by Slack's Cave in Scott County at 7,185 feet. Slack's Cave discharges into North Elkhorn about three miles due west from Royal Spring, a little to the southwest of Great Crossing, and is oriented northwest-southeast and parallel to the Royal Spring groundwater system. Slack's is of historical interest, because a brief account of the cave in the *Kentucky Gazette* for June 7, 1790, appears to be the first known description of a specific Kentucky cave:

> On the 3d May last, Mr. John Garnet near the mouth of Cain [Cane] Run in Woodford County [today Scott], lost a calf which was supposed to have gone into a Cave at the head of a spring. The Cave was examined some distance underground, but as they proceeded the passage was obstructed by a large current of water,

> upon which he had a boat built and proceeded by water up the stream about three quarters of a mile, when they overtook the Calf, which they recovered, and brought down to the mouth again. They saw no evidence of an end to the passage, the aperture as large where they stopped as at any other place. They were provided with candles to see their way.

Although the cave entrance at the spring can no longer be entered, having been blasted shut many years ago to keep cattle out, the cave stream flows out through the rubble to discharge into North Elkhorn, and Slack's Cave can be entered from another location. To the east, the adjacent Royal Spring system is potentially much longer than any other system in the Inner Bluegrass, but virtually the entire conduit is submerged or otherwise inaccessible.[11]

The decomposition of limestone bedrock produced the deep, fertile soils across much of the Inner Bluegrass that, in the past, supported the variety of plant communities encountered by early pioneers. Despite a wealth of firsthand descriptions by Kentucky pioneers, botanists of the first half of the twentieth century failed to delve deeply into this material and seemed rather at a loss as to how to characterize the presettlement vegetation of the region. Lucy Braun, in her classic 1950 work on American forests, was unable to draw any firm conclusions as to the nature of the vegetation at the time of Euro-American arrival. "Old forest trees, widely spaced in a carpet of Kentucky bluegrass, dot the extensive estates," she wrote. "From these it is not possible to construct a picture of the original condition. . . . Blue ash and bur oak may be thought of as most characteristic." From the few historical accounts Braun consulted, descriptions of extensive tracts of wild cane, rye, and clover led her to believe that the Bluegrass was but lightly forested. "That the Bluegrass was originally a forest region appears evident. That it was unlike any existing forest is also evident."[12]

Other investigators seized on the present-day distribution of large, ancient trees with wide-spreading branches and grassy meadows to develop an ecological misinterpretation that became widely accepted and repeated in nearly every modern-era description of the pioneer-era Bluegrass. The popular myth is that presettlement vegetation was dominated by savanna woodlands. Woodlands are different from forests. In a forest,

Ancient bur oak on fenceline between Kentucky Horse Park and Walnut Hall Farm. With a trunk diameter of 57 inches, this tree is an estimated 285 years old, predating Euro-American settlement. The presence of bur oak trees with wide-spreading limbs has been incorrectly interpreted as an indication that presettlement vegetation of the Inner Bluegrass region was a savanna woodland. Photograph by Gary O'Dell.

trees are closely spaced so that branches overlap to form a continuous—or closed—canopy; woodlands are more open, with trees spaced farther apart, allowing the growth of shade-tolerant understory vegetation. In a savanna woodland, trees are widely spaced, so that grassy undergrowth becomes the dominant form of vegetation. The savanna woodland interpretation of presettlement Bluegrass vegetation is, however, contradicted by the observations of pioneer explorers and settlers. According to Bluegrass ecologist Julian Campbell, the savanna myth originated as a seed planted by Ursula Davidson, a graduate student at the University of Kentucky. In her 1950 master's thesis, Davidson focused on the ancient bur oaks (*Quercus macrocarpa*) in an effort to determine the original vegetation of Lexington and vicinity. Because these oaks are widespread throughout the Inner Bluegrass and their seedlings are intolerant of deeply shaded conditions found in dense forest, Davidson concluded that the region, in the past, had been occupied by a rather open forest or woodland.[13]

This seed was later nurtured and the thesis greatly expanded by botanist and ecologist Mary E. Wharton, who had originally suggested the thesis subject to her former student, Ursula Davidson. In 1980, Wharton coauthored an article with William S. Bryant and others on presettlement vegetation of the Inner Bluegrass in the prestigious botanical journal *Castanea.* The authors analyzed the composition of a number of existing woodland tracts in the context of rather limited historical information, concluding that "savanna-woodland vegetation occupied the Inner Bluegrass at the time of settlement." The most prominent tree species of this savanna woodland were blue ash, bur oak, Shumard oak, and chinquapin oak, with a groundcover consisting of cane (*Arundinaria gigantea*), wild rye (*Elymus* spp.), other grasses, and legumes such as clover. In their opinion, the savanna woodland may have been initially developed from fires set by Native Americans as a hunting technique to provide grassland areas that would attract bison, and was thereafter maintained by the grazing habits of these large animals.[14]

The blue ash-oak savanna woodland model was further elaborated on by Wharton and Barbour in *Bluegrass Land and Life* (1991) but, as critiqued by Julian Campbell, the concept was exaggerated "with rather selective citing of particular pieces of evidence, without a critical evaluation of all the evidence, and without a realistic ecological model of how

An example of the iconic woodland pasture of the modern day in the Kentucky Horse Park, a few miles south of Georgetown, containing a number of ancient trees. Storm damage and lightning strikes have broken off the tops of many of these old trees. This is a landscape transformed by human activity rather than a remnant of the alleged presettlement savanna woodland. Photograph by Gary O'Dell.

the woodland was opened up." Nevertheless, the concept of savanna woodland has become firmly entrenched in the public and academic consciousness as representing the dominant plant community of the Inner Bluegrass present at the time of Euro-American settlement. The widespread, uncritical acceptance of the savanna hypothesis may be due in part, as Campbell observed, to its appeal as a "romantic notion that links the modern horse-farm landscape with a supposed past." In a 1990 paper on the landscape of the Bluegrass, Karl Raitz and Dorn Van Dommelen address the concept of the creation of symbols for popular consumption that represent "selected slices of reality." The modern-era grassy pastures of regional horse farms, dotted with ancient trees, represent an aesthetically pleasing stereotype of the Bluegrass. This is, however, a landscape that is created rather than natural. The savanna woodland hypothesis becomes easy to accept because, as Raitz and Van Dommelen point out, "we wish to associate with the aesthetic, the memorable, and the pleasant, the landscapes we build often represent ideals or 'myths' and are constructed so that they convey a desirable scene."[15]

Campbell has spent decades amassing evidence from which to draw informed conclusions about the nature of the Bluegrass landscape during pioneer times. Convinced that the accounts of the pioneers provided the best source of information, he examined hundreds of eyewitness descriptions from 1750 to 1805, including journals, letters, land surveys, land-trial depositions and other court records, and reminiscences, as well as published maps and descriptions in books based on firsthand accounts. Campbell also pursued additional lines of evidence. Data summarized by Gwynn Henderson (1998) from archaeological reports concerning Fort Ancient village sites across the region, circa 900–1700 A.D., identifies trees from wood fragments and ashes, indicating a wide variety of species with much hickory but no particular dominance by ash or oak.[16]

Using dendrochronology to assess tree ages and growth rates from annual growth rings, Ryan McEwan and Brian McCarthy (2008) found that ancient trees such as bur oak began to grow much faster after settlement, doubling or tripling radial growth and initiating massive spreading limbs—an effect that can be attributed to clearing away of surrounding trees. Bur oak seedlings can become established at forest or woodland margins and in clearings resulting from violent storm damage that takes out large trees. Campbell notes that while bur oak requires sun for seed germination, small trees can survive for decades under suppressed conditions, producing slow growth. A cut section of an old bur oak, observed by Campbell, exhibited very narrow growth rings for its first century, confined within a three-inch radius and representing presettlement growth. The early pattern was followed by much wider rings, indicating more rapid growth, interpreted as post-settlement, when clearing of forests allowed more sunlight to the trees. McEwan and McCarthy also found no evidence of fire scarring prior to settlement, which does not support a hypothesis of fires, natural or human-set, as a factor in producing a relatively open savanna woodland. Campbell has also assessed the occurrence of certain species found in woodlots, fencerows, and fields around the central Bluegrass, some of which are indicators of original species.[17]

From his extensive investigations, Campbell "soundly rejected" the savanna woodland model, noting that Wharton had overestimated the general age of the large, ancient trees, and mistakenly assumed that the wide-spreading open-grown form of bur oaks represented open conditions prior to settlement. Instead, these large trees had been preserved in the landscape by settlers to provide shade in pastures, and they developed their wide-spreading form as a result of the removal of competing trees. Campbell concluded that the Inner Bluegrass was characterized by a fairly diverse woodland, "ranging from deeply shady woods with 'sugar tree' to more open areas with much cane; ashes and oaks did not appear generally dominant." More specifically, 20–40 percent of the landscape was forested, with deep shade dominated by sugar maples and bitternut hickory. About 50–70 percent was in an intermediate condition between deep shade and more open woods, with ecological phases varying from relatively palatable (to wildlife) ash/elm, to more browsed-out walnut/buckeye, or locally oak/hickory on drier sites. More fertile soils had a great deal of maple, mostly sugar, along with walnuts, hickories, ashes, and oaks. Less fertile soils generally hosted oak-hickory forest dominated by white oak, or beech forest with some yellow poplar, mixed with species of more fertile soils. Significantly, only 1–10 percent of the Inner Bluegrass landscape possessed true openings in the canopy of trees, "with dense canebrakes, other shrubbery, or largely treeless grassland; it seems likely that these openings were concentrated along trails of larger animals (with humans) and around camp or village sites."[18]

Early descriptions of the Bluegrass indicate an extensive forest cover was present. Writing in 1795, David Barrow observed that "The growth in these parts is black walnut in great abundance, vastly large and tall sugar tree. . . . The growth of trees in these countries is so luxurious that they form a shade so universal and add there to the darkness of the soil." Samuel Matthew described the vegetation around Bryant's Station, about ten miles southeast of Georgetown, as it appeared in 1783: "Land that had not cane on it, was grown up with white blossoms, and the trees were tall ash, sugar-trees, elms, hackberry, tall and very thick." In the vicinity of Lexington, Asa Farrar recalled that, during the late 1780s, "forest of burr oak and black walnut" had to be cleared for roads. In 1793, botanist André Michaux left Lexington, traveling south toward the Kentucky River, and "went through portions of forest lands with very scattered Plantations."

Humphrey Marshall came to Kentucky in 1782, residing at Lexington, and in his 1812 *History of Kentucky* described the Elkhorn region as viewed by the first settlers: "the forest composed of oaks of various kinds, of ash, of walnut, cherry, buckeye, hackberry, sugar trees, towering aloft to the clouds, overspread the luxuriant undergrowth, with their daily shade; while beneath, the class of trees—the shrubs, the cane, the herbage, and the different kinds of grass, and clover, interspersed with flowers, filled the eye, and overlaid the soil with the forest's richest carpet."[19]

Although various types of open woodland mixed with canelands and a few pure grassy patches were mentioned in eyewitness accounts of the settlement era, according to Campbell "the terms savanna, glade, barrens, prairie, natural meadow, or grassland, were never used." While this is not strictly true, such terminology was rare. There were such plant communities, however, in adjacent areas. Filson's 1784 map of Kentucky depicted two areas of "natural meadows" in southern Ohio, and showed the "Big Barrens" region of western Kentucky. Generally, only in Ohio and Indiana, not Kentucky, did most accounts place natural meadows, prairies, or savanna landscapes. Thus, it would seem, the savanna woodland characterization is not supported by pioneer observations.[20]

There is no intent here to deny the existence of savanna woodland within the Inner Bluegrass. The presence of numerous ancient bur oaks in the modern landscape is sufficient to confirm that presettlement vegetation included a considerable amount of open space that allowed seedlings of these trees to become established. Instead, such savannah represents but a single element of a landscape featuring a mosaic of vegetative communities that also included a substantive forest cover, extensive canebrakes, and some open grasslands.

From the historical record, a rough approximation of the natural vegetation in the vicinity of Royal Spring at the time of settlement can be made. Several accounts of the pioneer era paint similar pictures, using broad strokes, of the vegetation of southern Scott County. Mary "Polly" Shipp came to Scott County in 1785 as a child six years old, first residing with her family at a fort built by her brother, Laban, on North Elkhorn. The Shipp station was located a little more than four miles due east from Royal Spring, along present-day Newtown Pike. The country about Georgetown, as she later recalled, "was a cane brake and a forest." A visitor to Georgetown and Lexington in 1834 solicited information about the history of the region from a number of residents who had been among the early settlers, and subsequently wrote, "Within the memory of living witnesses, the region which is now so splendidly embellished, and which supports a numerous and highly refined population, was covered with savage forests and vast cane-brakes." Levi Todd, describing the 1776 attack on McClelland's Station, noted that the Indians made "several attempts to draw our people into the woods," indicating forest or woodland conditions around the settlement.[21]

A more empirical approach to assessing presettlement vegetation is provided by investigation of pioneer land surveys conducted for claiming land in the vicinity of present-day Georgetown. These surveys, made by John Floyd and his group of surveyors in 1774, include descriptions of boundary or "witness trees." Boundary trees are trees used as reference points in the line of a survey or at a corner. An analysis of such boundary trees, most with two or three trees noted for each point, was made for me by Julian Campbell for land claims in the corridor along North Elkhorn Creek from the area of Royal Spring southeastward to the area of Russell Cave, north of Lexington (see map). The tree names used on the surveys provide an accurate indication of genus, and in some cases of species. Before commencing the Elkhorn surveys, Floyd ran a long baseline whose position corresponds exactly to the present-day Ironworks Pike. Most of the surveys taken off this baseline (including Floyd's Royal Spring survey) were rectangles of one thousand to three thousand acres, so that the points provide a random sample of trees in the landscape within about three miles of Elkhorn.[22]

Boundary tree data was obtained from the Kentucky Land Office website for eleven of the surveys shown on the map; the remainder could not be located in the documentary record but may be available from Virginia records or other sources. Excluded from the analysis were trees duplicated at corners shared by adjoining surveys. Boundary trees were not limited to large, mature trees, as some are recorded as being saplings. The analysis indicated that sugar maple (*Acer saccharum*) was the most frequent tree mentioned (21.8 percent), followed by hickory (*Carya* species, undifferentiated in the surveys, 12.7 percent), Ohio buckeye (*Aesculus glabra*, 11.8 percent), ash (*Fraxinus* species, undifferentiated, 10.9 percent), honey locust (*Gleditsia triacanthos,* 10.9 percent), elm (*Ulmus* species, undifferentiated, 6.4 percent), "hoopwood" or hackberry (*Celtis occidentalis,*

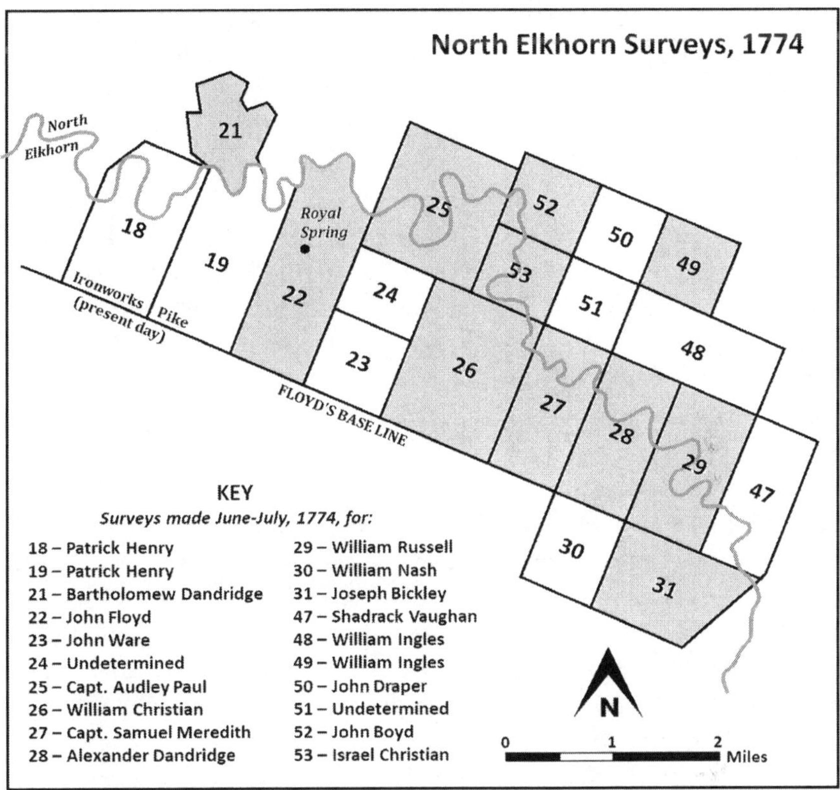

John Floyd and his party of surveyors laid out a series of land claims for prominent Virginians along North Elkhorn Creek during the summer of 1774. The shaded tracts are those for which information on boundary trees is available. These trees were recorded as waypoint markers along the survey lines, and their distribution can aid in reconstructing local presettlement vegetation. Map by Gary O'Dell, adapted from Hammon (1972).

6.4 percent), and walnut, most likely black walnut (*Juglans nigra*, 6.4 percent). Infrequently appearing boundary trees included white walnut, white oak, Spanish oak (probably Shumard oak), black oak, poplar, and cherry.[23]

Campbell's boundary tree analysis indicates that about a third of the Elkhorn landscape around Royal Spring was covered by relatively thick forest, with little disturbance, dominated by sugar maples and hickories, the latter most likely bitternut (*Carya cordiformis*). Greater species diversity appears to indicate shady woodlands, dominated by shade-tolerant species and occupying about 40 percent of the area. This condition was probably maintained largely as a result of herbivore disturbance and possibly occasional droughts or fires. Shade-intolerant species were less frequent, of which the major component was honey locust. Campbell noted that it was likely that "the honey locust, in particular, was concentrated in relatively open woods along buffalo trails and perhaps around old abandoned fields and villages of Indians." The surveys made no mention of bur oak, which, being very intolerant of shaded conditions, was probably concentrated in areas having a history of more intensive disturbance, such as described earlier. From the data, there is no evidence that oaks or ashes were prevalent, forming open woods or savanna-like communities.[24]

The only oaks recorded in the eleven parcels investigated were for tract #21, surveyed for Bartholomew Dandridge. The infrequency of oaks and ashes in the region seems unusual, since large specimens of bur oak (*Quercus macrocarpa*), chinquapin oak (*Quercus muehlenbergii*), and Shumard oak (*Quercus shumardii*) are common in the old "woodland pastures" of farms in the region. These woodland pastures are, as previously noted, created landscapes, deliberately produced by the more prosperous landowners who cleared the land but favored existing oaks and blue ash to provide shade for livestock. Campbell, however, cautioned that oaks were most likely locally frequent prior to settlement. As "long-lived [shade] intolerant species, they probably formed a much higher proportion of the larger canopy-sized class of trees than of the woods in general."[25]

On July 8, 1774, Floyd's party of surveyors continued to mark off land, beginning at a point seven or eight miles from the Forks of Elkhorn, and continued east along North Elkhorn Creek. By the morning of the next day, the party was very close to Royal Spring, and after working part of the day, the spring was discovered by Floyd and a companion, William Nash. In his journal, one of Floyd's assistants, Thomas Hanson, described the vegetation present in the Patrick Henry survey (#19) adjoining the Royal Spring tract on the western side: "Its timber is Honey Locust, Black Walnut, Sugar tree [sugar maple], Hickory, iron wood, Hoop wood [hackberry], Mulberry, Ash, & Elm, & some Oak." Many of these same species were also listed as boundary trees in John

Floyd's one thousand-acre survey of the land containing Royal Spring, which records multiple ash, buckeye, elm, hickory, honey locust, sugar tree, and walnut trees at various turning points along the survey. Hanson's notes on the North Elkhorn surveys suggest that there was a range of conditions in the region around Royal Spring, from deep woods to woodlands or openings.[26]

Hanson noted an "undergrowth" of "Clover pea vine Cane & Nettles—intermixed with Rich weed," the presence of which, except for the cane, also supports a wooded rather than savanna environment. Some of these species can occur in either shaded or lightly shaded situations, or in edge environments at the margins of woodlands. Lightly shaded or edge environments can be found in more open woodlands or along the banks of streams or woodland trails. Richweed (probably *Ageratina altissima*, aka white snakeroot) is typical of moist woodlands, as is the pea vine (*Amphicarpaea bracteata*, aka hog peanut). Nettle (either *Urtica dioica,* stinging nettle, or wood nettle, *Laportea canadensis*) is a plant that prefers locations in partial sun along rivers, lakes, and streams but is also found in shady woodland situations. The clover mentioned by Hanson, although possessing whitish flowers, is not the white clover (*Trifolium repens*), a species that was introduced to the New World from Europe and commonly seen as a weed in turfgrass. This is, instead, buffalo clover, annual (*Trifolium reflexum*) and running (*Trifolium stoloniferum*). The latter of these clovers was formerly listed as a federally endangered plant, and is considered threatened in Kentucky. Both types prefer a partly shaded environment, lightly wooded or at the edge of woods.[27]

The early explorers and settlers of Kentucky often commented on the presence of relatively large stands of wild cane, *Arundinaria gigantea*, a form of bamboo native to North America. Thomas Hutchins's 1778 map of the trans-Appalachian region, although inaccurate in many respects, depicts a large area of "Fine Cane Land" in what appears to be the central and eastern Bluegrass region. Filson's 1784 map of Kentucky notes several large areas as occupied by cane, including an area near the mouth of North Elkhorn shown as "Fine Cane." More significantly, the tributary of North Elkhorn known as Cane Run flows northward from Fayette County into southern Scott, joining North Elkhorn at Great Crossing 2.8 miles west of Royal Spring. During the early settlement

Abundant growths of wild cane were often noted by Kentucky explorers and settlers, but most of the cane has been eliminated from the state. This cluster sprang from seedlings planted in 1999 along Cane Run in Fayette County by ecologist Julian Campbell (pictured) in an effort to reestablish the species here. Photograph by Gary O'Dell.

era, the riparian corridor of this stream supported a rather extensive growth of *Arundinaria gigantea* for most of its length, possibly as far as Great Crossing, and may have been even more widespread locally. Pioneer Ben Guthrie recalled, "Where Geo. T. [Georgetown] is, was all a canebrake," likely referring to this caneland just south of the community. Cane prefers a habitat in full sun, although it is not very tolerant of hot temperatures and drought conditions; it also seems to grow well in partial shade. According to Campbell, cane is "typical of edges and other transitions from deep woods to full sun." Most of the wild cane in Kentucky was eliminated fairly early in the history of the commonwealth, save for isolated remnants, as a result of land clearing and grazing by cattle, who were very fond of cane foliage. All of the cane along Cane Run was eradicated in this manner.[28]

A number of historic accounts suggest that relatively open areas, harboring canebrakes or grassy meadows, may have been concentrated locally on the broader lowlands. On July 16, 1773, James and Robert McAfee crossed the Kentucky River, probably near the future site of Leestown, into present-day Franklin County, where James reported that they "surveyed one track of land for Robert McAfee containing 600 acres about 100 of that meadow land." Robert was more conservative, estimating the extent of meadow at about fifty acres. Floyd's 1774 survey for Dandridge (#21) noted a "meadow at the foot of a hill" near North Elkhorn, probably at the edge of the large bottom on the north side of the creek, west of the mouth of Cane Run. The Floyd surveys for Israel Christian (#53), Samuel Christian (#26), and Samuel Meredith (#27) recorded a canebrake at a shared corner. This was located near the Newtown Pike bridge over North Elkhorn, in the Lemons Mill area. Traveling from southeastern Franklin County through northern Woodford County in 1775, James Nourse made note of lightly timbered land, "the growth of grass under amazing—blue grass, white clover, buffalo grass and seed knee and waist high: what would be called a fine swarth of Grass in cultivated meadows, and such was its appearance without end—in little dells in this." Pioneer John Graves recalled in later life that, in 1787, there was a large blackberry patch near Robert Johnson's station at Great Crossing, just west of Georgetown: "Blackberries was a very rare thing, owing to the cane's being so thick." This was on tract #19 surveyed by Floyd for Patrick Henry and assigned to Johnson by Henry in the fall of 1793.[29]

When Dr. Thomas Walker came into Kentucky in 1750, skirting the edge of the Bluegrass region before heading back across the mountains, he noted the abundance of wild game in his journal. His party was frequently assaulted by black bears, although in return a number of these animals were shot, salted, and added to their provisions. After spending three months in the wilderness, Walker returned to Virginia, recording in his journal that, during this time, he and his companions had "killed in the journey 13 Buffaloes, 8 Elks, 53 Bears, 20 Deer, 4 wild Geese, about 150 Turkeys, besides small game. We might have killed three times as much meat, if we had wanted it." Of the Bluegrass, an Englishman visiting the region in 1775 later wrote of the abundance of wildlife, one of a very few early accounts referring to meadows or savanna in the region: "Game of all kinds is also exceedingly plenty; a man may kill six or eight deer every day. . . . Wild turkeys, very large and fat, are almost beyond number, sometimes five thousand in a flock, of which a man may kill just as many as he please. Elks are also very plenty, as well as raccoons, opossums, foxes and wolves. All these are found in the lofty woods, while in the savannahs or meadows buffaloes abound." Reports of the marvelous fecundity of wildlife in Kentucky was yet another inducement for immigrants from the eastern colonies, where most of the land was intensively cultivated and the wild game long hunted out.[30]

Buffalo trails crisscrossed the Bluegrass. One led from a ford of the Kentucky River near present-day Frankfort to a salt lick in central Scott County, where several trails converged and the earth had been so trampled that it became known as the "Stamping Ground." From here the buffalo trail led to the "Great Crossing" of North Elkhorn and continued eastward through the vicinity of Royal Spring. Thomas Hanson reported seeing a gathering of about three hundred buffalo in northern Kentucky in 1774, and others reported herds possibly numbering in the thousands.[31]

This was the land that lured so many immigrants from the colonies, portrayed as a land of "cane and clover," a veritable Eden bursting with promise. Nathan Reid was among many early arrivals who clearly understood the potential of the Bluegrass. Reid and John Floyd came from the same part of Virginia and had known each other for many years, and so became close friends. "Frequently have Floyd and I sat down on a log, or at the foot of a tree, and given a free rein to our heated imaginations, constructed many a glorious castle in the air," Reid later recalled. "We would, on such occasions, contrast the many discomforts that then beset us, with the pleasures we would one day enjoy in the possession of boundless wealth. Spread out before us lay the finest body of land in the world, any quantity of which, with but little exertion, we could make our own. We clearly foresaw that it would not be long before these lands would be justly appreciated, and sought after by thousands." Reid was quite correct in his prediction. At the time of which he was speaking, about 1775, Kentucky had only about 150 inhabitants; by 1790, in only fifteen years, the population had exploded to more than 73,000.[32]

The hope-filled immigrants who came to the Bluegrass were not disappointed by its bounty, for it was a lush and verdant land. In 1775, twenty-two-year-old Felix Walker came through Cumberland Gap and, in company with about thirty other men, assisted Daniel Boone in cutting a route into the Bluegrass, the Wilderness Trail. As he later recalled, approaching the Kentucky River,

> We arrived at the commencement of a cane country, traveled about thirty miles through thick cane and reed, and as the cane ceased, we began to discover the pleasing and rapturous appearance of the plains of Kentucky. A new sky and strange earth seemed to be presented to our view. So rich a soil we had never seen before; covered with clover in full bloom, the woods were abounding with wild game—turkeys so numerous that it might be said they appeared but one flock, universally scattered in the woods. It appeared that nature, in the profusion of her bounty, had spread a feast for all that lives, both for the animal and rational world. . . . The appearance of the country coming up to the full measure of our expectations, and seemed to exceed the fruitful source of our imaginary prospects.

Truly, the Inner Bluegrass was a "goodly land"—but it was not the paradise envisioned by so many immigrants.[33]

The majority of immigrants who blindly entered Kentucky expected to find "abundance in all desirable things and boundless liberty for all, thus a new life immeasurably superior to that before and equal to the idyllic modes of existence after which the human race has always yearned." The new land in the west did possess elements that lived up to pioneer expectations of a promised land. Here was a wilderness virtually unspoiled, the mark of Native Americans resting but lightly upon the land. It was a land of seemingly limitless bounty, teeming with wild game, the forests and woodlands filled with fruit and nut trees, well-watered by countless streams and clear-running springs, and with deep, fertile soils capable of producing bumper crops. And in this wilderness, filled with such gifts, one might anticipate an idyllic, classless life free from the social restraints of the civilized east.[34]

What these immigrants experienced after their arrival was an existence something far less than Edenic. For many years after settlement, the constant danger of Indian attack resulted in an unrelenting atmosphere of fear and apprehension. Under tremendous strain, pioneers were afraid to leave their fortified homes, stations, and forts to establish land claims, to hunt meat for the table, or to plant, tend, and harvest crops. "No place, no moment, was truly secure," commented historian Blake Smith; every activity was undertaken at great risk, the people afraid to move about in the very land they intended to possess. Ordinary tasks essential for survival were inherently dangerous and required extra labor and care. Crops, for example, could not be produced without setting men to guard and scout while others tended the fields. Under such conditions, and with the supply line from the east long and hazardous, hunger and privation were in constant attendance. Confined to tiny, crudely furnished rough cabins behind a stockade wall, destitute of nearly all possessions and often clad in rags, the settlers lived under primitive conditions in abject poverty. Josiah Collins, visiting Boonesborough in March 1778, described the inhabitants as "a poor distressed ½ naked, ½ starved people, daily surrounded by the savage."[35]

Away from the public forts, at isolated cabins and small stations widely scattered across the landscape, privation was accompanied by solitude and loneliness. While men ventured out to hunt, tend crops, or to counter Indian raiding parties, the women were cabin-bound, fearing to step outside their own walls. Many families had been decimated by Indian attacks, either during the difficult journey to Kentucky or from raids against isolated cabins, violent moments that left memories of unspeakable horror. In 1790, when Daniel Drake was about five years old and residing at May's Lick (near present-day Maysville, Kentucky), a party of travelers was attacked by Indians near the village and one man killed before the marauders were driven off. Drake recalled that "the alarm of my mother and aunts, communicated, of course, to all the children, was deep and the remembrance of the scene was long and kept vividly alive by talking it over and over." Being often cut off from all human contact, even neighbors, for days or weeks, haunted by unbearable loneliness and the constant pressure of fear and violence, had a significant psychological cost. Pioneer women confined to the emptiness of a dark cabin often descended into depression, plagued by nightmares and sometimes pushed beyond tolerance into breakdowns and even madness.[36]

A great many of the pioneer men responded to life in the wilderness by abandoning most of the rules of conventional society, regressing to a more primitive condition. "Wildness, abundance, and the lack of social restraints," Gaille McGregor observed, "were often just enough to bring out the worst in newly arrived emigrants." Led to expect a near-paradisical situation, the men of the frontier were instead presented with innumerable challenges to settlement, evoking a blind passion to conquer all obstacles. They became increasing prone to lawless, violent action. Some men became so enamored with warfare against Indian adversaries that they became, in effect, full-time warriors, taking every opportunity to join in retaliatory expeditions. The barbarity of their actions often matched or exceeded those of their opponents, atrocity for atrocity. The majority of the Kentucky settlers were of Scotch-Irish stock, aggressive and clannish: "indifferent to prior claims on the frontier land which sustained them, to the rights of Indians, and to the laws of colonial legislatures, they went about the business of mastering the wilderness and developing farms without much regard for any authority."[37]

As the frontier became more settled, these early pioneers who had sought to build a new life free of class distinctions now had to contend with antagonisms generated by an influx of lowland gentry who had been spared the worst hardships entailed in occupying the wilderness. Far more literate than most early pioneers, better acquainted with the land laws, and of sufficient means to retain legal counsel, the newer arrivals were shrewdly able to wrest much of the land away from prior occupants having defective titles. For most of the early seekers of paradise, even the land was denied to them.[38]

Although the land was certainly generous in its gifts, the climate was very un-paradisical, nothing like the pleasant tropical conditions suggested by the Edenic tradition and by some of the early writers about the area. Any such notion held by settlers was certainly dispelled by the unusually harsh winters from 1777 to 1780. On March 20, 1780, Colonel William Fleming, one of the commissioners assigned to Kentucky to judge land claims, made note of deadly winter conditions in his journal:

> The effects of the severe winter was now sensibly felt, The earth for so long a time being covered with snow and the water entirely froze, the Cane almost all killed, the Hogs that were in the country suffered greatly being frozen to death in their beds, the deer likewise not being able to get either water or food were found dead in great numbers, tirkies dropt dead off their roosts and

> even the Buffaloes died starved to death, the vast increase of people, near three thousand that came into this country with the prodigious losses they had in their cattle and horses, on their journey, and the severity of the winter after they got here killing such numbers, all contributed to raise the necessaries of life to a most extravagant price.

Kentucky experiences an average seasonal variation of about 95 degrees Fahrenheit between winter and summer, being considered a continental climate in the middle latitudes. The winter season is known for frequent and often extreme swings in temperature, and on rare occasions temperatures can plunge well below zero. Summer heat is less variable, with average daytime temperatures of midsummer in the middle to upper 80s, and often into the 90s. Heading into Kentucky by way of the Wilderness Road in the summer of 1785, Anna Christian complained about the heat, lack of water, and general fatigue in a letter to her sister-in-law: "Had I any Idea of its being half as bad as I found it no inducement on this earth, would have encouraged me to attempt it."[39]

The settlers were themselves agents responsible for the despoilation of paradise. From the onset of settlement, they set about to removing the forest with vigor and enthusiasm. The English colonists who first came to America had never experienced anything like the dense forests cloaking the coastal regions of the New World, those of their homeland having long ago been largely reduced to a few tame woodlands and hunting parks. They regarded the forests of America with considerable repugnance and apprehension. The more superstitious among them saw the dark and brooding forest recesses as the haunts of malignant spirits or ghosts, and those of a more rational nature, as abodes for bears and wolves or places where Indians might lurk in ambush. The attitude of many of the colonists was aptly summed up in 1662 by the Puritan poet Michael Wigglesworth, who described the great forest as "A waste and howling wilderness / Where none inhabited / But hellish fiends and brutish men." More significant, however, was the need to create arable land for pasture and crop production, and this was the primary motivation for the settlers of Kentucky. Entire forests disappeared rapidly, assaulted with axes, girdled or deadened with fire, and corn was planted among the remains of dead and dying trees. The ecological paradise so beloved by Daniel Boone was rapidly converted into "an agroecosystem geared toward maximizing the production of culturally favored species," as fields of crops such as corn, wheat, and rye replaced the diverse vegetation first encountered by the pioneers.[40]

Daniel Drake stated that, in Kentucky, "the great occupation was clearing off the forest and cultivating the rich & fresh soil." Recalling his Mason County childhood, he described his father's acquisition of two hundred acres near May's Lick in 1794. "The land acquired was covered with an unbroken forest, which must be cleared away, and a new cabin erected." Nine-year-old Daniel was "provided with a small axe; father had a larger, and a mattock for grubbing. Thus equipped . . . we charged upon the beautiful blue-ash and buckeye grove." The ongoing devastation of the land outraged Native Americans. In a grand council of Shawnee, Cherokee, Wyandot, and other tribes held at Chillicothe, Ohio, in early August 1782, the renegade white man Simon Girty sought to inflame the young warriors against the settlers in Kentucky, and delivered a memorable speech that included the following: "Brothers! They are planting fruit trees and ploughing the land where not long since were the cane break and clover field. Were there a voice in the trees of the forest, or articulate sound in the gurgling waters, every part of this country would call upon you to chase away these ruthless invaders who are laying it waste!" In the opinion of Arthur K. Moore, the architects of this destructive transformation, the white settlers invading the country, had in their hearts "no more consideration for the trees than for the game until the best of both were gone."[41]

Those who came into Kentucky—explorers, hunters, settlers—energetically slaughtered the wildlife with little consideration for the future. As early as 1775, there had been such a marked reduction of large game animals that Richard Henderson, addressing representatives from the four settlements at Transylvania on May 23, deplored "the wanton destruction of our game, the only support of life amongst many of us." In 1795, David Barrow observed that "Wild turkeys are much reduced on the settlements but plentiful in the borders. It is the same with deer, bear, etc." Writing in 1824, Joseph Doddridge mourned the loss of so much animal life on the former frontier: "The buffalo and elk have entirely disappeared from this section of the country. Of the bear and deer but very few remain. The wolves, formerly so numerous, and so destructive to the cattle, are now seldom heard of . . . the wild turkeys, which used to be so abundant as to supply no inconsiderable portion of provision for the first settlers, are now rarely seen." The slaughter was not limited to game animals. Bears, raccoons, wolves, wildcats, and birds of prey were all regarded as threats to agricultural production and were ruthlessly eliminated whenever possible. Competition from livestock and habitat destruction also contributed to the decline in wild populations.[42]

Deer were very abundant at the time of settlement, but when an elderly Daniel Boone returned to Kentucky in 1810 after more than a decade's absence, he "rambled about to see if a deer was still living in the land. But ah! Sir, what a difference thirty years make in the country," he told James Audubon. Now "only a few signs of deer were to be seen, and as to the deer itself, I saw none." By the time of Boone's visit, the buffalo, a primary staple for the pioneer table, was long gone. The buffalo had seemed inexhaustible to the first settlers, but wanton slaughter quickly depleted their numbers. On May 9, 1775, Richard Henderson noted in his journal with disgust "that we found it very difficult at first and indeed yet, to stop the great waste in killing meat. Many men were ignorant of the woods, and not skilled in hunting . . . would shoot, cripple and scare the game without being able to get much. . . . Others of wicked and wanton dispositions, would kill three, four, five or ½ dozen buffaloes, and not take a half horse load from them all." Pioneer William Clinkenbeard recalled, "They did destroy them and waste them then, at a mighty rate. If one wasn't young and fat, it was left, and they went on and killed another one." When André Michaux toured Kentucky and Tennessee in 1802, he observed that the buffalo were nearly all gone. The last sighting of free-roaming buffalo in Kentucky occurred in 1820, a small herd in Hart County near the Green River.[43]

Into this new and "goodly land" of bounty and hardship came the little party of Pennsylvanians and Virginians in 1774, led by John McClelland, who planted their hopes and dreams at Royal Spring, and to this place they would be followed in 1787 by Elijah Craig, who founded a city. They would reshape the wilderness, these dreamers, and they in turn would be transformed by the experience.

5

The Land of Springs

In all of Kentucky, there is probably no other spring that has been so intimately associated with the history, welfare, and very identity of a city or town than the Royal Spring of Georgetown in Scott County. Known also as the "Big Spring," this is certainly the largest spring in the Bluegrass region of central Kentucky, though by no means the largest in the state. From the pioneer era to the present day, Royal Spring has served as the community's primary water source, pouring out an abundant stream from beneath the limestone ledges of a low bluff. The flow from the spring provided power for water mills that stimulated early industry and growth of the town, and the picturesque setting served as a social nexus for the citizens of Georgetown. The spring lies within the boundary of the modern community and is readily visible from west Main Street. The prominence and importance of this spring to Georgetown was such that the city established a public park around it in 1975, commemorating the pioneer settlement of the community.

The spring has been known by many names through its long history. Called "Floyd's Spring" for about a year after its discovery in 1774, it was soon given the more refined designation of "Royal Spring" upon the establishment of a pioneer station above the spring head in 1775 in honor of its extraordinary flow and scenic appeal. The spring was also briefly called "McClelland's Spring" after the founder of the station. Following the Revolutionary War, given the antimonarchical sentiment prevalent in the country, some persons found the name "Royal Spring" to be objectionable. In a letter published in Lexington's *Kentucky Gazette* on March 8, 1788, a writer who styled himself "Agricola" observed that "At one time I had concluded to suffer my boys to drink at the Royal Spring, and try the efficacy of that wondrous font, but, being a very staunch whig, I hate even the name of Royal." Thereafter, many citizens of like sentiments began to refer to Georgetown's water source as the "Republican Spring." The two designations remained in equal competition for more than a century, so that references to the spring usually noted "the Royal or Republican Spring," although the latter fell into disuse shortly after the beginning of the twentieth century. Those who did not favor the pretensions of either label simply referred to the "Big Spring" of Georgetown. This approach was taken in a history of Scott County published in 1993, in which the authors justified their rationale as reflecting "the spirit of American democracy which prefers the language of logic to that of the crown." Nevertheless, the most durable of all these designations over time has been the "Royal Spring," by which term this remarkable spring is best known today.[1]

The association of Georgetown and Royal Spring was not by coincidence; the location of the future city was chosen specifically to make use of the spring. The distribution of springs suitable for water sources was in large part responsible for the pattern of settlement in pioneer Kentucky. During the pioneer era in Kentucky, mineral springs and the most prominent of the freshwater springs served as landmarks in the wilderness, the focal points of a network of trails created by bison in search of salt and by the Indians who traversed the region in search of game and to trade with other tribes. Throughout human history, spring water has been perceived as superior in quality to that of any other source, thought to issue in pristine form from the depths of the earth. A pure and reliable water supply was one of the most important criteria for any potential settlement, and the early explorers and settlers were eager to claim land containing a significant spring, which became the sites of pioneer homesteads and communities. The location of many cities and towns in Kentucky today can be attributed to the presence of a spring during the settlement period thought sufficient to supply the inhabitants.[2]

Natural springs are abundant throughout most of the landscape of Kentucky. A partial inventory of such springs in Scott and Bourbon counties conducted by me between 1997 and 1999 identified 436 springs in these two counties alone, most of which had been modified historically by addition of protective structures ranging from simple rock-walled enclosures to elaborate springhouses. There are thus uncounted thousands of free-flowing natural springs, large and small, across the length and breadth of the commonwealth. Small seeps and trickles may be found in all parts of Kentucky wherever there is fractured rock, but springs of sufficient flow to provide domestic and agricultural water supply sources are most numerous in those extensive areas of the state where cavernous limestone bedrock is present.[3]

The immigrants who sought a new life in Kentucky came into the region by way of the Cumberland Gap or from one of the landings on the north bank of the Ohio River. Either approach set pioneers upon a network of trails which had been used for millennia by animals and Indians to traverse the region. A profusion of narrow pathways had been developed in the wilderness by deer and Native Americans, but the most prominent trails, called "buffalo traces" by Euro-American settlers, were wide and well-trampled routes produced by the seasonal migrations of bison herds as they traveled between their foraging grounds and the many mineral springs of the region. Such trails had been in existence for millennia, as evidenced by the bones of prehistoric bison (immense shaggy creatures much larger than modern bison), mastodon, and other extinct animals found by the early pioneers at mineral springs such as Big Bone Lick and the Blue Licks. Many animals, large and small, were attracted by the salt-encrusted earth on the margins of such saline springs, which were termed "licks" by the settlers of the region because the animals would lick or consume the salty soil. Referring to the salt springs of Kentucky, John Filson wrote in 1784: "The amazing herds of Buffaloes which resort hither, by their size and number, fill the traveler with amazement and terror, especially when he beholds the prodigious roads they have made from all quarters, as if leading to some populous city; the vast spaces of land around these springs defolated [*sic*] as if by a ravaging enemy, and hills reduced to plains." Another traveler through central Kentucky, Nicholas Cresswell, observed in 1775 that the buffalo "eat great quantities of a sort of reddish clay found near brackish springs. I have seen amazing large holes dug or rather cut by them in this sort of earth."[4]

The "Buffaloes" encountered by the pioneers were relatively recent arrivals to the Ohio Valley region. Prior to the sixteenth century a combination of factors prompted movement of the plains bison into the eastern woodlands, including the Indian practice of setting fires to flush game and provide agricultural land that created, enlarged, and maintained prairie enclaves along the eastern margin of the Mississippi. The bison of the southeast were never as numerous as those of the Great Plains, seldom gathering in herds of more than a few hundred individuals, but their movements recreated the system of trails first developed by Pleistocene megafauna. These trails tended to traverse the ridges, as the herds were reluctant to ford water courses, with diversions to freshwater springs and canebrakes in the lowlands. "The buffalo seldom visited the licks in the winter," Nathan Boone wrote, referring to the hunting practices of his father, Daniel Boone. "They then would keep near the cane as the best winter's range and lived in summer mainly on grass." In the Ohio Valley, geographer John A. Jakle observed, the main objective of the buffalo was "always a salt lick, for basically, the traces were routes of maximum convenience connecting the larger salt springs."[5]

Eastern Kentucky is barricaded by two long, parallel ridges, each more than a hundred miles in length. The easternmost of these ridges is Cumberland Mountain, which reaches elevations of 2,200 to 3,500 feet. A little more than a dozen miles to the northwest, Pine Mountain's crests reach 1,800 to 2,200 feet. There are few significant breaks interrupting these ridges. Immigrants could have crossed Cumberland Mountain at Pennington Gap, but there was no equivalent gap in the vicinity allowing passage over Pine Mountain. Settlers instead traveled forty miles farther south through the Great Valley to Cumberland Gap, where a fortuitous alignment of notches through each of the two mountain ridges allowed access to Kentucky. Here, the movements of large animals and Native Americans had for ages been funneled through Cumberland Gap and along the Cumberland River northward through a water gap in Pine Mountain (site of present-day Pineville), developing a well-marked trail. Cumberland Gap thus became the primary gateway into Kentucky during the earliest years of exploration and settlement.

The buffalo trace forded Cumberland River at the Pine Mountain gap and followed the river eight miles farther to Flat Lick, a relatively level area with several salt springs that was a junction of several major trails. Indians of the region frequented the primary spring to make salt and to hunt buffalo attracted to the lick. The notorious British officer Henry Hamilton, captured at Vincennes, Indiana, by George Rogers Clark's men, was brought through Flat Lick in 1779 on his way to captivity at Williamsburg, Virginia, and noted in his journal that here was "a remarkable Buffaloe salt lick." Hamilton also observed that the trees bore markings and characters made by the Indians to describe their various exploits, the bark removed and the designs colored with red dye. The little stream in the vicinity was known as "Stinking Creek," allegedly from the habit of hunters, white and Indian, of leaving decaying carcasses and offal along the banks.[6]

Two primary trails split off from the vicinity of Flat Lick, the Warriors' Path and the Wilderness Trail. The Warriors' Path, a western branch of the long-established Great Indian Warpath, or "Athawominee," that traversed the length of the Great Appalachian Valley from upper New York State to Georgia, was a trade and war route linking the tribes of east Tennessee with those of the mid-Ohio Valley. The Kentucky branch of the Warpath followed the bison trace across Cumberland Gap to Flat Lick, and then cut northward to Eskippakithiki (Indian Old Fields) in eastern Clark County, an abandoned Shawnee town in the vicinity of several salt licks. The trail split again here, one fork running northwest to the Upper Blue Licks and on to the Ohio River, the other fork curving northeast and passing by Mud Lick (later, Olympian Springs) and Salt Lick in Bath County to the Ohio River opposite the mouth of the Scioto River, site of the Indian community known as Lower Shawnee Town. These and other licks led explorers to bestow the name "Great Salt Lick Creek" to the river upon which they were located, a designation later altered to Licking River. Thomas Hutchins, who came down the Ohio in 1766, later noted that "Great Salt Lick Creek is remarkable for fine land, plenty of buffalo, salt-springs, white clay, and limestone. Small boats may go to the crossing of the war-path without any impediment." The Warriors' Path mainly followed the river valleys, and some sections were developed along buffalo traces.[7]

The Wilderness Trail also began at Flat Lick, although the entire route through southwestern Virginia and into Kentucky was soon known by this name by Anglo-American settlers. The trace only skirted the Bluegrass; it was not until Daniel Boone blazed a trail to Boonesborough in March 1775, departing from the existing trail in Rockcastle County, that there was a direct route from the Gap into central Kentucky known as the Wilderness Trail and, later, as the Wilderness Road. From Flat Lick, the older trail followed hunters' paths and segments of buffalo traces to Knob Lick, near present Danville, and continued westward to the Falls of the Ohio, passing by Bullitt's Lick and Mann's Lick. Salt River, the major watercourse in this vicinity, was so designated because of these and numerous other licks along its tributaries. The buffalo trace continued on the north side of the Ohio, opposite the Falls, across southern Indiana to French Lick, and crossed the Wabash River at the site of Vincennes.[8]

With the near elimination of hostile Indian activity in Kentucky by 1783, the Ohio River became the preferred entry route into Kentucky. The trail known to the Indians as Alanant-o-wamiowee, or the "Buffalo Path," followed a semicircular course through northern Kentucky, from lick to lick, the endpoints connecting two Ohio River landings at the sites of present-day Covington and Maysville. This trail began at a ford near the mouth of the Licking River, used by the buffalo as they crossed into Kentucky from their winter range on the prairies of central Ohio. From the Ohio River ford, the trace headed southward to Big Bone Lick. George Croghan, in his journal entry for May 31, 1765, described the appearance of the trace as his party of explorers approached Big Bone Lick: "We went to the great lick. . . . On our way we passed through a fine timbered clear wood; we came into a large road which the buffalos have beaten, spacious enough for two wagons to go abreast, and leading straight into the lick." The trail continued south from Big Bone, passing by Drennon's Lick to Leestown, on the Kentucky River just north of Frankfort. Filson noted that the ford at Leestown was "worthy of admiration; a great road large enough for waggons made by the buffalo, sloping with an easy descent from the top to the bottom of a very large steep hill, at or near the river."[9]

From Leestown, the trace veered east to a salt lick in Scott County, where several trails converged and the herds so trampled the earth in the vicinity that it became known as the "Stamping Ground." The Alanant-o-wamiowee continued to the "Great Crossing" of North Elkhorn Creek and passed through the future sites of Georgetown and then Lexington. From downtown Lexington, the trace turned

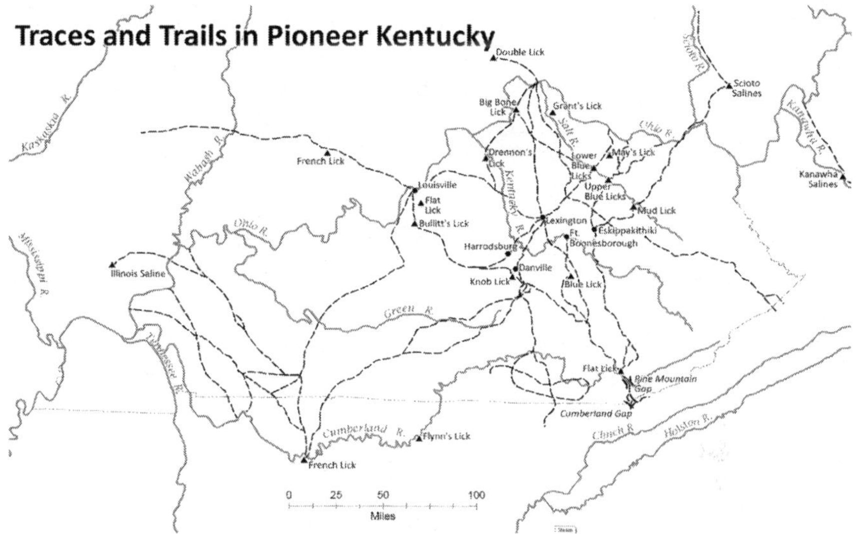

Map of buffalo traces and trails used by the pioneers during the settlement era. Derived from trail maps in Jakle ("The American Bison and the Human Occupance of the Ohio Valley," 300) and Ulack, Raitz and Pauer (*Atlas of Kentucky,* 53). Cartography by Jeffrey E. Levy, Gyula Pauer Center for Cartography and GIS, University of Kentucky.

northeast, following the present Limestone Street and Bryan Station Road, passing the pioneer fort known as Bryant's Station, and ran to the Lower Blue Lick and May's Lick before ending at the mouth of Limestone Creek, site of present-day Maysville. Traveler James Smith noted in 1795 that the old buffalo road between Lexington and the Lower Blue Lick was "generally 200 feet wide."[10]

Licks were especially numerous in Kentucky. Constantine Rafinesque, writing in 1832, identified 160 such springs located within the state, classifying them into three types: salt licks, possessing saline pools or encrustations; sulfur licks, dominated by sulfates rather than chlorides; and clay licks, where clay deposits are impregnated with salt. Of the latter, so-called "paint licks" were brightly colored ochres containing mineral oxides. Unlike the free-flowing freshwater springs throughout much of the state, salines are not karst springs. Most of the salt springs are located in areas where the surface bedrock is not conducive to the development of conduit systems and karst features. The sources for the saline waters of the Midwest are, even today, not well understood, but appear to be mainly derived from ancient seawater trapped in porous sedimentary rocks of early to late Paleozoic age, that surfaces at the licks through bedrock fractures and emerges from the soil. The strength of the brines at different licks varied considerably, but most Kentucky licks, such as those at Big Bone, the Blue Licks, and Bullitt's, contained less dissolved mineral than seawater and, when boiled down to produce salt, required as much as five hundred to a thousand gallons of brine to produce a single fifty-six-pound bushel, depending on the site. By comparison, evaporation of sea water requires less than two hundred gallons to produce a bushel.[11]

Native Americans had long visited saline springs to make salt as a condiment, although they did not use it for meat preservation. During the pioneer era, salt was often a scarce commodity for the Euro-American settlers, and so salt licks were seen as valuable assets and thus were promptly claimed by immigrants, who boiled the waters down to make salt. With the exception of the vicinity of Bullitt's Lick, however, such springs generally did not attract settlements. Salt was necessary, to be sure, but potable water was far more important to everyday life. If it was the location of the mineral springs that led to the establishment of a network of bison-generated trails, linking lick to lick, that guided pioneer movements in Kentucky, it was the location of the freshwater springs in the vicinity of these trails that determined where actual settlements were made. Many of the earliest settlers were under the initial impression that the country was poorly watered. Levi Todd recollected that, at Boonesborough in 1775, "We then thought springs of water scarce and that the country would be thinly inhabited." They soon learned that clear and free-flowing springs were abundant throughout central Kentucky.[12]

The most significant of the freshwater springs, as they were discovered by Euro-American pioneers, became reference points in the wilderness, serving hunters and explorers as navigational markers and locations for rendezvous with other frontiersmen. In the springtime of 1779, for example, John Pleakenstalver, Ralph Morgan, and a few others set out from Boonesborough to the vicinity of Elkhorn Creek, and along the way "encamped at Todd's spring," where Colonel John Todd had erected a cabin. Like the salt licks, freshwater springs were also good places to wait in concealment to hunt a deer or other wild game. Josiah Collins, one of the men who, in April 1779, helped erect the first fort at Lexington, recalled having trouble finding the spring where the settlement was to be located: "The old woodsmen about Boonesborough directed us how to find the camp. Old hunters knew where the spring was we were to build at. In truth they knew just where we were camped, and every big spring through the country, and just the place where this was."[13]

The Indians, who had been hunting in the region for generations and were well acquainted with the springs of Kentucky, used some of the same tactics on the pioneers that had been successful in hunting game for the larder. A raiding party might lie quietly at a well-known spring for hours or even days to ambush some luckless frontiersman as he came to drink. In the summer of 1780, a year after helping raise the Lexington blockhouse, Josiah Collins and a companion, Thornton Farrow, were approaching Hugh McGary's station on Shawnee Run in Mercer County on an errand for the commander at Lexington. Although Farrow claimed to have seen an Indian on the bank of the Kentucky River at the mouth of Shawnee Run, Collins scoffed, and believing themselves secure, recklessly they "lay down our bellies and drank" from a spring a few hundred yards from the settlement. No harm befell them from this, but Farrow had been correct, and the two men had been followed. On the very next day a man named Hinton, who had gone out to tend his field, was ambushed and killed by Indians when he drank from the same spring.[14]

Beginning about 1774, the region that would become Kentucky was invaded by swarms of would-be settlers as well as land speculators, who began to choose and survey prime tracts of land. Most of the initial claims were of lands in the central, or Bluegrass, region of the state; other areas were settled later. The land claims were made on the basis of crude surveys, which might constitute no more than corners marked by blazing or girdling trees, or carving initials into a tree or upon a boundary rock, and through "improvements," such as clearing an acre or two and planting a corn crop, or constructing a rough cabin. Surveys of these lands were based on the "metes and bounds" system, which consisted of bearings and distances from one physical landmark to another, and were further identified by the primary watercourse draining the land. Certificates were awarded by the Virginia government to those settlers who could establish a legally valid claim, and many certificates contain references to karst features. Pioneers used a well-developed terminology to describe such features as springs, "sinking springs," "lick springs," "boiling springs," "blue holes," "cave springs," and the like.

Since it was often difficult, in the wilderness, to locate markers for someone else's survey or even to determine if the land had been claimed at all, this led to a host of conflicting claims. In 1779, the Virginia government sent a commission to Kentucky to judge the land claims, resolve the conflicts, and issue certificates for valid claims. The certificates assigned by the commission were later affirmed by the Virginia government, which awarded grants or patents in Kentucky that included detailed property descriptions and surveys associated with the claims. A typical certificate might include a description such as the following, issued by the commission seated at St. Asaph's (Logan's Fort) on April 22, 1780: "Andrew Steele having obtained Certificate for preemption of 1000 Acres of land in the District of Kentucky [in] February 1780 now comes into Court and makes it appear that he is intitled also to a settlement by Virtue of raising a crop of Corn in the year 1776 lying about 2 Miles up from the mouth of Steel run waters of the South fork of Elkhorn to include a large Rocky Spring & his improvements ordered that a certificate issue accordingly."[15]

The uncertainty concerning overlapping claims led to extensive litigation that occupied Kentucky courts for decades and enriched a generation of lawyers. An example from the court records is indicative of the nature of depositions in the trials and the importance of springs to settlers claiming land. On April 5, 1801, Samuel Boggs testified in regard to a claim in present-day Scott County, Kentucky. In his deposition, Boggs made clear the competitive nature of land claiming and that settlers were well aware of problems with potentially conflicting claims: "That in year 1776 this deponent in company with William Lindsay deceased and others made an improvement by building a cabbin at the Cave spring where Henry Lindsay now lives which improvement was made for William Lindsay . . . also made several other improvements on the run above and below the Cave spring to keep other people from making improvements that might interfere with those at the Cave spring and this place."[16]

Although settlers chose their land mainly for its soil quality, sites for station and fort construction were selected on the basis of two important criteria: the defensibility of the location and access to a reliable source of potable water. Every station settlement in central Kentucky was situated near one or more freshwater springs. The first stations were erected at sites adjacent to the larger and more prominent springs of the region, particularly those in proximity to the trail system. As the region became settled, forts and stations quickly replaced the explorers' springs as navigational waypoints for travelers on the frontier, with the exception of the more prominent licks, such as Big Bone, the Blue Licks, and Bullitt's.[17]

In nearly every case, the fort or station was constructed at a short distance from the water supply, rather than being situated next to the source or including the spring within the stockade enclosure. Although this practice has long puzzled historians, since persons collecting water would be exposed to attack, there were some very practical reasons. If the spring was located in the residential area, traffic by people and livestock would soon transform the area about the water supply into an unpleasant mire, and the presence of mosquitos could be a significant annoyance. Another consideration was that nearly all of the larger springs were located in the valley bottoms, whereas ridgetops were more defensible and, for that reason, were preferred habitation locations. Valley bottoms, being prone to flooding by surface streams, would also be undesirable residential locations. The reasoning that determined which springs were considered desirable water supply sources by pioneer settlers is essentially the same rationale used by present-day residents of Kentucky's rural areas where water infrastructure is absent but springs are abundant. In a study of the water supply practices of a modern-day, self-supplied, rural population in a region of southeastern Kentucky lacking a public water system, I found that accessibility, reliability, and perceived water quality were the most important criteria determining which springs were used for household domestic water needs.[18]

Although siting the settlement at a distance from the water supply might pose a hazard during a time of active hostilities with Native Americans, it was thus deemed necessary in most cases to avoid fouling the source of potable water. The risks associated with conveying water from a spring that was not secured within the stockade were somewhat compensated for, when possible, by clearing away the intervening brush and trees to provide a clear field of fire from the dwelling place. However, separation of source and residential area did not necessarily ensure

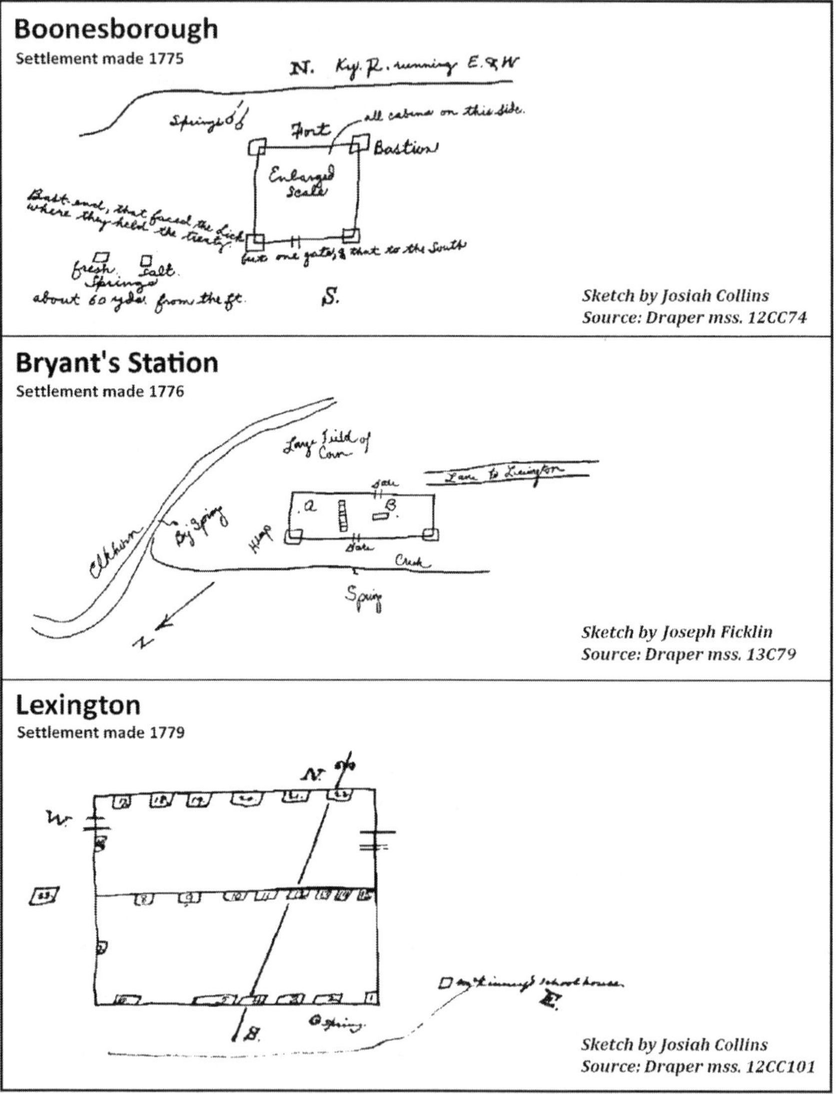

Water supply springs at known fortifications. Most pioneer fortifications were built so as to locate the water supply source outside the walls for hygienic reasons, as shown on these plans drawn by early Kentucky settlers who were familiar with their layout.

that the spring and its environs would be kept clean. Prior to the late nineteenth century, there was no comprehension of the role of microbes in transmitting waterborne disease, only a vague perception that sickness was somehow connected to "filth," and notions of sanitation were rudimentary at best. On a visit to Harrodsburg in February 1780, where the spring was outside the fort but close to the populated section, Colonel William Fleming noted with considerable distaste the condition of the water supply serving that community:

> The spring at this place is below the fort and fed by ponds above the fort so that the whole dirt and filth of the Fort, putrefied flesh, dead dogs, horse, cow, hog excrements and human odour all wash into the spring which with the Ashes and sweepings of filthy Cabbins, the dirtiness of the people, steeping skins to dress and washing every sort of dirty rags and cloths in the spring perfectly poisons the water and makes the most filthy nauseous potation of the water imaginable and will certainly contribute to render the inhabitants of this place sickly.[19]

Even after the country had long been settled, sanitation remained a problem at the springs that supplied communities with water for drinking and other needs. On August 15, 1790, the trustees of Lexington published an order in the *Kentucky Gazette* that "the public spring on Main Street and the one near the schoolhouse, no longer be used as washing places." No one paid much attention to this notice since, on July 3, 1795, the trustees threatened to prosecute "anyone doing washing at the public spring." Similar prohibitions intended to protect the water quality of Royal Spring were enacted by the Georgetown trustees early in the nineteenth century, and it is reasonable to suppose that other communities depending on spring water were equally concerned with the cleanliness of the source.[20]

As the country grew more populous, the original large tracts claimed by pioneers were divided and divided again and resold to newcomers. Real estate advertisements of the era were certain to emphasize the presence of a spring, a desirable feature that increased the value of the land. These springs were usually described as "never-failing," as in the case of an advertisement placed in the *Gazette* on December 7, 1793, by James Dunwiddie, who wished to sell two hundred acres located six miles north of Lexington. On this property were "two never-failing springs near to the buildings, which are a dwelling house twenty by eighteen, and two other cabins, the whole of hewed logs." John Bradford, publisher of the *Gazette* in Lexington, advertised for sale on April 24, 1804, the house and town lot upon which he resided, noting the presence of a brick spring house, from which the flow "never fails in the driest season," and in the back yard of the same lot, another "never-failing SPRING of cold water . . . equal to any in the state." Most springs used as household water supplies, both rural and in towns, were eventually enclosed by springhouses or other structures intended to protect the source and to provide cool storage for produce and dairy products.[21]

Many of the original forts and stations were eventually abandoned, but those more prudently situated continued to grow and became the towns and cities of present-day Kentucky. As the population of these communities increased, a single spring usually proved insufficient to meet the increasing demand for water. Communities were in time forced to develop other water supply sources; since there were no public distribution systems, individual households had to dig wells or collect rainwater in cisterns to meet their own needs. By the beginning of the twentieth century, community-based public systems based on artificial reservoirs or withdrawals from nearby rivers and streams were being developed to supply water to citizens of the largest towns.[22]

For those settlements that grew into substantial communities, most of the former water supply springs have been covered or destroyed as a consequence of urban development. Very few Kentucky cities obtain any part of their water supply from natural springs, and only Georgetown relies on the same spring that once supplied the pioneer community.

6

Floyd's Spring

The historical account of Georgetown's Royal Spring began on April 7, 1774, when John Floyd (1750–1783) set out from Smithfield Plantation near present-day Blacksburg, Virginia, on his first expedition to the fabled lands of Kentucky. Floyd was a remarkable man, destined to become, with Daniel Boone, Simon Kenton, and many others, a hero celebrated by settlers of the western frontier. In 1770, William Preston (1729–1783), the surveyor of Botetourt County, employed young Floyd as a schoolteacher and soon obtained a surveyor's license for him. John took up residence at Preston's Greenfield estate, and the two men soon became close friends. When Fincastle County, a vast area that included the Kentucky country, was formed in 1772, William Preston was commissioned as sheriff and surveyor of the new county. He moved to the New River Valley in the mountains of western Virginia, taking Floyd with him, and there established Smithfield Plantation. Preston arranged for his friend to be commissioned as a deputy sheriff and deputy surveyor. In 1774, Preston sent twenty-four-year-old Floyd across the mountains to the west to survey lands under military warrants, one of three such parties he dispatched at about the same time.[1]

Floyd's first excursion into Kentucky was chronicled by Thomas Hanson, who, along with Floyd and six other men, set out from Preston's home and followed the New River northward to its junction with the Kanawha, reaching the Ohio River on April 20. As they traveled,

Portrait of John Floyd. Courtesy of the Filson Historical Society.

they encountered other parties, including some friendly Delaware Indians, who informed them that the Shawnee intended to make war on the Pennsylvanians and Virginians. The sense of danger was heightened when they reached the mouth of the Kanawha and there met with a large group of settlers and explorers; one man warned them to "take care of their scalps." Undaunted, Floyd's company set off in canoes down the Ohio, their party now increased to more than thirty men. Stopping occasionally to survey particularly choice lands along the river, they reached the mouth of the Kentucky River (at present-day Carrollton) on May 13. Here eleven men left the company to head south along the Kentucky and join up with James Harrod, who was at that time engaged in laying out Harrod's Town (Harrodsburg), the first permanent settlement in Kentucky. Floyd and his men lingered in the vicinity for several days, surveying several thousand acres along the Ohio River bottoms.[2]

Floyd and his men employed the "metes and bounds" method in their surveys, the practice of which is still used for land surveys in the areas of the original thirteen colonies and in a handful of other states, including Kentucky and Tennessee. "Metes" refers to straight-line distances between two points, whereas "bounds" are lines that follow the edge of a linear landscape feature, such as a river or roadway. Surveys are run from turning point to turning point, which are identifiable features along the line or at the corners of a survey. These points might be a distinctive tree or cluster of trees, a pile of stones or a boulder, a stake driven into the ground, or even trees that have been marked with initials or a "blaze," where bark has been removed. Such boundary markers were, of course, rather temporary, since trees can die or be cut down and other markers removed or obscured, either accidentally or intentionally.[3]

Floyd, like other surveyors of his era, would have used a form of compass called a "circumferentor," which consisted of a circular brass box containing a magnetic needle, protected by a glass cover. The needle swings freely over an azimuthal scale divided into 360 degrees of direction. A pair of sights is located along the north-south axis of the instrument. Circumferentors were manufactured in several European countries and widely used for surveys until the early nineteenth century, when they fell out of favor and were replaced by theodolites. Compass directions were taken in the form of quadrant bearings, which give the angle in degrees away from north or south toward east or west directions. For example, a compass azimuth of 225 degrees would be a quadrant bearing of S 45 W, or 45 degrees to the west of South. Distance measurement was based on the English standard pole (also known as a rod), which was 16.5 feet long. Surveyors used the Gunter's chain, 66 feet long and made up of 100 standard metal links, each exactly 7.92 inches long and every tenth link marked with a brass ring. Twenty-five links equaled one pole, and four poles equaled a chain. The system of poles and chains was designed to be equivalent to many of the common units of distance and area used in Britain and, later, the American colonies. For example, 80 chains were equal to 5,280 feet, or one mile, and ten square chains equaled 43,560 square feet, or one acre.[4]

Floyd's party continued down the Ohio by canoe, reaching the Falls of the Ohio (at present-day Louisville) by May 29. The men spent a few days surveying here, and then set off over land to the east, traveling leisurely up the Salt River toward the central Bluegrass region and surveying select tracts of the best land they saw. On June 25, they reached the inland waters of the Kentucky River, and, believing hostile Indians to be in the vicinity, traveled three miles upstream under the cover of darkness and "lay without fire." The next day, they walked along the west bank of the river for seven miles, made a bark canoe, and crossed to the other side. Alarmed by a distant gunshot, the men "took off into the country" and traveled about twelve miles until they encountered Elkhorn Creek, "where we found some good land." During the next two weeks, Floyd and his men surveyed thousands of acres in the vicinity, Thomas Hanson noting on July 1 that "All the land we passed over today is like a Paradise it is so good & beautiful."[5]

Back at Smithfield, news from the frontier since Floyd's departure was alarming to William Preston. Dispatch after dispatch reported incidents of hostile encounters between Native Americans and whites in western Virginia and Pennsylvania, where tensions had been building for years. The Iroquois had ceded their claims to the lands south and east of the Ohio River in the 1768 Treaty of Stanwix; the Shawnee, Mingo, and other Ohio tribes had not been parties to the treaty, and became increasingly irritated as explorers, surveyors, and settlers began to swarm into the region. At the same time, occasional incidents in which travelers were robbed and sometimes killed by Indians elevated fear and anger among the whites. Murder by one side was matched from

Reenactors Willie Balderson and Bill Rose portray members of a colonial surveying party in the wilderness. Courtesy of the Colonial Williamsburg Foundation.

the other with retaliation of equal barbarity. The smoldering anger of the Indians was precipitated into a more active hostility on May 3, 1774, by the unprovoked slaughter of the entire family of Mingo Chief Logan, who had previously been very friendly to the whites.

It now appeared that all-out war was about to envelope the region. On June 10, John Murray, who carried the title of Lord Dunmore and was the colonial governor of Virginia, circulated a letter to county officials in which he stated that peace was no longer possible. The county lieutenants were to assemble their militias and prepare to defend their homes or march to the assistance of others. Preston was greatly concerned for the safety of the surveyors he had dispatched to Kentucky; he was truly fond of the young pioneer John Floyd. On June 20, Preston wrote to William Russell, captain of militia, at his residence on the Clinch River in present-day Russell County, Virginia, informing him of the situation and requesting that he send warning to the surveyors in Kentucky. Russell made the necessary arrangements and wrote back on the 26th: "I have Engaged to start immediately, on the occasion, two of the best Hands I could think of Danl. Boone, and Mich. Stoner, who have Engaged to search the country. . . . if it is not too late, I hope the Gentlemen will be appraised of the eminent Danger they are Daily in."[6]

In Kentucky, on July 6, John Floyd took three of his men and set off for the north branch of Elkhorn, arranging to meet the others of his party at James Harrod's cabin on the first day of August. He was accompanied by Hanson, Roderick McRae (one of the seven men who had made up Floyd's original company), and William Nash, who had joined the company on April 26 as they traveled down the Ohio. Hanson, in his journal, was greatly impressed by the lands they now encountered, writing that "the land is so good that I cannot give it its due praise." The party ran their surveys all through the week, tract after tract adjoining, until July 9, when Floyd decided to take a short break and, with Nash, "went in search of a spring, which they found." The exciting discovery of this huge spring was probably made by following the Royal Spring branch from its merger with North Elkhorn back to the source. Rejoining their two companions, the party continued surveying along North Elkhorn until July 18. Well satisfied with their labors, the party retired to Floyd's Spring, as it was now called, where they camped for several days.[7]

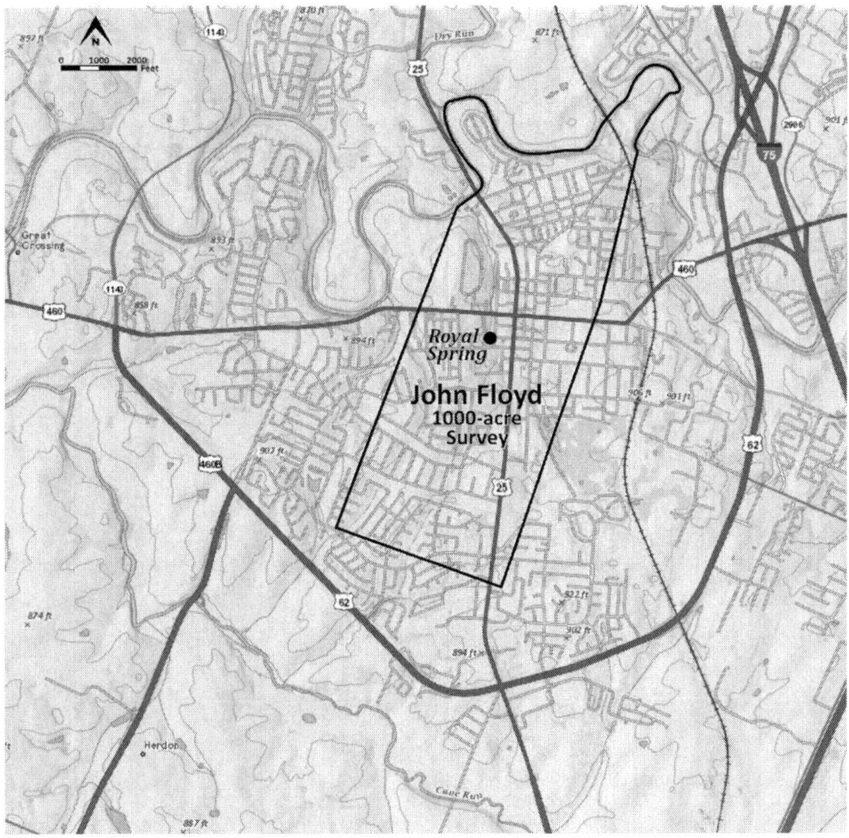

Floyd's survey of one thousand acres around Royal Spring. Map by Gary O'Dell.

On the 19th, the men mostly rested in their camp, but being surveyors, of course, could not resist taking the opportunity to measure the slope of the watercourse. The spring branch was found to have a fall of 13 feet 7 inches, from the springhead to the point where the flow joined Elkhorn, a distance of about three-quarters of a mile. Floyd's Spring, Hanson wrote, "is the largest I have ever seen, in the whole country and forms a creek of itself." During the following two days, the party surveyed one thousand acres around the spring for John Floyd. As recorded in the Virginia land office, the survey began "at two Sugar trees a honey Locust & ash by and below the mouth of a small draft [old term for an intermittent or seasonal stream] on the South Bank of the Creek near a buffaloe ford & runneth thence S 13 W 170 [poles] to an ash Buckeye & hickory saplin S 20 W 480 [poles] to two Elms & a honey Locust on a small creek and down it N 70 W 270 Poles Crossing the Creek to a hickory & walnut growing from one root & a single hickory on a flat hill side thence N 20 E 630 Poles Crossing the Creek to Elkhorn Creek & up the several Courses thereof to the Beginning." Breaking camp on July 21 and setting out for the rendezvous at Harrod's, Floyd subsequently obtained a grant for one thousand acres around the spring in his own name.[8]

When Floyd's party reached Harrod's cabin on July 24, they found the place deserted and some of the buildings still burning. Tacked to a tree (or carved into the wood) was a note that read, "Alarmed by finding some people killed we are gone down this way." Greatly distressed by this development, the surveyors traveled rapidly overland through the southeastern mountain country. Boone and Stoner evidently missed Floyd's small party, but spread the alarm through the Kentucky country, making a remarkable round-trip journey of eight hundred miles on foot through the wilderness in only sixty-one days. Daniel Boone later recalled, "On the 26th June [1774] I was employed by Gov. Dunmore to go out to that country and give the surveyors notice of the breaking out of the Indians war . . . and finding the surveyors well drove in by the Indians, I returned home." When Floyd and his men reached the Clinch River on August 9, "we found them forted in, prepared for war with the Shawnees." They finally returned to Smithfield on the 13th, "after an extreme painful and fatiguing journey of sixteen days, through mountains, almost inaccessible, and ways unknown."[9]

Floyd raised a volunteer company and set out on a march to join General Andrew Lewis on Dunmore's expedition against the Shawnee towns, arriving at Point Pleasant on the night of October 10, 1774, too late by mere hours to aid in the battle fought there that day. Only months later, Preston again dispatched Floyd to Kentucky to continue surveying Virginia's Crown lands.[10]

7

McClelland's Station

In late October 1775, Robert Patterson "left the Pittsburg country . . . with John McClelland and family and six other young men for the promised land, Kentucky." Patterson had heard about the beauty and bounty of Kentucky firsthand from such men as Daniel Boone, Simon Kenton, and James Harrod while serving with them in Dunmore's campaign against the Shawnee during the summer and fall of 1774. His companions were John McClelland (1745–1777) and his wife, Sarah (née Lowry); John's brothers Abraham and Alexander; the brothers William and Francis McConnell Sr.; Francis McConnell Jr.; a cousin, Andrew McConnell (the McConnells all being cousins to Patterson); and two others, David Perry and Stephen Lowry (Sarah's brother). Most of the party had been to Kentucky before and were eager to return and make permanent settlements. John and Alexander McClelland, William McConnell, Francis McConnell Jr., Andrew McConnell, and David Perry had just returned from an exploring trip that set out the previous April and spent several months surveying and making improvements in the vicinity of Elkhorn. William McConnell had first explored the Kentucky lands in 1774, and, as the most experienced, was probably the leader of this party.[1]

The McClellands were from the southwestern corner of Cumberland County, Pennsylvania (today Franklin County), in the vicinity of Mercersburg. Cumberland was, at the time, a very large county that occupied much of south-central Pennsylvania. The family was almost certainly previously acquainted with Patterson, whose home was about eight miles to the north, near present-day McConnellsburg (today in Fulton County). The Patterson farm was located at the southern toe of Cove Mountain, along the military road cut by General John Forbes during the 1758 campaign against the French at the site of present-day Pittsburgh. Robert Patterson, prior to leaving for Kentucky with the McClelland party, was courting Elizabeth Lindsay, who lived on her father's farm in Franklin County, four miles southeast from Chambersburg. It would be five long years, however, before the two were able to wed. John McClelland, thirty years old as the adventure began, was the eldest of a large brood of children born to John Robert McClelland and the former Margaret Chiswell. His wife, Sarah Louise, was a year younger than her husband and the only daughter of Abraham Scott Lowry and Sarah Sterrett. Additional friends and family would soon join them in Kentucky.[2]

Robert Patterson (1753–1827), then twenty years old, was outfitted by his father for a wilderness expedition with provisions, clothing, and a new saddle in exchange for a promise to survey some land for him in Kentucky. The party of ten men and one woman set off from Pittsburgh, some in canoes, into which they had loaded such goods and supplies as was thought necessary to set up households in a new land, while some, apparently including Patterson, kept pace along the bank of the Ohio, driving a few head of livestock. These would be the first stock imported into Kentucky, nine horses and fourteen cattle. In November, after a journey of nearly four hundred river miles, the party reached the mouth of Salt Lick Creek, presently the site of the community of Vanceburg, in Lewis County, Kentucky.[3]

Here, the party divided, arranging to rendezvous in a few weeks at Leestown, a ford of the Kentucky River located about a mile north of where Frankfort would later be established. Most of the party, including the McClellands, remained with the canoes and continued down the Ohio River, planning to turn up the Kentucky River and follow it southeastward to Leestown. This would require an additional journey of about 230 miles by water. Patterson, William McConnell, and Stephen Lowry bid farewell to the McClellands and, led by David Perry, turned their steps away from the Ohio River, driving the cattle and horses and scouting ahead for the best route for the animals. They headed almost due west, following Salt Lick Creek for a time, crossing Cabin Creek (present-day western Lewis County), to Stone Lick (now Orangeburg in Mason County, about nine miles southeast from Maysville), and striking the old buffalo trace at May's Lick (Mason County) that led from the Ohio River to the Lower Blue Licks. They crossed the buffalo road and continued to the west a few miles until they encountered another trail known as the Middle Trace, and then turned southward and followed the trace to the Lower Blue Licks. Here Patterson and company ran into Simon Kenton and John Williams, who told them that they knew of no other white person then in the country.[4]

Herding the livestock, they crossed the Licking River at this point and traveled westward along another buffalo trace that led to Hinkston's Station (just south of present-day Cynthiana in Harrison County), from there following Townsend Creek southwest to yet another buffalo trail, known to the Indians as Alanant-o-wamiowee or the "Buffalo Path." This trail took them westward to Leestown on the Kentucky River, passing very near to Floyd's Spring along the way. Patterson and the other drovers had managed to reach the rendezvous ahead of the McClelland party, and there waited for them several days; when the canoes arrived and the separate groups were reunited, they lost no time in striking off to the east, following the same buffalo road back to Floyd's Spring. Clearly the McClelland party knew exactly where they were going to establish their settlement. John McClelland had very likely discovered Floyd's Spring during his explorations of the Elkhorn region a few months earlier, and was unaware that the land about the spring had been surveyed and claimed by John Floyd. At this spring, which was renamed Royal Spring, Patterson and the other men "helped to build a house and made our home until April [1776] when the young men of us built a cabin two miles below Lexington where Wm. McConnel formaly lived." Before the end of the year, they would be joined by additional family and friends, including Benjamin McClelland (another brother of John), John McCracken, John Lowry (another brother of Sarah), and James Sterrett (likely Sarah's uncle). The settlement at Royal Spring certainly constituted a closely knit group.[5]

In April 1775, John Floyd returned to Kentucky at the head of a party of thirty-two men; on the first day of May they arrived at a prominent spring on the headwaters of Dick's (Dix) River, known as Buffalo

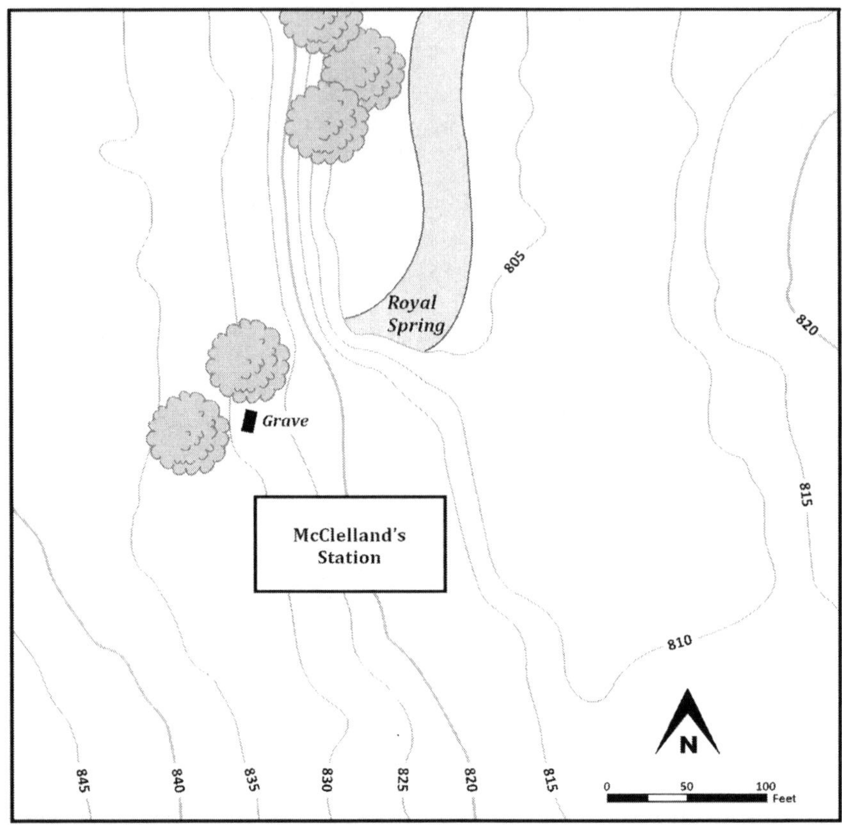

McClelland's Station. Size and position interpreted from notes by Lyman C. Draper, 1838, Draper mss., 16 J 35–36. Pioneer Levi Todd recalled a "woods" around the station. Although the settlers would have cleared most of the trees in the vicinity, according to Draper's notes some few were left standing in the locations indicated. Map by Gary O'Dell.

Springs. Among the members of Floyd's party were Joseph Drake, who five years earlier had been one of the long hunters who had first seen and named Dick's River and probably served as guide to this location, and Benjamin Logan, who was to become one of the most famous military leaders of the frontier militia. Here, on a slight rise overlooking the spring, they began to erect a number of cabins, naming the settlement "St. Asaph's" for a Welsh saint traditionally honored on May 1. For several years, Logan's Fort at St. Asaph's (today the site of Stanford in

Lincoln County), Harrod's Fort, and Fort Boonesborough were the only truly secure refuges in Kentucky, able to withstand a prolonged siege.[6]

Two days later, on May 3, Drake guided John Floyd twenty miles to Boonesborough, a little settlement that had been established on the Kentucky River only a few weeks before, the capital of Richard Henderson's infant Transylvania Colony. Floyd would use Henderson's settlement as his headquarters for the next eighteen months for surveying expeditions into the hinterlands until the partition of Fincastle County in December 1776 into Washington, Montgomery, and Kentucky counties. With Fincastle County abolished, Floyd lost his position as deputy surveyor and was recalled.[7]

In late April 1776, to his great distress, Floyd heard rumors that squatters had settled on the one thousand-acre Cave Spring tract (near the future site of Lexington) that he had surveyed for Preston in 1774 and on his own land around Floyd's Spring. On the first of May, Floyd, who was then camped at Powell's Valley on the Wilderness Trail en route back to Kentucky after a brief absence, wrote to Preston of the news he had been hearing from travelers heading back east. With the outbreak of the Revolution, a number of persons had fled from the virulent anti-loyalist sentiment of the East into the frontier. Floyd reported that eight Tories were now settled along the Elkhorn on William Russell's land and vicinity, and speculated, "I imagine some have got on yours, tho I can't learn for certain as yet." Before he completed the letter, he must have heard more, since he added a postscript, "The Cave Spring [Preston's] & my big spring are both settled & I don't know how to act." Soon after his arrival at Boonesborough, the rumors were confirmed. "My big spring," he wrote Preston on May 19, "is settled by a man who has his wife and family there, and has made large improvements and is determined, as I am told, to hold the land at the risk of his life."[8]

Almost immediately, an irate John Floyd set out to visit the Preston's Cave Spring tract and his own lands about the big spring to determine the circumstances and, if necessary, to evict the squatters. At the Cave Spring, he spoke with Francis McConnell, who appeared "very uneasy" in consequence of his unwitting infringement, but expressed a desire to purchase the land from Preston. At Floyd's Spring, the situation was not quite as he supposed, however, and when he confronted the McClellands, his anger quickly evaporated and was replaced by

John Floyd surveyed thousands of acres of choice Kentucky land for his patron, William Preston, including one thousand acres around Preston's Cave Spring in Fayette County (above). Preston never traveled to Kentucky and saw none of the land claimed in his name. Photograph by Gary O'Dell.

compassion. Upon his return to Boonesborough, he wrote to William Preston on June 8 that "I paid one McClelland a visit, who lives at the big spring. I went determined to drive him off, but on seeing his wife & three small children, who must have been distressed, I sold it for £300, to be on interest for that time, if not punctually paid. I believe he is able enough." Tragically, before the sale could be finalized, John McClelland was killed during an attack on the station at the end of the year.[9]

Floyd's comment about the McClelland children is significant. At this early date, the settler population in Kentucky was almost exclusively male; women were few, and children fewer still. The McClellands had at least three very young children living with them at the station at the time of Floyd's visit, and possibly more that he did not see. These children were five-year-old Abraham McClelland; Margaret "Peggy"

McClelland, nearly three years old at this time; and Mary Ann "Polly" McClelland, a few months short of her second birthday. These would have been the children observed by John Floyd, the youngsters perhaps peering curiously at the stranger from behind Sarah's skirt. There are two other children reported to have been born to John and Sarah, although this is not consistent across the sources consulted: James, born in 1774, and John, born on March 3, 1775. These latter two, one a newborn, may have been considered too young to be outside and so escaped Floyd's notice. Sarah would continue to bear more children after the death of her husband and her remarriage to Joseph Wilson. Certainly, the sight of these children, a rarity on the dangerous frontier, provoked Floyd's sympathy.[10]

The fall of 1775 and spring of 1776 were relatively peaceful in Kentucky, but there was a distinct air of unease throughout the western country. The inhabitants of the frontier were worried that the Shawnee might renew their attacks across the Ohio at any time, or that the Cherokee might raid from the southeast. Settlers and speculators alike worried about the validity of their land titles, given the vast presence of the Transylvania Colony on the south side of the Kentucky River and the efforts of Richard Henderson and the proprietors to establish there a government separate from Virginia.

Even so, in recent months there had been many new immigrants into Kentucky. On May 19, John Floyd wrote to Preston, "Families are settled scattering all over the country & appear to be under no apprehension of danger." Even as Floyd was writing this assurance, the Cherokee, incited by British agents and emissaries from the Shawnee, declared war on the settlements near their tribal lands. In concert with this outbreak of hostilities to the east, in Kentucky raiding parties of the Shawnee began first with attacks on isolated individuals, then with increasing boldness against the settlements. The first Bluegrass settlement to be raided was Leestown, where in late April a band of warriors waded across the large buffalo ford of the Kentucky River and attacked, killing Willis Lee and wounding Cyrus McCracken. This attack prompted a quick flurry of stockade building and improvements to fortifications across the region.[11]

Floyd's letter to his patron on July 21 reflected the heightened apprehension of the population: "The situation of our country is much altered since I wrote you last. The Indians seem determined to break up our settlement. . . . They have, I am satisfied, killed several which, at this time, I know not how to mention. Many are missing who, sometime ago, went out about their business who we can hear nothing of. Fresh sign of Indians is seen almost every day." Floyd informed his employer that the inhabitants of Boonesborough were engaged in finishing a large fortification about the settlement, and that he had heard forts were being erected at Harrodsburg and at Royal Spring. Hinkston's Station on the Licking River had been entirely abandoned, and to his knowledge, more than three hundred persons had fled the country in fear for their safety.[12]

Fortification of these stations was a united effort involving representatives from all of the settlements in the region working together. Among those helping to raise the fort on the bluff above Royal Spring (probably incorporating the McClelland house built in late autumn of 1775) were Robert Patterson, John Todd, and Simon Kenton. This was a strategic, if dangerously exposed, location, being then the only settlement north of the Kentucky River, more than forty miles in advance of any other.

Although there are a number of contemporary descriptions of the larger forts, such as those of Boonesborough, Harrod's Fort, and Bryant's Station, very little detail is available for smaller stations such as McClelland's. No archaeological excavations have ever been made here, and so there is no physical evidence. If the city of Georgetown were able to acquire the Kentucky Utilities property south of the spring, where the fortified station was located, archaeological investigation might be able to reveal more of the nature of the settlement from peripheral deposits. Because the modern building was apparently constructed directly atop the station site, it is unlikely that any traces of the actual station have been preserved. The following hypothetical description of McClelland's is derived in part from limited documentary evidence, and partly by drawing on more detailed descriptions of other pioneer forts and stations.

The best source of information concerning the characteristics of the pioneer station established at Royal Spring are the papers of Lyman C. Draper (1815–1891), an amateur historian and devoted chronicler of the trans-Allegheny region. As a child, Draper was regaled with the exploits of his grandfathers in the Revolutionary War and of his father in the War of 1812, and he developed a passion for history. In his readings, he discovered that different accounts of events were often inconsistent, and concluded that the best way to discern the truth was from the testimony of the original participants, the frontiersmen and women who had explored the wilderness, founded precarious settlements, and fought in the battles to subdue the region. Draper was concerned that the pioneers of the West were growing old, and that many would die with their stories remaining forever untold. Recording these stories became his lifelong obsession, and he corresponded with hundreds of early settlers and their descendants, and traveled extensively through the region to gain firsthand impressions of the territory.[13]

Draper visited Georgetown on August 25, 1838. The fortifications of the station had been dismantled long before, but there may have been some remnants or impressions in the soil, and at the time there were still persons living who were present during the attack in December 1776. Draper's notes for that date contain several sketches of the station in relation to the spring. When these sketches are evaluated in combination with his observations on the site and information from other sources, this allows a provisional reconstruction of some important aspects of the station: its location, size, shape, and internal layout. Of these, the greatest confidence can be attached to the location of the station. Draper describes the site: "The rocky cliff projecting over the spring is some 20 feet high, upon the top the ground ascends quite rapidly making the probable location of the fort some 40 feet higher or 60 feet above the level of the spring, ground then descending every way except to the west. From the summit immediately back, or south of the spring, is 40 paces, or about 120 feet, from the top of the cliff over the spring." The station was laid out on ground with a moderate incline. Kentucky archaeologist Kim McBride observed that it was not unusual for stations to be deliberately situated on sloping ground, as this provided a better view of the surrounding environment and so gave a defensive advantage. A position below the topographical crest on the slope toward a potential enemy is known as the "military crest" and allows maximum observation of the remainder of the slope. His sketches show the outline of the station on the hill above the spring with the long axis centered on the spring and perpendicular to the spring branch. Draper's calculation for the fort being 120 feet from the spring may be an overestimate of the length of a pace as being 3 feet long. I have taught "compass and pace" navigation as part of a course on maps for many years, and in my experience the average pace of a male is closer to 2.5 feet than to 3 feet, and even less over rough ground. Accordingly, this would locate the fort at approximately one hundred feet from the edge of the bluff.[14]

The size of the station is more problematic. McClelland's was routinely occupied by six to ten family groupings, and Nancy O'Malley, a noted Kentucky archaeologist and expert on pioneer fortifications, estimates that as many as thirty families may have been living at McClelland's Station when it was used as a sanctuary in 1776. Although the pioneers in the region were accustomed to living in crowded conditions, this still indicates that McClelland's Station was a sizable structure, larger than most family-based stations if not quite on the scale of a regional administrative center like Harrod's Fort. Draper's notes provide a means to roughly estimate the size and shape of the fort at Royal Spring. His sketches show the fort as a rectangle, with a length roughly twice the width. He made three sketches of the fort and spring in his notes in an effort to get the proportions correct, the third being the most crudely drawn. Draper observed that the spring, at the cliff line, was "3 rods" across, or 49.5 feet, since a "rod" is equivalent to a pole, the standard length of 16.5 feet. His first sketch, which showed the spring as being almost exactly two-thirds the width of the fort would correspondingly require the fort to be at least seventy-five feet through the long axis. Draper, however, found his first sketch to be unsatisfactory, adding a side note that stated, "I see that the spring is too large for the proportionate size of the fort." This is corrected in his further drawings, which show the spring of a lesser width relative to the fort. In these, the spring is about half the width of the fort's long side, the latter of which accordingly would be about one hundred feet long, giving the fort dimensions of about one hundred feet by fifty feet. These must be considered as very crude approximations, since Draper's sketches were made freehand without benefit of a ruler or straightedge, and in fact he placed the fort proportionately much closer to the spring than the 120 feet he indicated was the distance between the two locations. Given the number of reported inhabitants of McClelland's station and typical dimensions of cabins within pioneer forts, a minimum size of 120 feet by 80 feet seems more reasonable.[15]

Lacking any sort of documentary evidence, the construction and internal layout of McClelland's Station is the most difficult aspect to assess with confidence, although much can be inferred from what is known

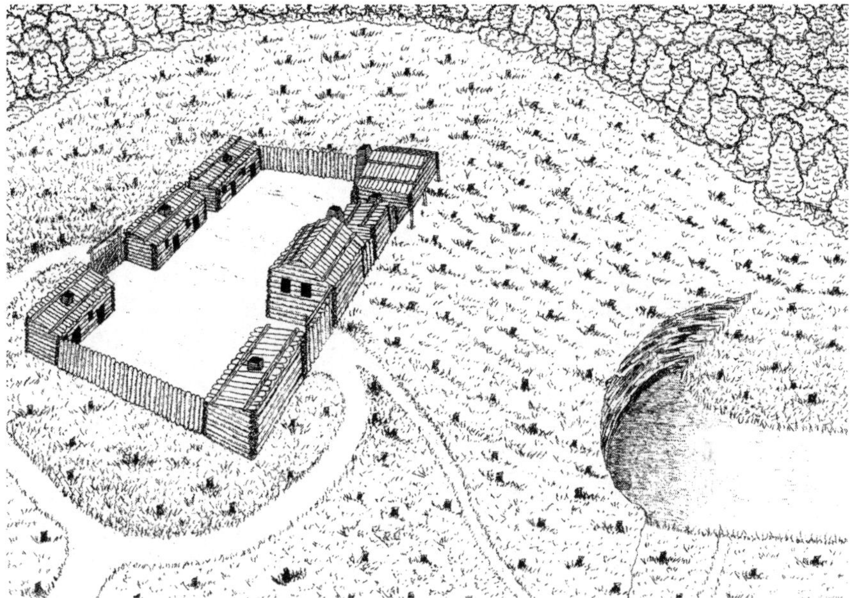

McClelland's Station. Interpretation by Anna Thornton, Georgetown, Kentucky, based on research by Gary O'Dell.

of other forts and stations built during the settlement period. Detailed descriptions and plan sketches for many of the major Kentucky forts were obtained by Lyman Draper, and modern archaeological surveys have been conducted for a number of sites, some of which involved excavations and recovery of cultural artifacts. Fort Boonesborough in Madison County, Harrod's Fort in Mercer, and Bryant's Station in Fayette are among the best-known pioneer fortifications, each possessing richly detailed historical accounts. Of these, only the Boonesborough site has been subjected to professional archaeological investigation in modern times. Other sites for which limited archaeological investigations have been conducted yielding cultural artifacts include Daniel Boone's station in Fayette County, John Grant's station in Bourbon, and Hugh McGary's station in Mercer. Physical evidence obtained from such stations combined with their historical accounts and the more limited information available on McClelland's allow some probable conclusions to be drawn about the station founded at Royal Spring in 1774.[16]

The station began as a large house, perhaps twenty by twenty feet, built above the spring in November or December 1775, intended to initially house the ten men and one woman of the McClelland party. As suggested by the orientation of the later stockade, the house faced toward Royal Spring and was centered perpendicular to the spring branch. Construction methods using round logs were first introduced to the American colonies during the 1630s by Finns and Swedes who settled in the New Sweden colony of Delaware; characteristics of European log structures are readily apparent in many New World structures. Pioneer cabins were typically built of logs stacked horizontally, with notches cut at the ends in which to fit other logs to make the corners. Builders usually stripped the bark from logs used in home construction because, if left intact, the bark would in time become infested with a variety of insects. Gaps between logs were filled with small stones or splits of wood and then plastered over with mud mixed with grass, moss, animal hair, or other binding materials. Dirt floors were the rule for these primitive dwellings, and roofing was generally composed of overlapping clapboards made from split logs, three to four feet in length, five to eight inches wide, and between one-half to three-quarters of an inch thick. These were laid with the slope of the roof on top of a series of parallel purlins or "rib poles," and held in place by substantial "weight poles" laid crosswise. As a free-standing structure when first erected, the McClelland house may have had a gable roof rather than the shed roof commonly built for houses enclosed within a fortification.[17]

Once the primary shelter was erected, the settlers would have turned their attention next to building additional cabins to relieve the crowded conditions, laying them out in two parallel lines (the McClelland cabin most likely occupying the center of the front row) in anticipation of the likely need for fortification. As more settlers moved to the station, more cabins were built. To save time and labor, these were likely double cabins, such as were built at Boonesborough, either in the "dog-trot" form, in which two cabins are separated by a walkway but share the same roof, or as "saddlebag" cabins that share an interior wall in common. Individual cabins would likely be smaller than the McClelland house in size; Boonesborough cabins measured sixteen feet square. If the station measured only fifty feet in width, as suggested by the Draper plan, sixteen-foot square cabins along both the north and south walls would leave a very cramped interior space of only eighteen feet between the rows; it seems more likely that the station width would have been eighty feet or greater to accommodate daily activities within the stockade. There may or may not have been cabins on the end walls. In one hypothetical arrangement, assuming a station length of 120 feet and double cabins measuring thirty-two feet, this would allow for three doubles along the back or north wall, separated by twelve-foot sections of stockade. The front, or south side, with the twenty-foot McClelland house in the center, may have had a double cabin and gate to one side, and a double and single cabin to the other. Altogether, the station was likely composed of at least a dozen cabins including McClelland's. Without either documentation or archaeological evidence, the number, type, and arrangement of interior cabins can only be speculative.[18]

Most—perhaps all—of the houses would have been provided with a chimney and hearth for cooking and heating. Various pioneer accounts describe chimneys as having foundations of dry-laid rock up to a height of about four feet, and built up from there with sticks daubed over with mud. Chimneys might be placed in the shared wall of a pair of cabins, a single chimney with hearths on each side opening out into the rooms, or each cabin might have its own chimney located on one of the exterior cabin walls. The cabin chimneys, as at Fort Boonesborough, would have been inside the stockade rather than along the outside perimeter. The same was true for doors, since a door opening from a cabin to the outside of the stockade would have been a weak point during an attack. As the first structure built, the McClelland cabin may have been an exception, possessing a door facing the spring; when the fortifications were erected, the McClellands may have sealed the exterior door and cut a new one facing inside. Alternatively, if the McClelland cabin was situated in the back of the stockade rather than the front, with another row of cabins built between it and the spring, the front door would have been facing to the inside.[19]

In the summer of 1776, rising tensions along the frontier cemented plans to fortify McClelland's Station. In the fortification of a station, a great deal of labor could be saved by using the outside wall of the cabins as part of the defensive perimeter and simply filling in the spaces between with log pickets. Cabins that served as corners provided part of two walls for the fort. To erect a section of stockade between cabins, the

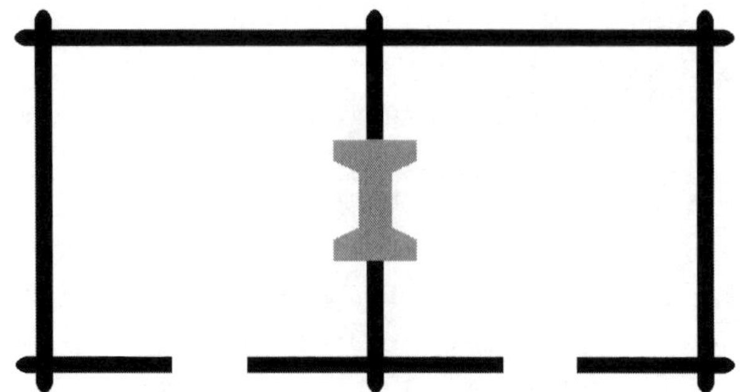

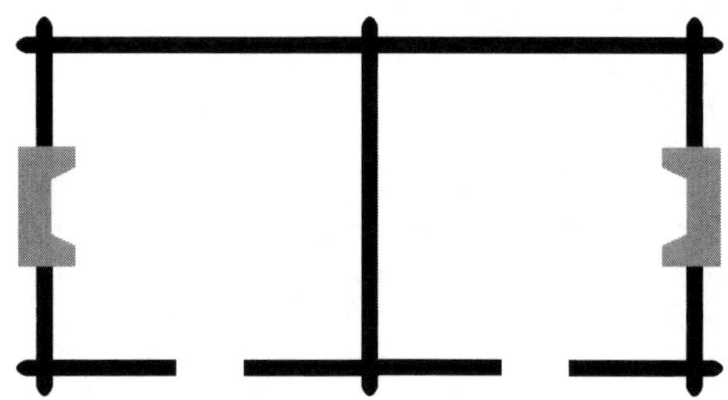

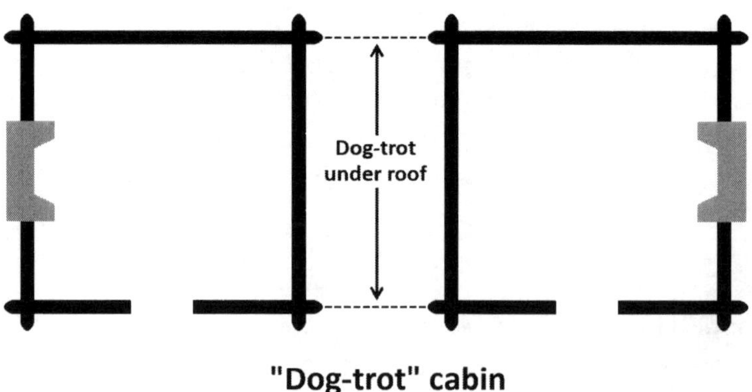

Pioneer cabin types associated with stockade enclosures. Adapted from O'Malley, *Boonesborough Unearthed.*

builders dug a shallow trench into which pickets made from logs about a foot in diameter and split lengthwise into halves were placed upright and kept from shifting by pinning other split sections to them horizontally at intervals. Stockades typically reached a height of ten to twelve feet, more or less level with the upper end of the cabin shed roofs. The overall appearance of a pioneer fort or stockaded station from the outside would thus present a somewhat regular pattern of broad swatches of horizontal logs (exterior cabin walls) alternating with narrow bands of vertical logs (the stockade pickets). Station residents cut slots and portholes in the stockade and cabin walls, normally plugged or covered over, to allow sharpshooters to fire at attackers from cover; when needed, additional holes could be knocked through the chinking between logs.[20]

Gates provided access to the interior, most likely a large gate in the front or north side of the stockade and a smaller one in the opposite wall, as was the case at Boonesborough and Bryant's Station; two gates were also present at Harrod's Fort, but located in the north and west sides rather than opposite sides. Because the McClelland house most likely occupied the central position in the front wall, the gate would have been placed off-center to the left or right.[21]

At public forts, such as Boonesborough and Harrod's, two or more corners were occupied by blockhouses, two-story structures in which the upper story projected outward over the walls of the fort, allowing defenders to direct enfilading fire along the walls. Although some stations without stockades built single structures in the form of a blockhouse, occupants of stations seldom went to the effort to construct blockhouses. McClelland's was larger than most stations, and here, Robert Patterson recalled, "I assisted in building blockhouse and stockade" in 1776. This statement suggests that McClelland's had only a single blockhouse. There was no indication as to which corner of the station was occupied by the blockhouse; because Royal Spring was a vital resource, it may have been positioned on the front so as to overlook the spring. Patterson also observed that defenders had erected "small sheltered enclosures at the corners" from which to fire, which implies structures that were less substantial than blockhouses, something like watchtowers. The defensive improvements made by residents of McClelland's Station with the assistance of Patterson and others in the summer of 1776 would not have been as substantial or as well-constructed as those erected at public forts, but would have provided protection against gunfire during an attack. The work transformed McClelland's into a miniature fort capable of withstanding most attacks. Cabins and stockades were, in any case, intended only to serve as temporary refuges until conditions in the country were deemed safe enough for residents to leave the safety of the forts and build more permanent abodes on their own land.[22]

Outside the stockade, settlers cleared away nearly all of the trees for a considerable distance. Much of the timber was used in construction of the cabins and stockade and to provide land for crop production, but the removal of trees was also intended to eliminate hiding places for potential attackers and to provide a clear line of fire. In colonial America, land clearing for agriculture was generally accomplished by the practice of "slash and burn," which required little initial effort. Settlers removed a strip of bark from around the circumference of a tree, a practice known as "girdling," which usually caused defoliation within a few days and the death of the tree soon afterward. Crops could then be planted beneath the leafless trees, which were later removed when convenient, piled up, and burned. The urgencies of frontier defense, however, dictated that standing trunks be removed almost immediately in order to prevent enemies from using them for concealment and cover. The landscape about McClelland's station would have been dotted with the stumps of cut trees that were too large to easily remove. Corn was the most commonly planted crop for Kentucky pioneer settlements, and because it grew to a height sufficient to provide concealment, cultivated fields were of necessity situated at some distance from the station. Defensive strategies were always paramount in the minds of station occupants.

The founders of McClelland's Station never envisioned their little settlement as becoming a town. This patch in the wilderness was John McClelland's land, and he had every reason to expect that, in due time, his claim to Royal Spring would be validated by the Virginia government. By his labors he planned to transform it into an agricultural estate that would support his family for generations. With the help of friends and family, from the moment he had arrived at Royal Spring McClelland had been diligently working to ensure that the legal requirements for his claim would be met. Building a house, clearing land, and planting crops were all among the necessary improvements required to establish possession under the law. Other occupants were engaged in the same activities, for each man and family desired to establish a claim to a homestead carved out of the wilderness. McClelland's Station was their shelter against the hazards of the new land. This was, after all, the primary function of a fort or a fortified station, to provide a secure base for settlers from which they could carry out surveys, claim land, and make the required improvements. Station residence was a temporary expedient, something to be endured until the ever-present threat of Indian attack receded and it was safe to move out onto their own lands.

A group sanctuary came with a price; it was crowded in the station and the tiny cabins were often occupied by more than one family. Residents of McClelland's had brought a number of enslaved people with them to help work the land, and housing must also be provided for these bondsmen. During this early settlement period, livestock was scarce in Kentucky, but the McClelland party had brought horses and cattle with them from Pennsylvania, and these, too, must be quartered within the stockade from time to time lest they be killed or stolen by an Indian raiding party. Yet, as Nancy O'Malley recently observed, "Families of the time period were used to crowding, both within a cabin and within a station enclosure. I can envision several kids piled into a single bed; parents sleeping with a baby; people bunked down on the floor in front of a fireplace." Circumstances in which numerous people are confined in close quarters can generate social unrest, and such was often the situation at the larger forts. Large public forts such as Harrod's Fort or Fort Boonesborough served as collection points for immigrants into Kentucky, hosting a transient population of settlers from many different places and backgrounds. There was less friction at privately held stations such as McClelland's, where the families were tied by kinship, marriage, or friendship.[23]

Supplies of all kinds were desperately low in that summer of 1776, but particularly powder and shot. At the beginning of October, Patterson and six others set off to Pittsburgh to bring back the badly needed items, but were attacked on the 14th in their camp on the bank of the Ohio near the mouth of the Hockhocking River (near Parkersburg, West Virginia) by a band of Shawnee. Two men were killed outright, two others wounded, and Patterson badly injured. George Rogers Clark and John Gabriel Jones (a friend of William Preston's who settled at McClelland's Station), who earlier set out from Harrodsburg on a similar mission, were more successful. At Harrodsburg in late June, the two men were elected as representatives to place a petition before the Virginia General Assembly requesting formation of a new county, in order to settle the Transylvania question.

Arriving in Botetourt County after a long and difficult journey through the mountains, Clark and Jones learned that the Assembly had already adjourned, and they would have to wait for the autumn session to present their petition. Jones temporarily returned to Holston, to participate in an expedition against the Cherokee, while Clark headed eastward to Williamsburg to discuss the pressing need for gunpowder and lead with Governor Patrick Henry. The governor was convinced, and he helped Clark persuade the Executive Council on August 23 to dispatch five hundred pounds of gunpowder to Pittsburgh for the settlements.[24]

Reunited with Gabriel Jones, the two men finally brought their petition to the Assembly and, after considerable argument, were able to convince the body to create a new county from Fincastle to be named Kentucky County, to go into effect on December 31, 1776. This effectively ended any claim the Transylvania Colony had for legitimacy. Clark and Jones next traveled to Pittsburgh to convey the gunpowder down the Ohio River to the settlements. They recruited a party of seven men to assist in this endeavor, but two hundred miles downriver they were pursued by a large body of Indians in canoes and were forced to land near the site of present-day Maysville, Kentucky. They managed to conceal the gunpowder in several different locations on Three Islands, and fled on foot, reaching Hinkston's abandoned settlement three days later. Here they encountered some surveyors, who told Clark that Captain John Todd was somewhere in the vicinity with a small party of men. Clark, with two of his companions, decided to press on to Harrodsburg for aid, leaving Gabriel Jones and the others to wait there for Todd.[25]

Soon after Clark's departure, Captain Todd arrived with a few other men on horseback. After some discussion, Todd decided to retrieve the gunpowder. Under his command, a party of ten rode off on December 25 following the buffalo trace northeast to the Lower Blue Licks. About five miles beyond Blue Licks, they encountered and were set upon by a larger group of Indians, a raiding party of forty or fifty warriors who were heading down the trace to attack the Kentucky settlements. Gabriel

Jones and another man were killed, and two others captured by the Indians; the remaining six men fled back down the trail to McClelland's.[26]

The Indians, a party of Wyandot led by the noted expatriate Mohawk warrior Pluk-kemeh-notee (corrupted to "Chief Pluggy" in frontier vernacular) continued down the buffalo trace and reached McClelland's Station on December 29. The station's defenders numbered only twenty-one men, generally inexperienced in warfare but considered "good gunners." The attack began at sunrise, Pluggy's warriors at first attempting to draw the defenders out of the fort into the open. John McClelland, who had been outside the fort when the firing began, was struck during the first shots. After the effort to decoy the station occupants from their refuge failed, the two sides continued to exchange fire for several hours. At the end of this period, to the dismay of the Indians, Pluggy was struck by several shots and killed. At sundown, the Wyandots broke off their direct attack but remained in the vicinity of the station for two more days, killing the livestock and sniping at the inhabitants. They then withdrew, traveling back up the buffalo trace to the Ohio River. Inside the fort, four men lay stricken, two with serious wounds. Edward Worthington was only lightly wounded. Robert Todd, John's brother, was badly injured but later recovered. Charles White died from his wounds on December 30, and, on the sixth day of January 1777 the station's founder, John McClelland, also succumbed.[27]

There remains today no trace of his gravesite, but some accounts indicate that McClelland was laid to rest "at the door of the fort," and it was this rationale that led Georgetown's Big Spring chapter of the Daughters of the American Revolution to place a granite monument in 1920 commemorating Scott County's Revolutionary War dead near the edge of the bluff above the spring. Lyman Draper's notes, however, state that McClelland was buried about twenty paces from the spring, and all of his sketches show the gravesite as being slightly to the west of the spring and fort. He noted that the spot was "covered with a large rough stone about seven feet in length." This tallies with the recollections of an early Georgetown resident, Sadie Bell, as reported by Katherine Bradley, one of the founders of the Big Spring chapter of the Daughters of the American Revolution in Georgetown: "She remembers to have seen often the tombstone of John McClelland, a slab the same length as the grave and lying on it, bearing an inscription that he was buried there in

1777. This stone was removed a few years ago and cannot now be traced. The grave was located on the West side and within fifty yards of the Spring itself." Local tradition holds that Pluk-kemeh-notee was buried by his followers in the ground over the spring before they retreated, although this seems unlikely as the warriors attending this task would have been in full view of the fort and exposed to gunfire; more probable is that the body of their leader was carried away with them, as it was the usual custom for Indians to retrieve their dead after raids.[28]

There was no longer any doubt in Kentucky after this: the Indian Wars had begun. McClelland's Station, isolated on the north side of the river a considerable distance from any other settlement, was considered too vulnerable. On January 30, 1777, the occupants abandoned McClelland's and moved to Harrod's Fort, assisted by the residents of that station. Samuel McMullen recalled, "I remember . . . the day McClelland's fort was broken up, or on the day following, which was in the month of Feb." Across Kentucky, the people huddled within only three forts: about twenty able-bodied men at Logan's Fort (St. Asaph's), about forty at Boonesborough, and seventy or eighty at Harrod's; with their families and enslaved people, less than 350 persons were left in the country. The gunpowder hidden at Three Islands, so desperately needed now, was recovered on January 2 by a party of thirty men led by Clark and Simon Kenton.[29]

Robert Patterson spent several months in a hospital in Pittsburgh recovering from his wounds, and then joined George Rogers Clark on his wildly successful expedition into the Illinois country. When he returned to McClelland's in October 1777 after a year's absence, Patterson was alarmed to discover it deserted. He cautiously "lay in the brush with the horse until morning and met the first who told of the alarm and distress from invasions the previous year, massacres of women and children, slaughter of livestock around stations, improvements destroyed, crops neglected, and a number of my acquaintances among the slain." Shaking his head in dismay, Patterson turned his horse southward to rejoin his comrades at Harrodsburg. Ten years would pass between the abandonment of McClelland's Station and the establishment of a new settlement at Royal Spring.[30]

After the death of John McClelland, since the land had not yet been paid for nor a deed of conveyance executed, John Floyd retained possession of Royal Spring and its abandoned fortification. On February 9,

1781, Floyd made an agreement with Stephen Trigg (1744–1782) to exchange the Royal Spring tract, plus an additional five hundred acres adjacent, for Trigg's settlement and preemption on Harrod's Creek and eight hundred acres on Gist's Fork of Brashear's Creek. Stephen Trigg was a member of the Virginia Land Commission, sent to Kentucky in 1779 to settle titles for land claims, who decided to remain in the new country and settled on Cane Run near Harrodsburg. Not too long after the deal was struck with Floyd, Trigg in turn sold the Royal Spring tract to John Cobbs (1740–1803). Trigg and Cobbs probably became acquainted by virtue of each making several neighboring land claims in Lincoln County; in particular, Cobbs obtained a treasury warrant in October 1781 for three thousand acres on Hammond's Creek on the Salt River (present-day Anderson County) "adjoining a survey of Colo. Stephen Triggs . . . of nine hundred acres on the west." Before the Royal Spring sale could be officially recorded, Colonel Trigg was killed in the ambush at Blue Licks on August 19, 1782.[31]

Yet another death would further complicate matters. On the morning of April 9, 1783, John Floyd set off down the Harrodsburg trail from his home at Floyd's Station in Jefferson County toward Bullitt's Lick, in company with his brothers Charles and Robert and five other men. After they had traveled about fifteen miles and had reached the vicinity of Clear's Station, they were ambushed by a small party of Indians, who fired on them from concealment at the edge of the trail. One man and all the horses but Floyd's were killed at the first volley; John Floyd, mortally wounded, reeled in his saddle. As he was about to slide to the ground, his brother Charles leaped up behind John and took the reins. The survivors raced back up the trail about five miles to Colonel Moore's cabin at the Fishpools, where John died on the following day.[32]

Life-and-death events on the dangerous frontier often occurred far more rapidly than documentation of mundane legal matters. The Royal Spring tract had been three times sold, but in each case either the seller or purchaser had been killed before the transaction could be recorded. Floyd's will, probated in Jefferson County on June 3, 1783, instructed his heirs to convey the Royal Spring property to the heirs of Stephen Trigg. The actual date when the will was made is unknown, but requiring conveyance to be made in this manner suggests that Floyd did not expect to be able to execute the deed properly and that the will was, in fact, executed as he lay dying in Moore's cabin. John Cobbs, meanwhile, removed to Richmond County, Georgia, sometime before 1784. In September 1785, Cobbs brought suit against Stephen Trigg's heirs for possession of the Royal Spring tract, which was granted by a decree of the Kentucky Supreme Court in November 1786. The actual deed of conveyance was not made by the Trigg heirs until March 1789, by which time Cobbs had already arranged to sell the tract to Elijah Craig. The actual conveyance to Craig, however, had to wait until Cobbs received legal title, and so was not recorded until June 1789.[33]

8

Serving God and Mammon

Elijah Craig (1743–1808) was among the last of his numerous family to immigrate to Kentucky from Virginia. In September 1781, virtually the entire clan, except for Elijah, packed up their belongings and, led by Elijah's brother Lewis Craig and Captain William Ellis, set out from a rendezvous near Fredericksburg in Spotsylvania County across the mountain wilderness to Kentucky. This was the near-legendary exodus made by the famous "Traveling Church," in which almost the entire congregation of the Upper Spotsylvania (Baptist) Church, nearly two hundred persons, set off for a new Canaan free from religious persecution. The entire Craig family had converted to the Baptist faith in 1765. Elijah and his brothers Lewis and Joseph were ordained as ministers, and at first used Elijah's tobacco barn as a meetinghouse. The brothers were each imprisoned several times for preaching in a manner contrary to the established Anglican Church of Virginia. Lewis Craig, the eldest of the three brothers, became the pastor of the newly established Upper Spotsylvania Church in 1770, and within a few years gathered several additional regional churches into the fold of the Separate Baptists, a faction of the Regular Baptists. The church greatly increased its membership and prospered, but longed to escape the repressive atmosphere and take their faith and church into the beckoning new lands of the west. This they accomplished literally, removing all but the actual church building, so that John Taylor, describing this journey in 1823, noted, "they were constituted, when they started, and was an organized Church on the road—wherever they stoped they were a house keeping at once." This was, in fact, a Traveling Church.[1]

The Craig party followed the Wilderness Road through Cumberland Gap and traveled through the mountains of eastern Kentucky until they finally reached the interior plains of the Bluegrass in early December, where they stopped at last and founded their new church at Gilbert's Creek, at the head of Dix River near present-day Lancaster. Over the next few years, members of the Traveling Church would establish new churches at several different locations in the Bluegrass. More immediately, most of the members of the Craig family were present at the siege of Bryant's Station in August 1782; the fort was commanded during the attack by Captain Elijah Craig, a nephew of the Reverend Elijah Craig, who at this time was still in Spotsylvania County.[2]

In May 1785, a Baptist church was organized at Great Crossings, on the settlement made by Robert and Jemima Johnson and others in 1783 where a well-trampled buffalo trail crossed North Elkhorn Creek. This location was just about two and one-half miles to the west of Royal Spring. Shortly after the Great Crossings Church was established, Elijah Craig came to Kentucky and became the church's first pastor. His arrival here would have been in late 1785 or early 1786; Bradley's 1876 history of this church states that "Craig removed to the neighborhood of Great Crossings Church during the first year of its existence." Ford's serial history of the early churches in Kentucky notes that during the first year at Great Crossings Church, "nothing of special importance occurred, except that Elijah Craig moved soon after into the neighborhood, and became pastor." Ford includes the minutes of the first conference for the Elkhorn Association of Baptist Churches, held June 25, 1785, at Lewis Craig's settlement on South Elkhorn, which recorded, "Elijah Craig, Augustus Easton and James Garrard, invited to seats." Although this may mean that representatives of the Association wrote to Elijah in Virginia with an invitation, it also suggests the possibility that Elijah arrived in Kentucky nearly a year earlier than attributed to him by most histories. Elijah Craig stated that he "settled on the frontiers on the north fork of Elkhorn in 1786," but he may have been present in Kentucky before this.[3]

In November 1787, John Cobbs, who won his suit in the Jefferson County Court against Trigg's heirs during autumn of the preceding year, appointed Samuel Taylor of Mercer County as his attorney specifically to convey "a certain tract of land in Fayette County State of Virginia containing one thousand acres more or less to Elijah Craig. . . . The said Land is known by the name of the Royal Spring." It is possible that Cobbs's 1786 lawsuit to obtain clear title was prompted by inquiries made by Elijah Craig into purchase of the land.[4]

Elijah did not wait to obtain official conveyance of the land title but moved onto the property and immediately began speculating in business ventures. He was a popular and gifted minister of the gospel, but in time lost some of his influence because of what was perceived as an entrepreneurial zeal that sometimes exceeded his devotion to matters spiritual. His first major undertaking, which probably provided the capital to invest in further opportunities, was to lay out a town on a part of his Royal Spring property and sell building lots. The former McClelland's Station was situated on some of the finest land in the Bluegrass, and possessed what most persons in the region believed to be the largest spring in Kentucky—in short, the perfect location for a town site. On November 3, 1787, Elijah published a notice in the *Kentucky Gazette* stating that "On repeated application from the public, I have at length condescended to dispose of a part of my land at the royal spring, near North Elkhorn, about two miles above Major Johnston's mill, for the purpose of erecting a town, which will consist of half-acre in-lots and out-lots proportioned of five acres each, the lots are already surveyed; any person inclining to purchase, are desired to attend at my house on Friday the sixteenth of November, when the terms of the sale will be known and equal lottery for choice will be made." Thus, a community was born, initially known as "Lebanon." On October 21, 1790, Elijah Craig petitioned the Virginia legislature on behalf of the inhabitants, who were all "very desirous that the village should be established as a town." Craig noted that the population of the village was about two hundred inhabitants. The Virginia government accordingly included "George Town," named in honor of the first president of the United States, among the communities established by a legislative act of December 16, 1790. Eighteen months later, Scott County was created out of Woodford County on June 22, 1792, as one of the first acts of the newly established Kentucky legislature.[5]

Having successfully founded a thriving new town, Elijah now turned his attention to launching several business enterprises. These

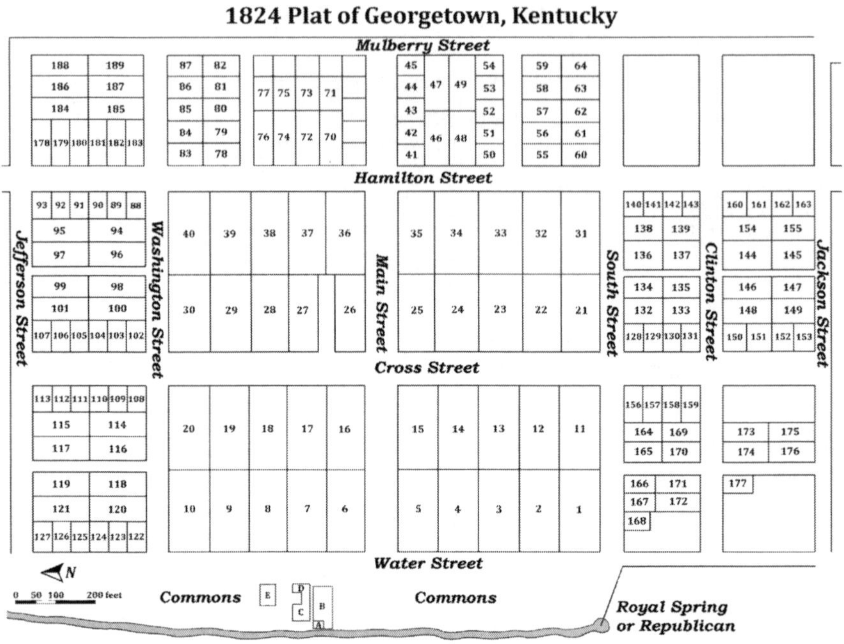

1824 Plat of Georgetown, Kentucky

Plat of Georgetown in 1824. From Scott County Line Book 1, redrafted from the original. Not shown are the larger "out-lots" in the eastern section of the community. The buildings labeled A through E were not identified on the original but are likely mills or similar structures. Map by Gary O'Dell.

endeavors were viewed by his fellow Baptists and by later generations of churchmen with mixed feelings, for all acknowledged that Craig was sincere and a true "child of God," but led astray by the temptations of the new land. John Taylor, writing in 1823, reported that Elijah was considered the greatest preacher of the three Craig brothers, but "his turn for speculation did him harm in every way." Spencer, in his *History of Kentucky Baptists* (1885), evaluated Elijah Craig's move to Kentucky as unfortunate, "both for the cause of Christ and himself." Craig, he stated, "was an enterprising business man. The country offered excellent facilities for profitable speculation. The temptation was too strong. He was soon overwhelmed in worldly business. . . . It seems that he had no intention to abandon the ministry, but vainly imagined that he could serve God and mammon both."[6]

Many of Elijah Craig's own congregation became dissatisfied with his leadership, and sought to replace him with another pastor. The subsequent dispute between the dissidents and Craig's supporters ultimately led to a split in the Great Crossings Church in 1795, when Craig led a sizable proportion of the congregation away to found another church nearby at McConnell's Run. Spiritual matters notwithstanding, Craig's foresight and business acumen were certainly instrumental to the growth and economic development of the region. Craig's vision for "Lebanon town" was not limited solely to "profitable speculation," since his very first act was to sponsor, in January 1788, establishment of a classical academy in the community, long before he entered any significant business venture. Modern historian Ann Bolton Bevins concluded that "Craig initially dreamed of establishing an industrial, Baptist oriented community where one could secure sound employment in a variety of tasks and where one's children could receive a good classical education."[7]

Historian Richard Collins, in his list of "first things" in Kentucky, gave Elijah Craig credit for the first fulling mill (1789); first ropewalk (1789); first paper mill (1791); and, by implication, manufacture of the first bourbon whiskey (1789). Although, in truth, none of Craig's ventures can be established with certainty as "first," they were among the earliest of their kind in Kentucky. The first mention of a Craig enterprise is from the *Kentucky Gazette* for June 13, 1789, which refers to "Craig's mill" without identifying the type; this may have been a saw mill or grist mill, or possibly the mill of his son-in-law. In the September 5, 1789, *Gazette*, Craig announced his intention to take over the fulling mill of Samuel Grant, "killed by savages." Samuel Grant (1762–1789) and his brother Moses Grant were both killed by Indians in an ambush in Indiana Territory on August 15, 1789. Samuel was a member of the Craig family, having married Elijah's daughter Lydia in Virginia in 1784. Since the mill was located on the Royal Spring tract, it probably would not have been established earlier than 1787, when Elijah Craig appears to have taken informal possession of the property from Cobbs. In a fulling mill, loose-woven woolen fabric is soaked in clean water and "fuller's earth," and pounded by heavy wooden hammers into a tighter knit. Ebenezer Stedman, an early resident of the community, locates the fulling mill on the west side of the spring branch, noting that the mill operation was powered by the flow from the spring for most of the year, but, during the dry months of summer, by horse power.[8]

The ropewalk was included as part of the fulling mill operation that Craig took over from his deceased son-in-law; the *Gazette* notice of September 5, 1789, referred to Grant's "fulling and hemp mill." Some details of Craig's ropewalk operation are available through the 1846 autobiography of formerly enslaved person William Hayden. Hayden, who was born to slavery in Virginia in 1785, was sold at the tender age of eight years in 1793 to Frederick Burdett (1768–1795) of Georgetown, Kentucky. In 1796, when William was eleven years old, his owner, Rebecca Cave Burdett (1772–1849), leased his labor to Elijah Craig for a six-year term. Long after, Hayden recalled:

> Soon after I came to reside with Mr. Craig, I was placed by him in the ropewalk, for the purpose of learning the rope-making business, and being very attentive, and quick of apprehension, I became a favorite with my employer, and set to work at spinning much sooner than is customary with the generality of boys; but being naturally good humored and quick on foot, I was frequently called from my work to run errands, and it appeared to me as if the fates were arrayed against me, for as soon as one "chore" was done—another stood ready waiting for my attendance. But this state of things was soon brought to an end, for it was soon discovered that I lacked but strength to be a first rate workman, and was accordingly sent with some others to Frankfort, Kentucky, to work in a "walk" of Mr. Craig's, under the management of a Mr. James Davis, with whom I had been but a short time, before I became a general favorite with my employer.[9]

At the end of 1802, Hayden's labor lease to Craig expired, and the young man was then sent as an expert rope-spinner to Lexington to work in the ropewalk of Peter January Sr. Hayden was manumitted in 1824 by his owner at that time, and moved to Cincinnati, Ohio. As a youth of exceptional intelligence, he had picked up rudiments of literacy at an early age and received some formal schooling, and so wrote his memoirs in Cincinnati in 1846.

The paper mill established by Craig at Royal Spring is, of all his endeavors, the most likely to have been a "first" in Kentucky, although there is still some doubt on this matter. Richard Collins reported that the Craig paper mill was established in 1791, but a notice in the April 7, 1792, *Kentucky Gazette* reported that Craig, Parker & Co. were at that time building a paper mill at Craig's fulling mill. In a further notice in the *Gazette* of March 30, 1793, the proprietors stated that they were now "actually making paper" at their mill. Accordingly, it appears that manufacturing operations began in early 1793. Five years prior to this, however, on August 25, 1787, Jacob Myers announced in the *Gazette* that he was erecting a paper mill on a branch of the Dick's River in Lincoln County. No subsequent mention of Myer's paper mill appears, so the effort may not have come to fruition.[10]

Ebenezer Stedman, whose father leased the Craig paper mill in 1818, wrote a short history of paper manufacturing in Kentucky. Drawing on both personal knowledge and *Gazette* advertisements, Stedman stated that the first paper mill in Kentucky commenced building in 1792 and was operated by Alexander and James Parker in partnership with Elijah Craig. The stimulus for erecting this mill appears to have been notices placed in the *Kentucky Gazette* on January 21, 1792, and regularly for many months afterward, by John Bradford of Lexington, editor and publisher. Bradford advertised to hire "anyone understanding the erection of a paper mill." Underscoring this appeal, on January 28 he published a letter to the public concerning the lack of good printing paper, which he had been obtaining from Pennsylvania but which was now in short supply because of difficulty in shipping downriver during the winter. On March 30, 1793, Bradford noted with satisfaction that the *Gazette* was now being printed on paper manufactured at Craig and Parker's George Town mill. According to Stedman, "the location at geotown on the Royal Spring Branch was on account of the pure clear watter, so necessary in Making paper." Craig's paper mill was located on the east side of the spring branch, about a half-mile downstream from the head of the spring, and almost directly across from his fulling mill and ropewalk.[11]

The most famous "first" popularly if incorrectly associated with Elijah Craig and Royal Spring is in the manufacture of "Bourbon" whiskey. There does not appear to be any historical documentation to substantiate

There are no known likenesses of Elijah Craig. This imaginative statue of Craig, carved by local chainsaw artisan Sandy Schu from a sycamore log, stood briefly in Royal Spring Park during the 1990s until it deteriorated. Craig is shown with a Bible in hand and a keg of whiskey at his feet. Photograph by Gary O'Dell.

this claim other than Richard Collins's 1874 assertion that "the first Bourbon Whiskey was made in 1789, at the fulling mill at Royal Spring." Elijah Craig certainly made whiskey, but he was not the first in Kentucky to do so; it is, however, the designation as "Bourbon" that is most problematic. Bourbon whiskey received its name from the region of Kentucky where good quality whiskey was first manufactured. Royal Spring was never in Bourbon County. Georgetown was first located in Fayette County; then, as Fayette was divided, in Woodford County, and finally became a part of Scott County in 1792. Bourbon County, created from Fayette County in 1785, was initially a huge expanse of land that occupied most of Eastern Kentucky. The Bourbon town of Limestone, today known as Maysville, was then the most important port on the Ohio River, and enjoyed a lively commerce. Bourbon County was split nearly in half in 1788 to form Mason County in the east, which included the port of Limestone. After statehood in 1792, Bourbon County continued to be subdivided into smaller and smaller counties until, by 1799, it had reached nearly its present configuration. The greater region continued to be referred as "Old Bourbon" for many decades, and whiskey was one of its most important exports, shipped to the outside world through the port of Limestone and identified as "Bourbon" whiskey. The designation of "Bourbon" whiskey thus at first referred to the place of origin, rather than to a particular process or manufacturer.[12]

Federal law dating from the end of the nineteenth century defines *bourbon* as whiskey that is made from a mash of at least 51 percent corn, distilled to less than 160 proof and barreled at less than 125 proof, and has been aged for at least two years in new, charred oak barrels. Tales crediting Elijah Craig with the invention of bourbon focus on his alleged discovery of the beneficial effect of aging in charred barrels. At least two variants on this story are promoted. In the first, Craig wished to use some old barrels, in which fish had been stored, to transport whiskey. To eliminate the fish odor, he burned out the inside of the barrels. When these barrels were used to convey whiskey to New Orleans, the whiskey had turned amber and had a more pleasing flavor as a consequence of contact with the charred oak. In the second variant, a barn in which Craig had stored some barrels caught on fire, and the barrels were partially charred by this; the results of storage in such barrels were the same, a great improvement in quality. Both stories are most likely apocryphal. That Elijah Craig made whiskey is certain, since in 1798 he was fined $140 by the US District Court for nonpayment of the federal excise tax on whiskey, but a great many other Kentucky residents were making whiskey prior to Craig. Since no mention of Elijah Craig's product ever appeared in the *Kentucky Gazette*, his distilling operation was most likely on a very small scale. The true inventor of bourbon whiskey will probably never be known, but to this day there is a friendly rivalry between Scott County and Bourbon County for the honor, the former of course claiming Craig and the latter usually asserting that Jacob Spears was the originator.[13]

The manufacturing operations founded by Elijah Craig may not, in every case, have been the first such in Kentucky, but each venture was launched successfully and outlasted its originator. These establishments formed an early industrial nucleus that was in large part responsible for the economic viability of the community and promoted its growth and future development. His reward was not wealth, for, as the *Gazette* noted on the occasion of his death in 1808, "his whole property was expended in attempts to carry his plans into execution," but, rather, the lasting legacy of one of the more prosperous and attractive cities of the Inner Bluegrass region. The parting eulogy of the *Gazette* is perhaps the most appropriate summary of the life of Elijah Craig: "If virtue consists in being useful to our fellow citizens, perhaps there were few more virtuous men than Mr. Craig."[14]

9

Clear Beautiful Spring Watter

Elijah Craig's will, probated in June 1808, divided his estate among his children, and appointed his son John Craig and "my good friends" John Hawkins and Josiah Pitts as executors. Josiah Pitts, likewise an early immigrant from Virginia, was married to Elijah's daughter Lucy, and the Pitts came into possession of a prime tract of Craig's land bounded on the east by the Royal Spring branch and adjacent to the city of George-town. Josiah and Lucy Pitts moved into Elijah's house on the hillside just to the west of Royal Spring, one of the first brick houses built in George Town. Little is known of Pitts's early life, but he may have come to Kentucky with Elijah Craig or shortly thereafter, since he was one of the residents of Lebanon who in 1790 petitioned the Virginia legislature for the establishment of George Town. Pitts was, for a time, one of the more successful merchants of the region, trading in such locally produced articles as tobacco, hemp cordage and bagging, whiskey, wheat flour, and bacon, which were shipped by flatboat to Natchez and New Orleans. He also operated the first tavern in Scott County, applying for a license in 1793. During the War of 1812, however, Pitts became over-extended and numerous judgements against him led to the loss of virtually his entire estate in 1813, including the Royal Spring property. Two years later, in 1815, Pitts died from an unknown cause.[1]

During the relatively brief period that Pitts owned Craig's Royal Spring tract, he made some fairly substantial improvements around the spring. In the western corner of the head of the spring, at the edge of the cliff line, he erected a dry-laid rock springhouse. This springhouse, which was aligned southwest-northeast, or at a diagonal to the outflow of the spring branch, was used as a "milk house," the cooler temperature within helping to preserve the milk. A long rock wall was built to mark the boundary between the Pitts' property and the George Town tract, since Pitts only owned one-half of the width of the stream. This presented the odd spectacle of a wall built straight down the center of the branch from the head of the spring, dividing the watercourse in half lengthwise.[2]

This situation resulted from the unusual manner in which Elijah Craig had divided his property in 1787 to establish Lebanon Town. Clearly he wished to promote the growth of the fledgling community by setting the boundary so as to provide access to the spring, but at the same time he also wished to preserve for himself and his heirs an indisputable legal right to use the water of the spring. Neither the original petition nor the 1790 act of the legislature establishing George Town described the town boundaries. The earliest extant property description referencing the division along the Royal Spring branch between the Craig tract and George Town is that of the June 24, 1813, sheriff's sale to Dr. William B. Keene of 129 acres belonging to Josiah Pitts, in which one of the survey calls extended from a point "near the head of the Big Spring thence North down the spring branch 35 poles to the Beginning."[3]

Despite the description provided by this deed, the exact bounds of George Town remained uncertain. In February 1816, the Kentucky legislature passed an act authorizing the trustees of the town to bring "suit in chancery" in the Scott County Circuit Court against "all the heirs of Elijah Craig, deceased, and all persons owning lands adjoining thereto" in order to establish the boundaries of George Town. According to this legislation, once all testimony had been heard and the court had issued its decision, the boundaries so fixed were to be considered the true boundaries of the town and a plat map to be deposited in the office of the county clerk. In accordance with this edict, a survey was made of the town and recorded by the county court in April 1824; the resulting map, the earliest such known for Georgetown, shows the streets and lots, the "Royal Spring or Republican [Spring]" and the town commons that lay between the spring branch and the town lots. Subsequently, on

February 22, 1834, the town boundaries were officially defined by an act of the legislature. According to the act, the George Town tract began at a point "at the head of the Republican spring" and the last boundary calls returned to the spring branch and proceeded "up the middle of the said branch to the middle of the head, thence around with the head of the spring to the beginning point of the Republican spring."[4]

In 1825, the town trustees paid John Cullen $439.74 to build a rock wall five hundred feet long against the east bank of the spring branch, from the head of the spring northward to the Main Street bridge across the branch. The branch now had two rock walls extending downstream from the spring, the older "cross-wall" dividing the stream lengthwise in half, and this newer retaining wall. On the west side of the cross-wall, Dr. Keene's livestock had ready access to the water of the branch. On the east side, the area between the retaining wall and Water Street, was the town commons, about seventy feet wide and five hundred feet long.[5]

The vicinity of the spring was a popular locale from the founding of the town to the present day. Writing to his daughter in 1878, Ebenezer Stedman, reminiscing about his life in the Bluegrass a half-century before, described the Royal Spring as it looked in 1818: "How Plainly Can i Se how things about Georgetown Looked at that Day: The old mill, the large pond above the Dam, the large flocks of wild Ducks that could Be seen on the clear Beautiful Spring watter." Waterfowl favored the spring branch, for, as Bill Gaines wrote in 1905, "Geese would be found in the spring at daylight. It was a beautiful sight in the hot days of August to see these geese sailing down this stream of ice cold water." In its natural state, the spring branch was no more than a foot or two in depth, flowing swiftly with the fall of the land to Elkhorn Creek. From an early date, however, the watercourse was impounded behind dams to provide waterpower to the machinery of the mills, so that "the water was deep enough to swim a horse." Elijah Craig built the first of these dams at his paper mill, which in later years served first a woolen mill (built on the same location after the paper mill burned in 1836) and then a grist mill. After this mill dam was taken down in 1895, Gaines complained that the water in the branch "now would hardly swim a duck." Main Street, where it crossed the spring branch on its way west to Frankfort, was supported by a massive bridge of dry-laid rock built in

The road from Georgetown to Frankfort crosses the rock bridge over the Royal Spring branch. The bridge was built between 1795 and 1799 and, with occasional repairs, continues to carry modern highway traffic. The bank inset to the right is the rebuilt baptismal steps, and visible in the center background is the roof of the old city jail. Photograph by Gary O'Dell.

1795–1799, so well-engineered and sturdy that it continues to carry the flow of modern traffic on US 460.[6]

During the long afternoons of summer along the banks of the spring branch could be seen old men drowsing over their cane poles, while barefoot boys, more alert, watched their own lines in hopeful anticipation of a tentative nibble that heralded a tasty bluegill or feisty smallmouth bass. Children raced back and forth in the grassy open space of the commons, absorbed in the endless incomprehensible games of childhood. One could hardly begin to reckon the number of toy boats crafted from wood and twigs and paper that have sailed forth valiantly upon the waters of Royal Spring, nor how many gangling adolescent boys, stripped to the waist, have plunged on a dare into the icy waters of the springhead, nor how many toddlers have inadvertently undertaken the same adventure, to be retrieved, scolded, comforted. Yet, in such a place, there was little real hazard to the little ones, for "drowning was impossible for there was not a minute in the day, but what some one was dipping a bucket of water out of the spring."[7]

Many immersions in the chilly waters of Royal Spring were deliberate and ceremonial. Although Elkhorn Creek was also used for this purpose, the deeper section of the spring branch, near the bridge where Main Street crossed the stream, was for many years site of most of the baptizing practiced by both white and Black churches of Georgetown. Here, the rock wall lining the eastern bank of the branch was breached, and steps built down to the water for ready access. On some occasions, particularly in the later nineteenth century, mass baptisms took place, and the crowds of participants and spectators numbered in the hundreds. The practice of baptism in the waters of Royal Spring generally ended after 1890, when most of the churches of the time installed baptismal fonts or pools.[8]

Royal Spring was of greatest significance as a water supply for the region, in the early days serving both Georgetown and the surrounding rural area, just as it continues to do today. James Y. Kelly (1831–1929), who came to Georgetown in 1846 as a youth of fifteen years, later recalled, "At the time when I first came here there were steps leading from the commons into the big spring from which everybody got their water, went down these steps and dipped up the water. . . . [The steps were] Right up at the head [of the spring]. . . . Everybody went there and got water just as they pleased . . . took buckets and barrells and wagons to haul it away. . . . people from the country would haul it." Kelly noted that the city took responsibility to keep the wall and spring access in good repair: "I have seen men there, time and again, and they would fix the stepping stones to enter the branch, they would repair the stepping stones at the wall of the spring, the city would fix up those walls." Gaines, writing in 1905, recalled how many Black women of the community would carry "three buckets of water at a time, one on her head and one in each hand. Many of these old negro women 60 or 70 years old, could carry three buckets brim full of water any distance within a mile and never spill a drop."[9]

From the earliest days of the community there were many persons who were willing to pay others to haul water from the spring to their homes, being elderly, infirm, or simply wishing to be spared the trouble. During the late nineteenth century, one such water hauler who made a modest living providing this service from 1870 to 1885 was Alexander "Elly" Elgin (1801–1885), an elderly Black man who with

The Big Spring of Georgetown, oil on canvas, 7½ x 11¼ inches, circa 1900, by Will T. Hunleigh. The spring was a favorite subject of the impressionist artist, who rendered several treatments. Courtesy of the Georgetown and Scott County Museum.

his "crooked-leg" mule, John, and cart was a common sight on the streets of Georgetown. Elly, who was too frail for the robust work of filling barrels with water, made his rounds with an assistant, his stepson David Bradford, who filled the barrels at the spring, and dipped it out into buckets to carry into the homes and businesses of the town. Elly received 15 cents per barrel delivered, and was considered such an asset to the community that, when the old mule John died, the *Georgetown Times* of February 8, 1882, lamented, "Elly Elgin's mule is dead, and our water works are seriously interrupted in consequence."[10]

Elly, who was the best-known of several men who earned their livelihood hauling water for local households, lived about five hundred feet from Royal Spring on a street that was named for him, Elly Alley. This alley ran southward from Clinton Street, a zigzag away from the spring, and Elly lived on the corner. The Water Street neighborhood, across the town commons from the spring branch, naturally attracted other residents who also made a living using water from the spring. Several of the town's washerwomen, who did laundry for others, resided on or near Water Street so as to have a convenient source of clean water for washing

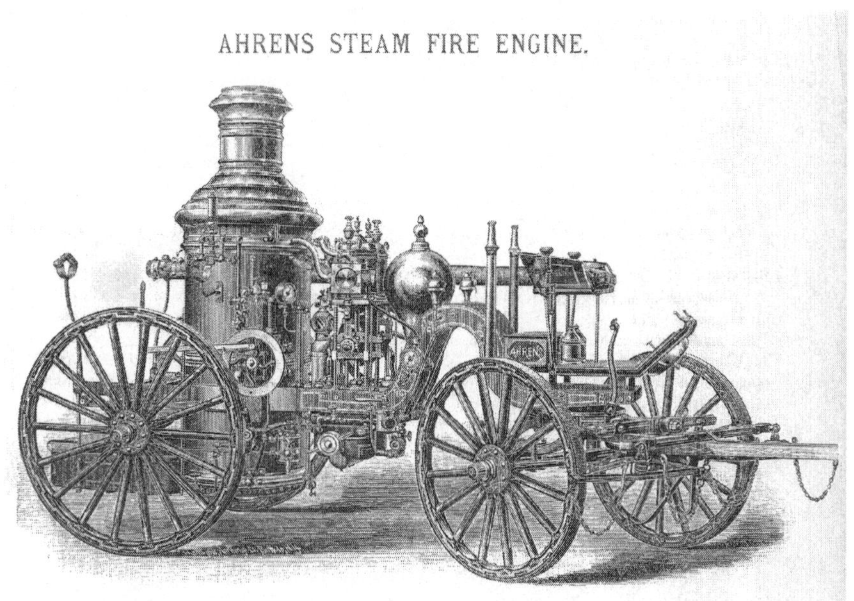

In 1877, the city of Georgetown purchased a steam-powered, horse-drawn Ahrens fire engine similar or identical to the one shown here. *Catalog, American Fire Engine Company* (Springfield, Mass., 1893), 12.

and rinsing, and hauled the water to their homes because of the ordinance that prohibited doing laundry in the spring branch. The census of 1860 lists a number of women with the occupation of "washerwoman" who owned property in the vicinity. Among these women was Nellie Green, a free Black who purchased a pleasant house at 126 South Water Street in January 1857, where she resided until her death in 1863 at the age of sixty. Susan Perry, who lived with Nellie and her husband, Ben Green, was also listed on the census as a washerwoman. Manual water transport was ultimately ended by the construction of a city water works in 1889, which, of course, withdrew its water from the Royal Spring.[11]

Although Royal Spring was the town's principal water supply source, its location on the western edge of Georgetown prompted the town trustees to have several public wells and cisterns constructed elsewhere in the community, primarily for fire protection. The first of these wells was excavated in 1805, on the grounds of the Public Square, a one-acre plot of land set aside for the community in 1787 by Elijah Craig and upon which the first courthouse was built during 1792–1793. This well was intended to provide water to livestock in the nearby "stray pen" and would also be convenient to the public and the fire department. The same 1816 legislative act which authorized litigation to determine the boundaries of the town also conveyed specific powers to the trustees to make infrastructure improvements and compel residents to contribute to common public safety and welfare. The trustees required each household and business to obtain one or more fire buckets, the number dependent on property value. In the event of a fire, these buckets, probably made of leather, were used either as part of a bucket brigade to pass water from a spring or well to the blaze, or to fill the barrels of a hand-pumped fire engine.[12]

The community purchased its first fire engine in 1807 through an appropriation of $200 made by the county court to the fire protection committee, of which Elijah Craig was a member; a lottery for the purchase of a second and somewhat larger fire engine was authorized by the legislative act of 1816. Since the engine house was located on the Public Square, the initial load of the engine was probably obtained from the well at that place, with refills made from whatever source was closest. Fire-fighting was exhausting work and required two brigades, one to carry water continuously to the reservoir of the engine and another to operate the two-handled pump and keep the water flowing. In 1865, the town obtained an engine with a suction hose that allowed refilling without the use of buckets, a side-handle outfit operated by six men on each side of the wagon, and, in 1877, a horse-drawn Ahrens steam-powered pumper, manufactured in Cincinnati.[13]

10

Blue Grass Park and the Civil War

Dr. William B. Keene (1775–1857), who purchased the land west of Royal Spring at the 1813 sheriff's sale, was one of the first physicians in Georgetown. Keene, originally from Maryland, opened his practice in the community in 1812. Medical care in Georgetown for many years was almost a family affair, since Keene's son Alexander was also a physician, as was Dr. William L. Richards, who married Keene's daughter Eleanora in 1826. William and Eleanora's only child, Alexander Keene Richards (1827–1881), was orphaned as a toddler; his mother died in 1830 and his father was carried away in the 1833 cholera epidemic at Georgetown. Keene Richards was taken in and raised by his doting grandparents, William and Hannah Keene.[1]

Dr. Keene was a wealthy man, and he lavished attention upon his grandson. The pivotal moment in young Keene Richards's life came in 1851 when, as a reward for completing his studies at Bethany College in Virginia, his grandfather sent him on a grand tour of Europe, a custom among the wealthy on both sides of the Atlantic. Twenty-four-year-old Keene apparently had little interest in the social life of the capitals, but was fascinated by horses. After first visiting the racecourses and breeders of England and France, Richards traveled to Spain, where his imagination was captured by the magnificent Arabian horses recently imported by

Keene Richards in Arab garb with the Arabian horse Mokhladi, purchased in Syria. Painted by Edward Troye in his studio at Blue Grass Park, Georgetown, in 1854. Original 36.5 by 47 inches, oil on canvas. Courtesy of the Georgetown and Scott County Museum.

Queen Isabella. Believing that the stamina of American Thoroughbreds could be improved by crossbreeding with Arabians, he next traveled to the Middle East, where he arranged to export Arabian horses from the Middle East to Kentucky and, later, some outstanding Thoroughbreds from England. Richards embarked on an ambitious breeding program, and soon became a well-known personage on the southern racing circuit.[2]

In April 1857, having owned the western half of the Royal Spring tract for more than forty years, William B. Keene died and left the eighty-acre property to his grandson, Alexander Keene Richards. Since Richards had been born and lived nearly his entire life in the brick house above Royal Spring and had invested so much time and energy into the breeding program, it was only natural that his grandfather would pass the Scott County acreage on to him. Although Dr. Keene had other children and grandchildren, to whom he made substantial bequests, the greater part of his estate, including a large plantation in northern Louisiana, was left to Richards, and so was a measure of the affection and regard he had for his orphaned grandson.[3]

With much of his grandfather's wealth now at his disposal, Keene Richards was able to pursue the gracious lifestyle of a Kentucky gentleman and to transform the Scott County farm into one of the nation's premier Thoroughbred breeding establishments. Almost immediately, he more than tripled the size of the estate by purchasing some adjoining farms, beginning in autumn 1857 with the 106-acre Webb Ross tract to the south. The acquisition of this land must have been particularly satisfying to Richards, since it had once belonged to his uncle, Alexander C. Keene, but was sold to Ross in 1845 when Keene moved to Louisiana. Two years later, Richards bought the Lunceford Herndon property of 135 acres, which adjoined the Ross tract to the southwest. The combined purchases brought Richards's holdings to 325 acres, and he commenced an ambitious building program, laying out a full-scale race track and erecting luxurious stables for his valuable equine stock. Many visitors considered Blue Grass Park, as it was known, to be one of the finest estates in Kentucky. One visitor in 1872, who by his own account had observed most of the breeding farms in America, lavished praise on Richards's establishment:

> There is a line of beauty in every swell of the meadows, and then the woodlands are absolutely perfect. The acres run up into the

> hundreds, and yet so few are the weeds on the domain that you can count them. The trees are magnificent specimens of the oak, the ash, the locust and the hickory, and nearly every one is as straight as an arrow, while all reveal a great length of trunk before putting forth a branch. Look in almost any direction, and you mark the horizon through long vista shadows. Pass into the open and the grass under your feet contrasts delicately with the blue sky over your head.[4]

Although there are no existing maps or plans of Blue Grass Park, nor have any photographs of the property been found that indicate the location and layout of various structures, some clues can be gleaned from period documents. As one of the foremost Thoroughbred breeders in the nation, Keene Richards often received visitors, who wrote glowing accounts for sporting journals of the magnificence of the Georgetown estate. The most detailed information is given for the house in which Richards lived, built by Elijah Craig in 1808, the year of his death. This was a substantial mansion of brick, stone, honey locust, and black walnut, sixty feet across the front and twenty feet deep, located about two hundred yards from the Frankfort Road on rising ground above and fifty yards from Royal Spring. This places the location of the former Craig house in the vicinity of 301 West College Street. An 1898 reminiscence fondly recalls "memories of golden sun-sets seen from its piazza," thus indicating that the house was oriented with its long axis north-south and facing Royal Spring. The house was surrounded by a well-kept lawn and gardens that extended down to the spring, and the acreage of the farm was divided into neatly fenced five-acre paddocks. Immediately to the right of the Craig house was the home of Pompey, the elderly enslaved person, who had been allowed to retire as a result of his advanced age and affliction with Alzheimer's disease; this was a new house built specifically as a reward for Pompey's years of service. On the other side of the main house were the house stables, in which during the summer were kept a matched pair of bay mares, Richards's buggy team; a pair of bay geldings sired by the famous Glencoe, his carriage horses; and a pair of grays. A road from the house led to a gate that opened on Water Street, next to Royal Spring. Not far from the mansion, beneath a giant oak, were buried the remains of two famous racehorses, Glencoe

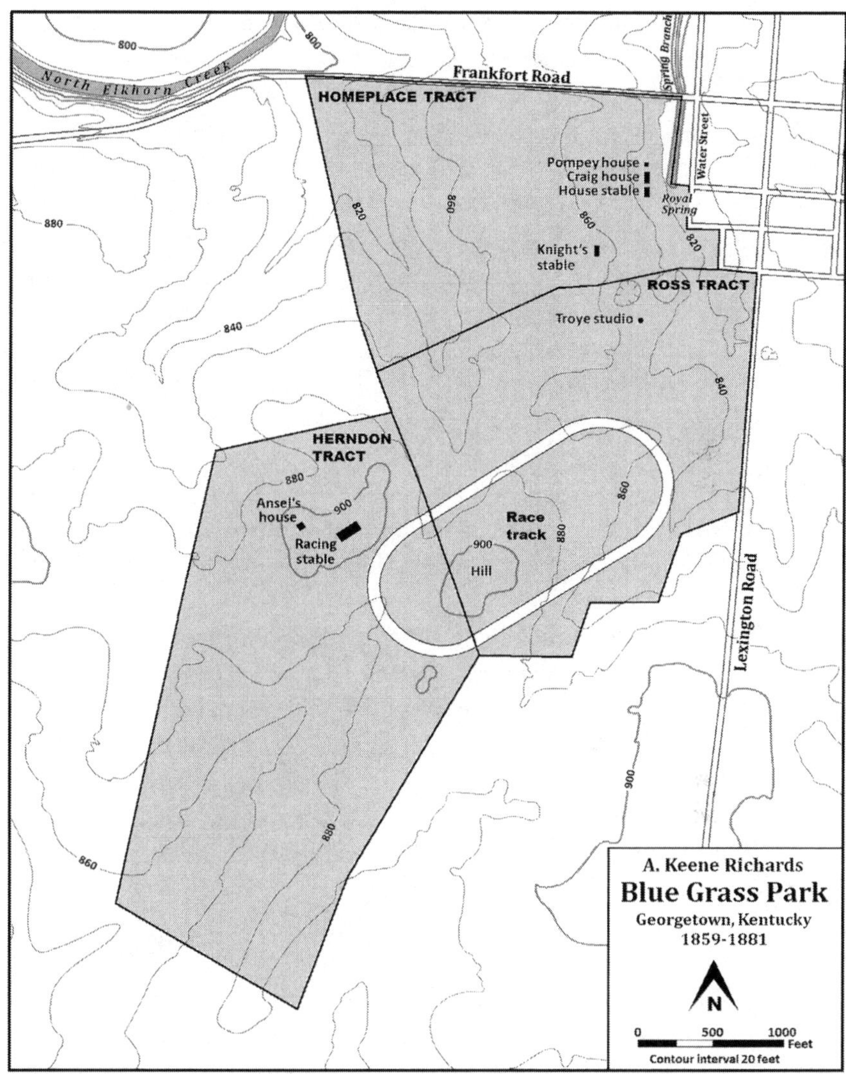

Richards's Blue Grass Park, a famous Thoroughbred breeding establishment during the nineteenth century. Based on Scott County property deeds and descriptions that appeared in sporting journals of the era. Map by Gary O'Dell.

and Peytona. An 1898 account noted that Glencoe was interred in the garden and the grave marked by a small stone.[5]

The property also contained many other structures, elegant and spacious stables, and a racetrack, as well as homes for workers; "There is no building upon the estate which has not a stamp of refined and cultivated taste upon it," as one visitor remarked. On the Ross tract, he laid out a mile-long oval training and exercise track, upon which his farm manager, Frank Sherritt, hosted a race meeting in May 1862 while Richards was away serving in the Confederate army. The presence of the track in this location is noted in a later property transfer. A visitor to the farm, heading southward from the main house to the track, would first encounter the stable, "built of brick with odd gables," of Knight of St George, a Thoroughbred imported from England in 1859 and the pride of Richard's breeding stock. A little farther along the farm road was the short path that led to the circular studio that Richards built for Edward Troye, his dearest friend and an accomplished artist. Troye (1808–1874) specialized in livestock portraits, and was noted for his many paintings of famous Thoroughbreds. He accompanied Richards on a trip to the Syrian desert in 1855 made to purchase Arabian horses, periodically spent time in residence at the Georgetown home of his friend and generous patron, and created many of his equine portraits at the studio.[6]

The racing stables, located behind the racetrack, were the largest on the estate. The stable contained "sixteen boxes, each large enough to contain four horses, stalled as is done North, with large water tanks, a wide passage between the two divisions, a loft above for hay, straw and corn, and a walk around the entire building wide enough to drive a buggy round, except at the corners, all of which is under the same roof. All the stables are built somewhat on the Gothic or Moorish style of architecture." The racing stable measured 147 feet long by fifty-six feet wide, and the interior from floor to roof was about thirty feet.[7]

A visitor in 1859 reported that the stables were provided with "clean and wholesome rain-water" from cisterns, which Richards preferred to spring water, to avoid any potential deleterious effects of a change of water when the horses were moved to tracks elsewhere, which generally were supplied with rain water. This policy was not always followed, since another visitor during the 1859 Christmas season observed that several stallions, after being briefly exercised, were brought down to a spring, where they were allowed to "drink a certain number of swallows, walked awhile, finish drinking, come into the stable, receive a little bundle of nice clean hay and bucket of chop feed, after they are rubbed off." There seems to have been another spring in addition to Royal Spring on the Richards property, since the visitor noted that the racing stable was situated on a "very beautiful rise, just above a nice spring of clear water, which courses its purling way through five or six lots of beautiful pasture land." This was evidently the spring at which horses were sometimes watered, not the Royal Spring. The racing stables were under the supervision of Ansel, an enslaved person who was widely acknowledged as one of the best horse trainers in the business, and his residence was located nearby. Ansel's home was described as having "as neat and pretty an exterior as many of our businessmen's cottages."[8]

The racetrack would have been "skinned," or bare dirt from which the sod had been removed, an American innovation believed to allow faster running as opposed to the custom in England, where horses ran on the turf of racecourses. The track was described as "hilly" and of a mile in length. A prominent hill of the infield obscured the back third of the course, beginning at about the half-mile post, from the view of spectators. It was rather thrilling for onlookers, as the leading horses disappeared from sight, forcing observers to speculate as to what they would see when the competitors rounded the hill and came back into view. One visitor to the May 1862 races at Georgetown wrote, "Bettie West jumped off with a commanding lead, which she held until they left our sight . . . on appearing again, Bettie West still leading. . . . This is the best mile race ever!"[9]

Keene Richards had very little time in which to pursue his breeding program, for his grand experiment was about to be interrupted by the convulsions of a nation at war with itself. The owner of a great Louisiana plantation and hundreds of enslaved people in the Deep South, Richards supported the rebel cause. In 1861, as Southern states seceded from the Union one after another and readied for war, Kentucky adopted a policy of neutrality, being politically divided on the question of secession. The neutral stance did not long survive, for in early September Confederate troops invaded southwestern Kentucky and Union forces moved into northern Kentucky. On September 18, the Kentucky legislature abandoned hopes of neutrality and officially adopted the Union side. On the following day, Keene Richards assisted the pro-Confederate US Senator from Kentucky, John C. Breckinridge, who, fearing imminent arrest, was in haste to depart Lexington. In November, Breckinridge was appointed a brigadier general in the Confederate army, and Richards joined his staff as a volunteer aide with the rank of captain, seeing action at the Battle of Baton Rouge in Louisiana in August 1862.[10]

During the summer of 1862, Union control of Kentucky appeared poised for collapse, beginning with an extensive cavalry raid through Kentucky by John Hunt Morgan in July. Morgan and his men, many of whom were from Scott County, were welcomed at Georgetown and made the city their headquarters for a few days before resuming their dash across the state. Following his successful raid, Morgan returned to the Inner Bluegrass a few weeks later when the state was simultaneously invaded from the west by General Braxton Bragg and from the southeast, through Cumberland Gap, by the forces of General Edmund Kirby Smith. Smith, a bolder general, pushed swiftly into the Bluegrass, routing Union troops in the vicinity of Richmond and entering Lexington on September 2, where the Confederate troops were greeted with enthusiasm. Confederate ambitions in Kentucky were dashed by the lack of coordination between Bragg and Smith, and the Southern forces were forced to retreat to Tennessee through Cumberland Gap after the Battle of Perryville, Kentucky, on October 8, 1862.

As the battle was being fought, the 103rd Ohio Volunteer Infantry was marching south from Covington on the Lexington Road. William T. Chapman, who had enlisted for three years of service on August 4 at Cleveland, kept a diary of the march. Water was a serious problem throughout the region; on September 21, Chapman noted, "all the springs and wells in this part of the country are about dry." In camp on October 12, the regiment received word of the battle at Perryville, and a few days later they pressed on toward Lexington. The Ohio troops arrived at Georgetown on the 20th and camped at Royal Spring for two days before resuming their march to Lexington. Chapman was greatly impressed with the locale and especially by the spring, writing, "The grounds we occupy are owned by Keene Richards, the most celebrated sportsman in Ky. Here is the most splendid spring of pure water I ever saw. It furnishes an abundance for an army." After weeks of scarcity, during which the troops often subsisted on foul and greenish water, the cool waters pouring from the springhead were most welcome.[11]

Breckinridge and the Kentucky troops under his command just missed participating in the Battle of Perryville. Breckinridge arrived at Knoxville on October 3 with about twenty-five hundred men, planning to set out on the 14th on a march through Cumberland Gap to rendezvous with Smith and Bragg. On the 17th, still short of the Kentucky border, Breckinridge was handed a dispatch from Bragg that gave the news of the defeat at Perryville and ordered him back to Knoxville. Keene Richards was, however, already in Kentucky, having been dispatched to Lexington to contact the general's wife, Mary C. Breckinridge. Richards was to arrange to have Mary escorted to Richmond to meet up with her husband, who expected to be in Kentucky in a short time. Richards made the necessary arrangements and took the opportunity to check on the condition of Blue Grass Park at Georgetown, returning to Lexington with a superb gelding, offspring of the celebrated Thoroughbred stallion Glencoe, which he presented as a gift to Confederate cavalry raider John Hunt Morgan. Soon afterward, Richards accompanied the combined forces of Smith and Bragg as they retreated from Kentucky after Perryville.[12]

Late in November, Breckinridge and his command marched with the remainder of Bragg's forces (weakened by detachment of several large units) to Murfreesboro. Richards, left behind in Knoxville because of illness, missed one of the most significant battles of the war. The Battle of Stones River at the beginning of the new year 1863 was one of the bloodiest conflicts of the Civil War, and the Confederate defeat was a major blow to Confederate aspirations and gave a much-needed boost to sagging Union morale.[13]

Discouraged by the turn of events, a slowly recovering Keene Richards wrote to Breckinridge from his sickbed with a plan that he believed might be a better use of his services. Having done his duty to this point, he proposed that he now travel to England, where he was well known among the aristocratic sportsmen, and use such influence as he possessed to arrange purchase of field artillery for his general. From Knoxville, Richards retreated to his Louisiana plantation, where he remained for a few weeks, and then traveled west across Texas to Matamoros, Mexico, just across the Rio Grande from Brownsville. From Matamoros, Richards took a ship to Havana and thence to London, England, where, his mission unsuccessful, he remained for the duration of the war. On June 16, 1865, on the advice of the American foreign minister, Richards left London and returned to Kentucky, where he "reported himself ready to abide by the laws of the United States of America and the Military laws of Kentucky." Richards signed the oath of allegiance to the Union at Lexington on July 11 and submitted his application for clemency to President Andrew Johnson. On September 8, 1865, Keene Richards was granted pardon for his actions during the war.[14]

Four years earlier, before departing Georgetown in September 1861, Keene Richards made arrangements to protect his property. On the very day, September 19, that he was to meet and escort John C. Breckinridge to the safety of Confederate territory, Richards visited the Scott County clerk's office. There, he executed a deed for his Blue Grass Park farm to his close friend, Edward Troye, for the sum of $12,200, and a further instrument conveying "all the interest I have in my Grand fathers Wm B Keenes Estate both real and personal & mixed in the State of Ky as devised to me by his last will and testament" to Troye for $3,000. Both of these deeds were produced to the county clerk on the 19th, and subsequently recorded in the county books on December 18, 1861. A marginal note beside the latter document states that it was not delivered to Troye until December 6, 1864.[15]

Troye's modern biographer, Alexander Mackay-Smith, suggested that the conveyance was no more than a legal fiction to forestall possible confiscation of Keene's estate, the property of an active Southern sympathizer. The premise was that Union officers would be less likely to appropriate the land from Troye, who remained a subject of the British Crown despite immigrating to the United States in 1831, particularly if he could produce a legal title. When Keene returned to Kentucky from overseas, he moved back into his home at Blue Grass Park and remained there for the rest of his life, through the kindness of his friend, and was the proprietor of the estate in fact if not by law.[16]

Keene Richards, like so many Southern gentry, was financially devastated by the Civil War. Early in the war he moved most of his horses to his Transylvania plantation in Louisiana, supposing, incorrectly as it turned out, that they would be safer in the Deep South than in Kentucky, a border state likely to be hotly contested. The Transylvania plantation was confiscated and his numerous enslaved people liberated by the Union army, eliminating his major source of income. Many of his horses in

Edward Troye, photographed in Lexington, Kentucky, 1872. Courtesy of the National Sporting Library and Museum, Harry Worcester Smith Archive.

Kentucky and Louisiana were appropriated by soldiers from both sides of the conflict, or given by Richards as gifts in support of the Confederacy. His breeding experiment with Arabian horses had barely gotten started before it was interrupted by the war, and in this short time had failed to produce a superior Thoroughbred endowed with greater stamina. After the war, Richards no longer had the financial means to import more stock from overseas to continue the experiment, though with the support of his friends he was able to partially recoup his fortunes, at least to the extent of rebuilding Blue Grass Park into a Thoroughbred breeding establishment of note.[17]

By January 1866, the sporting magazine *Turf, Field and Farm* was able to write that Richards "again has collected at his beautiful home, at Georgetown, Ky., a magnificent stable of racing stock. He will reappear upon the turf in the spring with some of the finest colts that ever strided around a race course." Richards's success at Blue Grass Park was offset by misfortune in other endeavors. Under the provisions of the presidential pardon, Richards was able to reclaim his Louisiana plantation almost immediately, but after two years of trying to raise cotton with paid laborers rather than enslaved people, he lost, by his own estimate, about $75,000. "The consequence of this," Richards wrote to Breckinridge in 1868, "was the Bank forced me to put in a claim of voluntary Bankruptcy." Richards declared bankruptcy in the federal court at Mount Sterling, Kentucky, on February 29, 1868. Despite an appearance of prosperity, the postwar Blue Grass Park operation was a house of cards. Richards, lacking the income from Transylvania Plantation, borrowed heavily in his effort to rebuild his breeding operation, and teetered constantly on the brink of financial disaster for the rest of his years.[18]

Richards's desperate—perhaps reckless—maneuverings to keep Blue Grass Park afloat and maintain the lifestyle of a gentleman ultimately collapsed. Immediately after the war, on his return to Kentucky in autumn 1865, Richards prevailed on his friend Edward Troye, the legal owner of the Georgetown estate, to mortgage the property to the Lexington bank of Grinstead and Bradley, cosigning a note for $4,400. Only a few months later, in the early spring of 1866, Richards mortgaged the horses of his stable to the same bank for $5,500. Meanwhile, he ran up substantial debts with local and regional merchants and borrowed heavily—very heavily—from Harvey C. Graves, his grandfather's close friend and executor of the estate. Late in 1866, Richards signed over to Graves a second mortgage on Blue Grass Park in the amount of $44,000. This latter amount probably represented money thrown into trying to raise cotton on his Louisiana plantation. In 1868, Troye sold all his right and title in the property to Graves for $1. In October 1871, Richards borrowed an additional $10,000 from the Sayre Bank of Lexington, assigning still another mortgage on the property jointly with Graves. Although Richards had not been the legal owner of the property since 1861, his ability to borrow against the property was probably the result of an unrecorded land contract made with Troye to buy back the land, which gave him a legal interest in Blue Grass Park. In the summer of 1868, Keene wrote to his friend General John C. Breckinridge, "The deed made Troye the day we had to start for the Mountains has stood the test of Law and reconstruction and I am working hard to get clear from Troye before either of us dies."[19]

Richards was apparently unable to make any payments to reduce his other debts, since between November 1865 and September 1873 he was assaulted by no fewer than fourteen separate lawsuits for minor debts. Then, in 1874, it all fell apart when the Sayre Bank brought suit against Richards in the Scott County District Court, immediately followed by Grinstead and Bradley, who lodged a cross petition. On September 12, the court, having determined that Richards remained indebted by the full amount of both mortgages, ordered the Blue Grass Park properties to be sold at public auction and the proceeds applied to the debts. In December 1875, nearly two hundred acres of Richards's estate, including the homestead tract beside Royal Spring, went under the gavel to Sayre for $17,000. The forced sale from Richards to Sayre was recorded in July 1876, and within a matter of weeks Sayre sold the eighty-acre homestead tract adjoining Royal Spring to James A. Grinstead of Lexington for $2,500.[20]

This was a very grim period in Richards's life. The loss of his estate was merely the latest, and perhaps most severe, of a series of personal tragedies. On July 25, 1874, Edward Troye died suddenly while visiting Richards in Georgetown and was buried in the Georgetown Cemetery. Then, in April 1875, a few months before the auction, the magnificent old brick house built by Elijah Craig above the spring, Richards's home, caught fire and was gutted, although nearly all of Troye's paintings and most of the family possessions were rescued.[21]

View of the Commons, taken in 1888. Royal Spring is obscured by trees at right of the picture. The white fencing is associated with Blue Grass Park, the Thoroughbred breeding farm of Keene Richards. Source: *Water Supply Company v. City of Georgetown*, KDLA.

Grinstead, co-owner of Grinstead and Bradley and a longtime friend of Keene Richards, apparently felt that his investment would be best served by allowing Richards to remain on the property and continue to direct the breeding operation. The report of the annual sale of Blue Grass Park yearlings for June 1877 (held in Lexington since the 1875 fire) referred to Richards as the proprietor of the establishment. His circumstances were greatly altered, of course, but by more than just the change in ownership. Richards remained in residence at Blue Grass Park, among his beloved horses, until his death from pneumonia on March 19, 1881, at the age of fifty-four.[22]

After Richards's death, the remaining stock and breeding records of Blue Grass Park were removed to the Walnut Hills Farm of James A.

Grinstead, a few miles south of Lexington. Richards was eulogized in the newspapers and the sporting magazines of the day. *Turf, Field and Farm* noted that Richards was a "courteous, pure minded, noble hearted gentleman" who had never been known to utter an oath or to wager a single dollar on a horse race; "The turf and breeding interests of America owe much to the memory of A. Keene Richards," the editor, Hamilton Busbey, concluded.[23]

The eighty-acre homestead tract underwent a relatively rapid series of conveyances during the next twenty years. The forced sale from Richards to Sayre was recorded in July 1876, and within a matter of weeks Sayre sold the land to James A. Grinstead of Lexington in August 1876 for $2,500. Grinstead held the property for nearly a decade, but assigned it to John T. Shelby, who conveyed it to John B. Graves of Scott County in January 1885 for $10,124. Graves immediately sold the property to William Payne of Scott County, taking a $500 profit on the transaction. Payne held onto the land for only four years, selling it in April 1889 to Jefferson D. Grover of Georgetown for the same price he had paid. Five years later, in October 1894, Grover conveyed the property to his older sister, Alice P. Montgomery, for $14,000. The following year, Alice and her husband, Henry P. Montgomery, founding president of the First National Bank of Georgetown, built a house on the high ground overlooking the spring. The Montgomerys soon began subdividing the property and selling the lots, marking the end of Blue Grass Park as farmland.[24]

11

The Water Works

Georgetown's first public water system was privately owned and was in large part prompted by the need for fire protection. The town, like many other communities of the era, suffered numerous destructive fires during the nineteenth century. Georgetown's most devastating fires occurred in 1869 and 1876; on both occasions, dozens of commercial buildings along Main Street were destroyed. In the aftermath of each major fire, the question of a water works to serve the community was raised, but no concrete action was taken on these discussions. The spectacular fire of 1876, during which the courthouse also burned to the ground, prompted the purchase of an Ahrens steam-powered fire engine for $5,000 during the following year. At that time, the trustees ordered that the Internal Improvement Committee place a barrel or make some other arrangement by which the steam pumper could be filled from the Royal Spring, and ordered that an opening be made in the wall at the head of the spring to allow the entrance of vehicles. During 1880–1881, the committee was instructed to "examine the spring branch and ascertain the cost for fixing for fire purposes." The subsequent report on building a wall for this purpose was ordered to be filed, but evidently no action was taken. In the fall of 1881, fire destroyed the Georgetown Hotel despite the new fire engine, for the operator, in a hurry to build up steam, neglected to fill the boiler with water before firing it up, and so damaged the engine that it could not be used to fight the blaze. After a fire in

Royal Spring, 1888. This photograph was taken prior to establishment of the Water Supply Company, and a citizen can be seen dipping water from the spring with a bucket. Source: *Water Supply Company v. City of Georgetown,* KDLA.

1887 destroyed four buildings on Main, including the office of the *Georgetown Times*, the town trustees made a feeble gesture to improve the water supply situation, ordering the Fire Department Committee to examine the spring-fed pond of S. M. Davis, north of Main Street, to see if the "available supply of spring-water, thereto, can be made to answer the purposes & uses for the fire Engine, of a Public cistern, for that section of town."[1]

At about this time, many Kentucky communities were investigating the feasibility of establishing water works systems. Georgetown's nearest neighbor, Lexington, constructed a municipal system in 1885, based on a reservoir built for the purpose. Thereafter, the Scott County community was inundated with proposals to erect water supply systems using the Royal Spring as a source. On January 15, 1889, a special meeting of the

Georgetown Board of Trustees was held to hear and consider a proposal by Frederick A. Cramer, formerly an engineer for Lexington's water company, and Robert J. Laws to construct and maintain a water works for the community. Cramer and Laws proposed a water plant located at the spring with a pumping capacity of 1.25 million gallons per day, water mains extending along the major thoroughfares of the town, and thirty fire hydrants to be located three hundred feet apart. A hydrant, located at the spring, would also be provided for the free use of all for domestic purposes, except that water vendors would be charged a fee not to exceed 1 cent per barrel. The board adjourned until the following day, and on further consideration made some alterations and amendments to the proposal. Cramer, who was present at this meeting, requested time to confer with his partner before any action was taken by the board on the proposal.[2]

At the February board meeting, the trustees heard Cramer's response to the requested changes in their proposal, but the meeting adjourned without taking any further action. At the very next meeting, on March 1, yet another party, John H. B. Davenport of Cincinnati, Ohio, stepped forward with a proposal to supply Georgetown with a water system. Davenport was acting as a representative for his brother, Edwin Rush Davenport of Middleport, Ohio, a civil engineer who built numerous water systems for cities across the United States during the latter part of the nineteenth century. As with Cramer and Laws, the trustees suggested alterations to the original proposal and asked Davenport to resubmit it. A special meeting was called on March 11 to hear the revised contract, but again, no immediate action was taken on the proposal.[3]

Although the trustees apparently did not care for the proposals they had heard, this seems to have motivated them to seriously consider the desirability of a water works for the community. At the April 5, 1889, regular meeting of the board, the chairman was instructed to place advertisements in the *Manufacturing Record* of Baltimore and the *Engineering News* of Chicago for water works proposals, with a deadline for submission of May 1, 1889. Given the almost impossibly tight deadline, this motion might have been made only for the sake of appearances; the trustees may have had someone else in mind. At the next meeting, on May 11, apparently without any prior formal meetings of the board for discussion, a provisional contract dated May 9 was made with John Nichols of Burgin, Kentucky, and Henry C. Patterson of Pineville,

Kentucky, to provide a water works for the community. A copy of the proposed contract was published in the *Georgetown Times*, and a public vote scheduled for the eighteenth day of May. The response was nearly unanimous in favor, and so the contract was made binding.[4]

Under the terms of the contract, for a period of fifteen years, Nichols and Patterson were to "take into possession and use for Water works purposes" a lot of ground bounded on the west by the "Big Spring" branch (i.e., part of the "Commons"), to supply the town with water for fire protection, domestic, and manufacturing needs. The company was granted the "perpetual, but not exclusive" right to take out water from the branch, and from the head of the spring. The company was to lay water mains, from four to eight inches in diameter, down the full length of Main Street and along a number of intersecting streets; to install and maintain no fewer than 60 hydrants for fire protection at locations designated by the trustees; to provide unlimited free water to the city public school and to the courthouse; and to maintain specified pressure in the lines. The contract made no specific mention of a hydrant near the spring for free use by the citizens, although this was later erected. The water rates were set at $12 annually for private households (with an additional $6 charge for a bathtub with a faucet) and most commercial enterprises, $36 for a restaurant, and $180 for a hotel. The community was to be charged a flat annual fee of $1,350 for use of the hydrants for fire protection. Nichols and Patterson agreed to begin construction of the water works within thirty days and to complete the works within six months. On the first day of June, Jeff Grover, who owned the western half of the spring and branch, agreed to lease the water rights to John Nichols in exchange for installation of a water line and hydrant near the residence on Grover's land and unlimited free use of the water. The Georgetown Water Company was incorporated on June 21, 1889, the first step in the turbulent history of the utility.[5]

The water works company quickly expanded into the general provision of utilities for the community. Within a few months, in September 1889, the company proposed to erect an electric plant to supply power to the community and, incidentally, to operate the water works machinery; the Georgetown Electric Light, Heat and Power Company was incorporated for this purpose in December. Construction of the electric plant, on the same site as the water works, began almost immediately.[6]

Meanwhile, in 1890, a group of partners petitioned the trustees for "free use" of a site on city property adjacent to the spring branch (north of the water works) upon which to build and operate an "Ice Factory Plant," drawing water from the branch. The proposal was approved and soon Georgetown residents could enjoy the novelty, soon to be indispensable, of ice for preservation of perishables and to cool their thirst. A short section of standard-gauge railway was constructed by the ice company to move coal and ice by mule-drawn cars between the ice factory and the power plant. In 1895, with organization of the Georgetown Street Railway Company by the ice company partners, tracks were extended through town and the system electrified, providing local streetcar transportation for the citizens. The original ice factory proved to be too small, having a capacity of only three tons per day, so the company constructed a larger facility in 1896 near the head of the spring. The new factory began producing ice on May 27. Under new ownership, as the twentieth century began, the ice company made approximately thirty-five tons of ice daily, which sold to the local trade for about a penny a pound and was shipped to other Bluegrass communities for $2.50 to $3.00 per ton. Ice from Royal Spring water was advertised as superior to all other sources simply by virtue of its origin in one of the finest springs in Kentucky.[7]

Nichols and Patterson were perhaps a little too ambitious, in terms of their financial resources, in attempting to construct both the water and electric utilities simultaneously. Having little capital of their own, in order to pay for all the improvements, the partners initially borrowed $10,000 from a Pineville bank, mortgaged their water works property to the Fidelity Trust and Safety Vault Company for $35,000 in April 1890, and subsequently borrowed another $10,000 from Fidelity in order to repay the Pineville loan. Having erected the water works, and begun work on the electric plant, they ran up large bills for materials and were unable to pay their suppliers. The Central Thompson-Houston Electric Company of Cincinnati brought suit against the company for a debt of $3,000, and the Georgetown water works and electric light plant were sold at public auction on May 2, 1892, to a group of wealthy Scott County investors headed by local banker Henry P. Montgomery. On June 8, 1892, the Water Supply Company of Georgetown was incorporated to supply water and electric power to the city and citizens of Georgetown.

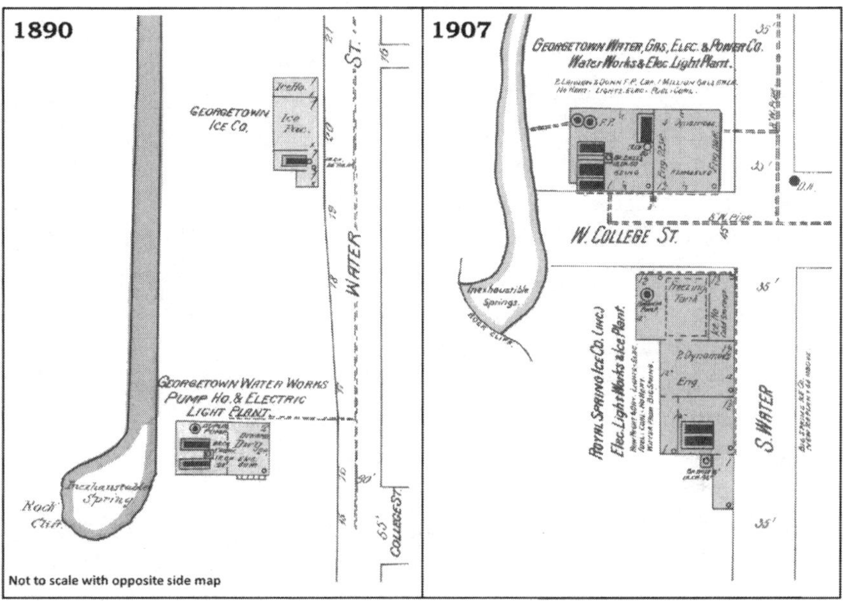

Georgetown Water Company and Ice Plant, 1890 and 1907. Details from Georgetown fire insurance maps, Sanborn Map Company.

This building, located at 214 South Water Street, was the ice storage warehouse across the street from the Royal Spring Ice Company. The structure was recently renovated and converted into a popular eating place called Local Feed. Photograph by Ann Bolton Bevins.

Montgomery was elected president, and the primary stockholders and company directors included Jeff D. Grover and his older brother, Horace M. Grover.[8]

Construction of the electric plant was completed during 1892, and after the city had been wired and gas lights converted to more modern fixtures, electric lights came on in Georgetown. The new owners of the Water Supply Company were just as ambitious as Nichols and Patterson to gain control of the city utilities. In April 1898, the company acquired the property and assets of the Georgetown Ice Company and the street railway, which was placed in receivership and sold at auction after becoming financially overextended. The Water Supply Company subsequently amended its charter to include the sale of ice and provision of power for transportation, but then, in August 1899, company stockholders organized two new and separate corporations, the Georgetown Electric Railway Company and the Royal Spring Ice Company, and transferred the appropriate assets to each of these. The city utilities were now represented by three different corporations, but for each company the board of directors was composed of the same persons.[9]

Nichols and Patterson were outraged by the forced sale of their water plant in 1892, and continued litigation through the Kentucky Court of Appeals to recover their investment. The higher court eventually ruled the forced sale to be valid, and the assets of the Water Supply Company and its subsidiaries were again sold at auction during the summer of 1900. Robert W. Nelson of Newport, Kentucky, purchased the property, and immediately the Georgetown Board of Council (established in 1894 to replace the trustees as the form of government) began negotiating with Nelson to lease or purchase the water and electric plants. Evidently Nelson was agreeable to the proposition, and the question was put to the voters of Georgetown at the regular election in the fall as to whether they would approve incurring a bonded indebtedness, not to exceed $50,000, to lease or purchase these utilities. On November 6, 1900, the citizens responded "yes" by a margin of four to one. The board appointed a committee to confer with Nelson as to the terms.[10]

In some manner, what had been thought to be a certain deal fell apart, so that in April 1901 the council solicited bids for purchase of the franchise to supply the city with water and electricity, publishing advertisements in the three Georgetown papers, in Louisville, and in Cincinnati. David J. Hauss of Cincinnati submitted the only bid in response. Hauss's initial bid was rejected as being far too low; his second, higher bid was accepted. Hauss was awarded a contract for a period of ten years, renewable for an additional ten; if either party chose not to extend the contract, the city reserved the right to erect its own water and electric plants just prior to expiration. Along with the contract, the council enacted an ordinance to establish rates and regulations governing the sale and use of water and electricity in Georgetown. In May 1901, Robert W. Nelson, David J. Hauss, and several affluent Georgetown citizens organized a new corporation, the Georgetown Water, Gas, Electric Light and Power Company to operate city utilities. On June 27, 1901, Nelson conveyed the water and electric plants to the corporation for $32,000. The old gas company, established in 1875, had suffered greatly when electric lights had generally replaced the smelly and unreliable gas lamps, and owner James P. Jackson was happy to merge his faltering company with the new corporation; Jackson was elected president of the utility company, which now combined water, gas, electric power, the street railway, and the ice companies under one umbrella.[11]

The water and power utilities of Georgetown remained under the same ownership for nearly three decades. Then, on January 9, 1927, Robert W. Nelson, the majority stockholder, passed away at his home in Newport, and control of his shares and of the company passed to his wife, Mary W. Nelson. As the new president of the Georgetown Water, Gas, Electric Light and Power Company, Mary Nelson almost immediately arranged the sale of the company's assets in June 1928 to the Lexington Utilities Company. In 1940, the Lexington Utilities Company was absorbed by Kentucky Utilities. Shortly afterward, in 1945, Kentucky Utilities divested itself of the water works, conveying possession to the city of Georgetown for $1 and "other good and valuable consideration," but retaining title to all assets associated with provision of electrical lighting and power.[12]

An important step toward reducing the industrial and commercial clutter around the springhead was taken in 1957, when the Georgetown Municipal Water Service plant on Water Street was moved nearly five hundred feet north to a new and more modern three-story facility on the west valley slope overlooking the spring branch. Pumps housed in the lowest level of the plant brought water from the spring to filters,

Water clarifier under construction in 1973, part of an extensive upgrade to the water treatment plant that took place during this period. A clarifier is used to remove solid particulates or suspended solids from raw water. Royal Spring is in right background, not visible. Photograph courtesy of the Georgetown Municipal Water and Sewer Service.

a clear well, and water tank, and on the middle level was the chemical mixing rooms, where the raw water was treated. The upper floor, which had a street entrance from Royal Spring Drive, contained the water testing lab and the office of the plant manager. During the mid-1970s, the city undertook a major expansion and upgrade to the water plant.[13]

12

Who Owns Royal Spring?

The closing decade of the nineteenth century and the beginning of the twentieth was a time when the Royal Spring itself was frequently the center of controversy and even litigation. Now that Royal Spring was being asked to serve a variety of demands, the troubles began: who really had legal priority to the waters of Royal Spring? In the past, the water had been ample for all needs and free for the taking, but now considerable financial stakes and the health and safety of a growing community were of concern. Councilman James Y. Kelly raised the question of the ownership of the spring at a February 1898 meeting of the town council, noting that both the ice company and the street railway asserted claims to the water.[1]

This was a legitimate concern. None of the land surrounding the head of the spring was actually owned by the city of Georgetown. All the land immediately west and south of the spring branch, the former Blue Grass Park, was purchased in 1894 by Alice Montgomery from her brother, Jefferson D. Grover. According to the property description in the deed, the survey ran west "to the middle of Big Spring," and thence "with the line of West wall of Big Spring Branch." In 1896, Montgomery sold a section out of the southeast corner of her tract, amounting to nearly three acres, to the Georgetown Street Railway Company; the northern line of this lot was the same boundary that ran "to the middle of the Big Spring." This lot was subsequently conveyed to the Royal

Spring Ice Company in 1899 as the site for a new plant of greater capacity. Earlier, in May 1889, the Georgetown trustees deeded a three-quarter-acre lot out of the town commons, just east of the spring branch and north of what would become the street railway property, to Paterson and Nichols as the site for the new water works. The grant for the land, bounded on the west by a line down the center of the spring branch, was to be "perpetual and exclusive." In 1890, the trustees also made a grant of land from the commons, north of the water works, to the ice company. When Kelly raised the question of ownership in 1898, the city could claim title only to one-half the width of the spring branch, on the east side from the discharge point downstream. This division of the watercourse had been in effect ever since Elijah Craig laid out the town boundaries in 1787.[2]

So, if all the land around the spring was in private hands, who really owned the spring itself and the rights to the flow of water? Long-established riparian doctrine allowed rights to the water to any landholder on the banks of the stream, but the members of the town council certainly believed that, based on long tradition, primacy belonged to the city of Georgetown, and were determined to exert control over the entire discharge. The council decided to test the waters, so to speak, by picking a fight with the ice company, beginning a conflict between the city and the Water Supply Company (parent company of the ice company) that continued to escalate, both sides adamant in their assertion of rights. The dispute really began in 1897, when the water resources of the spring were diminished by a regional drought.

The grant from the city to Nichols and associates gave the water company "permission to tap the spring branch by an underground pipe run from the power house . . . or along Water street and through the ground occupied by the ice company." The permit did not specify the point at which the ice company could extract water. The intake pipe for the water works and the pipe supplying the ice company and street railway were both set in the head of the spring, that of the ice company being closer to the outlet by a matter of mere inches. In its original location, north of the water works facility, the ice company plant was allowed the right to withdraw water from the spring branch opposite their building. After the new, larger plant was built in 1896, the mayor gave permission for the company to place an intake pipe in the head of the spring, under the condition that this pipe would be removed if requested by the city. In the fall of 1897, the Bluegrass was afflicted by a moderate drought that was more severe in the vicinity of Georgetown. The flow from Royal Spring was greatly reduced, to the point that, for one day during the first week of October, the spring was very nearly dry and the water works and ice plant were temporarily shut down. The ice company was asked to move its intake pipe from the head of the spring to a point downstream on the branch, but refused to do so.[3]

A return to adequate rainfall before the end of the year eased the imminent water supply crisis, but the town council remained incensed by the ice company's intractability. Early in February 1898, the city attorney was directed to take any necessary steps to have the intake pipe of the ice company and railway company removed from the spring "if they do not agree that the pipe is in said spring under permission of the City." Within weeks, however, the issue was postponed in consequence of the company's financial difficulties, and by the fall of 1898 the ice company was in the possession of the recently reorganized Water Supply Company. This presented the interesting situation in which one company was responsible for two competing uses of the same resource. On receiving the Water Supply Company's application for a five-year taxation exemption on the proposed supplemental ice plant, the city council seized on this opportunity to resolve the intake pipe issue and more firmly define its control of the spring.[4]

The exemption was approved at the November 11 council meeting, and a contract drafted that contained clauses requiring the Water Supply Company to acknowledge that the spring was the property of the city of Georgetown. The first priority was to ensure the citizens "a sufficiency of water for their necessary use" before taking water for manufacturing ice. The pipe or pipes for the ice company were, therefore, to be located downstream from the water works intake pipe, so as not to interfere with the water supply of the city. The city allowed that the ice company should not be denied its share of spring water unless the council judged it necessary for continued maintenance of a supply of water for fire protection and domestic use. In such circumstances, the Water Supply Company was to remove the ice plant's intake pipes on request, and, failing to do so, the city reserved the right to take action to have them removed.[5]

Royal Spring in 1901. At this time, there was a bitter contest, involving litigation, between the water supply and ice companies against the city of Georgetown over rights to the water from the spring. Water lines can be seen in the spring and next to the wall at left. Source: *Water Supply Company v. City of Georgetown,* KDLA.

The Water Supply Company rejected the contract, unwilling to grant ownership of the spring to the city. Annoyed by this response, in December 1898 the council voted unanimously to refuse the request for exemption from taxation. After further discussion, the council appointed a special committee to go and examine the spring and vicinity to determine what pipes had been placed in the head of the spring, and what obstructions might be hindering access to the spring. Since the council obviously already knew what sort of obstructions were present, and whose pipes were in the spring, the inspection was simply a formality to provide a legal argument against the Water Supply Company and its subsidiary. In what was apparently an immediate punitive measure, the council at their next meeting revoked the grant made to the original Georgetown Ice Company in 1890 for the tract of land north of the water works on the spring branch, site of the first ice factory, on the basis that the plant was no longer in operation.[6]

The conflict with the Water Supply Company over ownership of Royal Spring now began to dominate the council's agenda; monthly meetings were no longer sufficient to discuss the city's business, requiring the mayor to call special meetings on almost a weekly basis. During the first meeting of the new year, January 6, 1899, the council received a reply from the company that offered, perhaps spitefully, to relinquish their claim to Royal Spring in exchange for a ninety-nine-year exemption from taxes for the new ice factory. The man appointed to make a survey of Royal Spring and the vicinity next reported that Henry P. Montgomery, president of the Water Supply Company, had refused to allow him to proceed. Councilman James Y. Kelly, who had undertaken to trace the property and other legal records pertaining to ownership of the spring, made his report and gave a copy to the city attorney. The Improvement Committee, having made an inspection of College Street (which ended nearly at the head of the spring) and of Royal Spring, reported that the street was "obstructed by the cars and track of the Street Railway," which blocked access to the spring, and that a pipe belonging to the ice company ran down this street and into the spring pool, being placed above that of the water works. The council ordered that notice be given to the Water Supply Company to remove the obstructions and take the ice factory pipe from the spring, under threat of legal action, unless they request permission of the city to allow it to remain.[7]

This exchange of retaliatory actions continued through the remainder of January and February. At the January 6 meeting, a committee consisting of councilman Kelly and city attorney James F. Askew were appointed to confer with representatives of the Water Supply Company to see if it was possible to resolve the dispute over ownership of the spring. At this meeting, Kelly and Askew rejected the notion that the Water Supply Company had any rights to water from the spring except at the behest of the city, and dismissed the preposterous consideration of a ninety-nine-year exemption. The company made a more reasonable counteroffer, but once more asserted a claim to legal ownership of at least part of the spring and again offered to release this claim for a five-year relief of taxation. The committee was sent back to consult with company officials in a last effort to avoid taking the question to the courts. On January 23, the council received a final, written proposal from H. P. Montgomery: the Water Supply Company, in exchange for a five-year exemption from taxes on the proposed new ice factory and a three-years exemption on the ice plant built in 1896, agreed to convey to the city all their "right, title and interest" to the spring (a point on which they remained adamant), would place and keep the intake pipes for the ice factories downstream from that of the water works, and would cease making ice during a scarcity of water due to drought or other necessary consideration.[8]

The Georgetown Board of Council proved to be just as stubborn as the Water Supply Company on the ownership issue. James Y. Kelly, who above all others tended to take a hard line about this, recommended that the council reject the company's offer as written, and proposed an amendment that accepted all the other conditions but would require the company to sign a legal contract acknowledging "the Big or Royal Spring to be the property of the City of Georgetown." The council vote split evenly on this proposal, and Mayor Abner H. Sinclair cast the deciding vote in favor.

It would now seem to be more-or-less resolved—pending the response of the Water Supply Company, that is—but at the next meeting, only two days later on January 25, when attorney Louis L. Bristow read the newly drafted contract, James Y. Kelly now rose and objected to his own amendment! His objection was based on a number of minor legal technicalities and breaches of procedure, but primarily that the decision should be written in the form of a city ordinance, rather than a contract. Kelly's new motion was tabled for further discussion at the next meeting, on February 2, where it was carried and referred to attorney Bristow for a legal opinion. Bristow presented the proposed ordinance to the council on the next day, and it was laid over until the next regular meeting on March 3. The council then directed Bristow to execute the order, previously approved on January 6, requiring the company to remove the pipe from the spring pool and clear away the obstructions blocking College Street.[9]

At the March 3 council meeting, the proposed ordinance was read again, and carried by unanimous vote. The awkwardly titled "Big Spring, Street, or Commons Pipe-Obstructions" ordinance stated "That it shall be unlawful for any person or Corporation to place any pipe on or over any Street or common of the City of Georgetown, or in the Royal, Big, or Republican spring, without first having obtained permission from the Board of Council." The Water Supply Company refused to remove the ice factory pipe from the spring, and on April 21 the city filed suit against the company in the Scott County Circuit Court, asserting its ownership of Royal Spring and the right to control its use for the benefit of the citizens of Georgetown.[10]

Montgomery and the other officers and stockholders of the Water Supply Company must have felt themselves under siege. Ever since their acquisition of the water and electric utilities, and the street railway and ice company, as a result of the forced sale in 1892, they had been defending their interests in the courts. It was a demoralizing roller-coaster ride of apparent victories followed by setbacks; in 1894 the Montgomery County Circuit Court had set aside the sale in favor of John Nichols, but then in 1896 the lower court's decision was reversed by the Kentucky Court of Appeals, which confirmed the sale. Recently, however, the Fidelity Trust and Safety Vault Company, which had financed the original establishment and expansion of the first Water Company, had taken up the suit in the courts, attempting on behalf of their bondholders to revoke the sale of the water works. Now, not only were H. P. Montgomery and his partners in the Water Supply Company facing potential loss of their investment, even their perceived right to use the water of Royal Spring was being challenged. After the appeals court finally ruled the original sale invalid and Robert W. Nelson purchased the company assets at a forced sale in 1900 and subsequently helped organize the Georgetown Water, Gas, Electric Light and Power Company, the new corporation was made a defendant in the suit and subsequently filed a cross-petition asking for damages from the Water Supply Company.[11]

As the city's lawsuit slowly plodded through the legal system, meteorological variability intensified actual competition for the spring's water and fostered public resentment against the ice company for apparently squandering a valuable resource. The summer of 1899 marked the beginning of a prolonged period of moderate to severe drought in the Bluegrass. The region's streams and rivers shrank within their banks, and many springs dried up entirely. Although Royal Spring continued to flow, its discharge was greatly diminished. The mayor instituted a mild water rationing in early August, prohibiting the use of water for street sprinkling for dust control or for irrigation in yards and gardens. "Every year the demand on the Spring becomes greater," declared the *Georgetown Times* on August 9, noting that during a prolonged drought the spring was unable to meet all the many demands imposed by the city's growth in population and manufacturing. In the newspapers, and in the August council meeting, the Water Supply Company was castigated for continuing to pump thousands of gallons of water daily from the spring for its ice-manufacturing operation, most of which was sold outside the community. It was a "funny situation," the *Times* observed, that citizens should be required to cut back on their water use, the lawns and flowers to wither and die, a blanket of dust to coat the town, all the while the Ice Plant continues blithely to run "at full blast."[12]

The council directed the mayor and city attorney to bring suit (again!), if necessary, against the ice company to completely halt its use of water from Royal Spring if too much was being diverted from public use to ice manufacturing. Apparently, no further action was taken on this issue, so perhaps the company voluntarily reduced its water consumption during the drought crisis. The drought stretched into months and then years, occasionally interrupted by light to moderate rainfall that had little effect on stream levels and spring discharge, until on September 17, 1902, following several months of drought that today would be classified as "severe," the city council was at last forced to halt withdrawals of water from Royal Spring. For a few days, until the situation was relieved by a substantial rainfall, the ice company was ordered to cease intake of water, and the electric utility was ordered to shut down from midnight to 4:00 a.m. each day.[13]

Earlier that same year, the ice company attempted to circumvent the city's suit by boring a well on its property that would, if accurately located, intercept the conduit feeding Royal Spring. They thought that this would make the intake pipe issue legally moot, since the company would be able to withdraw water from the source on its own land, and so the question of city ownership would not apply. Alarmed, the council called a special meeting on January 24, 1902, to discuss the potential injury to Royal Spring engendered by the ice company's well. In March, the council passed an ordinance prohibiting the boring of any well near or over Royal Spring.[14]

In the suit in Scott County Circuit Court, *City of Georgetown v. Water Supply Company*, the ambiguous definitions of the boundary line at Royal Spring as described in various deeds dating back nearly to the founding of the city became the central point of contention. The water company claimed that they were the owners of part of the Royal Spring as well as owners of the adjacent land on which the ice plant was located. While the latter assertion was beyond doubt, the former was certainly open to interpretation. The land conveyances were particularly unhelpful. The survey description in the 1813 deed to William B. Keene commenced with "Beginning at the centre of the big spring branch," and the final survey calls concluded, "near the head of the Big Spring thence North down the spring branch." Succeeding transactions for the next seventy years simply made general reference to the Keene "Homestead" tract without providing further clarification, until, in 1885, the conveyance to John B. Graves once more gave a metes and bounds description, but very similar to that of 1813: "to middle of Big Spring, thence with the line of West wall of Big Spring Branch . . . to the Beginning." Subsequent transactions repeated this description verbatim. But when Alice P. Montgomery sold a 2.78-acre tract to the Georgetown Street Railway Company in 1896, upon which the second ice factory was built, the description read, "with College street N 83 W 170 feet to a point three feet West of the center of the Royal Spring," the boundary line thereby apparently passing through the head of the spring.[15]

The 1834 act of the Kentucky General Assembly, which was referred to frequently in the court proceedings, appeared to provide a more precise description. The act defined the town boundary as beginning at the head of the Republican Spring, and after outlining the town, returning "up the middle of said branch to the middle of the head, thence around with the head of the spring to the beginning point of the Republican Spring." Attorneys for both sides split the finest of hairs in interpreting the boundary descriptions to arrive at opposing conclusions supporting their respective clients.[16]

Attorneys for the city produced deposition after deposition by the most elderly citizens of the community to show that the spring had been historically considered *de facto* property of the city regardless of specific boundaries. From the beginning of the settlement, by all accounts, the spring had been used as a public water supply by the citizens of the community. Witnesses testified that Dr. William B. Keene, who held the land west of the branch for forty years after acquiring it in 1813, considered the spring to be for the benefit of and the property of the town, and that his grandson Keene Richards, when asked why he did not pump water from the spring to his stables, had stated, "I don't know whether the town would let me do it or not to water my stock." The defendant's case was substantially weakened when testimony from the 1893 Scott County Circuit Court case *A. K. Lair v. City of Georgetown and Georgetown Water Company* was introduced into evidence. The city had, at that time, stated that "the said spring was owned by said town, and the said town has owned it for one hundred and three years," and the water company had adopted the statement as its own, thus admitting that the town owned the spring.[17]

The defendants, the officers and stockholders of the Water Supply Company, were shocked when the circuit court rendered its verdict on May 22, 1903, for the judgement granted rights to the city far in excess of those requested by the plaintiff. The court adjudged that the Big Spring and branch "are the property of and belong to the city of Georgetown and have been for a time beyond which the memory of man runneth not to the contrary." The court ordered the intake pipe of the ice company removed, and the defendants forbidden to pump water from the head of the spring. Instead, they were required to place the pipe in the branch at a point greater than two hundred feet from the spring, adjacent to the site of the original ice factory (this being the terms of the original 1890 grant by the city). The railway company was further to remove forthwith the tracks and any other obstructions blocking access to the spring via College Street (which ran west from the city to near the head of the spring) or else, at their own expense, to build up the grade of the street to allow vehicles to be able to cross the tracks. The final provision, which the defendants found particularly offensive, granted the city the unasked-for right to build a movable dam across the branch at any point short of the original ice plant site so as to allow accumulation of water during low-flow conditions.[18]

The Water Supply Company immediately appealed the decision to the Kentucky Court of Appeals, which heard the case in 1904 and reversed the decision of the Scott County Circuit Court. The superior court chose to disregard the question of ownership of the spring altogether, save to rule that the company's adoption of the city's position of ownership in the

Lair case did not constitute an estoppel in the present case; in other words, it did not now preclude the company from claiming ownership of or rights to part of Royal Spring. "The petition of the city of Georgetown," the court ruled, "in so far as it claims to be the absolute owner of the entire spring, is dismissed without prejudice." The core issue, according to the court, was that the ice company was, in fact, pumping water from the spring under a permit issued by the city of Georgetown, and held that this permit could not be arbitrarily revoked. The Kentucky Court of Appeals did, however, rule that the pipe from the ice factory must be moved downstream to a point at least two hundred feet below the water works intake in the head of the spring. The city subsequently appealed the decision, seeking to clarify the ownership issue, but the appeal was dismissed. Over time, the city eliminated any basis for dispute over water rights by purchasing all the land surrounding the spring, gaining possession of the water works itself in 1945.[19]

13

Gulping Down Royal Spring Sewage

Even though the Georgetown community rejoiced when a privately owned company established a municipal water system in 1889, the water provided was raw, straight from the source and neither filtered nor treated. This was a certain formula for public health problems. From the earliest days of the community, the town trustees were, of course, concerned with the quality of the water from Royal Spring. In the era before germ theory, this concern was limited to aesthetic considerations, and even late in the century, after the connection between bacterial contamination and disease was widely known and accepted, a lack of understanding of the far-reaching nature of groundwater flow in karst systems limited efforts to control pollution to the immediate vicinity of the head of the spring.

In March 1812, the *Georgetown Telegraph* published a list of ordinances and regulations established by the trustees, including several that addressed water supply sanitation. A fine of $5 was to be levied on any person who placed "any filth or obstruction" into any spring of the community, and $2 per offense for any who should "bathe themselves, wash or rinse clothing within fifty yards of the Republican [Royal] spring or within twenty feet of any other spring." This latter directive was still in effect sixty years later, as noted in the minutes of the trustees in 1872.

These prohibitions were enlarged by a 1901 ordinance that forbade any person from depositing waste or dead animals in the spring or branch or near the water works, driving hogs and other animals into the branch, or swimming within the branch. The trustees also paid occasional visits to inspect the condition of Royal Spring and issued orders for thorough cleaning of the spring and the branch.[1]

The civic authorities had good reason to be concerned with the sanitary condition of the water supply. No one who had lived through one of the cholera epidemics of the nineteenth century would ever be likely to forget the horror of those days. This highly lethal bacterial disease is transmitted by consumption of water that has been contaminated by the fecal material of other cholera patients. The *Vibrio cholerae* bacterium has a very short incubation period, as little as twelve hours to a few days, before the appearance of symptoms. Infected persons experience massive watery diarrhea leading to severe dehydration, vomiting, rapid weak pulse, suppression of urine, muscle cramping, and weakness. Untreated severe cases often result in death within a few days after the onset of symptoms, sometimes in as little as a few hours. It was not unusual for a person to rise in the morning feeling well, and be dead of cholera by early afternoon. Death rates can exceed 70 percent, largely a result of dehydration.[2]

Of the four visits by cholera to Kentucky, in 1832–1833, 1848–1854, 1866, and again in 1872–1873, Georgetown was affected only by the two earlier epidemics. The first epidemic was the worst, both statewide and in Georgetown, in terms of the number of localities affected and the mortality of the disease. Cholera first appeared in the region at Cincinnati in the fall of 1832, and was likely spread from there to Maysville, Louisville, and other river ports by infected passengers on riverboats. The residents of the Inner Bluegrass, especially in Lexington, were not particularly apprehensive about the disease invading the area. In the late spring of 1833, a number of Lexington physicians asserted that the physical attributes of the region would deter cholera, the Bluegrass being distant from any large bodies of water, swamps, or lowlands and situated within a high, rolling, and well-drained country. Given that, at the time, there was no knowledge of the connection between germs and sickness and the prevailing medical theory of disease assumed an origin linked to filth and noxious vapors in the air, there was, perhaps, some justification in this belief. Daniel Drake, one of the most respected physicians of the region, dismissed the idea of waterborne disease, writing during the first epidemic: "The theory of [cholera's] aqueous origin, is equally unsatisfactory. In this city [Cincinnati], the inhabitants drink river water, in Lexington and Georgetown, well and spring water, issuing in veins from between limestone rock, yet the cholera prevailed in both; while many villages and country settlements, have remained comparatively exempt, although supplied with the same kind of water with others in their neighborhood, which were severely afflicted."[3] Lacking any knowledge of pathogenic microorganisms, even the brightest minds were perplexed as to how cholera could arise and spread. During the second epidemic, a theory of cholera origin was proposed that attributed the disease to the nature of the underlying bedrock. Specifically, advocates believed that the inhabitants of regions where water supplies were obtained from limestone aquifers were more likely to be stricken by cholera because the dissolved calcium carbonate in the water distressed the gastric system of persons consuming it. This conclusion was inferred from the global distribution of cholera outbreaks, which seemed to indicate a greater number and severity of cases in regions where the surface bedrock was limestone.

This idea seems to have originated with Charles T. Jackson, a prominent American geologist, who first presented the theory at a Boston lecture in 1834 and in an 1836 published paper on "The Natural History of Water." Jackson summarized the concept in an 1848 submission to the *New York Herald.* "The progress of the Asiatic cholera," he wrote, "shows also that there is such a thing as medical geology, for the cities situated on limestone soils have always suffered most severely from that scourge." Jackson's views came to the attention of Increase A. Lapham, a Wisconsin engineer and naturalist, who found himself in agreement. In the ensuing correspondence between the two men in the autumn of 1849, Jackson noted that he believed cholera to originate "from miasmatic effluvia probably of organic origin and perhaps may consist of living fungi or animalcules floating in the air near the surface of the earth," but that the "action of calcareous water" was the primary, if not sole "exciting cause of the disease." Writing to a medical journal in 1849, a Dr. H. B. Walton expressed his support of Jackson's theory based on his observations at Nashville, virtually a geological twin of the Inner Bluegrass region. Cholera had appeared in the city in January, he noted, and the worst effects had been confined to a locality in which most of the residents were supplied with water from springs and wells. Without reference to Jackson, Cincinnati resident John Lea similarly concluded that cholera was more likely to affect those who drank spring and well water from limestone formations, and published a lengthy expository in 1850.[4]

Although contemporary medical authorities tended to dismiss this theory, proponents such as Jackson and Lea came tantalizingly close to grasping the true nature of cholera transmission. Although both writers adhered to the idea that miasmas of the air infected persons whose digestive systems had been aggravated by drinking limestone water containing calcium carbonate, tiny "animalcules"—microbes—were indeed responsible for inflicting the disease on persons, and the local water supply had an important role in producing epidemic outbreaks. The nature of karst flow in regions of limestone bedrock ensured that pathogens contaminating groundwater were carried to wells and springs, infecting the populations who withdrew their water from such sources.[5]

Cholera made its first, brief appearance in the Bluegrass on November 6, 1832, as a fatal case involving a Black resident of Lexington. By the 11th, a total of five victims had succumbed to the disease in that city, and after a few days even mild cases had ceased to appear. According to Dr. Lundsford P. Yarnell, all of the cases originated in one section of Lexington, "near the margin of a small stream [Town Branch] which runs through the city, into which all the sewers empty." The ensuing winter remained cholera free in the commonwealth, lending support to the notion that the healthy climate and situation of the region would not permit cholera to take hold. Accordingly, residents of Lexington and most Bluegrass communities made no preparations to cope with an epidemic. The supposed immunity of the Inner Bluegrass quickly proved to be a tragically erroneous assumption.[6]

Cholera seems to have appeared in Scott County and Georgetown just prior to its outbreak in nearby Lexington. An 1892 reminiscence on cholera in the *Georgetown Times* stated that the first two victims in the county were two brothers, John and James Thompson, who owned and operated a sawmill on Dry Run near Georgetown. The Thompson brothers carted a load of lumber to Lexington, "where the disease had made its appearance, went home and died the following day." The first cholera cases of the year in Lexington occurred on June 3. This chronology of the initial Georgetown outbreak is contradicted by several accounts, which indicate cholera in Georgetown a few days earlier than in Lexington. On Wednesday, June 5, a Lexington paper reported that several cases of cholera were reported at Georgetown "up to Monday evening," or prior to June 3. In his memoirs, Ebenezer Stedman, who has proved a reliable source (if a poor speller) for much information about antebellum Georgetown and Scott County, also describes an earlier appearance of cholera in Georgetown. "In May the Collera broke out in Georgetown imeadetely After a uncommon heavy Rain which Caused a Big Freshit in Elkhorn. . . . This was on Satturday." The rain probably caused privies to overflow and contaminate neighborhood wells, triggering the outbreak. Not all citizens took their water from Royal Spring, especially if they lived some distance from the spring. Stedman continued, "In the Morning while I was in the Market house i met old Mr. Steffe. He looked as well as usual But had Bin much Concerned about The Collera. Thare had no Bin anny In Ky up to this time. As was goin to dinner Some one informed me that Mr. Steffee was down with the Colera . . . He was taken, the Second Case in Geotown, after Breakfast & Was dead Before dinner, & By this time thare ware Manny More Sick."[7]

Exactly who the first case may have been remains elusive, but by the end of the month the disease had run its course in Georgetown, resulting in a death toll whose number is uncertain but seems to have been about thirty persons. This was a little over 2 percent of the city's population. By contrast, with over five hundred deaths, Lexington suffered a much higher mortality, over 8 percent of its 1830 population of about six thousand inhabitants. A regional medical journal observed that Georgetown was among the Kentucky communities that had suffered most from the ravages of the disease, most of which were located in the Inner and Outer Bluegrass. Among prominent citizens who expired from the disease was Dr. William L. Richards, the father of horse breeder Alexander Keene Richards, who owned half of Royal Spring. Dr. Richards, who had purchased a large cotton plantation on the Mississippi in Louisiana, spent most of his time there, returning to Georgetown for the summer months. While in the South, he had observed the effects of cholera, which had struck Louisiana through the port New Orleans and spread from there to Kentucky. When the disease appeared in Georgetown, "the people sought to avail themselves of the advantages of his experience. Charging nothing for his services, the poor flocked to him for advice, and thus oppressed with business, he sunk under the Epidemic, in the midst of its reign."[8]

During the epidemic, a considerable body of the population fled from Georgetown to supposedly safe refuges elsewhere. Of those who remained, nearly a third contracted the disease, most recovering. Writing to Alexander Campbell on June 29 about cholera in the town, John T. Johnson observed, "It has disappeared some days in town, but still ravages the country. . . . It produced a prodigious panic, but our citizens bore it with considerable fortitude." Nearly all business in the community was suspended for the duration. There were no funeral services held for cholera victims because it was thought prudent to bury the dead as quickly as possible. Although most citizens obtained water from Royal Spring, many of the cases may have been derived from contaminated well water rather than from the spring. The recharge area of Royal Spring, from which the system is supplied by precipitation infiltration and surface runoff into sinkholes, was at the time outside the city in a rural area. A dispersed rural population in the recharge area meant fewer possible sources of fecal contamination from infected persons than for groundwater extracted from wells within the much more densely populated city boundary. Although it would require only the wastes from one patient to contaminate Royal Spring with pathogens, it would seem likely that a higher percentage of the population would have contracted the disease if the spring had been consistently or heavily contaminated during the epidemic.[9]

The pestilence returned to Georgetown in 1849, arriving at New Orleans in mid-December 1848 and traveling up the Mississippi by riverboat to the Ohio Valley within a few weeks. From the reports of deaths among the passengers, it appeared that every north-bound boat carried cholera to the interior. The terror and death experienced sixteen years before had shattered any illusions that the benevolent climate and situation of the Bluegrass provided any antidote to the ravages of cholera, and under the direction of local physicians and civic authorities, citizens in most of the larger cities and towns began to take what they believed to be preventative sanitary measures in anticipation of the arrival of the disease. Guided by the prevailing medical notion that cholera resulted from inhalation of foul miasmas generated by filth and rot, the citizens set to vigorously scrubbing the towns and cities. Numerous volunteers thoroughly cleaned cellars, stables, yards, streets, gutters, and sewers, drained ponds and wet areas, and applied liberal quantities of whitewash, lime, and nitrate of lead as disinfectants and to control odors. Residents were urged to practice strict personal hygiene. All of these were sensible sanitary practices but, of course, did not address the real and, as yet unknown, source of infection; there was no mention of the need for clean water.[10]

In Georgetown, Dr. William L. Sutton led community efforts to prevent cholera from taking hold in the town. Sutton was a Scott County native who had received medical degrees from both the Transylvania and Maryland medical schools and returned to practice in Georgetown in the autumn of 1833, just after the first epidemic subsided. He soon became one of the town's most prominent and respected physicians and a civic leader, elected to the board of trustees in January 1848, and as chair of the board in 1849. By this time, the presence of cholera along the Mississippi was well known, and it was only a matter of time before the scourge invaded Kentucky. One of Sutton's first acts as chair was to call a special meeting of the board for the purpose of "cleansing and purifying the town, in anticipation of a visit from the cholera." Dividing the town into five districts, he appointed a committee composed of a doctor and a layman for each district to implement the necessary sanitary measures.[11]

The disease first appeared in the Bluegrass on May 21, 1849, among the inmates of the Lunatic Asylum on the outskirts of Lexington. Within three weeks it was in the city, and throughout the Bluegrass shortly thereafter. Most communities of the region were afflicted, although with less severity than during the 1833 epidemic. In Lexington, about fifteen hundred persons fled the city in an attempt to escape the disease; about three hundred of those remaining succumbed to its effects. Cholera arrived in Georgetown in early spring, and intensified during the summer. Sanitary measures notwithstanding, there was still a strongly held belief among many physicians that consumption of certain foods was likely to precipitate the disease. The town board of trustees met on August 13 to pass an ordinance suggested by Sutton that prohibited sale of "any kind of vegetables, and fruits, veal, shoat, or fresh

William Loftus Sutton, M.D. (1797–1862), a prominent physician in Georgetown, organized the town's preparations against the 1849 cholera epidemic. The author of an important treatise on typhoid fever, Sutton led the founding of the Kentucky State Medical Society in 1851 and the passage of Kentucky's first vital statistics law in 1852. Oil on canvas by Spencer T. Bancroft, November 1852. Courtesy of the Georgetown and Scott County Museum.

fish" within the town limits, a measure that was repealed after the epidemic subsided. The death toll in Georgetown, as in most other Kentucky communities, was less than in cholera's first visitation; only about twenty souls perished from the disease.[12]

The year 1849 was the worst in cholera's second invasion of North America, but the disease continued to linger, with less impact, until 1854. The disease returned to Kentucky in 1866, and again during 1872–1873, but on both occasions Georgetown was spared the touch of this scourge. In 1866, cholera was reported at Louisville's Taylor Barracks among newly arrived army recruits from New York, and among recruits stationed at barracks at Bowling Green and Newport, but it did not make serious inroads among the civilian population. Cholera's final visit to Kentucky occurred in 1873. With nearly a thousand lives extinguished during that epidemic, the state was more severely affected than anywhere else in the nation. The disease, appearing first at Ohio River port cities, became widespread in many cities and towns across the state, although in the Inner Bluegrass region only Bourbon, Garrard, and Mercer counties were afflicted.[13]

The cholera epidemics of 1833 and 1849 took a deadly toll of Georgetown citizens, as elsewhere through the state, but not until the latter part of the century did physicians begin to recognize an association between certain diseases and contaminated water. The cholera epidemic of 1873 in the United States supplied ample evidence to support the theory of waterborne transmission of the disease, and afterward many communities throughout the country began to recognize that their water supplies were vulnerable to bacterial contamination.

In 1879, the Kentucky State Board of Health released a report that pointed out the vulnerability of water supplies to contamination and gave practical advice as to prevention of waterborne diseases. Much had been learned since cholera made its first appearance in the commonwealth, almost fifty years before. Although the role of microbes was not yet well understood, it was now quite clear that contaminated water was responsible for transmitting a number of serious diseases. The author of the report, William B. Rodman, observed that

> When we consider the house and kitchen refuse thrown upon the ground, the careless disposal of human and animal excreta, the filthy stable yard (too often in Kentucky used as a privy), the

> stinking pigpen, perhaps a graveyard, and, above all, the horrible privy, the contents above ground, or in a pit so shallow that every heavy rain causes the reeking mass to overflow, are we not surprised that diseases are not more prevalent than they seem? But this is a picture of the country. In the towns it is still worse. Here people and animals, being more crowded together, it follows that there is more decaying animal matter, and then the town sewers and drains, with their fearful masses of filth, must not be overlooked. Often these latter are merely some small ravine, open ditch, or small stream, by which the inhabitants expect to have the offal of their towns removed.

Referring to water supply, he noted that "It is barely possible that the water of springs and wells in towns, especially those situated near privies or sewers, will escape contamination." Rodman then made an important observation that is as true today as it was nearly a century and a half ago: "People may say that they know the water they use is pure, because it is clear, cold, perfectly tasteless, and free from all odor. . . . It is generally supposed, that because the water comes out of the ground it must necessarily be pure, whether drawn from a well or a spring." This is the common perception that has continued to foster sickness to the present day.[14]

Early in 1888, the Georgetown Board of Trustees took some initial measures to prevent contamination of the waters of Royal Spring. At their February 21 board meeting, the trustees instructed the Improvements Committee to see that culverts and drainage ways were constructed to prevent surface drainage from emptying into or near the headwaters of the spring. A week later, on March 2, the committee reported that William Payne, owner of the land on the west side of the spring branch, had consented to the removal of the rock wall that had long divided the branch into two linear halves. This discussion seems to have been prompted by a sudden realization that it might not be a good idea to allow cattle or horses to wade into the head of the spring, where so many people were accustomed to filling containers for their drinking water, and foul the water with their waste. A plank fence was built along the spring branch to block livestock from the vicinity of the head of the spring, while leaving a place for their access farther downstream. The old rock wall and the remains of the springhouse were subsequently removed.[15]

For the situation of most springs, measures taken to prevent pollution of the water downstream from the head of the spring might seem singularly ineffective, since these would not address contamination entering the groundwater aquifer upstream from the spring. For Royal Spring in the latter part of the nineteenth century, however, there was a very real danger that any contamination introduced into the spring branch would be taken up and distributed through the city water system. The waters of the branch were impounded by a mill dam built about three thousand feet north of the spring that was of sufficient height to form a pool that back flooded the head of the spring. Any pollution that entered the spring branch behind the dam would be likely to contaminate the entire pool all the way back to the spring.

At the trustees' meeting on February 21, 1888, a committee was appointed to examine the state of the mill dam on the spring branch, which belonged to Abraham K. Lair, to determine if the free flow of the water from Royal Spring was impaired by the height of the dam. The committee reported back at the next meeting that they had spoken to Lair, who admitted that he had recently raised the height of the dam by a few inches but would be willing to reduce it to its original elevation. The committee, however, believed that this would accomplish little to alleviate the problem. The impoundment constituted a health hazard, and the committee recommended that the dam should be entirely removed to allow the branch to flow freely. The trustees ordered the Finance Committee to look into the ownership and associated privileges of the dam. Negotiations with Lair over the dam were doubtless complicated by the fact that he had served several terms on the board of trustees and so had considerable leverage. Repeated requests for a removal or a significant reduction in the height of the dam proved fruitless, and the issue was tabled at meeting after meeting. In 1891 and again in 1892, committees were appointed to address the issue of the obstruction of flow by the dam, but in each case they obtained no satisfaction.[16]

The Lair flouring mill was located on the site where, nearly a century before, Elijah Craig had erected his paper mill, a short distance from Elkhorn Creek. The original mill burned in 1836 and was rebuilt and operated as first a woolen mill and then a flouring mill until 1866. In that year, the property was acquired by the Kentucky Baptist Education Society, who sold it to Lair in 1880. A water wheel at the dam provided power to the mill, and it had so operated for generations. Lair owned property on both sides of the spring branch and was incensed by the audacity of the trustees in requesting the removal of the dam. He filed suit in the Scott County Circuit Court against the town in early 1893, charging that the diversion of water by the recently established water supply system prevented him from operating his mill by water power. The case plodded through the court during 1893 and 1894; in 1894 the newly formed city council appointed a committee to negotiate with Lair for the outright purchase of his mill dam. In September 1895, Lair agreed to drop his suit and sell the dam to the town, reserving the right to take water out of the spring branch to power the steam engines of the mill, but he died on the last day of the month before the agreement could be finalized. The court-appointed estate administrator rapidly resolved the case. In the final judgement, the city of Georgetown was to pay $2,500 to the Lair estate, and in return it was given the right to remove "the Lair Mill dam and all alluvial deposits above said dam in the Big Spring branch." The special committee was directed to see to the removal of the dam, and on October 16, 1895, the *Georgetown Times* noted, "The Lair's mill dam has been torn away."[17]

With this pressing problem resolved, the town council, encouraged by the local board of health and other area physicians, began to direct their attention toward addressing potential contamination sources in the aquifer upstream from the discharge point. At this time, no one, not even geologists, had any real understanding of the nature of karst flow systems, and no one in Georgetown had any conception of how extensive the Royal Spring drainage basin really was, that the waters issuing from the spring originated many miles from the town. Those who were concerned with eliminating contamination of the spring limited their investigations to the immediate vicinity of the head of the spring, without venturing farther than the bounds of the community. Such efforts were not entirely misdirected, however, since at the time far more potential contamination was likely produced by the concentrated population of the community, served only in part by sanitary sewers and not at all in the vicinity of the spring, than derived from most of the largely rural upstream recharge area.

In January 1897 a special committee, headed by James Y. Kelly, was appointed by the council to examine all of the springs and drains of the city to determine if the drainage had a harmful effect on the water of the Royal Spring or any of the other springs used for drinking water. On the 5th of March, the committee reported that, in their opinion, all of the privies and cesspools in the area above the spring known as the "Rucker addition" (the southern part of the former Blue Grass Park) should be filled in, a system of sewerage installed, and residents forced to connect to the sewers. The committee also recommended that "the several sinks along said valley especially a well which was dug by Dr. Rucker, be stopped up so as to keep the surface water from running to the underground streams which we think are running to the Royal Spring."[18]

Dr. James F. Eastwood, professor of chemistry at Georgetown College, undertook to determine the actual quality of Royal Spring's water. He collected and analyzed water samples, finding "large quantities" of ammonia and salts, which he interpreted as indicating the presence of decayed "animal and vegetable matter." Eastwood thought it probable that the source of such contamination was the sinks and privies of the Rucker addition. At the council meeting on April 2, 1897, Eastwood made the very sensible suggestion that this connection might be proved by placing sawdust in some of the sinks, which would come out in the spring. A committee was appointed to assist him in making this test, which constituted a very early example of groundwater tracing. No report of the test results has been located. Although problem areas were identified, no further action was taken by the city council to protect the water supply for more than a decade, until the continued pollution of Royal Spring resulted in an epidemic with tragic results.[19]

In late fall of 1908 a serious outbreak of typhoid fever confronted the inhabitants of Georgetown. Typhoid was no stranger to the community, for it was present everywhere in urban settings throughout the nation during most of the nineteenth century and well into the first decades of the twentieth. In 1909, Dr. William Osler estimated that there were as many as half a million cases of typhoid in the United States each year, resulting in 35,000 to 40,000 deaths. Like cholera, typhoid is primarily a waterborne disease, caused by *Salmonella typhi* or *S. paratyphi* bacilli and capable of being transmitted in several ways, all involving transfer of pathogens from the feces or urine of infected persons to new victims.[20]

The most common mode of infection, leading to widespread epidemics, is through ingestion of water containing fecal matter from typhoid patients. Food and drink provide another source of infection, as microbes can be conveyed by uncooked fruits and vegetables grown in contaminated soil or washed in contaminated water, or handled by infected persons. Ice, unpasteurized milk and milk products such as cheese, ice cream, and butter, processed meat, sausage, poultry, fish, and shellfish can all serve to transfer typhoid. Food handlers and typhoid carriers are a major source of spread. Typhoid bacilli can persist for years, even decades, in the bile ducts, intestines, and bladders of asymptomatic and otherwise healthy persons, occasionally shed from their systems and contaminating everything they contact. About 5 percent of typhoid patients become carriers. The story of Mary Mallon ("Typhoid Mary"), who worked as a cook for several families in New York from 1900 to 1915, is the most famous example of a carrier. She is believed to have infected nearly fifty persons with typhoid, three of whom died. Direct contact with patients and their personal items, soiled by typhoid excreta, can result in new infections. The disease also can be spread by insects, such as flies and cockroaches, that feed or walk upon infected fecal material and then transfer the bacilli to foodstuffs and to persons.[21]

Typhoid has historically been a difficult disease to diagnose, and through most of the first half of the nineteenth century it often was confused with typhus, an equally serious, fever-inducing disease that is not waterborne but a vector-borne bacilli transmitted through the bites of body lice. They have similar symptoms, and in fact the term typhoid means "typhus-like." Not until 1836 was a clear distinction between typhus and typhoid as two distinct clinical entities made by William W. Gerhard, but misidentification of typhoid by physicians persisted for some decades afterward.[22]

Typhoid's diagnostic difficulty arises from the extremely complex symptomology of the disease. Unlike Asiatic cholera, which is readily identifiable in patients by its massive discharges of watery diarrhea, there is no single symptom or feature that is characteristic of typhoid. The disease tends to affect nearly every system in the body and manifest outwardly in many different forms; symptoms exhibited by some patients may not be present in others. Diagnosis is typically made on the basis of multiple symptoms. During the incubation period, which lasts one to two weeks, patients generally display no overt symptoms other than a general feeling of being unwell. The most constant feature of a typhoid infection is high fever, which may persist for several weeks, often accompanied by headache. In most but not all cases, the spleen is enlarged and tender, producing abdominal pain. Many patients will also develop small rose-colored spots, mostly on the abdomen but which may also be widely distributed on the chest and back, fading in a few days and reappearing. A typhoid infection can result in serious, sometimes lethal complications, such as massive intestinal hemorrhage or intestinal perforation, the latter being responsible for one-fourth to one-third of typhoid deaths. Without treatment, the overall mortality of the disease ranges from about 5 percent to nearly 30 percent.[23]

Georgetown's first major bout with the disease in epidemic form occurred during the 1840s, although certainly there must have been cases prior to this that were not identified as such. According to Dr. William L. Sutton, typhoid first appeared in the community during the winter of 1841, and "from that time, it has rarely been altogether absent from our neighborhood." The disease subsided after the initial outbreak, but it reappeared in strength during the winter of 1845–1846, when "twenty to thirty families of our village were attacked." Carefully reviewing his case notes, Sutton was perplexed by the many different circumstances under which typhoid had appeared among Georgetown and Scott County families, unable to determine if the disease was actually contagious or arose from other undetermined causes. In a well-documented and well-reasoned treatise on typhoid, he wrote:

> A contagious disease, whose infection may remain dormant in the system for seven months, or be quickened into life in as many hours; which may appear in half a dozen members of a family, in as many days, without any chance of introduction from without, and then spread no farther in that family, or neighborhood—which can originate in divers families in the same village or neighborhood, those families having no communication with each other—which can originate frequently at divers points in the country, and infect but one or a few persons—which, in one word, shall frequently be set at nought all the laws of contagion as usually understood, although it may at times seem to obey those laws, is a contagious disease which I do not profess to understand.

His frustration is clear, and the medical profession would remain frustrated in its efforts to understand and combat epidemic disease until the involvement of microbes with disease transmission became known much later in the century. In 1879, William B. Rodman warned Kentuckians that "those places, in both town and country, which have suffered with typhoid fever, will furnish a *cloud of witnesses* to the danger of using water fouled with the germs of those diseases"[24]

Typhoid could be a fatal affliction, and victims who recovered were often subject to health problems for the remainder of their lives. Nevertheless, typhoid had a lower mortality overall and did not inspire the same level of fear as that other, dreaded waterborne disease, cholera. Typhoid was simply an unremarkable aspect of urban life during the era, and a few cases were no great cause for alarm. Thus, on the 25th day of November 1908, the *Georgetown Times* casually observed, as a simple matter-of-fact, that a large number of cases of typhoid fever were present in the community. The town board of health recommended that citizens boil water used for consumption. At the time, typhoid was widespread through the commonwealth, characterized by many individual cases scattered among various communities. Under these circumstances it is often difficult to identify the beginning of an epidemic or to mark its ending. Severity can instead be gauged by increases and decreases in the number of persons afflicted in a particular locale. In Georgetown, the death on November 7 of Franklin Ferguson, son of the ex-mayor, signaled an intensification of the disease to epidemic proportions in that community.[25]

By the end of the first week in December, at the height of the epidemic, there were 120 cases of typhoid fever in Georgetown. As the weather grew colder, the disease subsided. Georgetown's population in 1908 was approximately forty-four hundred persons; in April 1909, Dr. Abraham C. Cook estimated that about three hundred of the community's inhabitants had contracted typhoid during the recent epidemic, and twenty-five had died. Early in December 1908, as more and more citizens were stricken, Dr. John A. Lewis, supported by Dr. John C. Thomasson, stated at the first monthly council meeting that "the first thing was to find the cause and in his opinion it was from one common center, the water supply from the Big Spring." Lewis noted that storm sewers were pouring filth into the spring branch below the spring and "the germs were polluting the water to the head of the spring." He recommended measures to prevent storm sewer drainage or surface runoff from entering the spring branch anywhere near the spring and suggested that the sinkholes above the head of the spring be "attended to." Recently appointed city health officer, Dr. Harry V. Johnson had taken samples from a faucet of the city water supply at Georgetown College and now reported that the water was contaminated with sewage.[26]

Early in the morning of the next day, Saturday, December 5, the mayor and council went to inspect the spring and examine the surrounding area. When they visited the sinkhole area above the head of the spring, they found that the largest sink, in the Royal Spring housing development, had been used as a dumping ground and was "full of filth." On Monday morning workers were set to cleaning out the spring and the sinkhole. James Y. Kelly, who probably knew more about the spring than anyone else in the community, produced a report detailing the various sinkholes in the vicinity and his observations on the probable subterranean course of the conduit feeding Royal Spring, which he presented to the council on December 8. In conclusion, he stated, "As I had given much attention to this spring I thought I would get down this information for the present and coming generations."[27]

By mid-December the epidemic had begun to moderate. At the Friday council meeting on December 18, the board of health made its official recommendations for improvement of the sanitary condition of the city. "It is our opinion," the statement read, "that the epidemic of typhoid fever is due to one cause—the pollution at some unknown point of the waters of the Royal Spring from which the city's water supply is drawn." While opinion was still divided as to whether the primary source of contamination was through infiltration from the land above the head of the spring, or from drainage into the spring branch below the spring, the board now appeared to be favoring the theory that the spring's underground waters were being contaminated before issuing forth. According to the board, a sanitary engineer should be employed at once "to look into the protection of the waters of the spring above its mouth and to lay out a system of sanitary sewers to take in the entire city." Every building, residential and commercial, should be forced to connect to the new sewerage system, and where sewer lines already exist, property owners who have not complied with orders to connect should be made to do so. The dumping ground on the commons near the water works should be cleaned up and put in grass and "maintained as a beautiful spot," and the ground on the west side of the branch also put into order and maintained. The board urged the city to purchase some suitable land, outside the community, to use as a dump site to eliminate the haphazard accumulation of rubbish and garbage within the city. Furthermore, the board suggested that, in addition to addressing potential sources of contamination, it would be wise to treat the water rather than to deliver it in a raw condition: "A system of filtration or water purification should be installed without delay." On the following Tuesday, Georgetown was briefly visited by a representative from the Kentucky State Board of Health, who, after inspecting the situation, gave his opinion that the source of the epidemic was from some case of typhoid above the spring, from which the pathogens had entered the water supply.[28]

The city government acted promptly on these recommendations. By the end of the month a dump site had been purchased and a sanitary engineer had been hired to deal with the situation. William P. Gerhard of New York City arrived in Georgetown on January 6 and spent several days in discussions with members of the board of health and inspecting Royal Spring and the surrounding area. His report supported the previous conclusions of the board:

> There are a number of sink holes in the hill to the South of the Spring and these have been used in the past as dumping grounds for all sorts of garbage and waste matter. On the same hill and directly over the rock formation from which the spring issues, a number of houses have recently been built which have no sewerage facilities and which are provided with ordinary surface closets. There is another large territory south East of the spring which naturally drains toward the same and must inevitably contribute to its pollution. I inspected this territory and found that while a portion of it is provided with a sanitary sewer, there are on the other hand numerous evidences of pollution, such as sink holes, surface closets and cesspools. In this way the water from the spring has without question been contaminated for a long time, and the contamination is constantly growing.

In his report to the council, Gerhard referred to a study made in 1906 by George C. Matson of the US Geological Survey, who had traced drainage from several sinkholes in the drainage area of the spring to the Royal Spring by placing large quantities of common salt in the sinks. Chemical tests showed that the salt was present in the spring water eight hours after one such experiment, and after sixteen hours in the second case. This, according to Gerhard, was conclusive evidence indicating the sinks as sources of contamination to the spring. Gerhard recommended measures similar to those advocated by the board of health to protect the immediate recharge area of the spring, and also emphasized the necessity of installing a system to filter or treat the water for pathogens before it is delivered to customers.[29]

Now that the experts had weighed in, unanimous in their recommendations, the matter would seem to be resolved and the necessary actions clear. Through the remainder of 1909, however, at meetings of the city council and in issues of the *Georgetown Times*, the citizens debated both the need for expensive remedies and exactly what sort of treatment system should be installed, if any. Notices by respected physicians of the community appeared in the *Times* with regularity, stressing the dangers of ignoring the situation and urging the installation of a treatment system. "Great masses of our population," scolded Dr. Abraham C. Cook, an ardent supporter of water purification, "swear by all that's good and bad that there is nothing the matter with the water of the big spring and never has been." Most people, he observed scornfully, would rather continue "gulping down the Royal Spring sewage" than see anything done which might add to their tax bill.[30]

In the meantime, as the city was receiving bids from northern firms for the installation of a filtering plant at the spring, a committee was appointed to investigate water treatment systems used in other regional communities. Some citizens favored the sand filtration system in common use; others, such as Dr. Cook, supported a more aggressive "electrical" method of water sterilization using ozone, rather than filtering water through "dirty sand." Cook, although correct in his criticism of sand filtration, was not entirely pure in his motive, since he was acting as a representative for an ozone purification company based in Philadelphia. Nearly every issue of the weekly *Times* during 1909 contained a lengthy exposition by Cook on the benefits of ozone treatment coupled with chastisement of the city government for delay on so urgent an issue.[31]

The Filter Committee appointed in mid-January made its report to the city council on March 30, recommending that additional bids for a treatment system be solicited. Their report concluded, "We are confronted at this time with the proposition of whose duty it is to install this filter," stating that the committee was unanimous in their opinion that such was the responsibility of the privately owned Georgetown water company, who should be compelled "at once" to begin installation of a system. The city attorney was directed to investigate whether the city had the authority to order the company to put in a filter, and accordingly, in late April the city of Georgetown filed suit in the Scott County Circuit Court against the Georgetown Water, Gas, Electric and Power Company to force the company to erect a filter plant and provide the citizens of the community with pure water. The petition by the plaintiff charged the water company with delivering water that was "foul, impure, filthy and full of disease germs, unfit for drinking purposes and dangerous."[32]

The case was dismissed from the circuit court after the water company filed a demurrer, and subsequently was taken up again in the Kentucky Court of Appeals, which rendered a decision against the city on September 23, 1909. In the court's opinion, the city of Georgetown, as owner of Royal Spring, was furnishing the water and the water company merely distributing that which was provided to it. Under these circumstances, the court held, the water company bore no responsibility for filtering or treating the water. The water company had not caused the pollution, and there was no provision in the existing contract between the city and company to provide for the erection of a treatment plant.[33]

Even before the appeal was settled, the city was considering how it would be able to finance a treatment plant should the case be decided for the water company. The estimated cost, based on bids received, would be about $20,000. The city simply did not have the funds, did not have the power to borrow this amount, and would not be able to put a bond proposition before the voters until the regular election in November. At a public meeting on July 21, 1909, a motion was proposed and carried to submit a proposal to the voters in November for a bond issue totaling $25,000: $20,000 for the treatment plant, and an additional $5,000 for sewer construction in the area above the head of Royal Spring for protection of the water supply. As election day approached, editorials and commentary in the *Times* appealed to the voters to support the bond issue.[34]

On November 2, 1909, Georgetown citizens voted by a substantial majority to finance construction of a filtration plant and new sewer lines, nearly 90 percent of voters favoring the projects. In September of the following year, the city council awarded the contract for the treatment plant to a Louisville firm, the low bidder at $17,026. The treatment plant began operating in late spring 1911 but had to shut down briefly in late May to correct mechanical problems. The original system was based on filtration and chemical treatment with soda ash and unslaked lime. By 1926, chlorination had become the method used in purification.[35]

Georgetown had relied on Royal Spring for more than 120 years as its primary water supply, trusting to the age-old misconception that spring water was always pure and safe, rising unblemished from the pristine depths of the earth. Advances in scientific and medical knowledge during the late nineteenth century, underscored by the typhoid epidemic of 1908, shattered that complacency. With the realization that disease-causing pathogens could be waterborne, the result of sewage contamination, the first measures were taken to eliminate contamination before it reached the aquifer. Though anecdotal evidence suggested that the Royal Spring drainage system extended far to the south, no one, not even through the middle of the twentieth century, realized that the underground watershed reached nearly into the urban heart of Lexington. As Lexington's population increased and its residential sections gradually expanded, more rapidly following the Second World War, urban development moved northward toward Georgetown. This development brought new threats to the water supply of the smaller community. Soon, Georgetown's water treatment processes intended solely to control pathogenic organisms would be insufficient as the water system's managers were forced to cope with a variety of chemical pollutants attendant with urban growth in the neighboring community. As officials of the Georgetown Board of Health and the expensive New York consultant pointed out, two separate strategies—preventative and remedial—were both needed to ensure safe drinking water: protection of the aquifer from contamination, and treatment of the raw water before it was supplied to consumers.

Not until the end of the twentieth century would there be a systematic effort made to protect the source of supply, through the creation of a groundwater aquifer "protection zone" that extended well into urban Fayette County.

14

Protecting Royal Spring

Before the Royal Spring water supply could be adequately safeguarded, the boundaries of the watershed had to be determined—no easy task for a subterranean drainage system. Many persons suspected that the spring waters originated as far south as Lexington. Robert Peter, writing in 1882, stated, "Some of the cavernous spaces in the limestones near Lexington are supposed to have subterranean connection with some of the Georgetown springs, since it is believed by some that substances thrown in at Lexington have made their appearance in the springs of Georgetown; however, the prevalent direction of the sink-holes, which mark the cavernous spaces beneath, is more frequently east than west." An account of Royal Spring published in 1897 in the *Georgetown Times* was even more tentative: "The source of the vast flow of water is absolutely unknown. It has been noticed that the waters of the spring become clouded when there are heavy rains 10 or 12 miles south of Georgetown. The spring cannot be a subterranean branch of any local watercourse, however, for it flows steadily when Elkhorn [Creek] and other neighboring springs are dry." This latter statement represented a significant misunderstanding of the situation, apparently reflecting a long-popular supposition that spring water originates from reservoirs deep within the earth and is not derived from the surface environment.[1]

Nearly seventy years later, the nature and extent of the Royal Spring aquifer still remained a mystery. In October 1964, in response to reports of detergent contamination of Royal Spring that produced a "sudsy" condition in the city's drinking water supply, the *Georgetown Graphic* published further speculation as to the source of the spring's waters. "It would seem," the paper observed, "that its source is between Elkhorn Creek and the Kentucky River to the south and east. . . . Since Lexington lies in this direction and has been expanding rapidly in recent years, it is logical to look there for the contamination." The author recalled that when, a few years previously, fluoride had appeared in the water supply, the city health department had traced it to a Lexington factory that had been discharging hydrofluoric acid into a tributary of Cane Run Creek. Cane Run originates in northern Lexington and flows northwest to discharge to North Elkhorn Creek at a point about two miles west of Royal Spring. "How acid got from creek to underground stream was never learned, but the contamination ceased after the factory stopped pouring acid into the creek." Based on this evidence, the author concluded that at least part of the flow of Royal Spring came from northern Lexington, and then began to carry his speculations much farther afield, supposing that the area of southern Fayette County and Jessamine County might be contributing to the spring's contamination, even though the area in question was twenty miles distant from the spring. The evidence for this was flimsy and wholly circumstantial, based on an observation that when the city of Nicholasville, in central Jessamine County, ceased pumping from deep wells and switched to the Kentucky River as a source, the flow from Royal Spring greatly increased. By 1968, the evidence increasingly began to point toward Cane Run as the source of at least some of the waters of Royal Spring. In that year, investigator Donald S. Mull came to this conclusion based on his analyses of water well data, groundwater chemistry, and local subsurface structural contours.[2]

Solving the Royal Spring puzzle would, however, soon be accomplished using dye-tracing methods unknown to investigators of earlier eras that would demonstrate that the spring was indeed "a subterranean branch" of a local watercourse. George Matson's crude 1905 experiments, using common salt (sodium chloride) to trace contamination from sinks in the vicinity of Royal Spring, were successful, but not a practical nor desirable method for long-distance tracing. Salt, in such quantities, is itself a pollutant harmful to aquatic life. At the end of the nineteenth century, water-tracing techniques involving nontoxic dyes were being developed in Europe, but it would be many decades before the procedures were refined and applied to investigations of American karst landscapes.[3]

Dye-tracing of groundwater involves placing dye in the bottom of a sinkhole or into the flow of a sinking stream and thereafter monitoring a suspected discharge point, a spring. In the past, monitoring was visual, which required use of a large quantity of dye in order for the colored water to remain visible many miles downstream. Modern dye-tracing methodology can detect minute quantities of dye, measured in parts per million, that would be invisible to the naked eye. Dye tracing can be qualitative, offering simple confirmation of a connection by the presence of dye in the outflow from the spring, or quantitative, which provides time-series measurements of the amount of diluted dye in the flow and thereby determines the dye discharge curve and its peak as it passes through the system. Qualitative tracing involves placement of receptors into the discharge point of a spring to absorb and retain dye that may be present in the flowing water. These are often packets of activated charcoal from which dye can later be extracted in the lab using a solvent. Formerly, the solvent solution was examined visually to confirm or reject the presence of dye. More recently, use of an instrument known as a spectrofluorophotometer has become the standard methodology, capable of detecting different dyes by the wavelength at which they fluoresce when struck by an intense beam of light. Common nontoxic dyes used for water tracing include fluorescein, eosin, and rhodamine WT. In quantitative tracing, a continuous sampling device automatically collects water samples at specified time intervals, and those samples are subsequently analyzed for dye content.[4]

Scientific confirmation of the extent of Royal Spring drainage and a first approximation of the basin boundaries was finally provided by University of Kentucky graduate students in geology working under the direction of Dr. John Thrailkill, as part of his long-term research program, initiated in 1976, to study karst hydrology in the Inner Bluegrass. After his retirement in 1992, these investigations continued under the direction of Dr. Lyle V. Sendlein. Thrailkill's student Joseph W. Troester began an investigation of the Royal Spring basin in 1977 by identifying potential recharge points in the region immediately southeast of the

Dr. John Thrailkill (far left) directed an extensive program investigating karst systems in the Inner Bluegrass during the 1970s and 1980s. With him at the entrance to Russell Cave in Fayette County are some of his geology students at the University of Kentucky. To the right of Thrailkill are Larry Spangler, Gary O'Dell (kneeling), Phil Byrd, and Lance Barron. Photograph by Gary O'Dell.

spring, along the course of Cane Run Creek. This stream has a watershed of sufficient size that it should carry a significant perennial flow, but instead, for most of its length through most of the year, the channel of Cane Run is dry. Along the length of the Cane Run channel are numerous crevices and holes that direct surface flow underground; only during times of very wet weather is flow continuous in the channel.[5]

Troester injected dye into three points located nearly in a straight line southeast from Royal Spring, the farthest from a swallow hole in the bed of Cane Run Creek approximately 5.6 miles distant. These traces were successful, indicating that the Royal Spring groundwater basin extended to at least this distance and received at least part of its flow from Cane Run. Following Troester's initial research, Lawrence E. Spangler, also a Thrailkill student, conducted a more extensive investigation of the spring basin. Spangler identified more than twenty well-defined

A: View of Cane Run Creek at high flow in the Kentucky Horse Park, Fayette County, following several days of rain in early May 2021. *B*: Same location two weeks later, following a period without significant precipitation. *C*: Same location and date as photograph B, swallet or "swallow hole" in creek bed, a fracture enlarged by acidic dissolution of limestone. Most of the Cane Run channel is completely dry during normal weather because of leakage through such bedrock crevices into the Royal Spring conduit system. Photographs by Gary O'Dell.

swallets along the Cane Run channel and on tributaries that sink just prior to joining the main channel, and observed that there was also substantial loss through bed seepage. I accompanied him in the field on many occasions. By 1982 Spangler had demonstrated that the Royal Spring basin had a narrow, linear shape and extended well into the corporate boundary of Lexington, more than nine miles from the spring. In succeeding years, additional traces by various parties, most recently by Randall Paylor, a graduate student at Eastern Kentucky University, further refined the limits of the basin boundary.[6]

Although the Royal Spring basin constitutes the most extensive groundwater system known in the Inner Bluegrass, until very recently

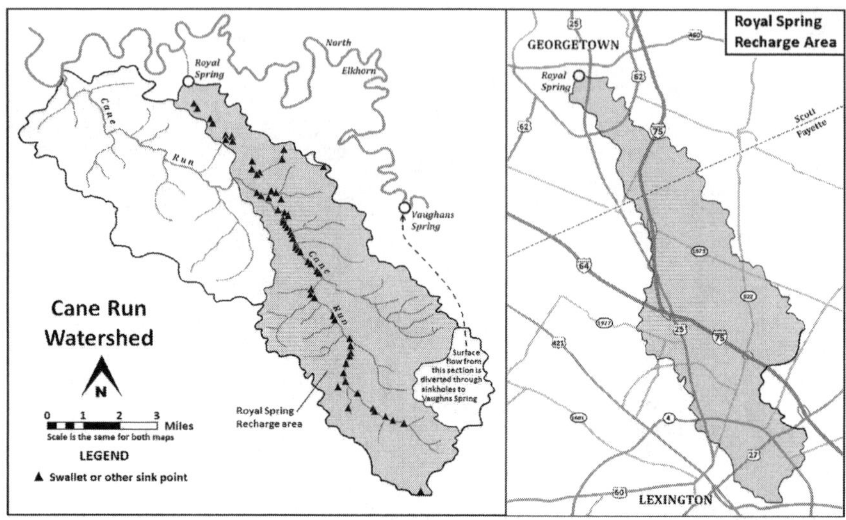

Cane Run watershed and Royal Spring recharge area. The flow pathways and basin boundaries were determined by dye traces carried out by several investigators, beginning in the late 1970s. Map by Gary O'Dell, adapted from Paylor, "Correlation of Spring Discharge with Groundwater Travel Time."

no part of the conduit system could be entered and explored. Many of the larger springs of the region are associated with caves, either in the upstream or downstream segments of the basin area. Certainly, such a large volume of flow as commonly discharges from Royal Spring indicates a master conduit of substantial size. The head, or discharge point, for Royal Spring cannot be entered, since it remains inundated even during low flow conditions. In 1997, Georgetown Municipal Water sent divers equipped with air tanks into the spring, a potentially hazardous undertaking. The divers were able to penetrate about a hundred feet into the spring, passing through what they described as a series of large chambers, apparently tens of feet in diameter since the beams of their powerful flashlights did not reach the walls of the passageway.[7]

In 1989, the late Douglas R. Graham, a University of Kentucky geology graduate student, entered and explored a lengthy section of the actual master conduit, located several miles upstream from the spring discharge point, as part of his thesis research. Graham had earlier

(1986–1987) conducted geophysical studies in the vicinity of the Kentucky Horse Park involving electrical resistivity in a deliberate and apparently successful attempt to locate the master conduit. During the summer of 1989, while hiking along Cane Run six miles south of Royal Spring in company with Karen Fitzmaurice (who was conducting a separate investigation), Doug discovered an open, natural shaft on the quarry property of the Vulcan Materials Company.[8]

The company began its Georgetown Road open quarry operation during the 1950s, and three decades later it inadvertently cut down into a cave containing a flowing stream. Freed from confinement, the cave stream began to fill the quarry pit. Vulcan tried to continue working the site, but pumps proved to be no match for the rising water and the company was forced to abandon the flooded pit. During periods of extreme drought, when the water level drops sufficiently, openings can be seen where the cave enters and exits the pit. With the former quarry now a small lake, the company moved north on the property and commenced preliminary removal of soil and surface rock, intending to open a new quarry. Unfortunately for their plans, the excavators again broke into a conduit in the new location, and Vulcan prudently called a halt to the operation. The site now lies abandoned, although the company intends to resume quarrying in the future by developing an underground mine located at a considerable depth below the breached conduit, similar to their extensive underground mine in Lexington that operates below the underground flow pathways of McConnell Springs.[9]

Following his discovery of the breakthrough feature, Graham returned, accompanied by Karen Fitzmaurice and James C. Currens of the Kentucky Geological Survey, with hard hats and lights to investigate the phenomenon. Descent into the twenty-foot shaft revealed a cave passage extending in both directions away from the surface opening. The passage contained a substantial stream flowing northward, toward Georgetown. The downstream passage quickly became impassible because of deep water, but Graham and his companions explored the upstream section, which averaged six to eight feet wide and about six feet high, for a distance of about fifteen hundred feet. Their ability to follow the cave so far southward without encountering any obstruction suggests that the conduit breached by the quarry pit was a tributary of the main Royal Spring conduit. A dye trace made from the stream

This collapse into the main conduit of Royal Spring occurred when the Vulcan Materials Company began removing the soil cover on their property near the junction of I-75 and US 25 in preparation for a new quarry operation. Standing behind the collapse is Jared Curry of Vulcan Materials. Photograph by Gary O'Dell.

inside the cave confirmed the connection to Royal Spring, and the cave almost certainly represents the primary conduit for the Royal Spring system. To date, this conduit has not been explored further, as the entrance fissure has since become unstable and dangerous.[10]

Additional studies of the Royal Spring conduit system were carried out on the grounds of the Kentucky Horse Park between 2011 and 2014 by James C. Currens of the Kentucky Geological Survey. Currens employed several geophysical methods, including electrical resistivity, shallow seismic, and microgravity sensing, to locate water-filled subterranean voids potentially representing the cave. This information was subsequently used to direct the drilling of wells through the bedrock into identified anomalies. Three of these wells were able to intercept the conduit at approximately fifty feet below the surface, allowing placement of equipment to monitor various water quality parameters. These

The interior of the Royal Spring conduit in 1990, entered at the Vulcan Quarry collapse feature. Photograph by Jim Currens.

included specific conductivity, water temperature, pH, turbidity, dissolved oxygen, and constituents such as fecal coliform bacteria, phosphorus, nitrate, and a limited number of pesticides. Bacterial and nitrate levels were of particular interest because these are unaffected by diversion underground and represent significant problems affecting the water supply at Royal Spring in Georgetown. A tiltable downhole camera was also lowered into the wells, allowing an estimation of the conduit size at this point: it is roughly 2.8 feet high and 18 feet wide.[11]

The research conducted by University of Kentucky graduate students and the Geological Survey, particularly the accurate delineation of the Royal Spring groundwater basin boundaries, made it possible to develop a strategic plan to protect the water supply of Georgetown. The motivation to accomplish this task was established by federal legislation in June 1986, an amendment to the Safe Drinking Water Act to provide additional protection from contamination for water systems where the source is groundwater from springs or wells. In most cases, the federal mandate to comply with the legislation descended to the states, which developed community-based programs generally known as Wellhead

Protection Programs, but in many cases instead termed Source Protection or Water Supply Protection programs, since not all water systems depended on groundwater from wells. In Kentucky, Georgetown was chosen as one of three communities, along with Elizabethtown and Calvert City, that the state Division of Water assisted in developing pilot Water Supply Protection (WSP) programs.[12]

For Georgetown, the program had three primary objectives: (1) to define the spring's groundwater recharge area boundary (the spring's drainage basin); (2) to identify and locate all potential sources of pollution within this area that might contaminate the water supply source; and (3) to designate zones in the protection area based on time of travel to the spring and the probable capability for attenuation of pollutants, primarily through dilution. Achieving these objectives would allow the development of management strategies and planning for future emergencies. The first of these goals had largely been accomplished through the dye-tracing projects of University of Kentucky students, although some areas on the margins needed to be more precisely defined. Since 80 percent of the nearly twenty-square-mile Royal Spring basin lies within Fayette County, a cooperative approach across jurisdictions was required. Accordingly, the Royal Spring Water Supply Protection Committee included planners and engineers representing both Georgetown and the Lexington-Fayette Urban County Government (LFUCG). Establishment of a planning group and determining basin boundaries constituted Phase One of the WSP program; Georgetown's pilot program was the first in Kentucky to receive Phase One approval from the Division of Water.[13]

The necessity for establishing protection for Georgetown's water supply was emphasized when, in late December 1989, Georgetown residents complained that their water smelled and tasted bad, and officials at the water plant detected minute traces of petroleum products in the raw water supply, including benzene, a known carcinogen. Although the quantities involved were not sufficient to constitute a health hazard, the water system was immediately shut down and remained out of operation for nearly ten months while efforts were made to track down the source of the contamination. The source, believed to be leakage from an underground gasoline storage tank, was never located, and contamination levels gradually diminished, only to reappear in 2002, again only in

Vehicular accidents involving hazardous cargos can endanger community water supplies derived from groundwater. Signs such as this, located on I-75/64 north of Lexington, were placed by the Kentucky Division of Water on major roads crossing into the Royal Spring karst basin. Similar signs help protect other communities in the state that use groundwater. Photograph by Gary O'Dell.

trace amounts not considered harmful. To deal with this recurring problem, the city invested a substantial amount of money in erecting a temporary treatment structure known as an "air stripper," which aids in removal of volatile substances such as benzene. Another scare occurred in 2001, when barely measurable traces of dioxin and PCBs were detected in the raw spring water.[14]

Alarms such as these propelled establishment of the groundwater protection program. The state Division of Water, which acted as technical consultant for the various WSP projects in Kentucky, applied to the Corporation for National and Community Service (established in 1993) for a grant to involve AmeriCorps volunteers in the inventory of potential contamination sources within the Royal Spring basin. The volunteers surveyed nearly two thousand industrial, commercial, and rural locations, focusing primarily on sites with sinkholes or where chemicals were present that could contaminate groundwater. In August 2001, the LFUCG Planning Commission approved the protection plan developed cooperatively with Georgetown. Among the key elements in the WSP plan is to educate property owners in the protection area about the importance of controlling pollution.[15]

Georgetown's Water Supply Protection Plan continues to be refined as more information about the groundwater flow system is provided by additional research. Initially, a basic model for water flow time-of-travel from various parts of the basin to the spring discharge was derived from the work of Thrailkill and Douglas R. Gouzie. Dye traces carried out by the principals suggested, reasonably, that in general flow velocity increased with increases in discharge (in response to precipitation events). A more thorough investigation carried out by Randall L. Paylor in 2003 confirmed this result and allowed the production of a series of maps showing expected travel time from different parts of the basin under various discharge volumes from Royal Spring. These maps comprise important tools for planning and for emergency response. According to Paylor, the fastest groundwater travel time from Lexington occurred during a major storm event, over a distance of about eleven miles, and took ten hours, or a velocity of about one mile per hour. The slowest travel occurred in low flow conditions produced by very dry weather, during which the average subsurface flow velocity was only 0.15 miles per hour and took three days to travel from Lexington to Georgetown.[16]

Although Royal Spring has faithfully (more or less) served the water supply needs of Georgetown for more than two centuries, few could have foreseen the demand placed on the source by the accelerated growth of the community in the last two decades of the twentieth century, growth largely in response to the construction of the huge Toyota Motor Manufacturing automobile assembly plant north of the city in 1986 and Georgetown's increasing popularity as a "bedroom community" for Lexington urban professionals. At the outset, planners knew that Royal Spring did not have the flow capacity to supply both Georgetown and Scott County and the enormous water demand that would be imposed by the Toyota facility. The spring's discharge averages twelve cubic feet per second, or about 8 million gallons per day, but is greatly diminished during summer months and, during periods of prolonged drought, can be reduced to a trickle. In

1986, the Georgetown water company served about forty-seven hundred customers, pumping about 2.1 million gallons per day on average, with a treatment capacity about double this. The new Toyota plant was expected to require 630,000 gallons per day initially, with that total projected to expand to more than 2.7 million gallons per day by 1992. To resolve the water supply problem, the state of Kentucky offered to pay for a twenty-four-inch main line to be constructed by the Kentucky American Water Company of Lexington from northern Fayette County to Toyota, at a cost of $5.5 million, as part of the incentive package intended to attract the Japanese firm to locate in Kentucky. Despite this solution, Georgetown and Scott County would still face increasing pressure on the spring-based water supply as a result of unprecedented population growth and development associated with establishment of the Toyota plant and the creation of more than eight thousand jobs.[17]

Three-quarters of a century earlier, the city council had, as local historian Lindsey Apple later observed, exhibited "a rare moment of progressive planning" by purchasing an unused mill dam and property on North Elkhorn Creek, once the site of Elijah Craig's saw and grist mill. Despite the best of intentions, however, the dam was allowed to deteriorate. In the late 1970s, when it began to become apparent that Royal Spring alone could not support additional community growth, hasty repairs to the dam proved insufficient. After considerable public debate, the city council settled on a location several miles north of Georgetown as a site for a large reservoir, and began to purchase land in the area.[18]

The 1988 drought, during which water rationing was imposed in Georgetown, as in several other Kentucky communities, brought the issue to a crisis point. Mayor Tom Prather, appointed to the office in 1986 to fill an unexpected vacancy, recalls that the people of Georgetown were angry over the water situation, and there were calls to sell the city water company to a private firm to solve supply problems and allow lower rates. The Lexington-based Kentucky American Water Company, in what Prather describes as a hostile takeover attempt, made a formal offer that was thought by some to be "insultingly low." The city hired a North Carolina engineering firm with a solid reputation, acceptable to both parties, to evaluate the offer. A representative of the firm subsequently presented an analysis of the water supply situation and the pros and cons of the Kentucky American offer. The Lexington water company was annoyed when the reporting engineer, who observed that "he who controls the water hole controls the valley," strongly recommended that Georgetown continue to operate its own water company.[19]

Spurred by the recent incidents of gasoline contamination, the city subsequently spent $2.8 million to bring Kentucky River water through a pipeline from the Frankfort water system to use as an emergency supply. The cost of water from Frankfort was considerably higher than Georgetown citizens had been accustomed to paying, and the reservoir plan assumed new importance. By 2004, the Scott County Fiscal Court had spent more than $3 million in acquiring about fifteen hundred acres of land, on which to site a 280-acre reservoir. During the long process of acquisition, however, environmental regulations had evolved to the point where justification of a dam had become extremely difficult. In that year, the US Environmental Protection Agency refused to approve the dam permit application, noting that the city had not made a sufficient case for the reservoir, when there were alternatives available. Some citizens questioned the wisdom of the great expenditures of the county's treasure for the reservoir project at the expense of other, equally pressing needs, and others noted that water was already being piped as needed from Frankfort and a regional water commission was being formed.[20]

The reservoir plan was finally shelved in March 2006, when the city learned that the US Army Corps of Engineers intended to reject the application. By withdrawing the application before the Corps made an official denial, the community avoided a lengthy appeals process. Furthermore, by this time, Georgetown, along with many other central Kentucky communities, had become a member of the new Bluegrass Water Supply Commission, which was officially created in August 2004. Participating communities intended to share equity in water plant and transmission lines with Kentucky American Water. Under this plan, the Lexington-based Kentucky American Water Company would build a new $160 million treatment plant on the Kentucky River north of Frankfort, sharing the water with members. The commission, however, was unable to raise its share of the expected project cost, and in 2008, with approval from the Public Service Commission, Kentucky American Water Company began construction of a new water plant on the same site with no intent to share the water with communities outside Lexington. The goal of regional water supply cooperation appeared to be at an end.[21]

Georgetown and Scott County planners and administrators recognize that significant increases in the water supply are essential to meet the needs of future growth, and that Royal Spring is not up to the projected demand. Georgetown Municipal Water and Sewer supplies water to the city of Georgetown and western Scott County, amounting to about 70 percent of the county population. Georgetown's population topped 37,000 in 2020, up nearly 25 percent from the 2010 census. The city is currently growing at a rate of 1.74 percent annually, and on this basis population will exceed 50,000 by 2040. Scott is the fastest-growing county in Kentucky. The county population is expected to nearly double during the next twenty years, from more than 57,000 in 2020 to almost 100,000 by 2040.[22]

City officials no longer consider a county reservoir to be a viable option to meet Georgetown's future needs. Water supply planning that included reservoir construction was conducted nearly two decades ago, and the continued rapid growth of Georgetown has made it clear that even adding a large impoundment to the system would be insufficient. A new and continuing water supply study funded by both the city and county has concluded that tapping into the Ohio River is the only realistic solution. Because the Ohio River is nearly equidistant to Georgetown from all possible directions, at the present time the best approach appears to be accessing the river via a pipeline from the Louisville water system. Finished water from an outside supplier, however, costs more and would mean higher water bills for Scott County residents. One option under consideration is to purchase raw water at relatively low cost, which can be finished by a local treatment plant. According to Mayor Prather, "all the cities along I-64 should have come together years ago to share a pipeline to the Ohio River." In his opinion, Kentucky American operates in a predatory manner, and has "just about roadblocked that approach. If cities remain isolated, Kentucky American can pick them off one by one." Obtaining water from Louisville is not an ideal solution, Prather says, simply because "We don't want another community to have their hands on our water spigot"; but Georgetown has to deal with financial reality.[23]

Although supplemental water sources are now needed from time to time and will become essential in the future, Royal Spring will undoubtedly continue to play a vital role in the future of Georgetown's water supply.

15

A Dumping Ground Since Time Immemorial

The pioneer explorers who came upon Royal Spring in the late eighteenth century found a locale that immediately invited settlement. With an apparently inexhaustible fount of sparkling water gushing out from beneath limestone ledges, the site possessed not only an intrinsic aesthetic appeal but, more importantly, represented a resource that would provide both water and power for development. The site soon lost much of its native charm, however, becoming a nexus for light industry shortly after settlement as the banks became lined by mills and manufactories and the spring branch was impounded by mill dams. The situation was exacerbated during the latter part of the nineteenth century as the watercourse became the focus of a cluster of utilities that provided water, electricity, gas, and ice to Georgetown. Many Georgetown residents were appalled by the blighted condition of the symbolic heart of the city. For more than a century afterward, both government officials and citizen activists made numerous efforts—largely unsuccessful—to transform this spoiled landscape back to a green space in which the community could take pride and celebrate its origins.

During the post–Civil War period in the United States, cities began to take an ever-increasing interest in the development of infrastructure and provision of services to their citizenry, a trend driven by a new awareness of the relationship between public health and sanitation and fostered by new technological innovations. Although Georgetown was a small, rural community, the sanitary reforms implemented by large cities were also adopted here, if somewhat later. The sanitation problems experienced by America's growing urban regions—garbage disposal, contaminated drinking water, and on-site sewage disposal into streams, cesspools, and privy vaults—were also manifest in Georgetown, if on a smaller scale. The condition of yards and streets during the nineteenth century would be appalling to modern sensibilities, since in common practice,

> nearly all urban households and businesses in American towns and cities discharged their wastes upon the land adjoining their dwellings and shops, principally within the confines of the private lot but also into the streets, especially in areas where little yard space existed. . . . Water spilled from pumps or cisterns muddied the ground, while privy vaults . . . functioned as receptacles for excrement. Kitchen slops and wash-water from a dwelling or shop either drained into these pits or into the street. Yards and, not infrequently alleys and streets became holding areas for rubbish and garbage until removed by workmen (often licensed as scavengers) or consumed by pigs, goats, cows, and other domestic animals.

A dramatic transformation of the urban landscape, both functional and aesthetic, resulted from the provision of city services, such as garbage collection, water-carriage sewerage, and public water systems, which eliminated the need for private space allocated to on-site waste disposal, and "freed much household yard space for new social functions, such as family recreation" and encouraged "small-lot householders to plant flowers, vines, and grass in their backyards in place of the waste and rubbish then customarily dumped there." Sanitary reforms were also linked to the development of "townsite consciousness," defined by urban historian Jon Peterson as "a generally heightened sensitivity to the health implications of a city's site and structure."[1]

One aspect of the increasing townsite consciousness was its influence on the creation of public spaces, or parklands. Nostalgic accounts often give the impression of the town commons beside Royal Spring as an idyllic garden spot; the reality during the late nineteenth century was that the area, at the edge of the community and bordered on the east by a low-income population, was essentially an industrial wasteland used as a dumping ground for refuse of all kinds. The scene was described in 1897 by an indignant citizen: "It would be a most picturesque and beautiful spot, but all that is unsightly in Georgetown seems to have gravitated toward it. Grimy, puffing boiler houses surrounded with heaps of cinders crowd about the virgin pool and draw the sustenance for the noisy giants within them through rusty pipes. The moss-fringed strata of weather-beaten rock overhanging the crystal water are daubed with the loudly colored letters of advertisements. There is something almost sorrowful in the rude disfigurement of the charming spot."[2] Twenty years before, there had been some agitation among the citizenry to develop the site as a city park, with landscaping and amenities for visitors. The sentiment appears to have been prompted by some minor improvements made by city workers during the summer of 1879. In June of that year, the trustees, in one of their occasional sanitary impulses, ordered the Internal Improvement Committee to see that the "Big Spring and branch" were thoroughly cleaned.

Rather more thought than usual seems to have been addressed to this enterprise, since the town surveyor was instructed to "make out specifications" for the work, which was carried out in July and August. As part of the effort, the wall along the eastern bank of the watercourse was raised and put into good repair. Subsequently, the Georgetown weekly paper *Every Saturday* briefly promoted the idea of converting the land into a city park, noting on August 23, 1879, that, despite the recent work, "the people want the flat improved and converted into a park." On September 13, the paper noted, "The Big Spring now presents a genteel appearance. You can take your friends to see it." An editorial in the same issue pointed out the advantages of a park in attracting tourists, providing recreation for young people, and bringing rural residents to town, concluding, "We have one of the most beautiful places in the State. Fence it off this Fall, get out shade trees, gravel the walks, build a band stand, erect a fountain, light it up, and you will have something to be proud of."[3]

Despite the efforts of the newspaper and concerned citizens, the fledgling movement faltered, and conversion of the commons into a park was not undertaken. During the next twenty years, the park question was raised periodically, until, in 1896, it appeared that there might be sufficient support from the mayor and town council to bring about development of the land as a park. In March 1896, the council directed the Improvement Committee to investigate and report on the feasibility and estimated costs of filling and leveling and planting of trees on the commons, "so as to make said vacant grounds desirable & suitable for a City Park." Evidently the committee's report was not in favor, since the park concept disappeared from the council's agenda and was not again raised for many years.[4]

The Georgetown women's Civic League was organized in 1909 under the leadership of Anne Payne Coffman (1872–1963), a progressive community activist. The League, whose membership mainly consisted of local women, first devoted its attention to improving conditions in the city and county school system, ultimately bringing about sanitary and educational reforms. The League also began to sponsor annual cleanup days for the community of Georgetown, and was responsible for arranging placement of garbage receptacles on prominent corners. In 1909, the busy League members chose to promote development of a park at Big Spring as one of its numerous projects for city beautification, and this time the movement was more successful in gaining support from the city council. Anne P. Coffman later recalled, "We didn't have bulldozers then, but Everett Marshall came with his two handsome horses and his equipment and leveled off the ground for us. We called in a landscape gardener to plan the grounds and lay out the paths. We planted shrubs and built a stone wall above the spring. Tables and benches were there for the public enjoyment." It took five years to bring the park into reality, from "a lot . . . used as a dumping ground since time immemorial," but by the summer of 1913 the grading and leveling and landscaping was complete, and the park opened as a pleasant retreat for all visitors. In the spring of 1920, the ladies of the Big Spring chapter of the Daughters of the American Revolution commissioned a granite monument to the memory of John McClelland and the original settlers of the site, which was placed on the ground just above the spring. The marker was inscribed with the names of thirty-six men and one woman, Polly Hawkins Craig, who were present when the station was attacked by Indian warriors led by Chief "Pluggy."[5]

Ann Payne Coffman in 1959, featured in an October 21 announcement by *Georgetown (Ky.) Times* celebrating October 23 as Ann Payne Coffman Day. Coffman led early efforts to establish Royal Spring Park. Courtesy of the Georgetown and Scott County Museum.

The year 1924 would mark the 150th anniversary of the discovery of Royal Spring by John Floyd and the planting of the seed that would become Georgetown. In recognition of this important date, in May 1923 Coffman addressed a meeting of the Scott County Woman's Club (successor to the Civic League), presenting a detailed history of the city and county from the settlement era to the present. She concluded by noting that "Some of us have a vision of a pageant to mark this interesting event, a pageant reproducing some of the stirring events of Georgetown and Scott County, staged on the banks of our beautiful Big Spring. Will you not all pledge yourselves to make this dream come true?" The club and community responded enthusiastically, with numerous civic organizations, including the Woman's Club and the Big Spring DAR, pledging their support. Unsurprisingly, on March 31, 1924, these groups chose Anne Coffman to plan and organize the proposed extravaganza, with a trained pageant director to be hired to oversee the actual staging of the show.[6]

Unfortunately, Coffman's original vision to host the event at Royal Spring could not be realized. Despite recent improvements to the grounds, the clutter of water company buildings greatly restricted the available space, and there were no trees on the commons. Venue notes by the Pageant Grounds Committee stated, "If possible for the pageant grounds choose a flat grassy space about 150 feet long and 50 feet wide with trees at the back and at each side. An outdoor amphitheater is, of course, best of all if it can be had." The committee further emphasized that "the trees are particularly necessary as they form screens for the pageant stage" as well as concealing set activities from the audience. With these criteria as guidance, the pageant planners had no choice but to move the event to the grounds of Georgetown College, which possessed not only the requisite open space and plenty of trees, but also provided changing rooms for actors. On May 14, Neva Summers Burgess of the John B. Rogers Producing Company in Fostoria, Ohio, arrived in Georgetown to direct the event. After her work here was completed, she would move on to Harrodsburg to direct an even larger pageant on June 16 celebrating Kentucky's pioneer history, staged at Graham Springs Park (today Young's Park) on a hill overlooking the former site of Harrod's Fort.[7]

The *Pageant of Scott County History* was presented on May 31 to a crowd estimated at more than fifteen hundred persons, gathered on the

Scene from *Pageant of Scott County History,* 1924, depicting pioneer women at McClelland's Station going to Royal Spring for water. Staged on the grounds of Georgetown College, the fortifications shown were a facade erected temporarily for the play. Courtesy of the Georgetown and Scott County Museum.

sloping lawn just north of Giddings Hall. Those in the central area made themselves comfortable on rugs and cushions on the ground, while to the sides and rear seating was provided by chairs and several sections of bleachers brought over from the Hinton athletic field. Backdrops for the performance included various decorated screens as well as a facade of log construction representing the stockade and blockhouses of McClelland's Station. More than 350 residents of Georgetown and Scott County played characters for the pageant, including nearly a hundred children. Responding to a call from the Big Spring DAR for descendants of early settlers to participate, more than two dozen performers assumed the roles of their ancestors. The producers made every effort to dress the cast in costumes that were historically accurate for the period represented, ordering the clothing from Mary Szwirschina, a Cincinnati costumer. The text of the pageant, except for the historical material, was written by Dr. Frederick W. Eberhardt, pastor of the Georgetown Baptist Church. A well-known author of several books of verse, he also wrote the lyrics for several poetic interludes presented during the pageant. In this task, Eberhardt was aided by Anne Coffman, who drew upon her research to write the historical vignettes. The Georgetown Band of Georgetown College, directed by Fred W. Bauer and supplemented by seven musicians from Lexington, provided music to accompany the performance.[8]

The pageant was presented as a series of eight episodes representing significant moments in Scott County history, from the presettlement era through World War I, some episodes consisting of two or more acts. The overriding theme was described in the prologue: "This is the storied pageant of the noble fountain which for untold centuries has poured its marvelous stream of life giving waters, refreshing, beautifying and making fruitful this favored spot on which our fair city is built." Accordingly, the greater part of the pageant focused on the settlement era. Intended as a patriotic celebration of Scott County's justifiably significant role in regional and national history, from a modern perspective the narrative is flawed by racial bias. Black persons are mentioned only briefly and only in reference to antebellum slavery, and in a manner perpetuating the myth that slavery existed in a mild and benevolent form in Kentucky: "Negro servitude is here shorn of the hardships of the cotton states. Alike for master and servant life is almost idyllic." There were no roles for Black characters in the pageant, even though enslaved Black pioneers had been instrumental in helping to tame the wilderness and nearly 40 percent of the Scott County population during antebellum times were enslaved people, and 20 percent of county residents at the time the pageant was presented were persons of color. The episode highlighting the antebellum period featured only a mock wedding of white elites and their white guests in 1860.[9]

The Civil War was mentioned only in passing—a single sentence—before the pageant moved on to introduce Scott County veterans of the First World War and a rousing finale with high school students from across the county posing as the forty-eight United States. Despite marginalizing a rather large proportion of the county population, the pageant served to remind citizens of their rich cultural and historical heritage and the long-standing importance of Royal Spring to the community.[10]

For many years the Woman's Club maintained a committee to oversee Royal Spring Park. Eventually, however, interest in the park declined, and it was used less and less as a recreational area by the citizens of

Royal Spring as it appeared in 1925. The new DAR monument can be seen at top left, above the spring. Samuel Wilson Collection, University of Kentucky Special Collections Research Center.

Georgetown. The shrubbery was cut down, and the appearance of the park area deteriorated through neglect. When, in 1952, the state highway department informed the community of plans to install a commemorative marker near the spring to inform passing drivers of the historical settlement of Georgetown, the Woman's Club, the Big Spring chapter of the DAR, and the city government cooperated in restoring the park to a presentable condition. At the time, Mayor Joe E. Johnson observed, "I don't know how many times I have passed there without even noticing the neglected condition of the Big Spring area. We won't let that happen again." At Johnson's instigation, the city council approved the installation of asphalt pavement near the head of the spring to allow vehicles to park nearby.[11]

Stimulated by the renewed interest in community history, in that same year the Georgetown chapter of the Jaycees established a committee

Former Georgetown Municipal Water and Sewer distribution warehouse, used to maintain water mains and elevated storage tanks. These structures were demolished in the summer of 1993 and the area repurposed as part of Royal Spring Park. Royal Spring is behind and to the right of the building. Photograph by Ann Bolton Bevins.

charged with building a replica of the McClellan fort on the hillside overlooking the spring. Members Virgil Pryor and Harold Parker successfully scouted the region for old logs to be used in the construction project. This ambitious undertaking was never realized. The Jaycees had counted on the willingness of local garages to haul the logs to the site, which they proved unwilling to do. The fund established for construction was too limited to pay for transportation of the logs, nor for most of the other necessary expenses involved in construction of the fort. Another major impediment was that the land above the spring was owned by Kentucky Utilities, not by the city of Georgetown. The project was regretfully abandoned. Mayor Johnson, whose term in office spanned 1950–1954, later recalled, "building the fort and park at the spring was one of my main objectives, but I just couldn't get it done then."[12]

16

Royal Spring Park

Despite the brief flurry of interest, the embryonic park soon returned to being a neglected and underutilized space in the heart of the city. In 1963, the Georgetown Junior Woman's Club voted to devote its profits to developing a park around the spring, but little concrete achievement came from this declaration. A few years later, in 1970, the "parent" organization, the Georgetown Woman's Club, once again took up the cause. It had been the club, in its former incarnation as the Civic League, that in 1909 had accomplished the initial establishment of a Royal Spring park, and now the club attempted to rally the city government and the citizens of Georgetown to complete the original vision, surrounding "Georgetown's most famous landmark . . . with an area so attractive that it will emphasize its historical significance, and attract local citizens as well as tourists." Soliciting contributions for this goal, the Woman's Club established a special account for the purpose at a local bank, with the stipulation that the funds be returned to the club if the project was not undertaken within three years.[1]

The club could not have picked a better time to make its appeal. At just this time there was a newly heightened appreciation of the nation's historical heritage as America prepared to celebrate its bicentennial in 1976. In anticipation of this landmark occasion, communities across the United States began to look to their historical roots. Patriotic sentiment was particularly robust in Georgetown, whose own birthday nearly coincided with that of the American nation, having been established as McClelland's Station in late autumn 1775 during the opening movements of the Revolution.

Local historian Ann Bolton Bevins took an important first step in the early spring of 1972 by preparing documentation nominating Royal Spring for inclusion in the National Register of Historic Places, a designation that was awarded to the site on April 2, 1973. As the paperwork was moving through the system, in January 1973 Thomas K. Shuff, president of the Scott County Historical Society, presented a plan to the mayor and city council intended to promote local tourism by developing the Royal Spring site as a historical park. The plan was favorably received, and shortly thereafter a joint city-county steering committee presided over by Bevins was named to bring this vision to fruition.[2]

For the first time in nearly a century of sporadic efforts, local government was wholeheartedly in support of the park movement. The committee recommended that professional planners be employed to develop the concept, and so the city and county funded a feasibility study by Scruggs and Hammond, Inc., of Lexington, planning consultants and landscape architects, whose report was released in November 1973. It was an ambitious plan to enhance the tourism potential of the community, one that not only recommended creation of a park around Royal Spring, but also development of the area north of the old stone bridge across West Main Street, connecting the two sections by means of a pedestrian tunnel. As envisioned, the long, narrow corridor between the springhead and the old stone bridge, a five-acre tract, would be converted to green space for passive and active recreation. A key element of the proposal was a reconstruction of the McClelland's Station fort. North of the bridge, a botanical garden would be planted and the old city jail converted to a museum and interpretive center. Reflecting the city's notable early industries, historical buildings would be constructed containing a mill operation, a distilling apparatus, and a ropewalk. The estimated price tag for the project, at nearly $500,000, was formidable. A comprehensive planning study conducted for the city more than a decade later also strongly recommended park development and extension of pedestrian access and green space along the Royal Spring branch north of the Main Street bridge.[3]

By late spring of 1975 an organization known as Big Royal Spring, Inc., a division of the Scott County Historical Society, had been appointed by the county judge and mayor to implement as much as possible of the park proposal. The first step was to request $30,000 from the city government to be applied toward reconstruction of the fort. The organization also applied to the Kentucky Bicentennial Commission for a matching grant. The reconstruction was soon designated as the official bicentennial project for Georgetown and Scott County by the city council, county fiscal court, and Scott County Bicentennial Commission. In mid-November, the Big Spring advocacy group launched a campaign to raise funds to rebuild McClelland's fort on the bluff overlooking the spring and develop a park along the associated stream corridor. By the end of the year more than $10,000 had been raised through private donations.[4]

Curiously, although reconstruction of the pioneer fort had long been the primary focal point of the intended park, after early 1977 reference to this plan all but disappeared from public notices. Work on establishing the Royal Spring park continued to advance, but a replica fort was no longer an active part of the agenda. The reason for this abrupt departure in purpose was the result of a physical obstruction that, while recognized, was simply ignored by the planners on the assumption that it could be dealt with when required. This proved to be an unrealistic expectation. Much of the space on the level ground above the spring is occupied by an electrical substation owned by Kentucky Utilities; only forty feet separates the substation fence from the limestone bluff from which the spring discharges, and there simply is not sufficient room for a replica fort in this area. In addition, the ground above the spring is crisscrossed by power lines serving the station. The only solution would be relocation of the substation, an enormously expensive undertaking, and while the Georgetown manager for Kentucky Utilities during the early 1970s was receptive to the possibility, his successor was not. In consequence, plans for the fort had to be abandoned.[5]

Construction of the replica fort on the ground above the springhead remains an important long-term goal for city planners, and may yet be accomplished in the near future. The current mayor of Georgetown, Tom Prather, believes that "planting seeds" with Kentucky Utilities is the best strategy to hasten the day when the electrical facility above the spring will be relocated to free up the space for the pioneer fort reconstruction. "We need to be pleasantly persistent," he observed

The Kentucky Utilities electrical substation located just above Royal Spring has, to date, thwarted Georgetown's goal of building a reconstruction of McClelland's Station in this location. Photograph by Gary O'Dell.

in 2016, to let the utility company know that there is a larger plan in which they can be a key partner. "There will be a point in time when KU will evaluate the yard and its need to be where it is. Our relationship with the corporation is such that KU should be receptive." Moving the yard would be a complex and expensive undertaking, but not impossible. "They will not rush to undertake such a relocation," Prather observed, "but it could happen."[6]

With the fort reconstruction in abeyance, park boosters in the late 1970s turned their attention to aspects of the plan that could be accomplished. The fort would have provided a highly visible evocation of the community's pioneer heritage, and so in May 1978 when local businessman Julian Feeback offered to donate a log cabin located about three hundred yards from the spring so that he could make better use of the property, project leaders jumped at the opportunity. Originally thought to have been built around 1794 by early Georgetown blacksmith Abram Scott, the eighteen-by-twenty-one-foot structure was transported at city expense in early June and settled onto a foundation of dry-stacked rock in its new location along the spring watercourse about halfway to the old stone bridge. When the logs were stripped in preparation for restoration, the supervising architect discovered that the cabin was not an original structure, but had been erected from reclaimed materials. Further research into the provenance of the cabin determined that it had been built about 1874 by former enslaved person Milton Leach of salvaged chestnut logs and other materials used by early settlers. Still, a log cabin was a log cabin, and upon formal dedication of the cabin on May 26, 1979, fully restored and equipped with displays of pioneer artifacts, the building became a showpiece for the emerging park. A second log cabin, originally built by Jesse Lewis (1768–1829) in 1820 near Christiansburg, Kentucky, was donated to the city in 1994 by Robert and Ginger Chapman of Shelby County and installed near the head of the spring. Unlike the Leach cabin, the interior of the Lewis cabin was not furnished but has instead been used for storage; among suggestions for potential utilization of the cabin has been setting it up to teach hearth cooking classes.[7]

Despite the great potential of the Royal Spring site as a sorely needed green space and as a cultural icon and tourist attraction for the city, two centuries of haphazard development had left the locale cluttered with unattractive utilitarian buildings that gave it an industrial character and nearly hid the spring and its watercourse from view. When Tom Prather first assumed the office of Georgetown's mayor in 1986 after the former mayor unexpectedly resigned for health reasons, rescuing the spring from its wretched circumstances was one of his top priorities. Prather, a city councilman prior to his mayoral appointment, grew up with an appreciation for the development issues facing the city, particularly those concerning water supply. His grandfather, Asa P. Prather, served four terms as mayor of Georgetown, from 1933 to 1949 and from 1953 to 1955, and during his time in office he arranged for the city to purchase the water company from the electric utility. Tom's father, Harold B. Prather, served as chairman of the water and sewer board for thirty-five years. Subsequently reelected to two full terms, during his eight years in office Tom had the time and the political will to accomplish much toward the renovation of Royal Spring as the birthplace of Georgetown.[8]

TOP: The Milton Leach log cabin in its original condition and location. This dwelling was built circa 1874 with materials salvaged from pioneer-era cabins. Photograph by Ann Bolton Bevins. BOTTOM: The Leach cabin after disassembly, transport, and restoration at Royal Spring Park. Photograph by Gary O'Dell.

Elected to a fifth term in 2018, Georgetown mayor Tom Prather has long been a strong supporter for developing Royal Spring Park as a valued city asset. Photograph by Arlene Wilson.

As Prather recalls, this was a time when there was a dawning realization that "water resources were something to be celebrated and embraced as part of community identity," and he was able to draw inspiration from the success of the citizens of Lexington in rescuing from destruction the historic spring that had been the birthplace of Georgetown's larger neighbor. In the spring of 1775, a party of explorers including William McConnell, John McClelland, and a number of other men who had founded the settlement at Royal Spring were in the vicinity of North Elkhorn Creek, in present-day Fayette County, making surveys and improvements for the purpose of land claims. According to tradition, while they were encamped around the "sinking springs" (later, McConnell Springs) they received news of the Battle of Lexington, Massachusetts, the conflict that opened the Revolutionary War, and in celebration of this victory the men decided to appropriate the name for the site. A few years later, when Robert Patterson established a settlement at a different spring about a mile and a half east of the explorer's camp, the name Lexington was chosen for the new community.[9]

Two hundred years later, the spring valley near Lexington was an obscure oasis of bubbling waters and greenery surrounded by sprawling urban and industrial development. James R. Rebmann, a senior city planner, recommended acquisition of the property as a city park, but no action was taken until 1990, when the very existence of the spring was threatened with obliteration by a planned industrial park. The development was halted by enforcement of a city ordinance that prohibited dumping in sinkhole areas, and upon foreclosure on the bankrupted property, the bank donated the land to the city and McConnell Springs Park was born. With financial support from a citizens' group, the Friends of McConnell Springs, the popular site now hosts an educational center, an amphitheater, and two miles of nature trails. Each year, the Friends of McConnell Springs sponsors Founders' Day, an annual celebration of Lexington's "birthday" and pioneer heritage.[10]

With the cooperation of the water company, Prather was able to remove much of the structural clutter that obscured the Royal Spring site, renovating some of the old buildings and tearing down others to open up the view of the spring face and spillway. Since the city depended on the spring for its primary water supply, however, it was not possible to return the spring and its initial watercourse to a "natural" state; the settling basins just downstream from the discharge point would have to remain, and the treatment plant had to be on site. Nevertheless, during his term in office Royal Spring was restored to a condition more appropriate for a city landmark and provided a pleasant, if yet underutilized, amenity for city residents. By the time Prather left office in 1993, he had accomplished much to manage economic development supercharged by establishment of the enormous Toyota manufacturing facility while working to preserve Georgetown's cultural and historic heritage.[11]

Despite improvements intended to improve access and public visibility, many Georgetown residents remained unaware of the existence of Royal Spring. The population boom stimulated by Toyota had brought in a large number of new citizens who knew little of the community's historical heritage, and Royal Spring's relatively obscure location along a side street of the west end formed a disconnect from Main Street that did not encourage public familiarity. At about this time, the early 1990s, Georgetown resident Eve Oakley had some ideas on how to propel Royal Spring Park into public consciousness while enhancing community culture. "Nobody used the park, nobody really knew it was there," Eve recalled, years later. "And we never had any music or anything like that in our community. And we have so many talented people here." With support from the city, Eve inaugurated "Arts in the Park," a series of concerts featuring local musicians held at Royal Spring Park every Sunday evening during the summer months. People brought lawn chairs and picnic dinners, and vendors sold funnel cakes and other treats. The Sunday concerts became a Georgetown tradition and did much to raise awareness of the little park at the spring.[12]

Both the 1973 park feasibility study and the 1987 city comprehensive planning document recommended extension of the Royal Spring Park to the north beyond the old Main Street stone bridge and the development of green space, botanical gardens, cultural areas, and a trail system along the stream corridor and North Water Street. As part of this vision, both plans suggested renovation of the old city jail building, located on the spring branch just north of the old stone bridge, converting it into either a museum and interpretive center or office space. The first step toward accomplishing this goal was realized, not as a result of the park planning effort, but rather as a fortuitous combination of circumstances. Erected in 1892 at a cost of $11,300 on the site of the

"Party in the Park" festival at Royal Spring Park, May 25, 2019. Courtesy of Georgetown-Scott County Parks and Recreation.

previous jail, the county jail complex consisted of the two-story Romanesque Revival-style jail building, very stern in appearance, and the Italianate-style jailer's house fronting on Water Street. The jail received national attention during 1900–1908 as the site where Kentucky's Secretary of State Caleb Powers and Henry Youtsey, a clerk in Powers's office, accused co-conspirators in the January 31, 1900, assassination of Kentucky's Governor William Goebel, were housed during a series of nationally publicized trials. At the time of its construction, the jail was a state-of-the-art facility with electrical lighting and a toilet on each floor, capable of housing a maximum of thirty-six prisoners. By the late twentieth century the building had deteriorated and was obsolete by modern penal standards. After the new Scott County Detention Center was completed in 1991, the last of the prisoners from the old facility were transferred there during the summer, and afterward the old jail building and jailer's residence stood abandoned.[13]

During the mid-1990s, a group of Georgetown citizens became concerned over the future of the historic jail complex. Not wishing to see

The old Scott County jail building, with jailor's house in front. Built in 1892, the jail is being renovated and repurposed as a welcome center. Photograph by Gary O'Dell.

the local landmark demolished by the city or sold as industrial property, the citizens instead organized the nonprofit Scott County Arts Consortium, Inc., in 1997 for the purpose of transforming the jail complex into a facility for community and cultural use and as a welcome center for Georgetown. Phase I of the project was designed to renovate the jailer's house. The newly formed citizens' group worked hard to raise money, holding bake sales, garage sales, and other fundraisers designed to raise public awareness of the project. The organization also sought and obtained grants from the Scott County Fiscal Court, the Kentucky Heritage Council, the Federal Highway Administration's Transportation Enhancement Activities Program, and from Georgetown Renaissance, Inc. The latter organization was established as a nonprofit corporation in 2000 to preserve and protect the historical downtown area of the community.[14]

By summer 2006, the renovated jailer's house was opened to the public as the Scott County Arts and Cultural Welcome Center. The center furnished visitors to Georgetown with maps and information on local businesses and cultural destinations and supported cultural activities for the community by hosting classes and workshops, receptions and meetings, and featuring galleries to showcase local and regional artists' and artisans' work throughout the year. Phases II and III for the proposed arts and cultural complex will, as funding becomes available, rehabilitate the old jail building to provide studios and meeting spaces, while preserving as much of its historic character as possible. Usage of the facility as an arts and cultural center ended in the summer of 2020, when the jailor's house was reallocated to Georgetown/Scott County Tourism to use as a welcome center primarily promoting local businesses. Accomplishment of Phase II of the project, renovation of the old jail structure, will in the future be under the management of the tourism department, an agency that has both funding and permanent staff.[15]

A great deal was accomplished in the three decades since Georgetown's bicentennial and the germination of the new park movement. Royal Spring Park was now a reality, a pleasant retreat for leisure and recreation much as the town founders had envisioned when they first laid out the "Commons" along the spring branch more than two hundred years before. North of the old stone Main Street bridge, rehabilitation of the old jail complex represented the first step in achieving the development of the riparian corridor that had been a consistent goal of the planning process since 1973. Continued investment in the park project, however, required a strong economy in which city resources could be expended on public amenities beyond provision of essential services. The long period of rapid national economic growth and perceived prosperity that began in the early 1990s ended in 2008 when the collapse of the housing industry triggered the worst financial crisis in US history since the Great Depression and led to a worldwide recession. In Georgetown, recently elected mayor Karen Tingle-Sames was confronted with a severely curtailed budget and the necessity to focus city resources on core services at the expense of cultural assets and programs. Plans for enhancement and expansion of Royal Spring Park were stalled, and even basic maintenance needs were neglected. The condition of the grounds began to deteriorate.[16]

In the autumn of 2010, an opportunity presented itself that had the potential to provide a temporary alleviation of the city's financial problems and restore attention to Royal Spring Park. For the first time, the World Equestrian Games were to be held in the United States, and the location selected was the Kentucky Horse Park, situated between Lexington and Georgetown, less than five miles from Royal Spring. The announcement came on December 6, 2005. The Horse Park, established as a state facility in 1978, is a working horse farm and educational theme park dedicated to showcasing the human relationship with the horse. Sprawling over more than twelve hundred acres of prime Bluegrass pastureland, the Horse Park was the only equine venue in America large enough to host all of the events typically associated with the games. The event, which would run from September 25 to October 10, was expected to draw more than 500,000 spectators and participants from all over the world, and state officials estimated that the games would pump more than $100 million into the local economy. Lexington and other Bluegrass communities began to prepare for the games well in advance, wanting to show off the region to its best advantage to the anticipated throngs of equi-tourists.[17]

The Bluegrass region, with some justification, is marketed as "The Horse Capital of the World." There are today approximately a quarter-million horses in Kentucky, approximately one horse for every eighteen human residents, of which more than 50,000 are Thoroughbreds. More than 450 Thoroughbred horse farms are located in only five counties of the Inner Bluegrass, nearly half of which are in Lexington and Fayette County alone. The Horse Park receives more than a million visitors each year, and the National Horse Center, which serves as the national headquarters for numerous equine organizations, is located at the Horse Park. Here, too, can be found the 45,000-square-foot International Museum of the Horse, committed to educating the public about the relationship between humans and horses through exhibits, publications, and programs. The office of the Thoroughbred industry's foremost international publication, *The Blood Horse*, is located in Lexington, and until recently the equally prestigious *Thoroughbred Times*. The Jockey Club, the principal governing body for Thoroughbred breeding and racing, maintains national offices in both New York City and Lexington, and on the campus of the University of Kentucky is the Maxwell H. Gluck Equine Research Center, one of the principals responsible for first successfully sequencing the horse genome in 2007.[18]

Georgetown is located in the core Thoroughbred breeding district and has a long history of association with the industry. Scott County was the site of at least two racetracks during the early nineteenth century, and local breeders such as Keene Richards were instrumental in helping to develop the bloodlines of both modern Thoroughbred and Standardbred horses. In 2017, Scott County was home to more than seven thousand horses and ranked sixth in the nation in sales of equines, with Fayette County in the number one position. In celebration of this heritage, in 1981 the Georgetown Chamber of Commerce inaugurated the "Festival of the Horse," a three-day event that has been held annually to the present day.[19]

Many Kentucky communities hold various types of themed fairs and festivals, featuring everything from pioneer heritage to craft shows to Bluegrass music, and Georgetown merchants wished to distinguish the city in such a way as to draw visitors to a special annual event as well as provide an enjoyable occasion for residents. Initially, during 1980, the Chamber sponsored a "Royal Spring Festival," which proved a disappointment. "Most people couldn't relate to the Big Spring," noted one resident. "If you weren't a native you didn't know that we got our water from the Big Spring." The Chamber recognized that there was a need to find a festival theme with a broader public recognition and appeal. "We decided that no one else had a horse festival," Chamber president John Fitch recalled. "We knew part of the Kentucky Horse Park was in Scott County, and the horse park said it would help with the idea. So we had the horse, something to build a festival upon and something people could relate to for a number of years." The festivals did not make use of Royal Spring Park as a venue, which being just slightly over one acre in size was deemed too small, but instead featured vendors and activities along Main Street and horse exhibitions and games at the larger Brooking Park in the northern part of the city. In 2009, the year before the World Equestrian Games, the Georgetown Festival of the Horse attracted an estimated 33,000 participants and visitors to the community.[20]

Since Georgetown was situated within minutes of the Horse Park, officials and residents of the community fully expected to benefit financially from the forthcoming World Equestrian Games, especially since their equine-themed annual festival could simply be moved a week or two to coincide with the games. The festival, normally held on East

The city of Georgetown has sponsored the popular Festival of the Horse annually for forty years; the Main Street scene above is from the 2020 event. Courtesy of Georgetown/Scott County Tourism.

Main Street, would be extended two blocks to West Main Street and to Water Street, and thus take in the Royal Spring Park. In addition, the city's Tourism Commission organized a new event specifically aimed at World Equestrian Games visitors, the Georgetown Equine Expo, to run during the same period as the games. The Expo would be situated at an outlet mall at the interstate exchange just to the east of the city, and was intended to be an "affordable, family-friendly alternative to the Games" featuring more than sixty national and international equine vendors along with nightly entertainment and special events sheltered in big-top tents erected in the parking lot. The commission allocated nearly $100,000 in preparing for the games, including funding a booth at the Horse Park, where tourism brochures and event information would be distributed to help lure visitors to Georgetown. Anticipating considerable air traffic into the county as visitors and participants arrived for the games, beginning in 2007 more than $8 million in improvements to the Georgetown-Scott County Regional Airport were fast-tracked to completion, using mainly federal funds.[21]

In the city of Georgetown, commission funds were also used to help spruce up the downtown area in anticipation of the flood of visitors, with new signs at entry points, new cast iron benches on Main Street, and displays of US and international flags to welcome visitors from abroad. Musical events were scheduled in the courthouse square. After several years of benign neglect, the park at Royal Spring also received a facelift, the grounds carefully groomed and a thirty-by-sixty-foot permanent roofed pavilion or picnic shelter for events constructed in the center of the park at a cost of about $30,000. During the games, the park and the shelter would be used mainly for children's events, including a petting zoo, pony rides, and "Paint Your Pony" using washable, nontoxic colors. A series of concerts were planned for the pavilion during the games, essentially a continuation of the summertime "Arts in the Park" musical events, but these were cancelled at the last minute, concerts instead to be held at a second bandstand set up on West Main Street near the park. The community now crossed its collective fingers and hoped that the games would, in fact, provide a sorely needed economic transfusion.[22]

The results were mixed, and in many ways disappointing. On the plus side, according to a subsequent analysis of the financial impact of the World Equestrian Games, visitors to the event brought more than $200 million into the Kentucky economy; direct spending alone accounted for $128 million. The greatest share of direct expenditures went to event spending at the Horse Park and to local lodging establishments, including hotels, motels, and campgrounds. Food and beverage businesses and retail shopping accounted for roughly one-fifth of total direct spending. The report also noted that several other local and regional businesses experienced increased revenues in consequence of the games. Direct tourism expenditures in Scott County for the year 2010 amounted to nearly $80 million, an increase of 10 percent over the previous year. During the period of the World Equestrian Games, lodging tax revenues for Scott County witnessed a significant increase, with collections more than double that of the previous October.[23]

The benefits were, however, far less than had been anticipated. There were far fewer visitors to the games than organizers had predicted. Initial estimates were that, given the prominence of Lexington and the Bluegrass region to the global Thoroughbred industry, more than a half-million visitors would converge on the area for the games. As it developed, however, about 420,000 tickets were sold or given out during September and October, but since visitors often bought tickets to multiple events, the actual number of visitors was likely between 150,000 and 200,000. Seventy percent of the visitors were from outside Kentucky, representing all fifty states and sixty-three different countries. The 2011 analysis noted that "The world-wide recession reduced their numbers from the initial expectation. . . . Many more international visitors were expected than were able to attend." John Simpson, director of tourism for Georgetown and Scott County at this time, recalled that the crowds at Georgetown's Festival of the Horse were slightly larger than usual during the games, but not by much. "People tended to stay at the Horse Park to watch events rather than visit local communities," he observed. In these circumstances, both Georgetown's Equine Expo and the similar International Equestrian Festival trade show at the Lexington Center proved to be dismal failures, failing to draw visitors away from the games. In Georgetown, Expo planners had expected four thousand daily visitors but were able on most days to attract less than a tenth of that number, and the nightly Wild West Show was often presented to no more than a couple dozen spectators. Angry vendors at the Expo began to abandon their booths long before the scheduled conclusion. In the opinion of the current director of Georgetown Tourism, the games were over-hyped and really did not have much of an impact on the community.[24]

Despite the brief flurry of interest by city government for sprucing up Royal Spring Park prior to the games, afterward the grounds were allowed to slowly degrade because of the ongoing shortage in funds that could be allocated toward maintenance. The turning point in the welfare of Royal Spring Park came just a few years later, partly because of the strengthening of the national economy and improvement of Georgetown's financial situation, but equally attributable to the 2014 election of Tom Prather to his third full term as mayor of the city. Prather, who narrowly defeated the incumbent, Everette Varney, had earlier proven to be a staunch advocate for the park, and when, early in his term, concerned citizens handed him a list of what they perceived to be the most pressing needs for the park, Prather was more than willing to do as much as the city budget permitted.[25]

View of Royal Spring Park looking north from above the spring. The Water Company facilities can be seen on the hillside to the left. Photograph by Gary O'Dell.

Despite significant progress, Royal Spring Park today still has accessibility issues that hinder realization of its full potential value to the citizens of Georgetown. In 2015, Prather was one of eight mayors chosen to attend the Eastern regional meeting of the Mayors Institute for City Design in Cincinnati, hosted by the University of Cincinnati School of Planning. Established in 1986, the institute is a leadership initiative of the National Endowment for the Arts in partnership with the US Council of Mayors with the goal of preparing mayors to be the chief urban designers of their cities. In a two-day technical assistance workshop, mayors present case studies concerning a design project or planning issue affecting their communities and engage with nationally renowned experts in architecture, landscape architecture, urban planning, transportation planning, and real estate development to find possible solutions. At the workshop, Mayor Prather presented a design project challenge for Royal Spring Park and Water Street. As he recalled, his goal was to "make it a destination, a world-class park."[26]

Prather's design challenge was taken up by a team from the University of Cincinnati's College of Design, Architecture, Art, and Planning, headed by faculty experts Conrad Kickert and Ryan Geismar. The two professors brought a group of twenty-seven talented graduate students to Georgetown in August 2016. Their mission was to study how downtown Georgetown could be revitalized, specifically focusing on connecting the existing Main Street with Royal Spring Park, but their effort would also entail planning for the future development of the entire downtown district. The students were divided into five teams, each of whom was tasked with conducting an analysis of downtown city functions based on specific themes ranging from infrastructure to administrative policies. Each team developed planning goals for downtown Georgetown, resulting in five different visions and directions for development to be presented to community decision makers. The student teams then each selected a quadrant of downtown to further focus on implementation of their vision into a site design; one of these teams was concerned primarily with Water Street and Royal Spring Park.[27]

The students also met with citizen groups to determine what the community perceived as planning needs. During one such meeting, a resident noted the difficulty involved in pedestrian access to Royal Spring Park: "Part of the problem is the streets downtown are so wide, it's not so easy to get across them. When walking west downtown, people often stop at Broadway because it is a particularly difficult intersection to cross with all of the traffic." By this the citizen meant that the lack of safe crossing points hindered pedestrian access to the park, reducing potential visitors. In their final project report, the students noted that Georgetown (like so many American cities) "prioritizes the car over the pedestrian . . . the walkable core of Georgetown is surrounded by moving and parked cars—cutting it off from surrounding neighborhoods and stifling further growth." Royal Spring Park, the report observed, was highly underutilized, being poorly integrated with the rest of the city. The disjointed nature of the streetscape had the effect of "discouraging walking outside the Main St. corridor, as it is not evident to the pedestrian (and potential shopper) anything exists beyond this." Recommendations to solve these problems revolved around creating new connections between downtown and its surroundings, thus encouraging more pedestrian traffic and less vehicular traffic and providing better access to Royal Spring Park.[28]

The Georgetown/Scott County 2017 Comprehensive Plan incorporated several of the recommendations for revitalizing downtown Georgetown provided in the University of Cincinnati Planning School report. The Comprehensive Plan included significant input from the community obtained through town meetings and focus groups. For Royal Spring Park, improved public accessibility would be addressed by establishing crosswalks at Main and Water streets and by plans to possibly extend the Legacy Trail to include the park. The first nine-mile segment of the Legacy Trail, a bicycle path twelve feet wide connecting Lexington to the Kentucky Horse Park, moving from the urban landscape to the rolling plains of the rural Bluegrass, began construction in 2009 and was completed a few weeks in advance of the World Equestrian Games. By late 2016, the trail had been run an additional 1.9 miles to reach Scott County, although funding was not available to extend it into the city. In the Comprehensive Plan, the trail could follow either of two possible routes to end at the Cardome Renaissance Center, a showcase for fine arts located along the North Fork of Elkhorn Creek opposite the point where the spring branch merges with the larger stream. One possible route would take the new section north to Elkhorn and then west to Cardome. A less expensive alternate would take the trail through Georgetown College, downtown Georgetown, and Royal Spring Park before heading north to Cardome. This alternate would utilize existing streets and pavement, using ride widenings and off-road sections where feasible, providing connections through highly used public areas.[29]

There can be no doubt that Royal Spring is a unique and important asset for the city of Georgetown, one whose value to the citizens has been enhanced in recent years by physical improvements, better maintenance, and increased public awareness of its cultural and historical significance. Even so, the site remains largely unknown outside Georgetown and Scott County, save to a handful of historians and karst hydrogeologists, and although providing intangible benefits as an amenity, it contributes little to the economy of the city. If suitably developed and publicized, Royal Spring Park has the potential to generate substantial economic benefits for Georgetown by tapping into an increasing public appetite for cultural heritage tourism.

The National Trust for Historic Preservation defines cultural heritage tourism as "traveling to experience the places, artifacts and activities that authentically represent the stories and people of the past and present. It includes visitation to cultural, historic, and natural resources." The Commonwealth of Kentucky hosts numerous historic sites and, in fact, ranks fourth in the nation in the number of listings on the National Register of Historic Places. Tourism is the state's third largest industry and second largest employer; visitor spending topped $10 billion for the first time in 2006. According to a recent national study, more than three-fourths of all leisure travelers (129.6 million) can be defined as cultural/heritage travelers, having participated in cultural/heritage activities on their most recent trip or within the past three years.[30]

There are two popular heritage attractions in Kentucky, at Harrodsburg and Boonesborough, that share a similar historical context with Georgetown's Royal Spring Park. Like McClelland's Station, the fortified settlement that gave rise to Georgetown, Harrod's Fort and Fort Boonesborough were the first trans-Appalachian settlements. Both are today state parks supported by government funding, and both contain replicas of the pioneer forts that were originally built to protect the inhabitants. The Harrodsburg site was initially established as the Pioneer Memorial State Park in 1927 and is today known as Old Fort Harrod State Park. In 1934, the bicentennial of the birth of Daniel Boone, Congress enacted legislation intended to acquire four sites associated with Boone: Boonesborough, Boone's Station, Bryant's Station, and the Blue Licks Battlefield, which had become a state park in 1927. Once acquired, a national highway would connect the Boone-related properties, which would become part of the National Parks System. Only the Boonesborough site could be acquired, and so, with Blue Licks, became part of the Kentucky State Parks system.[31]

The circumstances of Old Fort Harrod in Harrodsburg are a closer analog to those of the McClelland's Station site in Georgetown than is Boonesborough. The Boonesborough settlement never thrived and was soon abandoned, so that today the replica fort and visitor infrastructure stand alone on the banks of the Kentucky River, lacking an associated community. Old Fort Harrod, however, is embedded in the downtown heart of Harrodsburg much like the Royal Spring property, although more prominently and with better integration into the city's pedestrian network. The centerpiece of this park is a nearly full-scale replica of the fort built by James Harrod in 1774, in which cabins and blockhouses are furnished with hand-made furniture, implements, and tools used by the pioneer settlers. The state park enjoys several significant advantages over Royal Spring Park. As part of the Kentucky State Parks system, Old Fort Harrod receives financial support from the state, has a full-time park manager, and through long-standing publicity, including a dedicated website, has broad name recognition that encourages both in-state and out-of-state tourism. The fifteen-acre grounds of Old Fort Harrod are considerably larger than the 1.35 acres comprising Royal Spring Park and can thus support more diverse and larger-scale recreational activities.[32]

According to park manager David L. Coleman, the central location of Old Fort Harrod within the community allows the property to function as a city park as well as a historic attraction. "People can walk their dogs and enjoy the shade trees, gather with their families in the picnic shelter. They can attend some of our great fairs and festivals, attend an outdoor drama or listen to live music, much of which is free to the public." The state park provides significant economic benefits for Harrodsburg. "School groups by the thousands visit us here at OFH and many of these take their students to the local restaurants for lunch," Coleman notes. "Some of our events have people staying in our local hotels for two or three nights at a time. One festival alone contributes thousands into our local tourism board through the restaurant tax on food trucks. And then there are the thousands of history buffs that come to Harrodsburg annually to tour Old Fort Harrod State Park. Most of these will spend money in this town while here." According to Coleman, the park receives about 150,000 visitors each year, of whom an estimated 16,000 to 20,000 pay for admission into the replica fort. The price of admission ranges from $3 for school groups to $7 for adults; using $5 as an average, fort admission thus generates revenues for the state of approximately $100,000 annually.[33]

Royal Spring Park, as the site of McClelland's Station, is clearly of equal historical importance with Old Fort Harrod, and while it lacks some of the advantages of the state park, it does possess one outstanding feature not present at Harrodsburg: a large and attractive spring. The site of Harrod's Fort was selected for the presence of a large spring that is the origin for Town Creek, intended as a water supply for the settlement, but the fort was built six-tenths of a mile distant to provide a refuge for the inhabitants, and within its walls was only a small, unimpressive spring sunk into the hillside. Royal Spring is the largest spring in the Inner Bluegrass and, like McConnell Springs city park in Lexington, could provide an attraction to draw visitors from outside the community for its aesthetic qualities, historical connections, and potential for environmental education. If Royal Spring Park were to be developed as a historical heritage site featuring a replica of the McClelland's Station fort, it would also be far more accessible to tourists than any of the other pioneer fort attractions in Kentucky. Georgetown is much closer to the three primary metropolitan areas of the region—Lexington, Louisville, and Cincinnati—than any of the others, and is far better connected to the interstate highway system. Royal Spring Park is literally minutes away from interchanges on both I-75 and I-64, whereas the other pioneer forts are relatively distant from the interstate system and can be reached only after longer drives.[34]

While Royal Spring Park in its present form provides an attractive amenity for Georgetown residents, it has failed to generate any significant tourism despite an obvious potential to do so. The key to realization of this potential would appear to be providing the necessary magnet by constructing a replica of the McClelland's Station pioneer fort on the ground above the spring. As the settlement and fortification was smaller than that at Harrod's Fort, less ground would be required for laying out the replica. At present, ownership of the property above the spring by Kentucky Utilities is blocking achievement of this goal. One solution might be if the city could acquire all of the KU property between Royal Spring Avenue and Water Street, which would add an acre of ground to the park and provide more than enough space to construct the replica as well as ample parking for visitors. If construction costs are a consideration or if more space is needed on the periphery for other structures or functions, the replica could be scaled down and moved closer to the spring. This was the case when the state built the replica of Harrod's Fort; the original pioneer construction measured 264 feet square, but the reproduction was downsized to 200 feet square. Ideally, the present water treatment plant facility and settling basins at the spring should be relocated downstream to provide a more natural and aesthetically pleasing appearance, capable of evoking the pioneer era for visitors. Such a move, however, would be prohibitively expensive and is unlikely to be achieved in the foreseeable future.

A replica of Logan's Fort at Stanford, undergoing final stages of construction at this time, is the most recent addition to Kentucky's family of pioneer fort reconstructions. The project was conceived and largely driven by the efforts of Lincoln County resident Lynda W. Closson. Based on detailed research, as of this writing five of the original seven cabins and one of the three blockhouses have been built and partially stockaded. During 1997, a major archaeological investigation of the site was conducted by Kim and Stephen McBride of the Kentucky Archaeological Survey, which recovered numerous artifacts presumed to be associated with Logan's Fort as well as several backfilled pits or cellars containing artifacts of the period. The most astonishing discovery was made during excavation of a trench when human remains were uncovered, which proved to be those of a young man who, from cut marks on the skull, had been scalped. These have been identified as being most likely those of William Hudson, who was killed during an attack on the fort in June 1777 and buried within the stockade. This provides an interesting parallel to the situation at McClelland's, where the founder was killed during an attack and buried outside the fort. Should the city of Georgetown carry out its goal of reconstructing McClelland's fort, the experience gained by principals involved in bringing the replica to fruition at Stanford would be invaluable to planners.[35]

A better approach to establishing Royal Spring Park as a heritage site with a fort might be acquisition by the Commonwealth of Kentucky of the current property, the land belonging to Kentucky Utilities, and possibly several adjacent parcels to create a new Kentucky state park. As part of the state park system, this would allow Royal Spring a full-time manager, provide funding for a replica fort and visitor center, remove maintenance and operating costs from the city, and greatly enhance the tourism potential for this historic site. This would be of considerable economic benefit to Georgetown. The major obstacle to realizing this objective is the current state of the economy. As a consequence of the Great Recession of 2008, the Commonwealth of Kentucky was forced to make deep cuts to its operating budget, including funds formerly allocated to the Department of Parks. Basic maintenance and repairs to buildings in the park system were neglected for years, and facilities deteriorated, spawning numerous complaints from visitors. By 2016, the park system was facing a deficit of more than $240 million in deferred maintenance needs. Although state

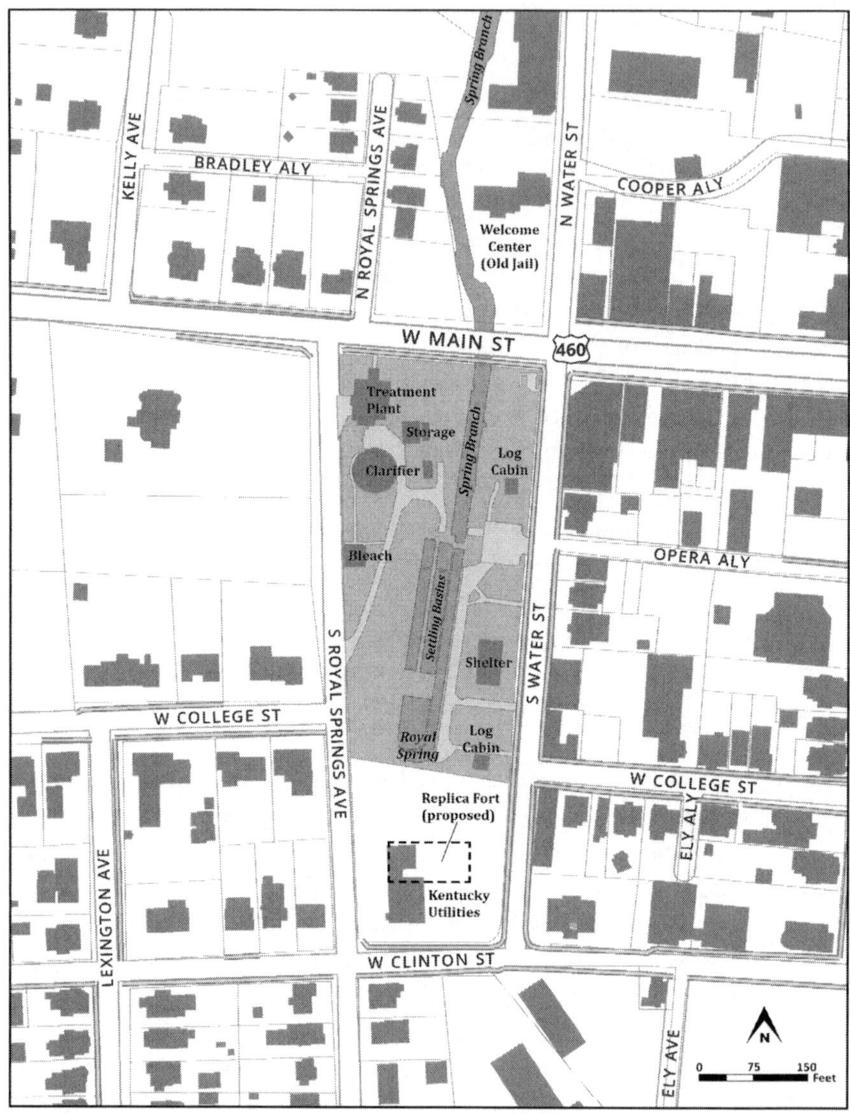

Royal Spring Park and its neighborhood, showing parcel boundaries. The lower part of the map depicts the McClelland Station fort in its historic location, where a replica might be built if the city is able to acquire the Kentucky Utilities property. Base map by Georgetown-Scott County Planning Commission, adapted by Gary O'Dell.

officials hope to make necessary repairs and improvements in order to showcase the state park system for its centennial anniversary in 2024, the onset of the COVID-19 pandemic has only served to exacerbate Kentucky's financial difficulties.[36]

Funding issues spurred Kentucky governors Steven Beshear (2007–2015) and Matt Bevin (2016–2019) to divest the state of a number of existing parks and to consider privatizing certain operations, such as hotels and golf courses. In 2009, the Department of Parks managed fifty-three state-owned properties; by 2021 this had been reduced to forty-nine by elimination of six parks from the system and the addition of two trail-based parks for hiking, biking, and horseback riding. Historic sites were particular targets, constituting four of the six eliminated parks. In 2012, the state transferred Constitution Square in Danville, the site of numerous constitutional conventions that led to Kentucky's statehood in 1792, to Boyle County. Boone's Station in Fayette County, home of Daniel Boone from 1779–1782, was given away in late 2018 to David's Fork Baptist Church, and the William Whitley house in Lincoln County, home to a noted Kentucky pioneer, was transferred to the Lincoln County Fiscal Court a few months later. Most recently, White Hall in Madison County, built in 1799 and former home to noted abolitionist Cassius Marcellus Clay, was turned over to Eastern Kentucky University in February 2019. Incorporating Royal Spring in the state park system may well be the best strategy, but such a goal does not appear capable of realization until the present economic circumstances and political climate are more favorable.[37]

Although expanding urban development now surrounds the spring, the park remains a tranquil oasis amid the hustle and bustle of a vibrant small city. The visitor can, with but little effort, still imagine the scene in April 1776 when two men stood in a clearing on the hill above the magnificent spring, behind them a handful of rough cabins. John Floyd had returned to his spring in anger, determined to drive the McClelland squatters off his land, but instead offered them the land at a fair price. Thus was the seed that became Georgetown planted, as an impulsive gesture by a man moved to a moment of compassion, a seed that was nurtured to fruition by Elijah Craig, a man of faith and industry.

In the fall of 2010, Georgetown booster Eve Oakley and city council member Don Hawkins attempted to secure funding to commission a bronze statue of Elijah Craig, to be positioned at the park entrance to greet visitors. More than a decade before, in 1997, local artisan Sandy Schu set out to sculpt a wooden statue of Craig from a sycamore log using a chainsaw, and turned to Eve for advice on how to portray the community founder. No likenesses of Craig were known to exist, so Eve and Sandy were free to exercise their imaginations. When completed, the seven-foot carving depicted the Baptist minister with a Bible tucked beneath his left arm and a whiskey barrel next to his right foot, thus commemorating two of his notable (if, in the latter case, alleged) achievements. Unfortunately, this was a period when maintenance at the park was minimal, and the wooden statute deteriorated so rapidly that, within a decade, it had completely rotted away. For the proposed bronze, Oakley and Hawkins envisioned a representation similar to the work created by Schu, and began to seek out contributions while discussing cost estimates with an artisan. Unfortunately the project never materialized, and so, today, the park commemorates the legacy of Elijah Craig only with a small plaque set in the ground at the entrance.[38]

However, the spirit of Craig lives on in the legend that surrounds his apocryphal role as the creator of the first bourbon whiskey, and this fame has made his name a valuable trademark. The Elijah Craig brand was first registered in 1960 by Commonwealth Distillers of Louisville, and was acquired by Heaven Hill Distillery of Bardstown in 1976, but it was not used until the company released a premium small-batch straight bourbon under that trademark in 1986. Elijah Craig bourbon, distilled in Louisville, has won numerous awards for excellence, and some have credited this particular brand as having helped spur a revival of consumer interest in whiskey, after decades of decline. In marketing the brand, Heaven Hill has not hesitated to proclaim Craig as the "father of bourbon," assuring consumers that their distillery "preserves the Bourbon making traditions developed by Elijah Craig. Each bottle of our bourbon is crafted with the same method used by Elijah over two hundred years ago."[39]

In Georgetown, a local entrepreneur was also inspired by the Elijah Craig legend to found a small business that began operation in 2015 in an old building located on Water Street directly across from Royal Spring. Earlier that year, David Adams relocated to Georgetown and began renovating the former A-1 auto parts store at 130 Water Street, outfitting it as a small craft distillery he called Royal Spring Branch Distillery. The impulse to open a distillery here came to Adams after reading the plaque in Royal Spring Park claiming bourbon as the invention of Elijah Craig. "The history of this street is why I wanted to open here," Adams observed. "I'm bringing [bourbon] back to its birthplace. Now that's a disputed birthplace, we know that. But we'll claim it." Although operating a distillery had long been a dream for Adams, who planned to produce brandy and moonshine (unaged whiskey) for immediate sale while his first batches of bourbon were properly aged, the financial realities in this very competitive industry proved to be overwhelming.[40]

Without ever having been able to initiate production of a house brand bourbon, in early 2017 Adams sold his operation to Jeff Mattingly, another distiller for whom he had been blending. Mattingly comes from a family with a long tradition of distilling, dating back more than 175 years, and has kinship ties with the Samuels family, the producers of Maker's Mark bourbon. He renamed the Water Street facility as Bourbon 30, commemorating a code phrase he and his brother had used as children when planning a secret raid on their father's bourbon supply, and also applied this term to his house bourbon. Primarily a blender rather than a distiller, Mattingly brings in select barrels of first-class bourbon from other distillers and carefully blends them to the taste of specific customers in batches ranging from a few bottles to several hundred bottles, all under the label J. Mattingly Bourbon. "Every bottle is crafted to be unique," Mattingly observes, and customers are able to select a bottle and label style and color that appeals to them. The company distills just enough of its own bourbon to satisfy the legal requirements to be registered as a distiller, and for this purpose Mattingly personally dips water out of Royal Spring and brings it across the street to use in production.[41]

Elijah Craig is best known to the world at large as the purported inventor of bourbon whiskey, a claim that Georgetown residents are happy to embrace. The true and enduring legacy of this Baptist minister and entrepreneur derives not from whiskey folklore, however, but from the city he founded on the ruins of McClelland's Station. Elijah Craig's astute judgement in selecting a town site that not only was set in some of the most fertile ground in Kentucky and lay astride a major buffalo trail, but possessed a magnificent and copious spring like no other in the

Two outstanding bourbons with a connection to Royal Spring. The Elijah Craig is distilled and bottled at Heaven Hill Distillery in Louisville, assuming the mantle of the legendary creator of bourbon. The J. Mattingly shown is one of many specialty bourbons blended at the Bourbon 30 operation across the street from Royal Spring, each small batch blended to satisfy a specific customer. Photograph by Gary O'Dell.

region, ensured that Georgetown would develop into one of the more significant communities of the Bluegrass. The ample flow from Royal Spring not only promoted light industry at an early date, but ensured an ample water supply for generations.

In August 1868, Lyman C. Draper, an inveterate romantic and a man driven to document the pioneer history of the West, visited Georgetown and stood on the town commons, marveling at the great fount of water gushing from the bedrock. He added a lengthy description of the spring to his collection of notes, observing "This is probably the noblest spring in Kentucky—the 'Royal Spring' indeed."[42]

Acknowledgments

I owe a great deal of appreciation to many fine citizens of Georgetown and Scott County, as well as others, whose contributions helped to bring this project to fruition. I cannot begin to express the debt that I owe to Ann Bolton Bevins, eminent Scott County historian, for her constant support and encouragement through the entire span of research and writing. Ann freely shared her encyclopedic knowledge of Scott County history, provided many significant documents, and read successive drafts of the manuscript, offering many valuable comments and suggestions. Frederick Johnston, coauthor with Bevins of *History of Scott County*, also read the manuscript and offered very useful suggestions. Discussions with Georgetown mayor Tom Prather, who has served multiple terms in office and has an abiding interest in the welfare of Royal Spring, provided considerable information about the water supply situation of the community and the efforts made to protect and preserve the spring.

Janis Atlee, a volunteer supporting the preservation of cultural heritage, provided valuable information about the restoration of the old city jail and insights on many topics related to Royal Spring and efforts being made for cultural enhancement in Georgetown. Eve Oakley, who provided occasional columns for the *Georgetown News-Graphic* and who had long been a staunch advocate for Royal Spring Park, shared her recollections in delightful conversations. I am also grateful to Lori Saunders, the current executive director of the Georgetown/Scott County

Tourism Commission, and John Simpson, the former director, for their observations on the significance of Georgetown's Festival of the Horse, particularly with respect to the World Equine Games held at the Kentucky Horse Park in 2010. Ms. Saunders has also been very helpful in other respects, as well, and provided pictures and video of activities at the park. James Long (director, recently retired) and Adam Terry of Georgetown Municipal Water and Sewer provided information about the history of the utility and helped to locate some historic photographs. Kimberly Rice, director of Parks and Recreation, was always ready to answer my questions about Royal Spring Park. Ruthie Stevens, director of the Georgetown and Scott County Museum, provided invaluable assistance in locating historic photographs and other materials. The excellent rendition of McClelland's Station was created by the very talented Anna Thornton, a Georgetown native and high school senior.

Many other residents of Georgetown and Scott County also provided useful information and insights, including Jane Offutt and Don Hawkins, former city council members; Ron Vance, volunteer curator at the Georgetown and Scott County Museum, Arlene Wilson of the mayor's office, Whitley Keltner, GIS analyst at the city/county planning commission, Maribeth Hambrick, Barbara Strippelhoff, Stephen Hockensmith, and Jeff Mattingly. I have spoken with so many wonderful people in Georgetown, in person, by phone, or via email, that I am certain that I have forgotten several who should be on this list!

Karst hydrogeologists James C. Currens, recently retired from the Kentucky Geological Survey, and Randy Paylor, also formerly with the KGS and now employed by the US Geological Survey in Nevada, freely shared their insights on Bluegrass karst and the drainage of the Royal Spring karst system. Rob Blair of the Kentucky Division of Water kindly supplied information on public water systems in the state that utilize groundwater sources. David Coleman, the manager at Fort Harrod State Park, provided information on the economic impact of heritage tourism for Harrodsburg. I have enjoyed reminiscing with my old friend Larry Spangler (and picking his brain for information). Many years ago he first showed Royal Spring to me and allowed me to assist him with his dye-tracing project to determine its underground pathways. Likewise, I have greatly enjoyed corresponding with another old friend, Nancy O'Malley, Kentucky archaeologist and expert on pioneer fortifications, concerning the probable appearance and characteristics of McClelland's Station. Bluegrass ecologist Julian Campbell provided me with a wealth of information and fascinating discussions on the presettlement vegetation of the region and, more specifically, of the area around Georgetown. He was kind enough to lead me on a little field trip to Cane Run to check on the welfare of wild cane he had reestablished along the stream. Another pleasant field trip was conducted for me by Scott County arborist David Leonard, who took me to view ancient trees in the Kentucky Horse Park.

Last but not least, I am always very grateful to my wife, Carol S. O'Dell, for her constant support, encouragement, and constructive criticism for all my projects, and who sensibly keeps me grounded in the present despite my tendency to dwell excessively in past centuries.

Notes

Preface

1. "Geo. W. Ranck Run Down and Killed by a Louisville & Nashville Passenger Train in the Lexington Yards," *Lexington Leader*, August 2, 1901; *G. W. Ranck's Extrx. v. L. & N. Ry. Co.*, Fayette County Circuit Court, Wilson Collection, University of Kentucky, 51W11.

2. Carolyn M. Wooley, *The Founding of Lexington 1775–1776* (Lexington, Ky.: Lexington-Fayette County Historic Commission, 1975). For an account of the establishment of McConnell Springs Park, see Gary A. O'Dell and James R. Rebmann, "The Rescue of McConnell Springs Historic Site: A Partnership Between Local Government and the Citizens of Lexington, Kentucky," *Proceedings of the 1995 National Cave Management Symposium*, G. Thomas Rea, ed., 255–66 (Indianapolis: Indiana Karst Conservancy, 1996).

3. Mary C. Kennedy and Patty Jo Watson, "The Chronology of Early Agriculture and Intensive Mineral Mining in the Salts Cave and Mammoth Cave Region, Mammoth Cave National Park," *Journal of Cave and Karst Studies* 59 (April 1997): 5.

4. Aristotle, *Politics*, book 7, section 1330b; James R. Smith, *Springs and Wells in Greek and Roman Literature: Their Legends and Locations* (New York: G. P. Putnam's Sons, 1922).

5. Tench Coxe, *A Statement of the Arts and Manufactures of the United States for the Year 1810*, part 3, *Tabular Statements of the Several Branches of American Manufactures* (Philadelphia: A. Cornman, Jr., 1814), 22. The quotation is from an advertisement in the collection of William M. Ambrose of Lexington; the identity of the periodical in which it appeared is unknown. The claim that

Wilson Spring (today known as McConnell's Spring) is the largest in Kentucky is a typical exaggeration.

6. Lawrence E. Spangler, "Karst Hydrogeology of Northern Fayette and Southern Scott Counties, Kentucky" (Master's thesis, University of Kentucky, 1982).

1. From Wilderness to City

1. Michael J. O'Brien, "The Roots of Frontier Expansion," in *Grassland, Forest, and Historical Settlement: An Analysis of Dynamics in Northeast Missouri*, ed. Michael J. O'Brien, Studies in North American Archaeology (Lincoln: Univ. of Nebraska Press, 1984), 59; Wilma A. Dunaway, *The First American Frontier: Transition to Capitalism in Southern Appalachia, 1700–1860*, Fred W. Morrison Series in Southern Studies (Chapel Hill: Univ. of North Carolina Press, 1996), 53–54; Daniel B. Smith, "'This Idea in Heaven': Image and Reality on the Kentucky Frontier," in *The Buzzel About Kentuck: Settling the Promised Land*, ed. Craig T. Friend (Lexington: Univ. Press of Kentucky, 1999), 77–79.

2. A. Gwynn Henderson and David Pollack, "Kentucky," in *Native America: A State-by-State Historical Encyclopedia*, vol. 1, *Alabama-Louisiana*, ed. Daniel S. Murphree (Santa Barbara, Calif.: Greenwood, 2012), 393–440; A. Gwynn Henderson, "Dispelling the Myth: Seventeenth- and Eighteenth-Century Indian Life in Kentucky," *Register of the Kentucky Historical Society* 90 (Bicentennial Issue, "The Kentucky Image," 1992): 1–25.

3. Henderson and Pollack, "Kentucky," 410–11; 414–15; Nancy O'Malley, "Frontier Defenses and Pioneer Strategies in the Historic Settlement Era," in *The Buzzel About Kentuck*, ed. Craig T. Friend (Lexington: Univ. Press of Kentucky, 1999), 62–63.

4. Clay Lancaster, "Planning the First Two Towns in Central Kentucky: Harrodsburg and Lexington," *The Kentucky Review* 9 (Autumn 1989): 3–28; Robert B. McAfee "The Life and Times of Robert B. McAfee and His Family and Connections," *Register of the Kentucky State Historical Society* 25 (January 1927): 23–24; Otis K. Rice, *Frontier Kentucky* (Lexington: Univ. Press of Kentucky, 1993), 61–62.

5. Nancy O'Malley, *Searching for Boonesborough*, Archaeological Report 193 (Lexington: University of Kentucky Program for Cultural Resource Assessment, 1990), 15–20; Charles G. Talbert, *Benjamin Logan, Kentucky Frontiersman* (Lexington: Univ. Press of Kentucky, 1962), 16–32.

6. Nancy O'Malley, *Stockading Up: A Study of Pioneer Stations in the Inner Bluegrass Region of Kentucky*, Archaeological Report 127, revised (Frankfort: Kentucky Heritage Council, 1994), 23–24; O'Malley, "Frontier Defenses," 64.

7. O'Malley, *Stockading Up*, 29, 36; O'Malley, "Frontier Defenses," 61.

8. O'Malley, *Stockading Up*, 28–29, 34, 161–66, 241–44, 292–94.

9. Ibid., 31, 292; Richard H. Collins, *History of Kentucky*, vol. 2 (Covington, Ky: Collins, 1878), 178; Colonel John Bowman to General Edward Hand, December 12, 1777, in *Frontier Defense on the Upper Ohio, 1777–1778*, ed. Reuben G. Thwaites and Louise P. Kellogg, (Madison: Wisconsin Historical Society, 1912), 181–83; Robert S. Cotterill, *History of Pioneer Kentucky* (Cincinnati: Johnson and Hardin, 1917), 111–16.

10. Henderson and Pollack, "Kentucky," 411, 416; *Encyclopedia of the North American Indian Wars*, vol. 1, *A–L*, ed. Spencer C. Tucker (Santa Barbara, Calif.: ABC-CLIO, 2011), 80, 269–71, 348–49; James C. Klotter and Craig T. Friend, *A New History of Kentucky*, 2nd ed. (Lexington: Univ. Press of Kentucky, 2018), 34–42, 79–80.

11. John C. Hudson, "A Location Theory for Rural Settlement," *Annals of the Association of American Geographers* 59 (June 1969), 365–81; Robert E. Warren and Michael J. O'Brien, "A Model of Frontier Settlement," in *Grassland, Forest and Historical Settlement: An Analysis of Dynamics in Northeast Missouri*, ed. Michael J. O'Brien (Lincoln: Univ. of Nebraska Press, 1984), 24–44; Michael J. O'Brien, "The Roots of Frontier Expansion," in O'Brien, ed., in *Grassland, Forest and Historical Settlement*, 58–94.

12. O'Malley, *Stockading Up*, 31–33, 310–12; O'Malley, "Frontier Defenses," 58–59, 66.

13. O'Malley, *Stockading Up*, 31–35, 312; O'Malley, "Frontier Defenses," 71–72.

14. US Decennial Census, 1800; Lewis W. McKee and Lydia K. Bond, *A History of Anderson County, 1780–1936* (Baltimore: Regional Publishing, 1975), 25–26, 33–34.

15. US Decennial Census, 1800–2000. Population data for many cities is not available for 1820, 1850, and 1890.

16. Jessica K. Graybill, Maureen Hays-Mitchell, and Donald J. Zeigler, "World Urban Development," in *Cities of the World: Regional Patterns and Urban Environments*, 7th ed., ed. Stanley D. Brunn, Donald J. Zeigler, Maureen Hays-Mitchell, and Jessica K. Graybill (Lanham, Md.: Rowman and Littlefield, 2020), 17–18, 42.

17. Joseph A. DiPietro, *Landscape Evolution of the United States: An Introduction to the Geography, Geology, and Natural History* (Amsterdam: Elsevier, 2014), 205–6. H. Roy Merrens, however, notes that the location of a number of so-called Fall Line cities, such as Philadelphia or Washington, D.C., is the result of other considerations rather than the Fall Line; see H. Roy Merrens, "Historical Geography and Early American History," *William and Mary Quarterly* 22 (October 1965): 533–38.

18. United Nations Human Settlement Programme, *State of the World's Cities, 2008–2009: Harmonious Cities* (London: Earthscan, 2008), 4–5; Griffith Taylor, *Urban Geography: A Study of Site, Evolution, Pattern and Classification in Villages, Towns and Cities* (1946; reprint, London: Routledge, 2007), 11–14; D. S. Mull, Robert J. Faust, and Gary R. Martin, *Water Availability and Vulnerability to Contamination in Northwestern Hardin County, Kentucky*, Water-Resources Investigations Report 90-4133 (Louisville: US Geological Survey, 1990).

19. Gary A. O'Dell, "Water Supply and the Early Development of Lexington, Kentucky," *Filson Club History Quarterly* 67 (October 1993): 451–54; Frances L. S. Dugan, *Rainfall Harvest: Gilbert Hinds King and the Lexington Hydraulic and Manufacturing Company* (Lexington: Self-published, 1953), 11–13, 22 (first quotation, 12–13); "Water Works," *Daily Transcript* (Lexington), July 15, 1879 (second quotation).

20. James C. Currens, "Karst: Shaped by Water from the Inside Out," in *Water in Kentucky: Natural History, Communities, and Conservation*, ed. Brian D. Lee, Daniel I. Carey, and Alice L. Jones (Lexington: Univ. Press of Kentucky, 2017), 116.

21. S. Pedley, M. Yates, J. F. Schijven, J. West, G. Howard, and M. Barrett, "Pathogens: Health Relevance, Transport, and Attenuation," in *Protecting Groundwater for Health: Managing the Quality of Drinking-Water Sources*, ed. Oliver Schmoll, Guy Howard, John Chilton, and Ingrid Chorus (London: World Health Organization, 2006), 61–76.

22. Fikret Kačaroğlu, "Review of Groundwater Pollution and Protection in Karst Areas," *Water, Air and Soil Pollution* 113 (July 1999): 338, 342–45.

23. Martin V. Melosi, *The Sanitary City: Urban Infrastructure in America from Colonial Times to the Present* (Baltimore: Johns Hopkins Univ. Press, 2000), 90–93, 151–53.

24. Joel A. Tarr, *The Search for the Ultimate Sink: Urban Pollution in Historical Perspective* (Akron, Ohio: Univ. of Akron Press, 1996), 8–10; Melosi, *The Sanitary City*, 90–93, 98–99, 151–53, 163–65.

25. *Lexington Leader*, September 17, 1902, April 13, 1905, and numerous other references in Lexington papers from 1894 to 1915. For establishment of water and sewerage in Georgetown, see chapter 13.

26. Helen Bridle, "Overview of Waterborne Pathogens," in *Waterborne Pathogens: Detection Methods and Applications*, ed. Helen Bridle (Amsterdam: Elsevier, 2014), 9–40. There are many other waterborne diseases in addition to those listed.

27. Charles-Edward A. Winslow, *The Conquest of Epidemic Disease: A Chapter in the History of Ideas* (Princeton, N.J.: Princeton Univ. Press, 1943, 236–66; John S. Chambers, *The Conquest of Cholera: America's Greatest Scourge* (New York: Macmillan, 1938), 34–36. Before malaria was used to describe a specific disease, the term simply meant "bad air," from the Italian *mal'aria.*

28. Chambers, *The Conquest of Cholera*, 24–334; Nancy D. Baird, "Asiatic Cholera's First Visit to Kentucky: A Study in Panic and Fear," *Filson Club History Quarterly* 48 (July 1974): 228–40; Baird, "Asiatic Cholera: Kentucky's First Health Instructor," *Filson Club History Quarterly* 48 (October 1974): 327–41.

29. John Snow, *On the Mode of Communication of Cholera*, 2nd ed. (London: John Churchill, 1855); Peter Vinten-Johansen, Howard Brody, Nigel Paneth, Stephen Rachman, and Michael Rip, *Cholera, Chloroform, and the Science of Medicine: A Life of John Snow* (Oxford, UK: Oxford Univ. Press, 2003), 199–339; Jason B. Harris, Regina C. LaRocque, Firdausi Qadri, Edward T. Ryan, and Stephen B. Calderwood, "Cholera," *The Lancet* 379 (June 30–July 6, 2012): 2466.

30. O'Dell, "Water Supply and the Early Development of Lexington," 450; *Covington (Ky.) Journal*, July 29, 1854.

31. O'Dell, "Water Supply and the Early Development of Lexington," 435–37; Lexington Town Trustees, *Minute Book 1781–1811*, 15, resolution, December 12, 1782, University of Kentucky Special Collections Research Center (first quotation); interview with Martin Wymore, Draper Collection, 11CC131 (second and third quotations). The "Town Spring" of Lexington is a different spring from McConnell's Spring, which is located about two miles to the west.

32. O'Dell, "Water Supply and the Early Development of Lexington," 450–60; Dugan, *Rainfall Harvest*, 2–75.

33. Theodore E. Lauer, "The Common Law Background of the Riparian Doctrine," *Missouri Law Review* 28 (winter 1963): 60–107; Anthony Scott and Georgina Coustalin, "The Evolution of Water Rights," *Natural Resources Journal* 35 (fall 1995): 821–979.

34. Joseph W. Dellapenna, "A Primer on Groundwater Law," *Idaho Law Review* 49 (spring 2013): 269–323 (first quotation, 273; second quotation, 272); Henry C. Black, "Waters," in *Cyclopedia of Law and Procedure*, vol. 40, ed. William Mack (New York: American Law Book Company, 1912), 625–28.

35. Black, "Waters," 49 (first quotation), 764–66, (second quotation, 766).

36. *Water Supply Co. v City of Georgetown*, *Kentucky Law Reporter*, vol. 26 (Frankfort, 1905), 327–32.

37. Walter Christaller, *Central Places in Southern Germany*, trans. Carlisle W. Baskin (Englewood Cliffs, N.J.: Prentice-Hall, 1966), originally published as *Die zentralen Orte in Süddeutschland* (Jena: Gustav Fisher, 1933); August Lösch, *The Economics of Location*, trans. W. H. Woglom and W. F. Stolper (New Haven, Conn.: Yale Univ. Press, 1954), originally published as *Die Raumliche Ordnung der Wirtschaft* (Jena: Gustav Fisher, 1940); Graybill, Hays-Mitchell, and Zeigler, "World Urban Development," 17–18; Leslie J. King, *Central Place Theory*, ed. Grant Ian Thrall (1985; reprint, Morgantown: West Virginia University Research Repository, 2020), 14, 20–25.

38. King, *Central Place Theory*, 14–17.

39. US Decennial Census, 1860, 2020.

40. Robert L. Kincaid, *The Wilderness Road* (New York: Bobbs-Merrill, 1947), 67–195; Craig T. Friend, *Along the Maysville Road: The Early American Republic in the Trans-Appalachian West* (Knoxville: Univ. of Tennessee Press, 2005), 1–58, 239–67.

41. Bettye L. Mastin, *Lexington 1779: Pioneer Kentucky as Described by Early Settlers* (Lexington: Lexington-Fayette County Historic Commission, 1979), 13–23; Charles R. Staples, *The History of Pioneer Lexington, Kentucky 1779–1806* (Lexington: Transylvania Press, 1959), 10–15, map opposite page 22, 309; John Todd to Thomas Jefferson, April 15, 1781, *The Papers of Thomas Jefferson*, vol. 5, *25 February 1781–28 May 1781*, ed. Julian P. Boyd (Princeton, N.J.: Princeton Univ. Press, 1952), 462–63.

42. Thomas Chapman, "Journal of a Journey Through the United States, 1795–6," *Historical Magazine* 5 (June 1869), 363 (first quotation); Lewis Condict, "Journal of a Trip to Kentucky in 1795," *Proceedings of the New Jersey Historical Society* 4 (January–October 1919): 120; Josiah Espy, *Memorandums of a Tour Made by Josiah Espy in the States of Ohio and Kentucky in 1805* (Cincinnati, Ohio: R. Clarke and Company, 1870), 8; Timothy Flint, *Recollections of the Last Ten Years* (Boston, Mass.: Cummings, Billiard, and Company, 1826), 68; William Darby, *The Emigrant's Guide to the Western and Southwestern States and Territories* (New York: Kirk and Mercein, 1818), 206 (second quotation); *Niles' Register*, January 28, 1815.

43. Reuben T. Durrett, "Origin of the City of Louisville," *Memorial History of Louisville from Its First Settlement to the Year 1896*, vol. 1, ed. Stoddard Johnson (Chicago: American Biographical Publishing Company, 1896), 37–44; Richard C. Wade, *The Urban Frontier: Pioneer Life in Early Pittsburgh, Cincinnati, Lexington, Louisville, and St. Louis* (Chicago: Univ. of Chicago Press, 1959), 13–27; Stuart S. Sprague, "The Canal at the Falls of the Ohio and the Three-Cornered Rivalry," *Register of the Kentucky Historical Society* 72 (January 1974): 38–54; Richard E. Banta, *The Ohio* (1949; reprint, Lexington: Univ. Press of Kentucky, 1998), 291–307; US Decennial Census, 1850.

44. Lindsey Apple, Frederick A. Johnston, and Ann B. Bevins, *Scott County, Kentucky: A History* (Georgetown, Ky: Scott County Historical Society, 1993), 50; *Acts Passed at the First Session of the Second General Assembly for the Commonwealth of Kentucky* (Lexington, 1793), 35–36; John B. Conrad, "Dry Ridge Trace," *Encyclopedia of Northern Kentucky*, ed. Paul A. Tenkotte and James C. Claypool (Lexington: Univ. Press of Kentucky, 2014), 284; Bill Gaines, *History of Scott County*, vol. 1 (Georgetown: B. O. Gaines Printery, 1905), 68, 103–4.

45. J. Winston Coleman, *Stage-Coach Days in the Bluegrass* (1935; reprint, Lexington: Univ. Press of Kentucky, 1995), 27; William N. Blane, *An Excursion*

Through the United States and Canada 1822–1823 (1824; reprint, London: Negro Universities Press, 1969), 104 (first quotation); Karl Raitz and Nancy O'Malley, "The Nineteenth-Century Evolution of Local-Scale Roads in Kentucky's Bluegrass," *Geographical Review* 94 (October 2004): 415–39 (second quotation, 425).

46. *Acts Passed at the First Session of the Twenty-Fifth General Assembly for the Commonwealth of Kentucky* (Frankfort, 1817), 197–200; *Acts Passed at the First Session of the Twenty-Sixth General Assembly for the Commonwealth of Kentucky* (Frankfort, 1817), 544–46; *Acts Passed at the First Session of the Twenty-Seventh General Assembly for the Commonwealth of Kentucky* (Frankfort, 1817), 721–25 (first quotation, 721); Raitz and O'Malley, "Nineteenth-Century Evolution," (second quotation, 428). The concept of macadam roads was developed by John McAdam in Britain about 1820.

47. Raitz and O'Malley, "Nineteenth-Century Evolution," 420 (quotation).

48. Apple, Johnston, and Bevins, *Scott County*, xx, 70 (combined in quotation).

49. Ibid., 72.

50. Charles F. Haywood, "Toyota Motor Manufacturing, Kentucky, and the Kentucky Economy," in *Japan in the Bluegrass*, ed. P. P. Karan (Lexington: Univ. Press of Kentucky, 2001), 155–57; Georgetown/Scott County Chamber of Commerce, "Georgetown/Scott County Community Profile 2018," https://www.gtown.org/economic-growth, accessed July 26, 2019.

51. US Decennial Census, 2020; Janet W. Patton and H. Milton Patton, "Dynamics of Growth and Change in Georgetown, Kentucky," in *Japan in the Bluegrass*, ed. P. P. Karan (Lexington: Univ. Press of Kentucky, 2001), 130–55. Kroger has been present in Georgetown since the 1920s, but opened its first large store in the early 1970s prior to the establishment of the Toyota plant. The city's Walmart store opened at about the time Toyota was under construction.

52. Apple, Johnston, and Bevins, *Scott County, Kentucky*, 384; Tom Prather, mayor of Georgetown, telephone conversation with author, April 21, 2016.

2. The New Frontier

1. US Bureau of the Census, "Colonial and Pre-Federal Statistics," *Historical Statistics of the United States: Colonial Times to 1970*, Bicentennial Edition, part 2 (Washington, D.C., 1975), 1168.

2. Alan Taylor, *American Colonies: The Settling of North America*, Penguin History of the United States, ed. Eric Foner (New York: Penguin, 2002), 308–9; H. Roy Merrens, "Historical Geography and Early American History," *William and Mary Quarterly* 22 (October 1965): 529–48.

3. Arthur K. Moore, *The Frontier Mind* (1963; reprint, Lexington: Univ. Press of Kentucky, 1957), 25–29; Smith, "This Idea in Heaven," 77–79.

4. Fredrika J. Teute, "Land, Liberty, and Labor in the Post-Revolutionary Era: Kentucky as the Promised Land" (Ph.D. diss., Johns Hopkins University, 1988), 2.

5. Richard Gross, "La Salle's Claim and the Ohio Valley," *Pennsylvania History: A Journal of Mid-Atlantic Studies* 87 (spring 2020): 338–63; Robert S. Weddle, "Tarnished Hero: A La Salle Overview," *Southwestern Historical Quarterly* 113 (October 2009): 164–70; George A. Wood, "Celoron de Blainville and French Expansion in the Ohio Valley," *Mississippi Valley Historical Review* 9 (March 1923): 164–70, 310–12; Wesley F. Craven, *The Virginia Company of London, 1606–1624* (Williamsburg, Va.: Virginia 350th Anniversary Celebration Corporation, 1957), 14; Lyon G. Tyler, *History of Virginia*, vol. 2, *The Federal Period* (Chicago, Ill.: American Historical Society, 1924), 12; William MacDonald, ed., *Documentary Source Book of American History, 1606–1913* (New York: Macmillan, 1918), 10; Fred Anderson, *Crucible of War: The Seven Years' War and the Fate of Empire in British North America, 1754–1766* (New York: Knopf, 2000), 23, 27–28; John Hrastar, *Breaking the Appalachian Barrier: Maryland as the Gateway to Ohio and the West, 1750–1850* (Jefferson, N.C.: McFarland, 2018), 78–80; Kenneth P. Bailey, *The Ohio Company of Virginia and the Westward Movement 1748–1792* (Glendale, Calif.: Arthur H. Clarke Company, 1939), 103–7, 125–38. In 1541, Hernan de Soto was the first European to discover the Mississippi River. Prior to La Salle, Father Jacques Marquette and fur trader Louis Joliet voyaged far enough down the river in 1673 to establish that the Mississippi flowed into the Gulf of Mexico.

6. Ellen C. Semple, *American History and Its Geographic Conditions* (Boston: Houghton, Mifflin, 1903), 37–40, 54–74.

7. Hrastar, *Breaking the Appalachian Barrier*, 23–24.

8. Ibid., 43–46; Semple, *American History*, 67–68. The Wilderness Road in Kentucky was separate from but connected to the Wilderness Road that traversed part of the Great Valley. A water gap is a notch that a river has carved through a mountain ridge. Most water gaps are believed to be superimposed, meaning the stream originally developed upon horizontal beds that overlie folded and faulted rock structures, eroding downward to imprint the river pattern on the evolving landscape. For example, the Cumberland River flows through a water gap in Pine Mountain near Pineville in eastern Kentucky. Wind gaps, such as Cumberland Gap, can be produced when a stream cuts partway across a ridge and then abandons its channel to flow elsewhere, or when the headwaters of one river captures, or diverts, part of the course of another river through headward erosion. The course of the captured river below the point of intersection no longer carries water and ceases downward erosion, leaving a "wind gap" through which only the wind moves. See discussion in Joseph A. DiPietro, *Landscape Evolution in the United States: An Introduction to*

Geography, Geology, and Natural History, 2nd ed. (Amsterdam: Elsevier, 2018), 337–40.

9. J. Stoddard Johnston, ed., *First Explorations of Kentucky*, Filson Club Publication No. 13 (Louisville: John P. Morton, 1898), xv–xvi, 5–7.

10. Thomas Walker, "Journal of Doctor Thomas Walker, 1749–1750," in *First Explorations of Kentucky*, ed. J. Stoddard Johnston, Filson Club Publication No. 13 (Louisville: John P. Morton, 1898), 33–75.

11. Johnston, ed., *First Explorations*, 88–90.

12. William M. Darlington, *Christopher Gist's Journals with Historical, Geographical and Ethnological Notes* (Pittsburgh: J. R. Weldin, 1893), 31–66, 128–34.

13. Anderson, *Crucible of War*, 31–45; George Washington, *The Journal of Major George Washington* (Williamsburg, Va.: William Hunter, 1754).

14. Anderson, *Crucible of War*, 45–49.

15. Ibid., 267–85, 505–6; Eric Foner, *Give Me Liberty: An American History* (New York: Norton, 2017), 169–71.

16. Anderson, *Crucible of War*, 560–65.

17. Colin G. Calloway, *The Scratch of a Pen: 1763 and the Transformation of North America* (Oxford: Oxford Univ. Press, 2006), 92–97; Anderson, *Crucible of War*, 565–71.

18. Anderson, *Crucible of War*, 566–616; Darrell J. Kozlowski, *Colonialism*, Key Concepts in American History (New York: Chelsea House, 2010), 71–72.

19. Calloway, *Scratch of a Pen*, 98–100, 111.

20. Ibid.; Anderson, *Crucible of War*, 568–69, 634–37.

21. Thomas P. Abernethy, *Three Virginia Frontiers* (1940; reprint, Gloucester, Mass.: Peter Smith, 1962), 29–62; Warren R. Hofstra, "'The Extention of His Majesties Dominions': The Virginia Backcountry and the Reconfiguration of Imperial Frontiers," *Journal of American History* 84 (March 1998): 1281–1312; Fairfax Harrison, *Virginia Land Grants. A Study of Conveyancing in Relation to Colonial Politics* (Richmond, Va.: Old Dominion Press, 1925), 16–42; "An Act Concerning the Granting, Seating, and Planting, and for Settling the Titles and Bounds of Lands," October 1705, in *The Statutes at Large; Being a Collection of All the Laws of Virginia*, vol. 3, ed. William W. Hening (Richmond, Va.: Samuel Pleasants, 1812), 304–29 (quotation, 313); Neal O. Hammon, "Land Acquisition on the Kentucky Frontier," *Register of the Kentucky Historical Society* 78 (autumn 1980): 299.

22. Warren R. Hofstra, *The Planting of New Virginia: Settlement and Landscape in the Shenandoah Valley* (Baltimore: John Hopkins Univ. Press, 2004), 112; Harrison, *Virginia Land Grants*, 11–12, 42–59 (quotation, 52).

23. Hofstra, *Planting of New Virginia*, 53–54 (first quotation, 53); Abernethy, *Three Virginia Frontiers*, 41–62; Richard L. Morton, *Colonial Virginia*,

vol. 2, Westward Expansion and Prelude to Revolution, 1710–1763 (Chapel Hill: Univ. of North Carolina Press, 1960), 536–51 (second quotation, 544); Hofstra, "'Extention of His Majesties Dominions,'" 1282–84.

24. Smith, "This Idea in Heaven," 79; Stephen Aron, *How the West Was Lost : The Transformation of Kentucky from Daniel Boone to Henry Clay* (Baltimore: Johns Hopkins Univ. Press, 1996), 59–61.

25. Aron, How the West was Lost, 61–62; Archibald Henderson, "Richard Henderson and the Occupation of Kentucky, 1775," *Mississippi Valley Historical Review* 1 (December 1914): 342–51; Richard Henderson, "Proposals for the Encouragement of Settling the Lands Purchased by Rich'd Henderson & Co.," December 5, 1774, *Colonial Records of North Carolina*, vol. 9, ed. William L. Saunders (Raleigh, N.C.: Josephus Daniels, 1890), 1129–131.

26. William S. Lester, *The Transylvania Colony* (Spencer, Ind.: S. R. Guard, 1935), 29–39; Nancy O'Malley, *Boonesborough Unearthed: Frontier Archaeology at a Revolutionary Fort* (Lexington: Univ. Press of Kentucky, 2019), 9–10; Treaty of Watauga, in *Boonesborough: Its Founding, Pioneer Struggles, Indian Experiences, Transylvania Days, and Revolutionary Annals*, ed. George W. Ranck (Louisville, Ky.: John P. Morton, 1901), 151–56 (quotation, 151).

27. Smith, "This Idea in Heaven," 80; O'Malley, *Boonesborough Unearthed*, 10–11; John Murray, Earl of Dunmore, "A Proclamation by Governor Dunmore, of Virginia," March 21, 1775, *Colonial Records of North Carolina*, vol. 9, 1169–70; Josiah Martin, "Proclamation by Josiah Martin Against Richard Henderson and the Transylvania Purchase," February 10, 1775, *Colonial Records of North Carolina*, vol. 9, 1122–25; Letter from Governor Martin to the Earl of Dartmouth, November 12, 1775, *Colonial Records of North Carolina*, vol. 10, 321–28 (quotation, 324). William Legge, the second Earl of Dartmouth, served as secretary of state for the American colonies from 1772 through November 1775.

28. Smith, "This Idea in Heaven," 80–81; Henderson, "Proposals for the Encouragement of Settling the Lands," 1129 (quotation).

29. Lester, *Transylvania Colony*, 127–49; Aron, *How the West Was Lost*, 62–68; Smith, "This Idea in Heaven," 81–82; Compact Between the Proprietors and the People, May 27, 1775, in Ranck, ed., *Boonesborough: Its Founding*, 208–10; Henderson, "Richard Henderson," 361.

30. Floyd to Preston, May 27, 1776, Draper mss., 33 S 296, State Historical Society of Wisconsin.

31. John E. Selby, *The Revolution in Virginia, 1775–1783* (Williamsburg, Va.: Colonial Williamsburg Foundation, 1988), 8–43.

32. Carl H. Laub, "Revolutionary Virginia and the Crown Lands (1775–1783)," *William and Mary Quarterly* 11 (October 1931): 305–6.

33. Ibid., 306–8; Hammon, "Land Acquisition," 307, 310; *Proceedings of the Convention of Delegates* [May 1776] (Richmond, Va.: Ritchie, Trueheart,

and Duval, 1816), 63 (first quotation); "The 5th, 9th, 10th and 11th Sections of an Act, Entitled, 'An Act for Raising a Supply of Money for Public Exigencies,'" *Revised Code of the Laws of Virginia*, vol. 2 (Richmond, Va.: Thomas Ritchie, 1819), 350–53; "An Act for Adjusting and Settling the Titles of Claimers to Unpatented Lands Under the Present and Former Government, Previous to the Establishment of the Commonwealth's Land Office," *Revised Code of the Laws of Virginia*, vol. 2 (Richmond, Va.: Thomas Ritchie, 1819), 354–65 (second and third quotations, 358). "Pre-emption" refers to the right of a settler to purchase public land from the state.

34. "Act for Adjusting and Settling Titles," 360–64; Hammon, "Land Acquisition," 309–12.

35. "An Act for Establishing a Land Office, and Ascertaining the Terms and Manner of Granting Waste and Unappropriated Lands," *Revised Code of the Laws of Virginia*, vol. 2 (Richmond, Va.: Thomas Ritchie, 1819), 365–75.

36. Aron, *How the West Was Lost*, 70–72; Laub, "Revolutionary Virginia," 310; Paul W. Gates, *Landlords and Tenants on the Prairie Frontier: Studies in American Land Policy* (Ithaca, N.Y.: Cornell Univ. Press, 1973), 16–17.

37. Aron, *How the West Was Lost*, 70–71; Hammon, "Land Acquisition," 312–14.

38. Aron, *How the West Was Lost*, 71–81; Brandon M. Robison, "Pioneers, Proclamations, and Patents: A Narrative of the Conquest, Division, Settlement, and Transformation of Kentucky" (Master's thesis, University of Louisville, 2013), 7 (quotation).

39. Teute, "Land, Liberty, and Labor," 185, 254–301 (quotation, 261).

40. Moses Austin, "A Memorandum of M. Austin's Journey from the Lead Mines in the County of Wythe in the State of Virginia to the Province of Louisiana West of the Mississippi, 1796–1797," *American Historical Review* 5 (April 1900): 525–26 (first and second quotations).

3. Bluegrass Paradise

1. O'Malley, *Stockading Up*, 19–20; O'Malley, "Frontier Defenses," 57–75.

2. Humphrey Marshall, *History of Kentucky*, vol. 1 (Frankfort, Ky.: Henry Gore, 1812), 8–9; Henderson and Pollack, "Kentucky," 405–14; Betty A. Smith, "Distribution of Eighteenth-Century Cherokee Settlements," in *The Cherokee Indian Nation: A Troubled History*, ed. Duane H. King (Knoxville: Univ. of Tennessee Press, 2000), 46–60; Moore, *Frontier Mind*, 17–18 (quotations, 18).

3. William C. Rive, ed., *Journal of an Exploration in the Spring of the Year 1750* (Boston, Mass.: Little, Brown, 1888); Thomas Pownall, *Topographical Description of North America* (London: Printed for J. Almon, 1776); Archibald Henderson, "Dr. Thomas Walker and the Loyal Company of Virginia,"

Proceedings of the American Antiquarian Society, n.s. 41 (April 1931): 91; Darlington, *Christopher Gist's Journals*, 30. Gist's journal is found in the appendix to Pownall's book, 7–16.

4. Henderson, "Dr. Thomas Walker," 79–94; Darlington, *Christopher Gist's Journals*, 30; Bailey, *Ohio Company*, 85 (quotation).

5. Lucien Beckner, "Eskippakithiki: The Last Indian Town in Kentucky," *Filson Club History Quarterly* 6 (October 1932): 371–72; Nicholas B. Wainwright, *George Croghan: Wilderness Diplomat* (Chapel Hill: Univ. of North Carolina Press, 1959), 3–13; Klotter and Friend, *A New History of Kentucky*, 9–10. Although historians have spelled Findlay's name variously as Finley, Finlay, and Findley, Lyman Draper settled upon "Findlay" for his biography of Daniel Boone. His first name is sometimes given as James rather than John.

6. Beckner, "Eskippakithiki," 372–73, 375.

7. Walter O'Meara, *Guns at the Forks* (Pittsburgh, Pa.: Univ. of Pittsburgh Press, 1979), 109–26; Paul Kopperman, *Braddock at the Monongahela* (Pittsburgh, Pa.: Univ. of Pittsburgh Press, 1992), 17, 32–33, 40, 293n33; Henderson, "Dr. Thomas Walker," 94–96; Neal O. Hammon, ed., *My Father, Daniel Boone: The Draper Interviews with Nathan Boone* (Lexington: Univ. Press of Kentucky, 1999), 13–14.

8. O'Meara, *Guns at the Forks*, 126–51; Kopperman, *Braddock at the Monongahela*, 148; Lyman C. Draper, *The Life of Daniel Boone*, ed. Ted F. Belue (Mechanicsburg, Pa.: Stackpole Books, 1998), 14; Michael Lofaro, *Daniel Boone: An American Life* (Lexington: Univ. Press of Kentucky, 2003), 12–15.

9. Hammon, *My Father, Daniel Boone*, 17, 19; Lofaro, *Daniel Boone*, 24–25, 27–28.

10. Lofaro, *Daniel Boone*, 27–30; Draper, *Life of Daniel Boone*, 207–8, 210; John Filson, *The Discovery, Settlement and Present State of Kentucke* (Wilmington, Del: James Adams, 1784), 40 (quotation).

11. Lofaro, *Daniel Boone*, 30–38.

12. Ibid., 150–59; Daniel Boone, "Memorial of Daniel Boone," January 18, 1812, reprinted in *Niles Weekly Register* 4 (March 13, 1813), 36–38 (quotation, 36).

13. Thomas Hanson, "Hanson's Journal," in *Documentary History of Dunmore's War, 1774*, ed. Reuben G. Thwaites and Louise P. Kellogg (Madison: Wisconsin Historical Society, 1905), 129 (first quotation); John Brown Sr. to William Preston, May 5, 1775, Draper mss., 4 QQ 15 (second quotation); Felix Walker, "Narrative of an Adventure in Kentucky in the Year 1775," *DeBow's Review* 41 (February 1854): 150–55 (third quotation, 150; fourth quotation, 152); Samuel Meredith Jr. to John Breckinridge, May 2, 1791, quoted in Lowell H. Harrison, "A Virginian Moves to Kentucky, 1793," *William and Mary Quarterly* 15 (April 1958): 206.

14. Francis Asbury, *The Journal of the Rev. Francis Asbury*, vol. 2 (New York: N. Bangs and T. Mason for the Methodist Episcopal Church, 1821), 74 (first quotation); Harry Toulmin, *The Western Country in 1793: Reports on Kentucky and Virginia* (San Marino, Calif.: Printed by Grant Dahlstrom at The Castle Press, 1948), 73; Patrick Scott, interview by Lyman C. Draper, Draper mss., 1 CC 6 (second quotation); David Meade to Judge Prentis, December 12, 1796, quoted in Teute, "Land, Liberty, and Labor," 154 (third quotation); Thomas D. Clark, ed., *Bluegrass Cavalcade* (Lexington: Univ. of Kentucky Press, 1956), 2–3 (fourth quotation).

15. Moore, *Frontier Mind*, 3–38.

16. John Walton, *John Filson of Kentucke* (Lexington: Univ. of Kentucky Press, 1956), 1 (quotation).

17. Ibid., 16–27, 29–30; Irene Tichenor, "Tracking the Mysteries: The Legacy of John Filson's 1784 Book and Map," *Ohio Valley History* 9 (winter 2009): 6–10; Filson, *The Discovery, Settlement and Present State of Kentucke*, front matter (quotation), 6.

18. Filson, *The Discovery, Settlement and Present State of Kentucke*, 6 (first quotation); Willard R. Jillson, *Filson's Kentucke*, Filson Club Publication No. 35 (Louisville, Ky., 1939), 119–37, (second quotation, 125; third quotation, 124; fourth quotation, 130; fifth quotation, 129).

19. Walton, *John Filson*, 24–28, 64–67 (first quotation, 28); Curtis Dewees, *George Washington's Kentucky Land* (Lake Orion, Mich.: Lake Orion Books, 2005), 20 (second quotation). Tichenor ("Tracking the Mysteries") provides a great deal of interesting detail on the production of Filson's book and map; see 6–10, 12–22.

20. Walton, *John Filson*, 34–35; Filson, *The Discovery, Settlement and Present State of Kentucke*, 11–28 (first quotation, 17, second quotation, 44, third quotation, 81–82). Filson probably intended "finest people" rather than "first people; possibly a printer's error.

21. Dewees, *George Washington*, 21–22; Tichenor, "Tracking the Mysteries," 11–12; Walton, *John Filson*, 40–44; Gilbert Imlay, *Topographical Description of the Western Territory of North America* (London: J. Debrett, 1792).

22. Walton, *John Filson*, 116–19, 125–26

23. Austin, "A Memorandum of M. Austin's Journey," 526.

24. Ibid., 526.

4. A Goodly Land

1. US Department of Agriculture, *Soil Survey of Scott County, Kentucky* (Washington, D.C.: GPO, 1977).

2. Mary E. Wharton and Roger W. Barbour, *Bluegrass Land and Life: Land Character, Plants and Animals of the Inner Bluegrass Region of Kentucky, Past, Present and Future* (Lexington: Univ. Press of Kentucky, 1991), 5–18.

3. John F. Watkins and Gary O'Dell, "Kentucky's Physical Regions and the Inner Bluegrass," in *Lexington and Kentucky's Inner Bluegrass Region*, ed. Richard Ulack, Karl B. Raitz, and Hilary L. Hopper, Pathways in Geography (Indiana, Pa.: National Council for Geographic Education, 1994), 5–6; Michael C. Pope, Steven M. Holland, and Mark E. Patzkowsky, "The Cincinnati Arch: A Stationary Peripheral Bulge During the Late Ordovician," in *Perspectives in Carbonate Geology: A Tribute to the Career of Robert Nathan Ginsburg*, ed. Peter K. Swart, Gregor P. Eberli, and Judith A. McKenzie, International Association of Sedimentologists, Special Publication No. 41 (Chichester, UK: John Wiley and Sons, 2009), 255–76; William J. Frazier and David R. Schwimmer, "The Tippecanoe Sequence: Middle Ordovician-Lower Devonian," in *Regional Stratigraphy of North America* (Boston, Mass.: Springer, 1987), 135–53. See also Frank R. Ettensohn, ed., *Changing Interpretations of Kentucky Geology: Layer-Cake, Facies, Flexure, and Eustacy*, Miscellaneous Report No. 5. (Columbus: State of Ohio, Dept. of Natural Resources, Division of Geological Survey, 1992). Erosion of the Nashville Dome over time has produced the broad physiographic feature known as the Nashville Basin.

4. David Barrow, "Diary of David Barrow," typescript copy of original, Manuscripts and Folklife Archives, Paper 2351, Western Kentucky University, 22; Wayne R. Newell, "Physiography," in *The Geology of Kentucky: A Text to Accompany the Geologic Map of Kentucky*, ed. Robert C. McDowell, Geological Survey Professional Paper 1151-H (Washington, D.C.: GPO, 1986), H66; Wharton and Barbour, *Bluegrass Land and Life*, 5–15.

5. Basil W. Duke, *Reminiscences of General Basil W. Duke, C. S. A.* (Garden City, N.Y.: Doubleday, 1911), 21 (first quotation); Draper, *Life of Daniel Boone*, 406; Draper mss., 4 B 67–68 (second quotation).

6. Arthur N. Palmer, *Cave Geology* (Dayton, Ohio: Cave Books, 2007), 21, 27–31.

7. Ibid., 31–33.

8. James Nourse, "Journey to Kentucky in 1775," *Journal of American History* 19 (July–August–September 1925): 252; Barrow, "Diary of David Barrow," 24.

9. William E. Ellis, *The Kentucky River* (Lexington: Univ. Press of Kentucky, 2000), 33–52; William M. Andrews Jr., "Geologic Controls on Plio-Pleistocene Drainage Evolution of the Kentucky River in Central Kentucky" (Ph.D. diss., Univ. of Kentucky, 2004).

10. Richard Taylor, *Elkhorn: Evolution of a Kentucky Landscape* (Lexington: Univ. Press of Kentucky, 2018), 19, 23; Samuel Wilson, "McClelland and His Men" (Lexington: University of Kentucky Library Associates, typescript, 1956), 9.

11. James C. Currens and Randall Paylor, "The Bluegrass Region, Central Kentucky," in *Caves and Karst of the USA*, ed. Arthur N. Palmer and Margaret V. Palmer (Huntsville, Ala.: National Speleological Society), 103–7; Gary A. O'Dell and Lawrence E. Spangler, "Slack's Cave Bicentennial 1790–1990," *NSS News* (National Speleological Society) 48 (March 1990), 60–63.

12. E. Lucy Braun, *Deciduous Forests of Eastern North America* (Philadelphia, Pa.: Blakiston, 1950), 125–31, 26 (first quotation), 28 (second quotation).

13. Julian Campbell, "Rebuilding the Concept of Bluegrass Woodland," *The Lady Slipper* (Kentucky Native Plant Society) 25 (spring 2010), 6–9; Ursula M. Davidson, "The Original Vegetation of Lexington, KY. and Vicinity" (Master's thesis, University of Kentucky, 1950), 23–31; Mary E. Wharton and Roger W. Barbour, *Trees and Shrubs of Kentucky* (Lexington: Univ. Press of Kentucky, 1973), 514. Most of Campbell's published and unpublished papers on Bluegrass vegetation can be downloaded from his Bluegrasswoodland website: https://bluegrasswoodland.com/.

14. William S. Bryant, Mary E. Wharton, William H. Martin, and Johnnie B. Varner, "The Blue Ash-Oak Savanna-Woodland, a Remnant of Presettlement Vegetation in the Inner Bluegrass of Kentucky," *Castanea* 45 (September 1980): 149–64, 158 (quotation).

15. Wharton and Barbour, *Bluegrass Land and Life*, 28–33, 59–60; Campbell, "Rebuilding the Concept," 6 (first quotation); Julian Campbell, "NOT a Savanna, the Bluegrass Woodland of 1775 was Eutrophic and Probably Much Browsed but Little Opened," 8 pages, unpublished notes, February 2014, personal communication, May 9, 2021, 1 (second quotation); Karl Raitz and Dorn Van Dommelen, "Creating the Landscape Symbol Vocabulary for a Regional Image: The Case of the Kentucky Bluegrass," *Landscape Journal* 9 (fall 1990): 109–21, 109 (third quotation), 110 (fourth quotation).

16. Julian Campbell, "Historical Quotes on Vegetation in the Bluegrass and Some Adjacent Regions," 107 pages, unpublished notes, February 2014, personal communication, May 9, 2021; A. Gwynn Henderson, "Middle Fort Ancient Villages and Organization Complexity in Central Kentucky" (Ph.D. diss., University of Kentucky, 1998). Journals that provide significant descriptions of settlement-era Kentucky and Inner Bluegrass vegetation include those of David Barrow, Nicholas Cresswell, William Fleming, Christopher Gist, Thomas Hanson, James and Robert McAfee, botanists Francois and André Michaux, James Nourse, Nicholas Parry, James Smith, and Thomas Walker. The voluminous materials collected by Lyman Draper and John Dabney Shane represent an important source of pioneer recollections. Significant books include Thomas Hutchins's *A Topographical Description of Virginia, Pennsylvania, Maryland, and North Carolina* (1778), John Filson's *Discovery, Settlement and Present State of Kentucke* (1784, reprinted in Imlay, 1792, and successive editions), Gilbert Imlay's *Topographical Description of the Western Territory of North America* (1792), and Draper's *Life of Daniel Boone* (originally in manuscript form, edited and published in 1998 by Ted F. Belue). Early maps of Kentucky that include notes on vegetation include those produced by Thomas Hutchins (1778), John Filson (1784), and Elihu Barker (1795, included in the 1797 edition of Imlay's book).

17. Ryan W. McEwan and Brian C. McCarthy, "Anthropogenic Disturbance and the Formation of Oak Savanna in Central Kentucky, USA," *Journal of Biogeography* 35 (May 2008): 965–75; Campbell, personal communication, August 21, 2021.

18. Campbell, "Rebuilding the Concept," 6; Campbell, "NOT a Savanna," 1 (quotations).

19. Barrow, "Diary of David Barrow," 22 (first quotation); Samuel Matthew, interview by John D. Shane, Draper mss., 11 CC 158 (second quotation); Asa Farrar, interview by John D. Shane, Draper mss., 13 CC 2 (third quotation); André Michaux, "Journal of André Michaux," in *Early Western Travels 1748–1846*, vol. 3, *Travels West of the Alleghenies*, ed. Reuben G. Thwaites (Cleveland, Ohio: Clark, 1904), 38 (fourth quotation)

20. Julian Campbell, *The Land of Cane and Clover: Presettlement Vegetation in the So-Called Bluegrass Region of Kentucky: A Report from the Herbarium* (Lexington: University of Kentucky, 1985), 12 (quotation); Marshall, *History of Kentucky*, 1:5–6.

21. Mary "Polly" Hawkins, "Life and Times of Aunt Polly Hawkins," typescript, Scott County Public Library, Local History Box 1, Folder 2010KR204 (first quotation); O'Malley, *Stockading Up*, 296–97; Ann B. Bevins, *A History of Scott County as Told by Selected Buildings* (Georgetown, Ky.: privately printed, 1981), 7–9; Anonymous, "Travels in Hot Weather, No. 2," *Western Monthly Magazine* 2 (October 1834), 539 (second quotation); Levi Todd's narrative, Draper mss., 15 CC 160, (third quotation). Levi Todd's brother was Robert Todd, who was seriously wounded defending McClelland's Station during the Indian attack on December 29, 1776.

22. Julian Campbell, "Evidence of the Original Woodland along Elkhorn Creek, Based on Surveys in 1774," typescript, n.p., 2021, personal communication, August 26, 2021; Neal O. Hammon, "The Fincastle Surveyors in the Bluegrass," *Register of the Kentucky Historical Society* 70 (October 1972): 283; Hanson, "Hanson's Journal," 130 (quotation). The web address for the Kentucky Land Office, Virginia and Old Kentucky Patent Series, is https://web.sos.ky.gov/land/vakypatentseries.aspx.

23. Campbell, "Evidence of the Original Woodland."

24. Ibid. (quotation).

25. Ibid. (quotation).

26. Hanson, "Hanson's Journal," 130 (quotation).

27. Thomas G. Barnes and S. Wilson Francis, *Wildflowers and Ferns of Kentucky* (Lexington: Univ. Press of Kentucky, 2004), 172, 196; Ronald L. Jones, *Plant Life of Kentucky: An Illustrated Guide to the Vascular Flora* (Lexington: Univ. Press of Kentucky, 2005), 361, 379, 410, 563, 674; Michael A. Vincent, M. A., "The genus *Trifolium* (Fabaceae) in Kentucky," *Journal of the Kentucky Academy of Science* 62 (spring 2001): 10, 12–14.

28. Ben Guthrie, quoted in [Ann P.] Coffman, "Big Crossing Station, built by Robert Johnson," *Filson Club History Quarterly* 5 (January 1931): 9 (first quotation); Julian Campbell, "Growth of Cane (*Arundinaria sensu stricto*), the Mysterious Native Bamboo of North America," in *Combined Proceedings of the International Plant Propagator's Society* 61 (2011): 334–45, 340 (second quotation); Campbell, "Bluegrass Woodland and Its Eutrophic Nature," 30 pages, unpublished notes, personal communication, May 9, 2021. Julian Campbell has, at his own expense, undertaken to restore cane to the Cane Run corridor; between 1999 and 2002 he planted 150 five-year-old seedlings he had raised, in rows along both banks. After a slow start, the cane is now prospering

29. Campbell, "Evidence of the Original Woodland"; James McAfee, "Journals of James and Robert McAfee," appendix in Neander M. Woods, *The Woods-McAfee Memorial* (Louisville, Ky.: Courier-Journal Job Printing Company, 1905), 434; Nourse, "Journey to Kentucky," 252; Otto A. Rothert, transcr., "John D. Shane's Interview with Colonel John Graves of Fayette County," *Filson Historical Quarterly* 15 (October 1941): 43–44 (quotation); O'Malley, *Stockading Up*, 288–89.

30. Walker, "Journal of Doctor Thomas Walker," 33–75, 75 (quotation); John F. D. Smyth, *A Tour of the United States of America*, vol. 1 (London: G. Robinson, 1784), 337–38 (quotation).

31. Hanson, "Hanson's Journal," 122; Ted F. Belue, *The Long Hunt: Death of the Buffalo East of the Mississippi River* (Mechanicsburg, Pa.: Stackpole Books, 1996), 97–134.

32. Anna M. Cartlidge, "Colonel John Floyd: Reluctant Adventurer," *Register of the Kentucky Historical Society* 66 (October 1968): 336; Draper mss., 10 NN 149 (quotation); Evarts B. Greene and Virginia D. Hamilton, *American Population Before the Federal Census of 1790* (1932; reprint, Gloucester, Ma.: Columbia Univ. Press, 2006), 192.

33. Walker, "Narrative of an Adventure," 152 (quotation).

34. Moore, *Frontier Mind*, 3 (quotation).

35. Smith, "This Idea in Heaven," 88–95 (first quotation, 89); Josiah Collins, interview by John D. Shane, Draper mss., 12 CC 67 (second quotation).

36. Smith, "This Idea in Heaven," 91–94; David W. Kennedy and Lizabeth Cohen, *The American Pageant*, 16th ed. (Boston, Mass.: Wadsworth Cengage Learning, 2016), 278; Daniel Drake, *Pioneer Life in Kentucky: A Series of Reminiscential Letters from Daniel Drake, M. D. of Cincinnati to His Children*, ed. Charles D. Drake (Cincinnati, Ohio: Robert Clarke, 1870), 22–23 (quotation).

37. Gaille McGregor, *The Noble Savage in the New World Garden: Notes Toward a Syntactics of Place* (Toronto: Univ. of Toronto Press, 1988), 109 (first quotation); Moore, *Frontier Mind*, 48–56, 63–67 (second quotation, 52).

38. Moore, *Frontier Mind*, 70–75.

39. William Fleming, "Colonel William Fleming's Journal of Travels in Kentucky, 1779–1780," in *Travels in the American Colonies*, ed. Newton D. Mereness (New York: MacMillan, 1916), 636; Jerry Hill, *Kentucky Weather* (Lexington: Univ. Press of Kentucky, 2005), 40–50; Ann Christian to Ann Fleming, September 13, 1785, quoted in *Running Mad for Kentucky: Frontier Travel Accounts*, ed. Ellen Eslinger (Lexington: Univ. Press of Kentucky, 2004), 36 (quotation).

40. Michael Williams, *Americans and Their Forests: A Historical Geography*, Studies in Environment and History (Cambridge: Cambridge Univ. Press, 2004), 10–14; Michael Wigglesworth, "God's Controversy in New England," in *American Poetry of the Seventeenth Century*, ed. Harrison T. Meserole (University Park: Pennsylvania State Univ. Press, 1993), 43–54 (first quotation, 44); Andrew P. Patrick, "Birth of the Bluegrass: Ecological Transformations in Central Kentucky to 1810," *Register of the Kentucky Historical Society* 115 (spring 2017): 175 (second quotation).

41. Drake, *Pioneer Life*, 34 (first quotation), 181 (second quotation); John Bradford, "Bryan's Station," reprinted from *Kentucky Gazette*, November 17, 1826, in *The Voice of the Frontier: John Bradford's Notes on Kentucky*, ed. Thomas D. Clark (Lexington: Univ. Press of Kentucky, 1993), 49–54 (third quotation, 50); Moore, *Frontier Mind*, 56 (fourth quotation).

42. Wharton and Barbour, *Bluegrass Land and Life*, 37–39; Patrick, "Birth of the Bluegrass," 170, 176–77; Ranck, *Boonesborough*, 201 (first quotation); Barrow, "Diary of David Barrow," 126 (second quotation); Joseph Doddridge, *Notes on the Settlement and Indian Wars of the Western Parts of Virginia and Pennsylvania, from 1763 to 1783* (Albany, N.Y.: 1876), 104–5 (third quotation).

43. John James Audubon, *Delineations of American Scenery and Character* (New York: G. A. Baker, 1926), 115 (first quotation); Ranck, *Boonesborough*, 176 (second quotation); William Clinkenbeard, interview by John D. Shane, Draper mss., 11 CC 61 (third quotation); André Michaux, "Journal of André Michaux," 37, 73; Belue, *Long Hunt*, 156.

5. The Land of Springs

1. *Kentucky Gazette* (Lexington), March 8, 1788 (first quotation); Apple, Johnston, and Bevins, *Scott County, Kentucky*, xvi (second quotation).

2. Much of the material in this chapter is taken from Gary A. O'Dell, "Springs and the Settlement of Pioneer Kentucky," in *Water in Kentucky: Natural History, Communities, and Conservation*, ed. Brian M. Lee, Daniel I. Carey, and Alice L. Jones (Lexington: Univ. Press of Kentucky, 2017), 27–39.

3. Groundwater database, Kentucky Division of Water, Frankfort, Kentucky.

4. Stanley Hedeen, *Big Bone Lick: The Cradle of American Paleontology* (Lexington: Univ. Press of Kentucky, 2008); Filson, *The Discovery, Settlement and Present State of Kentucke*, 32–33 (first quotation); Nicholas Cresswell, *The Journal of Nicholas Cresswell, 1774–1777* (Carlisle, Mass.: Dial Press, 1924), 85 (second quotation).

5. Erhard Rostlund, "The Geographic Range of the Historic Bison in the Southeast," *Annals of the American Association of Geographers* 50 (December 1960): 395–407; John A. Jakle, "The American Bison and the Human Occupance of the Ohio Valley," *Proceedings of the American Philosophical Society* 112 (August 1968): 299–305 (second quotation, 302); John A. Jakle, "Salt on the Ohio Valley Frontier, 1770–1820," *Annals of the American Association of Geographers* 59 (December 1969): 687–709; Belue, *Long Hunt*, 7–10; Draper mss., 6 S 103 (first quotation).

6. John D. Barnhart, *Henry Hamilton and George Rogers Clark in the American Revolution, With the Unpublished Journal of Lieut. Gov. Henry Hamilton* (Crawfordsville, Ind: R. E. Banta, 1951), 198; Kincaid, *Wilderness Road*, 70, 75.

7. Willard R. Jillson, *Pioneer Kentucky* (Frankfort, Ky.: State Journal Company, 1934), 37–39; Kincaid, *Wilderness Road*, 30; Karl B. Raitz, Jeff E. Levy, and Richard A. Gilbreath, "Mapping Kentucky's Frontier Trails Through Geographic Information and Cartographic Applications," *Geographical Review* 100 (July 2010): 312–35; Thomas Hutchins, *A Topographical Description of Virginia, Pennsylvania, Maryland, and North Carolina*, ed. F. C. Hicks (1778; reprint, Cleveland, Ohio: Burrows Brothers, 1904), 95 (quotation).

8. Kincaid, *Wilderness Road*, 101–5; Jakle, *American Bison*, 302; Robert E. McDowell, "Bullitt's Lick: The Related Saltworks and Settlements," *Filson Club History Quarterly* 30 (July 1956): 241–69.

9. Jakle, *American Bison*, 302; Jillson, *Pioneer Kentucky*, 46; George Croghan, "The Journals of George Croghan, 1750–1765," ed. Reuben G. Thwaites, in *Early Western Journals 1748–1765*, vol. 1 (Cleveland, Ohio: Arthur H. Clark, 1904), 135 (first quotation); Filson, *The Discovery, Settlement and Present State of Kentucke*, 30 (second quotation).

10. Neal O. Hammon, "Pioneer Routes in Central Kentucky," *Filson Club History Quarterly* 74 (spring 2000): 129–31; Joshua Morrow, ed., "Tours into Kentucky and the Northwest: Three Journals by the Rev. James Smith of Powhatan County, Virginia, 1783–1795–1797," *Ohio State Archaeological and Historical Quarterly* 16 (1907): 372 (quotation).

11. Constantine S. Rafinesque, "Licks and Sucks of Kentucky," *Atlantic Journal, and Friend of Knowledge* 1 (summer 1832): 74–77; Michael C. Hansen, "The Scioto Saline: Ohio's Early Salt Industry," *GeoFacts No. 7*, Ohio Department of Natural Resources, Division of Geological Survey (March 1995), 1–2; Deidre M. McCartney, Megan A. Finney, and J. Barry Maynard, "Sources of the Salt in the Big Bone Lick Springs, Northern Kentucky," *Geological Society*

of America Abstracts with Programs 37, no. 5 (2005): 34; Jakle, "Salt on the Ohio Valley Frontier," 700.

12. Draper mss., 15 CC 157.

13. Collins, *History of Kentucky*, vol. 2, 179 (first quotation); Draper mss., 12 CC 100 (second quotation).

14. Alexander S. Withers, *Chronicles of Border Warfare* (Clarksburg, Va.: Joseph Israel, 1831), 144; Draper mss., 12 CC 68 (quotation).

15. Kentucky Historical Society, *Certificate Book of the Virginia Land Commission 1779–1780* (Greenville, S.C.: Southern Historical Press, 1992), 290 (quotation).

16. Fayette County Circuit Court, *Complete Record Book A*, 381 (quotation).

17. O'Malley, "Frontier Defenses," 61.

18. O'Malley, *Stockading Up*, 36; Gary A. O'Dell, "The Search for Water: Self-Supply Strategies in a Rural Appalachian Neighborhood" (Master's thesis, University of Kentucky, 1996), 88–92. Among exceptions to the general practice of water supply springs being located external to a settlement enclosure is that of William Miller's station in Garrard County. According to O'Malley (*Stockading Up*, 236), the station contained a cave spring, which was accessed by stairs cut down from the entrance.

19. Fleming, "Colonel William Fleming's Journal," 630.

20. *Kentucky Gazette* (Lexington), August 15, 1790 (first quotation), July 3, 1795 (second quotation).

21. *Kentucky Gazette* (Lexington), December 7, 1793 (first quotation), April 24, 1804 (second quotation).

22. O'Dell, "Water Supply and the Early Development of Lexington," 431–61.

6. Floyd's Spring

1. Cartlidge, "Colonel John Floyd: Reluctant Adventurer," 317–25.

2. Hanson, "Hanson's Journal," 110–33 (quotation, 115). All subsequent direct references to Floyd's 1774 expedition to Kentucky, unless otherwise cited, are taken from this source.

3. Linda Marie Pett-Conklin, "Cadastral Surveying in Colonial South Carolina: A Historical Geography" (Ph.D. diss., Louisiana State University, 1986), 98–102.

4. Sarah S. Hughes, *Surveyors and Statesmen: Land Measuring in Colonial Virginia* (Richmond, Va.: Virginia Surveyors Foundation, 1979), 31–32; Pett-Conklin, "Cadastral Surveying in Colonial South Carolina," 70–80.

5. Hanson, "Hanson's Journal" (first three quotations, 128; fourth quotation, 129).

6. Dunmore to county lieutenants, Williamsburg, Virginia, June 10, 1774, in Thwaites and Kellogg, eds., *Documentary History of Dunmore's War, 1774*, 33–35; William Russell to William Preston, Clinch River, June 26, 1774, in Thwaites and Kellogg, eds., *Documentary History of Dunmore's War, 1774*, 49–51.

7. Hanson, "Hanson's Journal" (quotations, 130).

8. Ibid. On December 1, 1779, Thomas Jefferson, governor of Virginia, issued a grant for one thousand acres in the name of John Floyd, Virginia Land Office patents B, 1779–1780, 197, reel 43. The tract was described as "in the county of Kentucky on elk horn creek a north branch of the Kentucky River." Floyd was listed as the assignee of William Preston, who was in turn the assignee of Alexander Waugh. This was a subterfuge arranged between these parties to award the land to Floyd, since John Floyd was not old enough to have participated in the French and Indian War and was thus not eligible for a military land patent under the terms of the Proclamation of 1763. The spring was not mentioned in the property description.

9. Hanson, "Hanson's Journal" (first quotation, 131; third quotation, 133); deposition of Daniel Boone, Point Pleasant, April 24, 1794, Fayette County, Kentucky, Circuit Court, *Complete Record Book A*, 621 (second quotation); William Preston to Lord Dunmore, Fincastle, August 13, 1774, in *American Archives: A Documentary History of the English Colonies in North America*, series 4, vol. 1 (Washington, D.C.: M. St. Clair Clarke and Peter Force, 1837), 707–8. Preston also refers to Floyd's return in: William Preston to George Washington, August 15, 1774, *Letters to Washington, and Accompanying Papers*, vol. 5, ed. Stanislaus M. Hamilton (Boston, Mass.: Houghton Mifflin, 1902), 46.

10. John Floyd to William Preston, Point Pleasant, October 16, 1774, in Thwaites and Kellogg, eds., *Documentary History of Dunmore's War, 1774*, 266–69.

7. McClelland's Station

1. Charlotte Conover, *Concerning the Forefathers* (Dayton, Ohio: Winthrop Press, 1902), 134–36, 138–39; Jefferson M. Patterson (youngest son of Robert Patterson) to Lyman C. Draper, Dayton, Ohio, n.d., probably 1843, Draper mss., 1 MM 16–21 (quotation). The letter is also reproduced in part in Eliza H. Brevoort, *McClelland-Harper: Settlers in the Wabash Valley 1774–1954* (Lawrenceville, Ill.: Bey Printing Office, 1955), 6–7. This letter contains an account of the travels and activities of Robert Patterson during the settlement era, written in the first person, that has often been referred to by historians as Patterson's "diary" or "journal." This is inaccurate; the account appears to be a synthesis of various depositions of Robert Patterson that was drafted and sometimes paraphrased by Jefferson Patterson for Draper's collection. Jefferson earlier wrote Draper on March 23, 1843, stating that "My father left no biographical sketches of his life. All the facts, incidents and adventures, are picked

up from old depositions about land claims in Ky and his Memorial to Congress for a pension" (Draper mss., 1 MM 15). Jefferson Patterson had many of his father's papers, and thus presumably had access to a number of depositions that could not be located by the author of this account. Charlotte Conover, however, stated that she based many of the "intimate details" of her biography of Patterson on two autobiographical sketches, the first written in 1816 and the second circa 1826, "when Robert Patterson was confined to his home with the beginning of what was his last illness" (Conover, *Concerning the Forefathers*, 3). Existing depositions by Patterson note his departure from Pittsburgh and some details of his route and travels, but do not specifically note all of his companions on the journey. Richard Collins collected numerous depositions of the settlement era, and in his *History of Kentucky* (vol. 2, 178) provides the names of those traveling to Kentucky in this party. Patterson, in a deposition dated October 19, 1818, names William McConnell, David Perry, and Stephen Lowry as being among his traveling companions (Draper mss., 15 CC 2).

2. Conover, *Concerning the Forefathers*, 121–27, 160–61, 195–97; Robert M. Torrence, comp., "Presbyterian Church, Mercersburg, Franklin County, Pennsylvania, Marriages by John King, D.D. 1769–1812," *Pennsylvania Vital Records*, vol. 2 (Baltimore: Genealogical Publishing Company, 1983), 146; Virginia S. Fendrick, comp., *American Revolutionary Soldiers of Franklin County, Pennsylvania* (Chambersburg, Pa.: Historical Works Committee of the Franklin County, Chapter, Daughters of the American Revolution, 1944), 126, 152. Published information on McClelland family genealogy is sparse, and I have been required to compile and cross-check information from websites such as Ancestry.com and FamilySearch (operated by the Genealogical Society of Utah) to establish family connections.

3. Deposition of Robert Patterson, January 31, 1801, *Complete Record Book A*, 307–13; Jefferson M. Patterson to Lyman C. Draper, Dayton, Ohio, n.d. (probably 1843), Draper mss., 1 MM 16–21.

4. Deposition of Robert Patterson, Fayette County, September 16, 1802, Draper mss., 1 MM 67–68; deposition of Robert Patterson, Dayton, Ohio, October 19, 1818, Draper mss., 15 C 25.9–25.10; Jefferson M. Patterson to Lyman C. Draper, Dayton, Ohio, n.d. (probably 1843), Draper mss., 1 MM 16–21. Subsequent direct references to the journey of the two separate groups to Royal Spring, unless otherwise cited, are derived from these sources.

5. Patterson to Draper, Draper mss., 1 MM 16–21 (quotation); Wilson, "McClelland and His Men," 12. The cabin "two miles below Lexington" would be McConnell's cabin at McConnell Springs, now within the bounds of Lexington.

6. John Floyd to William Preston, Kentucky Levels [plains of the Bluegrass region], May 30, 1775, Draper mss., 33 S 270–75; John Floyd to William Preston, Powell's Valley, April 21, 1775, Draper mss., 17 CC 167–69. This letter

identifies "Mr. Drake" as one of the party. Dick's River, later corrupted to Dix, was named in 1770 by a party of hunters, which included Drake, who were invited by a friendly Cherokee warrior known as Captain Dick to visit "his" river.

7. Journal of Richard Henderson, Boonesborough, May 3, 1775, Draper mss., 1 CC 34.

8. John Floyd to William Preston, Powell's Valley, May 1, 1776, Draper mss., 33 S 291–92 (first and second quotations, 292); Floyd to Preston, Boonesborough, May 19, 1776, Draper mss., 33 S 292–95 (third quotation, 293).

9. John Floyd to William Preston, Boonesborough, June 8, 1776, Draper mss., 33 S 298 (quotations). Francis McConnell was not specifically named in this letter as the settler on Preston's Cave Spring property, but is placed on this site at the time in question by several depositions—for example, deposition, William McConnell, July 22, 1789, *Kenton v. McConnell*; deposition, John McCrackin, August 4, 1790, *Kenton v. McConnell.* Original depositions not located, quoted in Carolyn M. Wooley, *The Founding of Lexington 1775–1776* (Lexington: Lexington-Fayette County Historic Commission, 1975), 48–49, note 91.

10. Information about the McClelland children was obtained from the genealogical websites mentioned previously.

11. John Floyd to William Preston, Boonesborough, May 19, 1776, Draper mss., 33 S 292–95 (quotation, 295); F. Paul Pacult, *Buffalo, Barrels, and Bourbon: The Story of How Buffalo Trace Distillery Became the World's Most Awarded Distillery* (Hoboken, N.J.: John Wiley and Sons, 2021), 25; Klotter and Friend, *A New History of Kentucky*, 35.

12. John Floyd to William Preston, Boonesborough, July 21, 1776, Draper mss., 33 S 300–305 (quotation, 300). Hinkston's Station in present-day Harrison County was established in 1775 by John Hinkston, and in 1779 the abandoned station was reoccupied by Isaac Ruddell and known by his name.

13. William B. Hesseltine, "Lyman Copeland Draper, 1815–1891," *Wisconsin Magazine of History* 35 (spring 1952), 163–66, 231–34.

14. Draper mss., 16 J 33–36, quotation, 35; Kim McBride, personal communication to Gary O'Dell, January 8, 2022.

15. O'Malley, *Stockading Up*, 293; Draper mss., 16 J 35–36, quotation, 36.

16. *Stockading Up* (1987), by Nancy O'Malley, remains the single most important reference on pioneer stations in the Inner Bluegrass region. See also O'Malley, *Boonesborough Unearthed*, for a detailed account of the Boonesborough settlement and the information gleaned by archaeological investigation. Many scholars consider Nancy O'Malley to be the leading authority on pioneer settlements and fortifications in Kentucky.

17. Terry G. Jordan, *American Log Buildings: An Old World Heritage* (Chapel Hill: Univ. of North Carolina Press, 1985), 44–45, 55; Terry G. Jordan and

Matti Kaups, *American Backwoods Frontier: An Ethnic and Ecological Interpretation* (Baltimore: Johns Hopkins Univ. Press, 1992), 137–77; O'Malley, *Stockading Up*, 24–30; O'Malley, *Boonesborough Unearthed*, 74–75; O'Malley, personal communication, May 3, 2021.

18. O'Malley, *Boonesborough Unearthed*, 75–76; William L. Montell and Michael L. Morse, *Kentucky Folk Architecture* (Lexington: Univ. Press of Kentucky, 1976), 8–25.

19. O'Malley, *Boonesborough Unearthed*, 75–76.

20. Ibid., 77.

21. O'Malley, *Stockading Up*, 24, 183.

22. Conover, *Concerning the Forefathers*, 146; Charlotte R. Conover, *Builders in New Fields* (New York: G. P. Putnam's Sons, 1939), 26

23. Nancy O'Malley, "Settling a Station," lecture, Kentucky Woodsmen's Weekend, Fort Boonesborough State Park, November 5, 2005; O'Malley, personal communication, May 3, 2021 (quotation).

24. Petition of Robert Patterson to the Congress of the United States, n.d., Draper mss., 1 MM 1–7; petitions dated June 15, 20, 1776, in *Petitions of the Early Inhabitants of Kentucky to the General Assembly of Virginia 1769 to 1792*, ed. James R. Robertson (Louisville, Ky.: John P. Morton, 1914), 36–42; George Rogers Clark to John Brown ("Clark's Memoir"), 1791, in *George Rogers Clark Papers 1771–1781*, ed. James A. James (Springfield, Ill: Illinois State Historical Society), 209–14. Clark and Jones probably first stopped at Richfield, General Andrew Lewis's estate in what is presently Roanoke County, then Botetourt. At the time, Lewis was away to the east on Chesapeake Bay, having just defeated Governor Dunmore at Gwynn Island.

25. James, *George Rogers Clark Papers*, 214–15.

26. Ibid., 20, 215; narrative of General Levi Todd, "Transactions in Kentucky from 1774 to 1777," Draper mss., 15 CC 160. Levi Todd does not appear to have been present, but was the brother of John Todd (later killed in the ambush at Blue Licks in August 1782. There are discrepancies between Clark's and Todd's accounts. Clark stated that four men were killed; Todd listed two killed and two captured.

27. James, *George Rogers Clark Papers*, 20, 215; Levi Todd's narrative, Draper mss., 15 CC 160 (quotation); Robert B. McAfee to Lyman C. Draper, November 30, 1847, Draper mss., 4 CC 84–85; John Bradford, "Opening the Great Western Road," reprinted from *Kentucky Gazette*, September 15, 1826, in *Voice of the Frontier*, 14. The latter contains the recollections of Elizabeth Thomas, who was twelve years old and a resident of Harrodsburg at the time of the attack on McClelland's Station. Ebenezer Stedman, who moved to Georgetown in 1818, wrote, "In the fall of 1826 one of the McClenan on a visit to Geotown pointed out the graves of his Relataves that had Bin killed & Buried thare." Ebenezer H. Stedman, *Bluegrass Craftsman: Being the Reminiscences of*

Ebenezer Hiram Stedman, Papermaker: 1808–1885, ed. Frances L. S. Dugan and Jacqueline P. Bull (Lexington: Univ. Press of Kentucky, 1959), 213.

28. Draper mss., 16 J 35–36, 36 (first quotation); Brevoort, *McClelland-Harper*, 20 (second quotation); Gaines, *History of Scott County*, vol. 2, 409; Federal Writers' Project, *Kentucky: A Guide to the Bluegrass State* (New York: Harcourt, Brace, 1939), 264–65. The statement by Sadie Bell was contained in a report by Katherine Bradley that cannot now be located, but was also quoted in Anne P. Coffman, "Mrs. W. H. Coffman Reviews Early History of Georgetown and County," *Georgetown Times*, May 23, 1923. The *Guide to the Bluegrass State* claimed that "For many years, superstitious inhabitants of the settlement believed that the echo in the spring was the death cry of the Indian chief."

29. Levi Todd's narrative, Draper mss., 15 CC 160; deposition of Samuel McMullen, Fayette County Circuit Court, *Complete Record Book D*, 15 (quotation); Edna Kenton, *Simon Kenton: His Life and Period 1755–1836* (Garden City, N.Y.: Doubleday, Doran, 1930), 80–81.

30. Robert Patterson, petition to Congress, Draper mss., 1 MM 1–7; quotation from unlocated deposition by Robert Patterson, quoted in Conover, *Concerning the Forefathers*, 161–62, and in Samuel Wilson, *McClelland and His Men*, 23–24.

31. *John Floyd's Heirs & Dev. v. John Adams, et. al.*, in *Decisions of the Appeals Court of Kentucky*, vol. 1, ed. Alex K. Marshall (Louisville, Ky.: George G. Fetter Printing Company, 1899), 72–74; Stephen Trigg, 900 acres, Virginia Land Office Grants F, 1781–1782, 368 (reel 47); John Cobbs, 3,000 acres, Virginia Land Office Grants No. 2, 1786, 355 (reel 68). The properties traded to John Floyd were the 1,400-acre Harrods Creek settlement and preemption located near the Ohio River in present-day Jefferson County and 800 acres on Guist Creek in present-day Shelby County.

32. Fleming, "Colonel William Fleming's Journal," 672–73. The ambush took place just past Clear's Station, which was abandoned at the time, at the point where the present-day Bluelicks Road dips down to cross Clear Run in Bullitt County. The Fishpools was located in the vicinity of present-day Okolona, Jefferson County. Fleming, however, states that Floyd was taken to the Salt Works (Bullitt's Lick, near present-day Shepherdsville). See also Cartlidge, "Colonel John Floyd: Reluctant Adventurer," 363–65.

33. Kentucky Supreme Court, *Order Book A*, 179, September 12, 1785, *John Cobbs v. William Trigg* filed. Additional references to the suit are found in Supreme Court, *Order Book A*, 394, 511; Supreme Court, *Order Book D*, 96, 97, 112, 185, 342; and Supreme Court, *Order Book F*, 290, spanning the period from 1786 to 1792. The date—November (not recorded) 1786—on which the suit was settled in favor of John Cobbs is known only by reference contained within Kentucky Supreme Court, *Deed Book B*, 35–38, March 9, 1789, quit claim, John Floyd's executors to John Cobbs. This deposition should be found recorded in

Supreme Court, *Order Book B*, but Books *B*, *C*, and *F* have been lost and are not available for consultation. Additional links in the deed trail are: Kentucky Supreme Court, *Deed Book B*, June 4, 1789, power of attorney executed November 13, 1787, by John Cobbs of Georgia to Samuel Taylor of Virginia to convey Royal Spring tract to Elijah Craig, 44–45; Kentucky Supreme Court, *Deed Book B*, 29–31, deed, John Cobbs to Elijah Craig. The chain of conveyances of the Royal Spring property was first worked out by Samuel M. Wilson and presented in a speech given in 1920 to the Big Spring chapter of the Daughters of the American Revolution, subsequently published in limited form as a typescript as "McClelland and His Men." Although Wilson provided a chronological list of names involved in these transactions, he did not give citations, and so considerable additional research was required to document this properly.

8. Serving God and Mammon

1. John H. Spencer and Burrilla B. Spencer, *A History of Kentucky Baptists: From 1769 to 1885, Including More Than 800 Biographical Sketches* (Cincinnati, Ohio: J. R. Baumes, 1885), 81–89; John Taylor, *A History of Ten Baptist Churches of Which the Author has been Alternately a Member.* (Frankfort, Ky.: J. H. Holeman, 1823), 42 (quotation); Samuel H. Ford, "First Church, Its Origin, Virginia, Lewis Craig," chapter in series "History of the Kentucky Baptists," *Christian Repository* (February 1856): 69–77; George W. Ranck, *The Traveling Church: An Account of the Baptist Exodus from Virginia to Kentucky in 1781 Under the Leadership of Rev. Lewis Craig and Capt. William Ellis* (Louisville, Ky.: Press of Baptist Book Concern, 1891), 5–13.

2. Ranck, *The Traveling Church*, 14–38; Reuben T. Durrett, "First Act in the Siege of Bryant's Station," in *Bryant's Station, and the Memorial Proceedings*, ed. Reuben T. Durrett (Louisville, Ky.: John P. Morton, 1897), 46–49.

3. John N. Bradley, *History of Great Crossings Church* (N.p.: N.p., 1876), 2 (first quotation); Samuel H. Ford, "South Elkhorn, Clear Creek, and Big Crossing Churches," chapter in series "History of Kentucky Baptists," *Christian Repository* (May 1856), 269 (second quotation), 271 (third quotation); petition of Elijah Craig to the Virginia legislature, October 21, 1790, in *Petitions from Kentucky to the Virginia Legislature 1776 to 1791: A Supplement to Petitions of the Early Inhabitants of Kentucky to the General Assembly of Virginia 1769 to 1792*, comp. John F. Dorman (Easley, S.C.: Southern Historical Press, 1981), 285 (fourth quotation). Sections of the buffalo trail are still visible in the field on the north side of US 460 near the intersection with KY 227 and on the west side of KY 227 south of Great Crossing near the Baptist Church.

4. Kentucky Supreme Court, *Deed Book B*, 44–45, June 4, 1789, power of attorney executed November 13, 1787, by John Cobbs of Georgia to Samuel Taylor of Virginia (quotation).

5. *Kentucky Gazette* (Lexington), November 3, 1787 (first quotation); petition of Elijah Craig, Woodford County, October 21, 1791, Legislative Petitions of the General Assembly, 1776–1865, accession number 36121, box 288, folder 19, Library of Virginia, Richmond, Va. (second quotation); "An Act to Establish Several Towns," December 16, 1790, in *The Statutes at Large: Being a Collection of All the Laws of Virginia*, vol. 13, ed. William W. Hening (1823; reprint, Charlottesville, Va.: Univ. Press of Virginia, 1969), 170; "An Act for Dividing the County of Woodford," in *The Statute Law of Kentucky*, vol. 1, ed. William Littell (Frankfort, Ky.: William Hunter, 1809), 61, boundary description 626.

6. Taylor, *A History of Ten Baptist Churches*, 280 (second quotation); Bradley, *History of Great Crossings Church*, 3; Spencer and Spencer, *History of Kentucky Baptists*, 88 (third and fourth quotations), 89 (first quotation).

7. Bradley, *History of Great Crossings Church*, 2–3; Spencer and Spencer, *History of Kentucky Baptists*, 88 (first quotation); *Kentucky Gazette*, January 28, 1788; Ann B. Bevins, *The Royal Spring of Georgetown, Kentucky* (Georgetown, Ky.: Scott County Historical Society, 1970), 26.

8. Collins, *History of Kentucky*, vol. 1, 516; *Kentucky Gazette* (Lexington), June 13, 1789, September 5, 1789 (first quotation), January 23, 1790; Hazel A. Spraker, *The Boone Family: A Genealogical History of the Descendants of George and Mary Boone, Who Came to America in 1717* (Rutland, Vt: Tuttle, 1922), 64, 114; Stedman, *Bluegrass Craftsman*, 32. Richard Collins's *History* is an expanded version of that of his father, Lewis Collins, whose own *Historical Sketches of Kentucky* was published in 1847. Unlike Richard, the elder Collins did not single out Elijah Craig for a list of "firsts," though he did note (on page 510) that Craig and Parkers erected the first paper mill in Kentucky in 1795. This suggests that Lewis Collins's source for this was early issues of the *Kentucky Gazette.* Richard Collins's source, however, may have been from an account published in Frankfort's *Argus of Western America* on September 19, 1827, of a dinner near Frankfort in honor of presidential candidate Andrew Jackson. During the dinner, the following toast was given by Lewis Sanders: "The memory of *Elijah Craig*, the founder of Georgetown, Kentucky. A philosopher and Christian—a useful man in his day. He established the first fulling-mill, the first paper-mill and the first rope-walk in Kentucky" (italics in original). Grant County and Grants Creek (Switzerland County) in Indiana were named for the slain Samuel and Moses Grant; in Kentucky, there is some uncertainty whether Grant County is named for Samuel or for one of his brothers, John Grant or Squire Grant. Grant's Lick in Campbell County is named for John Grant. Elijah Craig entered into partnership in December 1789 with James Logan to operate the fulling mill. The partnership lasted until March 1795, when it was dissolved (*Kentucky Gazette*, April 4, 1795). Craig continued operation of the mill afterward.

9. *Kentucky Gazette* (Lexington), September 5, 1789 (first quotation); William Hayden, *Narrative of William Hayden, Containing a Faithful Account of His Travels for a Number of Years, Whilst a Slave, in the South* (Cincinnati, Ohio: N.p., 1846), 24 (second quotation).

10. *Kentucky Gazette* (Lexington), August 25, 1787, January 21, 1792, March 30, 1793 (quotation)

11. Stedman, *Bluegrass Craftsman*, 211–17, (second quotation, 212); *Kentucky Gazette* (Lexington), January 21, 1792 (first quotation), January 28, 1792.

12. Collins, *History of Kentucky*, vol. 1, 516 (quotation); Henry Crowgey, *Kentucky Bourbon: The Early Years of Whiskeymaking* (Lexington: Univ. Press of Kentucky, 1971), 124–36; Charles K. Cowdery, *Bourbon Straight: The Uncut and Unfiltered Story of American Whiskey* (Chicago: Made and Bottled in Kentucky, 2004), 22–29.

13. John C. Tramazzo, *Bourbon and Bullets: True Stories of Whiskey, War, and Military Service* (Lincoln, Nebr.: Potomac Books, 2018), 15–17; Willard R. Jillson, *Early Kentucky Distillers 1783–1800* (Frankfort, Ky.: Standard Printing Company, 1940), 46; Crowgey, *Kentucky Bourbon*, 129–30; Michael R. Veach, *Kentucky Bourbon Whiskey: An American Heritage* (Lexington: Univ. Press of Kentucky, 2013), 22, 24.

14. *Kentucky Gazette* (Lexington), May 24, 1808. Craig departed this life on May 18, "after a long and painful illness."

9. Clear Beautiful Spring Watter

1. Scott County, *Will Book A*, 410, will of Elijah Craig, made May 13, 1808, probated June 1808; Stephen F. Gano, "Georgetown: Growth and Development," in *History of Bourbon, Scott, Harrison and Nicholas Counties, Kentucky*, ed. William H. Perrin (Chicago: O. L. Baskin, 1882), 188; Scott County, *Order Book A*, 9, January 22, 1793, Josiah Pitts granted tavern license; Scott County, *Deed Book B*, 137–42, June 24, 1813, deed, William Shortridge, Deputy Sheriff, to William B. Keene; Scott County, *Deed Book N*, 23–24, October 1837, deed, William Shortridge, Deputy Sheriff, to William B. Keene [recopied from original]. The record in *Deed Book B* is fragmentary, as this volume consists of burned records that were recopied after the 1837 fire that destroyed the courthouse. The document in *Deed Book N* is a replacement deed, recorded from a copy produced in the Scott County Court of October 1837 by William B. Keene.

2. There has been some controversy as to when the "cross-wall," as it was known, was built. Testimony in *City of Georgetown v. Water Supply Company* (see "Water Supply Co. v. City of Georgetown," *Southwestern Reporter*, vol. 81 [St. Paul, Minn.: West Publishing Company, 1904], 661), suggests that the wall and springhouse may have been built by William B. Keene sometime after

1813, but none of the witnesses possessed firsthand knowledge and were therefore uncertain as to the date of construction. The original court record for this case could not be located, but is duplicated in *Water Supply Company v. City of Georgetown*, Kentucky Court of Appeals, 1904, box 1555, case number 32652, Kentucky Department for Libraries and Archives (hereafter KDLA), Frankfort, Kentucky. Bill Gaines, in his 1905 *History of Scott County* (Georgetown), asserted that the springhouse and cross-wall were built during the ownership of Josiah Pitts (pages 232, 251,252). The most detailed descriptions of the springhouse and cross-wall are found in the testimony of James Y. Kelly, in the case cited above, who stated that the wall "was there in '46 [1846]" when he first came to Georgetown.

3. Scott County, *Deed Book B*, 137–42, June 24, 1813, deed, William Shortridge, Deputy Sheriff, to William B. Keene (quotation); Scott County, *Deed Book N*, 23–24, October 1837, deed, William Shortridge, Deputy Sheriff, to William B. Keene [recopied from original]

4. "An Act Increasing the Powers of the Trustees of the Town of Georgetown, and for Other Purposes," *Acts Passed at the First Session of the 24th General Assembly for the Commonwealth of Kentucky* (Frankfort, Ky.: Gerard and Berry, 1816), 616–20 (first quotation, 617); Scott County, *Lines Book 1*, 39–40, April 1824, plat of the town of George Town; Scott County, *Order Book B-2*, 181, April 1824; "An Act to Amend an Act, Entitled an Act to Enlarge the Boundaries of Georgetown, and for Other Purposes," *Acts Passed at the First Session of the Forty-Third General Assembly for the Commonwealth of Kentucky* (Frankfort, Ky.: Albert G. Hodges, 1835), 98–104 (second quotation, 103–4).

5. The only extant source for this information is from "Notes on Georgetown, No. 8," *Every Saturday* (Georgetown, Ky.), August 9, 1879, which referred to a March 1825 resolution by the town's board of trustees. These records can no longer be located; the earliest minutes of the Georgetown trustees in recent possession by the city began in 1850 with *Book A. Books A* and *B* are, however, now missing from the vault of city hall, and their whereabouts are unknown.

6. Stedman, *Bluegrass Craftsman*, 28 (first quotation); Gaines, *History of Scott County*, vol. 2, 463 (second and third quotations); Scott County, *Order Book A*, 53, October 27, 1795. In May 2017, the city of Georgetown received a Transportation Alternatives Program (TAP) grant from the Federal Highway Administration to make needed repairs and improvements to the stone bridge, totaling $1.1 million after subsequent amendments and supplemented by $277,000 in local matching funds. Work on the Georgetown West Main Streetscape Project began in 2022, and will repair bridge walls, rebuild sidewalks, improve the storm drainage system, and provide new street lighting and landscaping. Arlene Wilson (Georgetown Mayor's Office) to Gary O'Dell, personal communication, April 18, 2022. This communication was in response to my query on the subject

and contained summary information provided by Devon Golden (city attorney) and Eddie Hightower (city engineer), along with supporting documents.

7. Gaines, *History of Scott County*, vol. 2, 461 (quotation).

8. Ibid., 463.

9. Testimony of James Y. Kelly, 1903, *City of Georgetown v. Georgetown Water Company* (first quotation); Gaines, *History of Scott County*, vol. 2, 461 (second quotation).

10. Gaines, *History of Scott County*, vol. 2, 466–67; *Georgetown (Ky.) Times*, February 8, 1882 (quotation), June 10, 1885. The 1880 US Census lists the occupation of Alexander Elgin as "water carrier," and that of his sixteen-year-old stepson, David Bradford, as "cart driver." See O'Dell, "The Search for Water," for a discussion of the many creative ways in which rural people provide themselves with water for domestic use, including purchase of hauled water.

11. Ann B. Bevins, personal communication, June 6, 2021; Ann B. Bevins, unpublished notes on Water Street, personal communication, May 10, 2021; Scott County, *Deed Book 3*, John Sheehan to Nelly Green, January 13, 1857, 262; US Decennial Census 1860.

12. Scott County, *Order Book A*, 2–3, October 1792; Scott County, *Order Book A*, 259, February 25, 1805; Scott County, *Order Book A*, 288, February 24, 1806 (original date on document obliterated; determined from context); Scott County, *Order Book A*, 295, June 23, 1806; "Act Increasing the Powers of the Trustees of the Town of Georgetown," 619–20.

13. Gaines, *History of Scott County*, vol. 2, 220, 471; "Act Increasing the Powers of the Trustees of the Town of Georgetown," 619; Georgetown Trustees, *Minute Book C*, May 4, 1877, 263; May 15, 1877, 264; June 1, 1877, 268; "Fire Fiend!" *Georgetown Weekly Times*, October 19, 1881.

10. Blue Grass Park and the Civil War

1. *Georgetown (Ky.) Telegraph*, March 19, 1812.

2. A. Keene Richards, *The Arab Horses, Mohkladi, Massoud and Sacklowie: Imported by A. Keene Richards, Georgetown, Kentucky* (Lexington: Kentucky Statesman Printing, 1857); Thornton Chard, "Keene Richards' Arabian Importations," *The Horse* (November/December 1934), 12–18; (January/February 1935), 21–25); Thornton Chard, "Arabian Blood for Stamina," *The Horse* (November/December 1935), 3–7; (January/Febuary 1936, 6–9); Alexander Mackay-Smith, *The Race Horses of America, 1832–1872: Portraits and Other Paintings by Edward Troye* (Saratoga Springs, N.Y.: National Museum of Racing, 1981). The Keene Richards item, above, is a very rare exhibition catalog in which Richards describes how his interest in horse breeding came about and provides brief accounts of his importations of horses from the Arab lands and Europe. The text of the catalog, sans illustrations, was later reprinted in "The

Breeding Stud of A. Keene Richards, Esq., of Georgetown, Ky," *Spirit of the Times* 27 (August 8, 1857), 303–4. Racetracks, as opposed to racecourses, are an American invention in which the turf has been removed to produce an allegedly faster running surface on bare dirt; racecourses in which the grass has been left in place were the form used in Europe.

3. Scott County, *Will Book M*, 666–70, will of William B. Keene, made September 27, 1856, probated May 1857.

4. Scott County, *Deed Book T*, September 15, 1845, 172; Scott County, *Deed Book 3*, October 14, 1857, 375; Scott County, *Deed Book 5*, December 1, 1859, 254; "H.B." [Hamilton Busbey], "Closing Notes of a September Holiday," *Turf, Field and Farm* 37 (October 4, 1872), 209–10 (quotation, 209).

5. "Breeding Establishments of Kentucky," *Spirit of the Times* 18 (July 11, 1868), 370; "Residence of A. K. Richards, Georgetown," *Spirit of the Times* 30 (July 28, 1860), 299–300; "Visit to A. K. Richards' Racing Stables, near Georgetown, Ky," *Wilkes' Spirit of the Times* 1 (January 21, 1860), 306–7; Gaines, *History of Scott County*, 446; "A. K. Richards' Stud," *Spirit of the Times* 18 (July 11, 1868), 370; Anon., "Death of Glencoe," *Georgetown (Ky.) Times*, January 19, 1898 (quotation). The *Spirit of the Times*, a weekly sporting newspaper founded in 1831, was known by several different names during its existence due to changes in ownership. At one time, the paper split, resulting in two competing papers under the same name, until later re-merging.

6. "Residence of A. K. Richards, Georgetown," 300 (first quotation); "Georgetown, Ky, Spring Meeting," *Wilkes Spirit of the Times* 6 (June 7, 1862), 219; Mackay-Smith, *The Race Horses of America*, 101, 104, 199; Scott County, Mortgage Book 4, October 6, 1871, 32; Gaines, *History of Scott County*, 446 (second quotation); "Breeding Establishments of Kentucky," 370.

7. "Visit to A. K. Richards' Racing Stables," 306 (quotation); "Residence of A. K. Richards, Georgetown," 300.

8. "Visit to A. K. Richards' Racing Stables," 306 (first three quotations); "Residence of A. K. Richards, Georgetown," 300 (fourth quotation).

9. "Georgetown, Ky, Spring Meeting," 219 (quotation).

10. *New York Herald*, March 20, 1881, obituary of Keene Richards; Keene Richards to John C. Breckinridge, July 8, 1868, Breckinridge Family Papers 1752–1965, box 572, Library of Congress.

11. MS652, William T. Chapman Papers Transcripts (August–September, October, 1862), Bowling Green State University Libraries, lib.bgsu.edu/finding_aids/items/show/2038, accessed August 31, 2019.

12. William C. Davis, *Breckinridge: Statesman, Soldier, Symbol* (Baton Rouge: Louisiana State Univ. Press, 1974), 325–29; US War Department, *War of the Rebellion: Official Records of the Union and Confederate Armies* [hereinafter *O.R.*] (Washington, D.C.: GPO, 1880–1901), ser. 1, vol. 16, part 1, 455–56.

13. Davis, *Breckinridge*, 329–49; Grady McWhiney, *Braxton Bragg and Confederate Defeat*, vol. 1, *Field Command* (New York: Columbia Univ. Press, 1969), 337–73.

14. A. Keene Richards to John C. Breckinridge, October 30, 1862, National Archives and Records Administration, *Compiled Service Records of Confederate Officers and Enlisted Men*, M331; amnesty application for A. Keene Richards, August 20, 1865, National Archives and Records Administration, Confederate Amnesty Papers, Amnesty Applications, reel 1003-26 (quotation). Keene Richards was granted a pardon by President Andrew Johnson on September 8, 1865.

15. Scott County, *Deed Book 6*, 17–18 (quotation, 18), September 19, 1861, deeds, A. Keene Richards to Edward Troye.

16. Mackay-Smith, *Race Horses of America*, 226, 229.

17. "H.B." [Hamilton Busbey], "Closing Notes of a September Holiday," 209–10; "A. Keene Richards," *Turf, Field and Farm* 32 (March 25, 1881), 184; "Death of Col. A. Keene Richards," *Kentucky Live Stock Record* 13 (March 26, 1881), 200. The *Kentucky Live Stock Record* was renamed in 1895 as the *Thoroughbred Record* and continued to be published in Lexington until 2012, at which time the journal filed for bankruptcy.

18. "The Georgetown Stable," *Turf, Field and Farm* 2 (January 6, 1866), 9 (first quotation); Richards to Breckinridge, July 8, 1868, Breckinridge Family Papers (second quotation); A. Keene Richards bankruptcy case file #842, US District Court, Western District of Kentucky, Louisville Term, February 29, 1868.

19. Scott County, *Mortgage Book 3*, 218, October 16, 1865, mortgage, Edward Troye to Grinstead and Bradley; Scott County, *Mortgage Book 3*, 231–32, March 28, 1866, mortgage (horses), Keene Richards to Grinstead and Bradley; Scott County, *Mortgage Book 3*, 250, October 13, 1866, mortgage, Alexander Keene Richards to Harvey C. Graves; Scott County, *Deed Book 9*, 363, December 22, 1868, mortgage, Edward and Camelia A. Troye to Harvey C. Graves; Scott County, *Mortgage Book 4*, 32, October 6, 1871, mortgage, A. Keene Richards and Harvey C. Graves to E. D. Sayre; Richards to Breckinridge, July 8, 1868, Breckinridge Family Papers (quotation).

20. Scott County, *Order Book 31*, 519–21, September 12, 1874, *Sayre v. Richards*; Scott County, *Deed Book 15*, 55–57, July 22, 1876, deed, A. Keene and Mary E. Richards and Harvey C. and Martha Graves to E. D. Sayre; Scott County, *Deed Book 15*, 90, August 29, 1876, deed, E. D. Sayre to James A. Grinstead; Scott County, *Deed Book 15*, 278–79, October 18, 1876, quit claim, W. B. Keene [Jr.] of Louisiana to James A. Grinstead.

21. "Death of Edward Troye, Esq.," *Georgetown (Ky.) Times*, July 29, 1874; "Fire," *Georgetown (Ky.) Times*, April 19, 1875.

22. "Blue Grass Park," *Kentucky Live Stock Record* 1 (June 23, 1877), 392; *Lexington Daily Press*, March 20, 1881.

23. Samuel Y. Keene, "LeComte—Edith Filly," *Thoroughbred Record* 63 (June 16, 1906), 394; "A. Keene Richards," *Turf, Field and Farm* 32 (March 25, 1881), 184 (quotations).

24. Scott County, *Deed Book 21*, 442, January 8, 1885, deed, John T. Shelby, assignee of James A. Grinstead, to John B. Graves; Scott County, *Deed Book 21*, 449–50, January 22, 1885, deed, John B. and Mary Graves to William Payne; Scott County, *Deed Book 25*, 85–86, April 9, 1889, deed, William and Elizabeth Payne to Jeff D. Grover; Scott County, *Deed Book 29*, 203–4, October 9, 1894, deed, J. D. Grover to Alice P. Montgomery; Ann B. Bevins, *A History of Scott County, as Told by Selected Buildings* (Georgetown, Ky.: Kreative Grafiks Ink, 1981), 236–37. The quit claim from W. B. Keene Jr. was in response to a stipulation of W. B. Keene Sr.'s will that reverted the property to him in the event that Keene Richards died without "male issue of his body."

11. The Water Works

1. Gaines, *History of Scott County*, 437–38, 443–45; Georgetown Trustees, *Minute Book C*, May 4, 1877, 263; July 6, 1877, 274; August 2, 1878, 336; September 6, 1878, 340; September 9, 1878, 341; Georgetown Trustees, *Minute Book D*, November 5, 1880, 104 (first quotation); June 3, 1881, 135; July 1, 1881, 137; November 4, 1887, 451 (second quotation); "Fire Fiend!" *Georgetown Weekly Times*, October 19, 1881.

2. O'Dell, "Water Supply and the Early Development of Lexington," 456–60; Georgetown Trustees, *Minute Book D*, January 15, 1889, 529; January 16, 1889, 530.

3. Georgetown Trustees, *Minute Book D*, March 1, 1889, 538; March 11, 1889, 539. Obituaries of Edwin Rush Davenport in the August 18, 1897, *Pomeroy (Ohio) Tribune-Telegraph* and in the August 20, 1897, *Middleport (Ohio) Republican-Herald* describe Davenport as a civil engineer who "built water works at Alton, Illinois; Hannibal, Missouri; Stillwater, Duluth and Fergus Falls, Minnesota; Wahpeton, N. D.; Oskaloosa, Iowa; Charleston, W. Va." and at Pomeroy, Ohio. J. H. B. Davenport was mentioned as a surviving brother, a resident of Chicago, Illinois.

4. Georgetown Trustees, *Minute Book D*, April 5, 1889, 546; May 11, 1889, 550; May 18, 1889, 552; "Water Works Election Notice," *Georgetown (Ky.) Times*, May 15, 1889; Scott County, *Deed Book 25*, 127–30, May 9, 1889, contract between chairman and Board of Trustees of Georgetown and E. H. Patterson [*sic*] and John Nichols.

5. Scott County, *Deed Book 25*, 127–30, May 9, 1889, contract (quotations); Scott County, *Deed Book 25*, 134–35, June 1, 1889, water lease, Jeff D. Grover to John Nichols; Scott County, *Record of Corporation Book 1*, 60–62, June 21, 1889, Articles of Incorporation, Georgetown Water Company.

6. Georgetown Trustees, *Minute Book D*, 571, September 6, 1889; October 4, 1889, 575.

7. Georgetown Trustees, *Minute Book D*, March 7, 1890, 599 (quotations); "The Ice Factory in Operation," *Georgetown (Ky.) Times*, July 2, 1890; "Plant and Electric Railway," *Georgetown (Ky.) Times*, February 26, 1896; Scott County, *Deed Book 30*, 462–63, March 2, 1896, deed, Alice P. and H. P. Montgomery to Georgetown Street Railway Company; "Ice Plant and Street Railway," *Georgetown (Ky.) Times*, May 27, 1896; Gaines, *History of Scott County*, vol. 2, 468–70; Apple, Johnston, and Bevins, *Scott County, Kentucky: A History*, 236.

8. "Georgetown Water Co. v. Fidelity Trust & Safety Vault Co. Montgomery &. v. same," *Reports of Civil and Criminal Cases Decided by the Court of Appeals of Kentucky*, volume X, volume 117 (Louisville, Ky., 1906), 330–34; "Sale of Water Works," *Georgetown (Ky.) Times*, May 4, 1892; Scott County, *Record of Corporation Book 1*, 81–83, June 8, 1892, Articles of Incorporation, The Water Supply Company.

9. "Receiver to be Appointed: Street Railway and Ice Plant to be Sold," *Georgetown (Ky.) Times*, February 16, 1898; "Sale of Street Railway and Ice Plant," *Georgetown (Ky.) Times*, April 20, 1898; Scott County, *Record of Corporation Book 1*, 129–31, May 25, 1898, Articles of Incorporation, Amendments, The Water Supply Company; Scott County, *Record of Corporation Book 1*, 132–34, August 8, 1899, Articles of Incorporation, Georgetown Electric Railway Company; Scott County, *Record of Corporation Book 1*, 134–36, August 8, 1899, Articles of Incorporation, Georgetown, Royal Spring Ice Company; Scott County, *Record of Corporation Book 1*, 137–38, August 8, 1899, Articles of Incorporation, Amendments, The Water Supply Company; Scott County, *Deed Book 33*, 271–72, September 1, 1899, deed, The Water Supply Company to the Royal Spring Ice Company; Scott County, *Deed Book 33*, 272–73, September 1, 1899, deed, The Water Supply Company to the Georgetown Electric Railway Company.

10. Scott County Board of Council, *Minute Book G*, August 3, 1900, 398, 399; August 10, 1900, 404; November 2, 1900, 434; November 7, 1900, 442. Numerous subsequent deeds make reference to the conveyance, on August 1, 1900, of the assets of the Water Supply Company and subsidiaries by Master Commissioner Robert E. Roberts to Robert W. Nelson, but none list the book and page, and, despite diligent investigation, I have been unable to locate this transaction in the Scott County records.

11. Georgetown Board of Council, *Minute Book H*, April 8, 1901, 64–65; April 19, 1901, 67; April 23, 1901, 70; April 26, 1901, 72; April 30, 1901, 73; May 3, 1901, 87–91,92–100; Scott County, *Record of Corporation Book 1*, June 19, 1901, Articles of Incorporation, Georgetown Water, Gas, Electric and Power Company, 153–54; Scott County, *Deed Book 34*, 370–71, June 27, 1901,

deed, R. W. and Mary W. Nelson to Georgetown Water, Gas, Electric and Power Company; Scott County, *Record of Corporation Book 1*, 157–58, August 19, 1901, Articles of Incorporation, Georgetown Water, Light and Power Company.

12. "Col. R. W. Nelson Famous Lawyer Dies in Newport Ky," *Cincinnati (Ohio) Enquirer*, January 10, 1927; Scott County, *Deed Book 56*, 519–22, June 20, 1928, Georgetown Water, Gas, Electric and Power Company to Lexington Utilities Company; Scott County, *Deed Book 65*, January 3, 1940, Lexington Utilities Company to Kentucky Utilities Company, 69–80; Scott County, *Deed Book 70*, 476–80, October 23, 1945, Kentucky Utilities Company to City of Georgetown.

13. "Survey of Water and Disposal Plants Ordered," *Georgetown (Ky.) Times*, April 13, 1955; "Georgetown Water Company Nears Completion of New Plant," *Georgetown (Ky.) Times*, February 13, 1957; "City Will Honor Former Mayor, City Attorney," *Georgetown (Ky.) Times*, July 31, 1957.

12. Who Owns Royal Spring?

1. Georgetown Board of Council, *Minute Book G*, February 4, 1898, 16.

2. Scott County, *Deed Book 29*, 203–4 (first and second quotations, 204), October 9, 1894, deed, J. D. Grover to Alice P. Montgomery; Scott County, *Deed Book 30*, 462–63, March 2, 1896, deed, Alice P. and H. P. Montgomery to Georgetown Street Railway Company; Scott County, *Deed Book 33*, 271–72, September 1, 1899, deed, Water Supply Company to Royal Spring Ice Company; Scott County, *Deed Book 25*, 127–30 (third quotation, 127), May 9, 1889, contract between chairman and Board of Trustees of Georgetown and Paterson and Nichols.

3. *Georgetown (Ky.) Times*, October 6, 1897; *Water Supply Co. v. City of Georgetown*, *Kentucky Law Reporter* 26 (August 15, 1904), 327 (quotation).

4. Georgetown Board of Council, *Minute Book G*, February 4, 1898, 16 (quotation).

5. Georgetown Board of Council, *Minute Book G*, November 11, 1898, 116 (quotation); "New Ice Plant Exempted from Taxation," *Georgetown (Ky.) Times*, November 10, 1898.

6. Georgetown Board of Council, *Minute Book G*, December 2, 1898, 123; December 9, 1898, 131; December 17, 1898, 135.

7. Georgetown Board of Council, *Minute Book G*, January 6, 1899, 143–44 (quotation, 144).

8. Georgetown Board of Council, *Minute Book G*, January 13, 1899, 147; January 20, 1899, 158; January 23, 1899, 159–61 (quotation, 160).

9. Georgetown Board of Council, *Minute Book G*, January 25, 1899, 162; February 2, 1899, 163–64; February 3, 1899, 171

10. Georgetown Board of Council, *Minute Book G*, February 3, 1899, 171; March 3, 1899, 188 (quotation); "Petition in Equity: City of Georgetown by Its Mayor and Board of Council vs. The Water Supply Company," April 21, 1899, in *Water Supply Company v. City of Georgetown*, Kentucky Court of Appeals, 1904, box 1555, case number 32652, KDLA.

11. *Georgetown Water Company v. Central Thompson Houston Company*, Kentucky Court of Appeals, 1899, box 1230, case number 27887, KDLA; *Fidelity Trust and Safety Vault Company v. Georgetown Water Company*, Kentucky Court of Appeals, 1900, box 1537, case number 32401, KDLA; Scott County Circuit Court, *Order Book 40*, 335, October 11, 1901.

12. "The Big Spring" and "A Funny Situation," *Georgetown (Ky.) Times*, August 9, 1899; Georgetown Board of Council, *Minute Book G*, August 4, 1899, 269.

13. Georgetown Board of Council, *Minute Book G*, August 4, 1899, 269; *Minute Book H*, September 17, 1902, 363; *Georgetown (Ky.) Times*, August 9, 1899 (quotations). Drought classification is based on the Palmer Drought Severity Index (PDSI), which uses several indicators, including precipitation and soil moisture, in a complex formula to determine categories.

14. Georgetown Board of Council, *Minute Book H*, January 24, 1902, 244; Georgetown Board of Council, *Minute Book H*, March 22, 1902, 271.

15. Scott County, *Deed Book B*, 137–42, June 24, 1813, deed, William Shortridge, Deputy Sheriff, to William B. Keene (fragmentary), and Scott County, *Deed Book N*, 23–24 (first quotation, 33), October 1837 (re-recorded); Scott County, *Deed Book 21*, 442 (second quotation), January 8, 1885, deed, John T. Shelby, assignee of James A. Grinstead, to John B. Graves; Scott County, *Deed Book 30*, 462–63 (third quotation, 463), March 2, 1896, deed, Alice P. and H. P. Montgomery to Georgetown Street Railway Company.

16. "Act to Enlarge the Boundaries of Georgetown," *Forty-Third General Assembly for the Commonwealth of Kentucky*, 98–104 (quotation, 103–4).

17. *City of Georgetown v. Water Supply Company*, included with *Water Supply Company v. City of Georgetown*, Kentucky Court of Appeals, 1904, box 1555, case number 32652, KDLA (first quotation, n.p., handwritten). Documents from *A. K. Lair v. City of Georgetown* are also included in the appeal (second quotation, n.p., handwritten). See also "Water Supply Co. v. City of Georgetown," *Southwestern Reporter* 81 (St. Paul, Minn.: West Publishing Company, 1904), 660–63. Pertinent, but not admitted into evidence in the case, was a statement that had appeared in print forty years earlier, written by a visitor to Blue Grass Park: "The lawn and gardens are very neatly laid out, and extend to the right to a large spring of delicious cool water, issuing from an immense rock, which a former owner had divided by a stone wall, so as to form a running stream separating the town from the estate; this stream was ceded to the town

on the understanding that the Richards estate should never be brought within the corporation limits, but the papers being destroyed at the burning of the Court-house, the compact has been broken, and the present owner has no redress," *Spirit of the Times* 30 (July 28, 1860), 299.

18. Scott County, *Circuit Court Book 41*, judgement in *City of Georgetown vs. The Water Supply Company*, May 22, 1903, 211–14 (quotation, 211).

19. *Water Supply Company v. City of Georgetown*, Kentucky Court of Appeals, 1904, box 1555, case number 32652, KDLA; *Water Supply Co. v. City of Georgetown*, *Kentucky Law Reporter*, 332 (quotation).

13. Gulping Down Royal Spring Sewage

1. *Georgetown (Ky.) Telegraph*, March 19, 1812 (quotations); Georgetown Trustees, *Minute Book C*, November 1, 1872, 15; "Ordinance No. 85, Establishing Rates and Regulations With the Georgetown Water, Light & Power Company for the Use of Water, Electric Light and Power," *Minute Book H*, May 3, 1901, 87–91. Orders by the trustees of Georgetown, later the city council, directing the cleaning of the Royal or Big Spring, are found in the following *Minute Books*: *A*, September 4, 1852, 165; *A*, May 15, 1854, 202; *C*, October 5, 1877, 284; *C*, November 2, 1877, 288; *D*, June 11, 1879, 22; *D*, June 20, 1879, 25; *D*, July 7, 1879, 28; *E*, June 5, 1891, 42; *E*, September 19, 1892, 170; *F*, October 8, 1895, 198; *F*, July 2, 1897, 371; *G*, April 27, 1899, 223.

2. Harris et al., "Cholera" 2467–70.

3. Baird, "Asiatic Cholera's First Visit," 228; "The Cholera," *Lexington Observer and Kentucky Reporter*, June 1, 1833; George W. Ranck, *History of Lexington, Kentucky: Its Early Annals and Recent Progress* (Cincinnati, Ohio: Robert Clarke, 1872), 325; Daniel Drake, "Miscellaneous Observations—Historical, Statistical, Aetiological and Therapeutic, on the Prevailing Epidemic," *Western Journal of the Medical and Physical Sciences* 7 (July, August, and September 1833): 165–66 (quotation).

4. Charles T. Jackson, "The Natural History of Water," in *Scientific Tracts for the Diffusion of Useful Knowledge* (Boston, Mass.: Light and Stearns, 1836), 129; Charles T. Jackson, "The Cholera in the United States," *New York Herald*, November 2, 1848 (first quotation); Lapham to Jackson, August 7, 1849, and Jackson to Lapham, September 6, 1849, in John H. Voje, "Two Interesting Letters Concerning the Causes of Cholera, as Understood in 1849," *Wisconsin Medical Journal* 8 (February 1915): 365–67 (second quotation); Anon., "Cholera in Nashville—Relation to Limestone," *Western Journal of Medicine and Surgery*, 3rd series, 3 (March 1, 1849): 271–72; John Lea, *Cholera, With Reference to the Geological Theory: A Proximate Cause—A Law by Which It Is Governed—A Prophylactic* (Cincinnati, Ohio: Wright, Ferris, 1850; reprinted in *International*

Journal of Epidemiology 42 (February 2013): 30–42. See also David M. Morens, "Commentary: Cholera Conundrums and Proto-Epidemiologic Puzzles. The Confusing Epidemic World of John Lea and John Snow," *International Journal of Epidemiology* 42 (February 2013): 43–52.

5. Rather than upsetting the digestive system, calcium carbonate is beneficial, used as an antacid in solid or liquid formulations to provide symptomatic relief of heartburn, acid indigestion, and upset stomach. For this purpose, chalk has been chewed for centuries. One regular strength Rolaids tablet contains 550 mg of calcium carbonate, roughly equal to the amount that would be ingested by drinking 5 liters (1.3 gallons) of water from a typical karst spring in limestone.

6. Lunsford P. Yandell, "Notices of the Diseases of the Summer and Fall of 1832," *Transylvania Journal of Medicine and the Associate Sciences* 6 (April, May, and June, 1832): 503–6 (quotation, 504); Lunsford P. Yandell, "An Account of Spasmodic Cholera, as It Appeared in the City of Lexington, in June 1833," *Transylvania Journal of Medicine and the Associate Sciences* 6 (April, May, and June, 1833): 197.

7. "The Cholera in 1833 and 1849," *Georgetown (Ky.) Times*, June 5, 1833 (first quotation); "Cholera in Georgetown," *Lexington (Ky.) Observer and Reporter*, June 5, 1833 (second quotation); Stedman, *Bluegrass Craftsman*, 148–49 (third and fourth quotations).

8. "The Cholera in 1833 and 1849"; Baird, "Asiatic Cholera's First Visit," 231; Drake, "Miscellaneous Observations," 162; "Medical Obituary: William Richards, M.D.," *Western Journal of the Medical and Physical Sciences* 7 (June 30, 1833): 159–60 (quotation); "Notes on Georgetown," *Every Saturday* (Georgetown, Ky.), August 2, 1879.

9. "The Cholera in 1833 and 1849"; John T. Johnson, Georgetown, to Alexander Campbell, June 29, 1833, *Millennial Harbinger* 7 (July 1833), 328 (quotation).

10. Chambers, *The Conquest of Cholera*, 197–234; "The Cholera in 1833 and 1849"; Ethelbert L. Dudley, "Editorial," *Transylvania Medical Journal* 1 (June 1849): 94–96; Baird, "Asiatic Cholera: Kentucky's First Health Instructor," 327–32.

11. Carrie T. Goldsborough and Anna G. Fisher, *William Loftis Sutton, M.D., 1797–1862: Father of Kentucky State Medical Society and of Kentucky's First Vital Statistics Law* (Lexington, Ky.: The Thoroughbred Press, 1948), 22–25, 30–35, 131–32.

12. Ibid., 132–33.

13. Baird, "Asiatic Cholera: Kentucky's First Health Instructor," 333–41; Ely McClellan, *An Account of the Epidemic of Cholera, During the Summer of 1873, in Eighteen Counties of the State of Kentucky* (Cambridge, Mass.: Riverside Press, 1874); Joseph K. Barnes et al., *Cholera Epidemic of 1873 in the United States*

(Washington, D.C.: GPO, 1875), 258–325. See also Chambers, *The Conquest of Cholera*, 252–59, 269–334. Cholera continues to claim lives globally in the twenty-first century despite overall improvements in sanitation. The United States experienced its last cholera outbreak during 1910–1911, which was confined to New York City and resulted in eleven deaths. Cholera is endemic in many countries, with the highest incidence in Sub-Saharan Africa. Although the majority of cases are not reported, recent research estimates that approximately 2.9 million cases occur annually, resulting in about 95,000 deaths. See Mohammed Ali, Allyson R. Nelson, Anna L. Lopez, and David A. Sack, "Updated Global Burden of Cholera in Endemic Countries," *PLOS Neglected Tropical Diseases* 9 (June 2015), https://doi.org/10.1371/journal.pntd.0003671, accessed September 12, 2021.

14. William B. Rodman, "Contamination of Water Supply as a Cause of Disease," *First Annual Report of the State Board of Health of Kentucky* (Frankfort, Ky.: Kentuck Yeoman Office, 1879), 27–34 (first, second, and third quotations, 29; fourth quotation, 30). A serious local epidemic of waterborne hepatitis occurred in 1983 in Meade County, Kentucky, affecting more than fifty people who drew water from a large spring near Brandenburg known as Buttermilk Falls that was contaminated with human fecal material (*Louisville Courier-Journal*, January 6, 1983).

15. Georgetown Trustees, *Minute Book D*, February 21, 1888, 471, and March 2, 1888, 474–75.

16. Georgetown Trustees, *Minute Book D*, February 21, 1888, 471, and March 2, 1888, 474–75; *Minute Book E*, July 3, 1891, 53, and April 1, 1892, 126.

17. Scott County, *Deed Book 18*, 26–27, June 22, 1880, deed, Trustees of the Kentucky Baptist Education Society to A. K. Lair; "Suit Against the Town and Water Company," *Georgetown Times*, April 26, 1893; Petition in Equity, *A. K. Lair v. The Chairman & Board of Trustees of Georgetown and The Water Supply Company*, included with record for *Water Supply Company vs. City of Georgetown*, Kentucky Court of Appeals, 1904, box 1555, case number 32652, KDLA.; Scott County Circuit Court, *Order Book 37*, 528, October 10, 1895, and 541, October 11, 1895; Georgetown Trustees, *Minute Book F*, December 7, 1894, 116, September 9, 1895, 188–89, and October 8, 1895, 197.

18. Georgetown Trustees, *Minute Book F*, January 16, 1897, 322, and March 5, 1897, 329 (quotation).

19. Georgetown Trustees, *Minute Book F*, April 2, 1897, 342 (quotations).

20. William Osler, *The Principles and Practice of Medicine*, 7th ed. (New York: D. Appleton and Company, 1909), 58.

21. Ibid., 61–62, 97; S. N. Khosla, *Typhoid Fever: Its Cause, Transmission and Prevention* (New Delhi, India: Atlantic Publishers, 2008), 13; Naomi Rogers, "Germs with Legs: Flies, Disease, and the New Public Health," *Bulletin of the History of Medicine* 63 (winter 1989): 599–617. Many books have been

written about Typhoid Mary; among the best accounts is that by Judith W. Leavitt, *Typhoid Mary: Captive to the Public's Health* (Boston, Mass.: Beacon Press, 1996). Typhoid remains a serious problem today in developing countries, with a worldwide incidence of about 12.5 million cases, the majority in India and other Asian countries and in Africa (Khosla, *Typhoid Fever*, 7).

22. Osler, *Principles and Practice of Medicine*, 57; Khosla, *Typhoid Fever*, 3.

23. Osler, *Principles and Practice of Medicine*, 70–96; Khosla, *Typhoid Fever*, 23–45.

24. William L. Sutton, *History of the Disease Usually Called Typhoid Fever, as It Has Appeared in Georgetown and Its Vicinity, With Some Reflections as to Its Causes and Nature* (Louisville, Ky.: Maxwell, 1850), 6–28 (first quotation, 7; second quotation, 18; third quotation, 28); Rodman, "Contamination of Water Supply," 32.

25. *Georgetown (Ky.) Times*, November 25, 1908; "Funeral," *Lexington (Ky.) Leader*, November 11, 1908.

26. "The Typhoid Fever Situation," *Georgetown (Ky.) Times*, December 9, 1908 (quotations); A. C. Cook, "Toes Up," *Georgetown (Ky.) Times*, April 21, 1909; "City Council Meeting. Fever Situation Discussed, Action Taken," *Georgetown (Ky.) Times*, December 9, 1908. The estimated 1908 population of Georgetown is interpolated from US Census reports that show a 1900 population of 3,823 persons and 4,533 in 1910.

27. Untitled notice, *Georgetown (Ky.) Times*, December 9, 1908 (quotation); "City Council Meeting," *Georgetown (Ky.) Times*, December 9, 1908; James Y. Kelly, "About the Big or Royal Spring Georgetown Ky," December 8, 1908, handwritten note in possession of Georgetown Mayor's Office.

28. "City Council. Report and Recommendations of Board of Health," *Georgetown (Ky.) Times*, December 23, 1908 (quotations); "Dr. McCormack Talks on Typhoid Fever Epidemic," *Georgetown (Ky.) Times*, December 23, 1908.

29. "Filtration Necessary. Sanitary Expert Looks Over the Ground and Makes Report," *Georgetown (Ky.) Times*, January 13, 1909 (quotation); George C. Matson, "The Big Spring: Possibilities of Pollution," *Georgetown Times*, January 16, 1907. Matson briefly refers to the traces he conducted here in his 1909 published report *Water Resources of the Blue Grass Region, Kentucky* (Washington, D.C.: GPO, 1909), 80: "In the examination of the big spring at Georgetown, Ky., from 2 to 4 barrels of salt were used with good results."

30. A. C. Cook, "Sterilized Water to Eliminate Typhoid," *Georgetown (Ky.) Times*, February 3, 1909 (quotations).

31. "Electric Water-Purification System," *Georgetown (Ky.) Times*, January 20, 1909; "The Filter Commission," *Georgetown (Ky.) Times*, January 27, 1909; "City Council. Report of Filter Commission," *Georgetown (Ky.) Times*, March 31, 1909; "Public Meeting in Interest of Pure Water Supply," *Georgetown (Ky.) Times*, July 14, 1909.

32. "City Council. Report of Filter Commission," *Georgetown (Ky.) Times*, March 31, 1909 (first quotation); "City Filed Suit," *Georgetown (Ky.) Times*, April 28, 1909 (second quotation).

33. *City of Georgetown v. Georgetown Water, Gas, Electric and Power Company*, Scott Circuit Court, 1909, box 1005, case number 17458, KDLA; *City of Georgetown v. Georgetown Water, Gas, Electric and Power Company*, Kentucky Court of Appeals, 1909, box 1934, case number 37962, KDLA; "Court of Appeals Decision," *Georgetown (Ky.) Times*, October 13, 1909.

34. "Public Meeting in Interest of Pure Water Supply," *Georgetown (Ky.) Times*, July 14, 1909; "Public Meeting in Interest of Pure Water Supply," *Georgetown (Ky.) Times*, July 21, 1909; "To the Voters of Georgetown," *Georgetown (Ky.) Times*, October 27, 1909; "To the Citizens of Georgetown," *Georgetown (Ky.) Times*, October 27, 1909.

35. Georgetown City Council, *Minute Book 10*, January 19, 1912, 42; "Will Purify Water with Liquid Chlorine," *Georgetown (Ky.) Times*, July 23, 1924.

14. Protecting Royal Spring

1. Robert Peter, *History of Fayette County, Kentucky, With an Outline Sketch of the Blue Grass Region*, ed. William H. Perrin (Chicago: O. L. Baskin, 1882), 32 (first quotation); "Nature's Wonder! The Big Spring at Georgetown," *Georgetown (Ky.) Times*, June 2, 1897 (second quotation).

2. "Detergent Found in Water from City's Royal Spring," *Georgetown (Ky.) Graphic*, October 29, 1964; "The Prospect of Drinking Purified Sewage Isn't One to Relish," *Georgetown (Ky.) Graphic*, October 29, 1964 (quotation); Donald S. Mull, *The Hydrology of the Lexington and Fayette County, Kentucky, Area* (Lexington, Ky.: Lexington and Fayette County Planning Commission, 1968), 17.

3. Matson, *Water Resources of the Bluegrass*, 80; Richard B. Dole, "Use of Fluorescein in the Study of Underground Waters," in *Underground-Water Papers*, ed. Myron L. Fuller, US Geological Survey Water-Supply Paper 160 (Washington, D.C.: GPO, 1906), 75; Markus Flury and Nu Nu Wai, "Dyes as Tracers for Vadose Zone Hydrology," *Reviews of Geophysics* 41 (March 2003): 2-7–2-9, https://agupubs.onlinelibrary.wiley.com/toc/19449208/2003/41/1, accessed September 14, 2019.

4. Thomas Aley, *Ozark Underground Laboratory's Groundwater Tracing Handbook* (Protem, Mo.: Ozark Underground Laboratory, 2002). I assisted Lawrence E. Spangler in 1981 with traces that helped determine the groundwater basin for Royal Spring and more recently has carried out a number of groundwater flow system investigations using dye-tracing in Boyle, Carter, Fayette, and Rockcastle counties in Kentucky.

5. Lawrence E. Spangler, "Karst Hydrogeology of Northern Fayette and Southern Scott Counties, Kentucky" (Master's thesis, University of Kentucky,

1982), 5; John Thrailkill, Joseph W. Troester, Lawrence E. Spangler, and Steven J. Cordiviola, "Nature of a Groundwater Basin Divide near Georgetown, Inner Bluegrass Karst Region, Kentucky," in *Hydrogeology of Karst Terrains—Case Studies, International Contributions to Hydrogeology*, vol. 1, ed. A. Burger and L. Dubertret (Hanover, Germany: Verlag Heinz Heise, 1984), 76–79.

6. Spangler, "Karst Hydrogeology," 23–26; John Thrailkill and Douglas R. Gouzie, *Discharge and Travel Time Determinations in the Royal Spring Groundwater Basin, Kentucky*, Research Report No. 149 (Lexington: Kentucky Water Resources Research Institute, 1984); John Thrailkill, Stephen B. Sullivan, and Douglas R. Gouzie, "Flow Parameters in a Shallow Conduit-Flow Carbonate Aquifer, Inner Bluegrass Karst Region, Kentucky, USA," *Journal of Hydrology* 129 (December 1991): 87–108; Randall L. Paylor, "Correlation of Spring Discharge with Groundwater Travel Time in the Royal Spring Karst Basin, Georgetown, Kentucky" (Master's thesis, Eastern Kentucky University, 2007).

7. James Long, Georgetown Municipal Water and Sewer, personal communication, October 22, 2007.

8. C. Douglas R. Graham, personal communication, August 19, 2005; C. Douglas R. Graham, *Electrical Resistivity Studies in the Inner Bluegrass Karst Region, Kentucky*, Kentucky Geological Survey, Thesis Series 1, Series XII, 1999 (Lexington: Kentucky Geological Survey, 1999), reprint of master's thesis, University of Kentucky, 1995.

9. Phillip W. O'Dell, personal communication, May 11, 2021.

10. C. Douglas R. Graham, personal communication, August 19, 2005.

11. James C. Currens, "Karst Hydrogeology of the Royal Spring Groundwater Basin and Calculation of the Annual Load of Indicator Water Quality Constituents 2011–2014 Water Year," unpublished paper in author's possession, 35 pages.

12. "Safe Drinking Water Amendment of 1986," Public Law 99-339, Section 1428, US Statutes at Large, vol. 100, part 1 (Washington, D.C.: GPO, 1989), 660–63; Karen P. Fitzmaurice, "An Analysis of the Kentucky Wellhead Protection Programs for Georgetown, Elizabethtown, and Calvert City, Kentucky" (Master's thesis, University of Kentucky, 1990)

13. Fitzmaurice, "An Analysis of the Kentucky Wellhead Protection Programs"; Sara D. Evans and Beverly Oliver, "Georgetown, Kentucky, Water Supply Protection Project" (Frankfort: Kentucky Division of Water, 1996), internal document prepared for Governor's Environmental Excellence Awards.

14. Tonya Richards, "Petroleum Contamination Found in Georgetown's Water Supply," *Lexington (Ky.) Herald-Leader*, December 19, 1989; "Gas Derivatives in Scott Water," *Lexington (Ky.) Herald-Leader*, March 17, 2002; Mary Meehan, "Fayette Approves Clean-Water Plan," *Lexington (Ky.) Herald-Leader*, August 31, 2001; Jim Warren, "Georgetown Water Deemed Safe After Toxins Detected in Supply," *Lexington (Ky.) Herald-Leader*, September 22, 2001.

15. Evans and Oliver, "Georgetown, Kentucky, Water Supply Protection Project"; Holly E. Stepp, "Georgetown Water Supply Dangers Are Cataloged," *Lexington (Ky.) Herald-Leader*, December 18, 1996; Meehan, "Fayette Approves Clean-Water Plan"; Lexington-Fayette Urban County Government, Division of Planning, "Royal Spring Wellhead Protection Plan," *2001 Comprehensive Plan Update*, Lexington-Fayette Urban County (Lexington, Ky.: Lexington-Fayette Urban County Government, 2001), 4-15–4-18, copy at Lexington Public Library.

16. Thrailkill and Gouzie, *Discharge and Travel Time Determinations*; Paylor, "Correlation of Spring Discharge with Groundwater Travel Time," 49.

17. US Geological Survey National Water Information System, Current Water Data for Kentucky, https://waterdata.usgs.gov/ky/nwis/rt, accessed July 12, 2019; Robert Kaiser and Andy Mead, "Shifting Gears in Scott County Community Makes Effort to Adjust to Toyota," *Lexington (Ky.) Herald-Leader*, August 10, 1986; Patton and Patton, "Dynamics of Growth and Change in Georgetown, Kentucky," 123–30; Clyde J. Sholar and Pamla A. Wood, *Evaluation of the Drought Susceptibility of Water Supplies Used in the Kentucky River Basin in 1988*, US Geological Survey Water-Resources Investigations Report 91-4105 (Louisville, Ky: USGS, 1991), 19; agreement between the Commonwealth of Kentucky and Kentucky American Water Company, June 30, 1986, https://psc.ky.gov/Home/Library?type=Tariffs; Kentucky Public Service Commission, case number 19009628, "Commonwealth of Kentucky Before the Public Service Commission," July 21, 1986, Commission Records, https://psc.ky.gov/PSC_WebNet/CommissionRecords.aspx, accessed July 12, 2019.

18. Apple, Johnston, and Bevins, *Scott County, Kentucky: A History*, 289 (quotation); Todd Pack, "Scott County Reconsiders $5 Million Reservoir," *Lexington (Ky.) Herald-Leader*, July 16, 1988; Laura Yuen, "Fighting for His Lifestyle," *Lexington (Ky.) Herald-Leader*, November 25, 2001; Steve Lannen and Andy Mead, "EPA Isn't Ready to OK Reservoir—Scott Officials Insist Water Supply Needed," *Lexington (Ky.) Herald-Leader*, August 9, 2004.

19. Apple, Johnston, and Bevins, *Scott County, Kentucky: A History*, 384; Tom Prather, personal communication, June 29, 2021.

20. Lannen and Mead, "EPA Isn't Ready to OK Reservoir."

21. Andy Mead, "Water Plan Faces Challenge," *Lexington (Ky.) Herald-Leader*, November 12, 2007; Andy Mead, "PSC Picks Ky. River Plan, Kentucky American Can Build Plant, Pipeline," *Lexington (Ky.) Herald-Leader*, April 26, 2008; Andy Mead, "Water Plant Deadline Passes, Proposed Facility Won't Include Cities Around Lexington," *Lexington (Ky.) Herald-Leader*, June 3, 2008; Andy Mead, "Group Might Bill Water Company, Spent $500,000 Looking at Water Supply Options," *Lexington (Ky.) Herald-Leader*, April 21, 2010. The property is still owned by the Scott County Fiscal Court, and currently is being used only for horseback riding.

22. US Decennial Census 2020; Matt Ruther, Tom Sawyer, and Sarah Ehresman, *Projections of Population and Households State of Kentucky, Kentucky Counties, and Area Development Districts 2015–2040* (Louisville: Kentucky State Data Center, 2016), 7, 226; Tom Prather, interview by Gary O'Dell, April 21, 2016.

23. Tom Prather, personal communication, June 29, 2021.

15. A Dumping Ground Since Time Immemorial

1. Jon A. Peterson, "The Impact of Sanitary Reform upon American Urban Planning, 1840–1890," *Journal of Social History* 13 (autumn 1979): 85 (first quotation, 85, second and third quotations, 95, fourth quotation, 84).

2. "Nature's Wonder! The Big Spring at Georgetown," *Georgetown (Ky.) Times*, June 2, 1897.

3. Georgetown Board of Trustees, *Minute Book D*, June 11, 1879, 22; June 20, 1879, 25; July 7, 1879, 28; July 18, 1879, 31.

4. Georgetown Board of Trustees, *Minute Book F*, March 6, 1896, 28 (quotation).

5. Apple, Johnston, and Bevins, *Scott County, Kentucky: A History*, 287–88, 317–18; "The Spring . . . Royal? Big? or Floyds?" *Georgetown (Ky.) News*, August 18, 1972 (first quotation). This article is a reproduction of an address to the Scott County Historical Society by Ann Bolton Bevins on August 1, 1957. The quotations attributed to Anne Payne Coffman were based on interviews made in 1952 by the author of the address. "City Council," *Georgetown (Ky.) Times*, June 9, 1909; Josephine G. Marks, "One Year's Footprint in Georgetown's Sands of Time," *Georgetown (Ky.) Times*, June 26, 1912 (second quotation); "Civic League," *Georgetown (Ky.) Times*, June 11, 1913; "Royal Spring," *Lexington (Ky.) Herald*, June 4, 1920; "Big Spring Chapter," *DAR Magazine* 56 (January 1922), 53.

6. "Mrs. W. H. Coffman Reviews Early History of Georgetown and County," *Georgetown (Ky.) Times*, May 23, 1923; "Propose Historical Pageant for County," *Georgetown (Ky.) Times*, April 2, 1924.

7. "Duties of Grounds Committee," Royal Spring box, Scott County Public Library (quotations); "Director Arrives to Begin Work on Historical Pageant," *Georgetown (Ky.) Times*, May 14, 1924; "Historical Pageant Will Be Staged on Campus at College," *Georgetown (Ky.) Times*, May 28, 1924; "Pageant of Kentucky's Historic Past," *Danville (Ky.) Advocate-Messenger*, June 13, 1924. At this time, the state historic park at Harrodsburg had not yet been established nor the replica fort constructed.

8. "Early History of Scott Graphically Shown in Pageant," *Georgetown (Ky.) Times*, June 4, 1924; Notes of Costume Committee, Royal Spring box, Scott County Public Library; "Historical Pageant Will Be Staged on Campus at College," *Georgetown (Ky.) Times*, May 28, 1924.

9. Anne P. Coffman and Frederick W. Eberhardt, *Pageant of Scott County History 1774–1924* (Georgetown, Ky.: Georgetown College, 1924), (first quotation, 5, second quotation, 41); US Census 1850, 1920.

10. Coffman and Eberhardt, *Pageant of Scott County History*, 41–47.

11. "The Spring," *Georgetown (Ky.) News*, August 18, 1972.

12. Ibid.; "Campaign Begins to Rebuild Fort," *The Graphic* (Georgetown, Ky.), November 20, 1975.

16. Royal Spring Park

1. "Mrs. Penn Speaks on 'Big Spring' to Scott Women," *Lexington (Ky.) Leader*, June 6, 1963; "'For Royal Spring Park' Woman's Club Makes Initial Contribution," *Georgetown (Ky.) News*, March 27, 1970.

2. National Register of Historic Places, Royal Spring Park, Georgetown, Scott County, Kentucky, National Register 73000842; "Historical Society Asks Park and Restoration of Fort," *The Graphic* (Georgetown, Ky.), January 18, 1973; Ann B. Bevins, "Georgetown-Scott County Committee Named to Initiate Development of Royal Spring," *Lexington (Ky.) Herald*, May 24, 1973.

3. Scruggs and Hammond, Inc., *Big Royal Spring, Georgetown, Kentucky: An Examination into the Feasibility of Park Development* (Lexington, Ky.: Privately printed, 1973); "Planners Report Favorably on Spring Park," *The Graphic* (Georgetown, Ky.), January 24, 1974; Kentucky Society of Architects and the Kentucky Chapter of the American Society of Landscape Architects, *Georgetown/Scott County, Kentucky Kentucky Design Assistance Team* (Georgetown, Ky.: Georgetown College, 1987).

4. "Matching Funds Sought for Spring Project," *The Graphic* (Georgetown, Ky.), June 26, 1975; "Reconstruction of Outpost Is Bicentennial Project," *The Graphic* (Georgetown, Ky.), November 13, 1975; Ann B. Bevins, "Campaign to Finance Fort to Open Tuesday," *The Graphic* (Georgetown, Ky.), November 13, 1975; "Campaign Begins to Rebuild Fort," *The Graphic* (Georgetown, Ky.), November 20, 1975; "$10,000 Donated in Fort Campaign," *The Graphic* (Georgetown, Ky.), January 1, 1976. Due to the active efforts of Georgetown citizens, the city was the first in Kentucky to become designated as an official bicentennial community by the National American Revolution Bicentennial Administration in Washington, D.C. (*The Graphic* [Georgetown, Ky.], November 13, 1975).

5. Ann Bolton Bevins, personal communication, December 2015.

6. Prather interview, April 21, 2016.

7. "Royal Spring Park Getting Log Cabin," *The Graphic* (Georgetown, Ky.), May 4, 1978; *Lexington (Ky.) Leader*, Ann Bevins, "Old Log Cabin Finds New Home in Georgetown," June 22, 1978, "Dedication of Log Cabin Puts Georgetown Park Step Closer," May 25, 1979; "Architect Restoring Scott County Cabin," *Lexington (Ky.) Herald*, August 21, 1978; Ann Bevins, "Furnishing of

Big Spring Cabin Nearly Complete," *Georgetown (Ky.) News and Times*, November 1, 1979; Maribeth Hambrick, personal communication, March 29, 2016; Janis Atlee, interview by Gary O'Dell, April 7, 2016.

8. "Georgetown Council Member Made Mayor," *Lexington (Ky.) Herald-Leader*, September 30, 1986; Prather interview, April 21, 2016; "Georgetown Mayor Comes Home Again and Again," Bluegrass Area Development District, July 7, 2016, http://bgadd.org/georgetown-mayor-comes-home-again-and-again/, accessed July 10, 2019.

9. Prather interview, April 21, 2016; Nancy O'Malley, "McConnell Springs in Historical Perspective," unpublished report, Department of Anthropology, University of Kentucky, 2006; Wooley, *The Founding of Lexington 1775–1776*, 9–14; Mastin, *Lexington 1779: Pioneer Kentucky as Described by Early Settlers*, 9–23.

10. Gary A. O'Dell and James R. Rebmann, "The Rescue of McConnell Springs Historic Site: A Partnership Between Local Government and the Citizens of Lexington, Kentucky," in *Proceedings, 1995 Cave Management Symposium*, ed. G. T. Rea (Indianapolis: Indiana Karst Conservancy, 1995), 255–66; O'Malley, *McConnell Springs*, 70–72.

11. Prather interview, April 21, 2016.

12. Naomi Faulkner, "Arts Bring Park Alive," *News-Graphic* (Georgetown, Ky.), July 29, 2010 (first quotation); Eve Oakley, telephone interview, August 3, 2019 (second quotation).

13. Gaines, *History of Scott County*, vol. 1, 23, vol. 2, 99–100; Bevins, *History of Scott County*, 285–86; James C. Klotter, *William Goebel: The Politics of Wrath* (Lexington: Univ. Press of Kentucky, 1977); National Register of Historic Places, Scott County Jail Complex, Georgetown, Kentucky, National Register 020000923; Janis Atlee, interview, April 7, 2016.

14. Atlee interview, April 7, 2016; Barbara Strippelhoff, personal communication, March 30, 2016.

15. Barbara Strippelhoff, personal communication, March 30, 2016; Scott County Arts and Cultural Center, http://www.scottcountyartworks.org/scac/, accessed July 3, 2016; Janis Atlee, interview by Gary O'Dell, Georgetown, Kentucky, May 21, 2021.

16. Barry Eichengreen, *Hall of Mirrors: The Great Depression, The Great Recession, and the Uses and Misuses of History* (New York: Oxford Univ. Press, 2015); Atlee interview, April 7, 2016.

17. Kevin Hall, "City Begins Planning for 2010 Games," *News-Graphic* (Georgetown, Ky.), October 18, 2006; Maryjean Wall, "Questions and Answers About the Games," *Lexington (Ky.) Herald-Leader*, December 7, 2005; Jim Jordan, "State Economy Will Get a Boost," *Lexington (Ky.) Herald-Leader*, December 7, 2005; Ryan Alessi, "How the State Wooed, Won Games," *Lexington (Ky.) Herald-Leader*, December 11, 2005.

18. *2012 Kentucky Equine Survey* (Lexington: University of Kentucky Agricultural Equine Programs, 2013), https://uknowledge.uky.edu/equine_reports/1, accessed July 17, 2019; Kentucky Horse Council, *Guide to the Kentucky Horse Industry* (Lexington, Ky.: Kentucky Horse Council, 2009). The five Inner Bluegrass counties and Thoroughbred farm numbers are Fayette (211), Woodford (114), Bourbon (98), Scott (40), and Jessamine (23).

19. Apple, Johnston, and Bevins, *Scott County, Kentucky: A History*, 59–70, 127–31, 228–29; *2012 Kentucky Equine Survey*, 15; US Department of Agriculture, "2017 Census of Agriculture County Profile: Scott County, Kentucky," https://www.nass.usda.gov/Publications/AgCensus/2017/Online_Resources/County_Profiles/Kentucky/index.php, accessed July 18, 2019.

20. Royal Spring Festival schedule of events, typewritten, Scott County Public Library, History of Scott County, box 1, folder 2010KR004; Raewyn A. Graham, "'Equi-cultural Identity': A Case Study of the Scone and Upper Hunter Horse Festival and the Georgetown Festival of the Horse" (Ph.D. diss., University of Sydney, 2013), 103–9; Wayne Boblitt, "John Fitch Jr. Heads up Another Horse Festival," *Georgetown (Ky.) Graphic*, October 2, 1986; Shawntaye Hopkins, "Festival of Horses and Homecoming," *Lexington (Ky.) Herald-Leader*, October 2, 2009; Rick Capone, "No Better Weekend," *News-Graphic* (Georgetown, Ky.), October 6, 2009.

21. Shawntaye Hopkins, "Georgetown Equine Expo to Run During WEG," *Lexington (Ky.) Herald-Leader*, January 10, 2010; Shawntaye Hopkins, "Georgetown Is Saddling Up: City, Scott County Leaders Plan Big Welcome to Games Visitors," *Lexington (Ky.) Herald-Leader*, September 22, 2010; Shawntaye Hopkins, "Scott County Unveils $8 Million Airport Renovation," *Lexington (Ky.) Herald-Leader*, September 24, 2010; John Simpson, former director, Tourism Commission, telephone interview by Gary O'Dell, July 25, 2019; Lori Saunders, executive director, Georgetown/Scott County Tourism Commission, telephone interview by Gary O'Dell, July 22, 2019.

22. Hopkins, "Georgetown Is Saddling Up"; Atlee interview, April 7, 2016; Simpson interview, July 25, 2019; Saunders interview, July 22, 2019.

23. Certec, Inc., *Economic Impact of the Alltech FEI World Equestrian Games, Kentucky 2010*, prepared for Kentucky Tourism, Arts and Heritage Council (Versailles, Ky.: Certec, Inc., June 2011), 1–3; Certec, Inc., *Economic Impact of Kentucky's Travel and Tourism Industry, 2008 and 2009*, and *Economic Impact of Kentucky's Travel and Tourism Industry, 2010 and 2011*, prepared for Kentucky Tourism, Arts and Heritage Council (Versailles, Ky.: Certec, Inc., May 2012); John Simpson. "WEG: Hotel Tax Revenue Rose Sharply During Games," *News-Graphic* (Georgetown, Ky.), June 30, 2011.

24. Certec, Inc., *Economic Impact of the World Equestrian Games*, 7 (first quotation); Simpson interview, July 25, 2019 (second quotation); Saunders interview, July 22, 2019; Scott Sloan, "Upbeat Downtown," *Lexington (Ky.)*

Herald-Leader, October 4, 2010; Shawntaye Hopkins, "Georgetown Trade Show Closes Shop," *Lexington (Ky.) Herald-Leader*, October 8, 2010.

25. Atlee interview, April 7, 2016

26. Prather interview, April 21, 2016; Mayor's Institute on City Design, "What Is the Mayor's Institute," https://www.micd.org/about/, "Events," https://www.micd.org/events/micd-east-2015, accessed November 16, 2019. The institute is a leadership initiative of the National Endowment for the Arts in partnership with the American Architectural Foundation and the US Conference of Mayors, with support from United Technologies.

27. Conrad Kickert and Ryan Geismar, *Core of Georgetown: Planmaking Workshop Fall* 2016 (Cincinnati, Ohio: University of Cincinnati School of Planning, 2016), 5, 8.

28. Kelli Stokes, "Making Water Street a Destination," *News-Graphic* (Georgetown, Ky.), September 1, 2016 (first quotation); Kickert and Geismar, *Core of Georgetown*, 5 (second quotation), 6, 16 (third quotation); Kelli Stokes, "UC Students Unveil Potential Downtown Design Overhaul," *News-Graphic* (Georgetown, Ky.), December 3, 2016.

29. Georgetown-Scott County Planning Commission, "Great Scott! The 2017 Comprehensive Plan for Georgetown-Scott County, Kentucky," 96–97, https://www.gscplanning.com/comprehensive-plan, accessed November 16, 2019; Anon., "Legacy Trail Would Improve Health, Community," *Lexington (Ky.) Herald-Leader*, October 28, 2008; Jack Brammer, "Hitting the New Legacy Trail—Governor Joins the Crowd to Celebrate Opening," *Lexington (Ky.) Herald-Leader*, September 13, 2010; Dan Adkins, "Legacy Trail Extension Will Stop at Scott County Line for Now," *Georgetown News-Graphic*, July 28, 2016.

30. National Trust for Historic Preservation, https://savingplaces.org (first quotation); John I. Gilderbloom, Erin E. House, and Matthew J. Hanka, *Historic Preservation in Kentucky*, Preservation Kentucky, 2009, http://preservationkentucky.org/historic-preservation-in-kentucky/, accessed September 29, 2019; Mandala Research, LLC, "The Cultural and Heritage Traveler 2013 Edition," Travel and Tourism Research Association: Advancing Tourism Research Globally, 2017, https://scholarworks.umass.edu/ttra/2013marketing/White_Papers/10, accessed October 11, 2019. Leisure travelers are defined as travelers who have taken at least one trip in the past twelve months for pleasure, vacation, or personal purposes within the United States that was fifty-plus miles away from home one-way, or where the traveler spent at least one overnight and have shared or sole responsibility for travel planning.

31. Kentucky State Parks, "Old Fort Harrod History," https://parks.ky.gov/parks/recreationparks/fort-harrod/history.aspx, and "Fort Boonesborough History," https://parks.ky.gov/parks/recreationparks/fort-boonesborough/history.aspx, both accessed on October 6, 2019. The Boone Station property remained in private hands, but in 1992 the owner, Robert C. Strader, gave the land to the

Kentucky State Parks System in his will. Later that year, it became the Boone Station State Historic Site, but it remained in the system for only a short while, closed as a park, and was given to David's Fork Baptist Church in late 2018 as a cost-saving measure. See Tom Eblen, "State Officials Quietly Gave Away Park Where Daniel Boone Lived," *Lexington (Ky.) Herald-Leader*, January 30, 2019.

32. "Old Fort Harrod," https://parks.ky.gov/parks/recreationparks/Fort-Harrod/, accessed October 6, 2019. The Royal Spring parcel of 3.5 acres is all city property, but Georgetown Municipal Water and Sewer occupies 2.15 acres of the total, leaving the park with 1.35 acres to the east of the Royal Spring branch.

33. David L. Coleman, Old Fort Harrod State Park Manager, personal communications, August 27 and September 17, 2019.

34. Willard R. Jillson, "Harrod's Old Fort, 1791," *Register of the Kentucky Historical Society* 28 (January 1930): 104–14; Robert B. McAfee, "The Life and Times of Robert B. McAfee and His Family and Connections," *Register of the Kentucky Historical Society* 25 (January 1927): 23; Roger Recktenwald, "Water and Wastewater Service for the Commonwealth of Kentucky," in *Water in Kentucky: Natural History, Communities, and Conservation*, ed. Brian D. Lee, Daniel I. Carey, and Alice L. Jones (Lexington: Univ. Press of Kentucky, 2017), 40. The original McAfee autobiography was a handwritten manuscript authored in 1845.

35. Lynda W. Closson, interview by Gary A. O'Dell, December 16, 2021; Kim A. McBride and W. Stephen McBride, *Archaeological Investigations at Logan's Fort, Lincoln County, Kentucky*, Research Report 3, Kentucky Archaeological Survey (Lexington, Ky.: University of Kentucky, 2000), 28–59; Talbert, *Benjamin Logan*, 37–39.

36. Jason Bailey, "Lessons from the Great Recession: Kentucky and Other States Need More Federal Relief," Kentucky Center for Economic Policy, April 29, 2020, https://kypolicy.org/wp-content/uploads/2020/04/Lessons-from-Great-Recession-Final.pdf, accessed April 10, 2021; Bill Estep, "$18 Million Targeted for Freshening of State Parks," *Lexington (Ky.) Herald-Leader*, June 3, 2016; Andy Beam, "Kentucky Senate Committee Rejects New Spending for Parks," *Louisville Courier-Journal*, March 6, 2019; Anon, "Gov. Bevin Signs $50 Million State Parks Improvement Bill at Cumberland Falls Resort," *The Lane Report*, April 18, 2019, https://www.lanereport.com/112537/2019/04/gov-bevin-signs-50-million-state-parks-improvement-bill-at-cumberland-falls-resort/, accessed April 10, 2021; Mary Potter, "Privatization of State Parks: A Bad Idea Supported by Bevin and Conway," *West Kentucky Journal*, August 26, 2015, https://www.westkyjournal.com/news.php?viewStory=5571, accessed April 10, 2021.

37. Eblen, "State Officials Quietly Gave Away Park"; Linda Blackford, "EKU Board Votes to Accept Ownership of White Hall Estate," *Lexington (Ky.) Herald-Leader*, February 24, 2019; Jack Brammer, "Bevin Gives Away a Third State Historic Site to Locals," *Lexington (Ky.) Herald-Leader*, March 30, 2019.

38. Thomas Musgrave, "Residents Seek Monument for Elijah Craig," *News-Graphic* (Georgetown, Ky.), September 2, 2010; "Statue Honors Preacher Who Invented Bourbon," *Lexington (Ky.) Herald-Leader*, September 4, 1997; Eve Oakley, telephone interview, August 3, 2019.

39. Sam Komlenic, "The True Story of Elijah Craig," *Whiskey Advocate*, http://whiskyadvocate.com/the-true-story-of-elijah-craig/, accessed September 22, 2019; Elijah Craig Bourbon, https://elijahcraig.com, accessed September 22, 2019.

40. Journey McAndrews, "New Distillery Gets Ready to Shine," *News-Graphic* (Georgetown, Ky.), November 1, 2014; Journey McAndrews, "Georgetown Transplant Looks to Bring Bourbon Back Home," *News-Graphic* (Georgetown, Ky.), November 26, 2014 (first quotation); Kayla Pickrell, "New Family Businesses Find Roots, Stay Local," *Georgetown, Scott County, Kentucky: Our Past Reflects Our Future* (Georgetown, Ky.: Georgetown Chamber of Commerce, 2015), 6 (second quotation); David Adams, telephone interview by Gary O'Dell, October 12, 2019.

41. Jeff Mattingly, interview by Gary O'Dell, May 5, 2021 (quotation).

42. Draper mss., 16 J 35, August 25, 1868.

Index

Page numbers in *italics* refer to illustrations.

Acer saccharum (sugar maple), 86, 87, 88, 89, 91, 121
Adams, David, establishes Royal Spring Branch Distillery, 270–71
Adams, James, printer of Filson's *Kentucke*, 70
Aesculus sp. (buckeye), 86, 87, 91; *Aesculus glabra* (Ohio buckeye), 88
Ageratina altissima (richweed, white snakeroot), 91
agriculture: Bluegrass, productivity for, 67–68, 71, 74, 95; clearing of forests for, 6, 98–99, 138; crop production, 6–7, 67, 95, 98–99, 138; eastern colonies, declining yields in, 36; eastern colonies, lack of available land for, 36; settlers guarding fields, 95–96; slash and burn practice, 138; tree girdling, 138
Alanant-o-wamiowee. *See* Buffalo Path
Albemarle County, Virginia, 41
Allegheny Plateau, 38
Allegheny River: Forks of the Ohio and, 42; French fortifications on, 42, 43; Monongahela River confluence with, 42
Ambrose, William M., collection of whiskey advertisements, 279n5
American colonies: agricultural land, lack of, 36; appeal of western frontier in, 36; European immigration to, 35, 36; opportunities lacking for young people in, 36; population 1640, 1770, 35; population growth of, 35–36; population pressure in, 36; poverty in, 36; soil fertility reduced in, 36; standard of living compared to England, 36; tenant farming in, 36; unemployment in, 36
AmeriCorps, and Royal Spring, potential contamination sources, 229–30
Amphicarpaea bracteata (pea vine, hog peanut), 91
Anderson County (Kentucky): John Cobbs, land in, 143; Inner Bluegrass, included in, 75; Lawrenceburg, county seat of, *8* (map), 11
Anglican Church of Virginia, 145

Index

Ansel (enslaved person): house of, 169; as trainer at Blue Grass Park, 169
Appalachian Basin, Bluegrass geologic structure and, 75
Appalachian Mountains, 3; Appalachian Basin and, 75; as barrier to western settlement, 36, *39* (map), 60; Great Appalachian Valley in, 38, *39*, 40, 105; natural gateways, 38, 43, 60; origin, 75; prohibition on settlement west of, 35, 44, 53
Apple, Lindsey, on Georgetown's purchase of dam, 231
archaeology: of Boone's Station, 133; in ecological assessment, 85; of Fort Ancient sites, 85; of Fort Boonesborough, 133; of Hugh McGary's Station, 133; of John Grant's Station, 133; of Logan's Fort, 257; of McClelland's Station, 130
Aristotle, on water supply springs, xi
Arts in the Park, concerts in Royal Spring Park, 252
Arundinaria gigantea (wild cane): bison and, 104; on Cane Run, 91, *92*, 295n28; on Filson's map, 71, 91; at Georgetown, vicinity of, 88, 91, 92; habitat, 92; on Hutchins's map, 91; of Inner Bluegrass, 74, 81, 83, 86, 87, 91, 93, 94, 95, 99; of Kentucky, 71, 91, 95; of Kentucky, most eliminated from, 92; killed by harsh winter, 97; as livestock fodder, 92; reports of early explorers, 91–93; on Salt River, 4; savanna woodland, as component of, 83
Asbury, Rev. Francis, on soil fertility, 67
Ash, blue. See *Fraxinus quadrangulata*
Ashland, Kentucky, 25, 76
Askew, James F., as Georgetown city attorney, 191
Ater Spring, visited by Ranck, viii
Athawominee. *See* Great Indian Warpath
Audubon, James, and Daniel Boone, 100
Augusta, Georgia, on Fall Line, 14
Austin, Moses, remarks on immigrants to Kentucky, 58–59, 72, 73
Austin, Stephen F., colonization of Texas and, 58

Ballinger, Richard, way station of, 58
Barbour, James, land commissioner, 55
Barron, Lance, student of John Thrailkill, *222*
Barrow, David: on decline of wildlife, 99; observations on forest trees, 86; on quality of Bluegrass soils, 76; on streams and springs, 79
Battle of Baton Rouge (Louisiana), 170
Battle of Blue Licks (Kentucky): Daniel Boone at, 264; described, 9; John Todd killed at, 302n26; Stephen Trigg killed at, 143
Battle of Fallen Timbers (Ohio), 9
Battle of Lexington (Massachusetts), viii; and naming of Lexington, Kentucky, 251
Battle of Perryville (Kentucky), 170, 171
Battle of Point Pleasant (Virginia), 49, 122. *See also* Dunmore's War
Battle of Richmond (Kentucky), 170
Battle of Stones River (Tennessee), 171
Bauer, Fred W.: Georgetown Band, directed by, 241; Pageant of Scott County History and, 241
bears. See *Ursus americanus*
Bedflord County, Virginia, 41
beech, American. See *Fagus grandifolia*
Bell, Sadie, on John McClelland gravesite, 141
Beshear, Steven (governor), and reduction of state park sites, 269
Bettie West (Thoroughbred horse), 169
Bevin, Matt (governor), and reduction of state park sites, 269
Bevins, Ann Bolton: Big Royal Spring, Inc., president of, 245–46; on Elijah Craig's vision for Georgetown, 149; Royal Spring, nominates for National Register, 245; Royal Spring Park and, 245–46

Big Barrens, natural meadows of, 87
Big Bone Lick, Kentucky, 29; Buffalo Path (Alanant-o-wamiowee) and, 106; as landmark in frontier, 111; mineral concentration of waters, 108; and prehistoric animals, 103
Big Royal Spring, Inc.: Ann Bolton Bevins and, 245; established, 245–46; fundraising for fort replica, 246
Big Spring, 101, 102, 181, 187, 192, 193, 195, 196; park movement for, 237. *See also* Republican Spring; Royal Spring
Big Spring Chapter, DAR: historical pageant and, 239, 240; Revolutionary War dead monument and, 141, 237; Royal Spring historical marker and, 242
bison, 74; abundance of, 77, 93, 94, 103; cane and, 104; decline in numbers, 99, 100; eastern woodland, spread into, 104; hunted by Daniel Boone, 66; hunted by Floyd and Reid, 77; hunted by Thomas Walker, 93; Kentucky River ford of, 93, 94, 106, 124, 125, 129; last free-roaming herd in Kentucky, 100; migrations of, seasonal, 104; prehistoric, 103; salt licks, influence on movements, 104, 108, savanna woodland hypothesis and, 83; starved during winter of 1780, 97–98;trails created by, 4, 27, 29, 41, 86, 90, 94, 103–8, 125, 140, 141, 146, 271; slaughter of, 100; winter range of, 106. *See also* trails
Blacks, 41; as cholera victims, 201; churches, 159; historical pageant, not represented in, 241; as pioneers, 241; Scott County, population of, 241; as water carriers, 159–61. *See also* slavery/enslaved people
Blacksburg, Virginia, 115
Blainville, Pierre Joseph Celoron De, and French claim to Ohio Valley, 37
Blane, William, describes Maysville Road, 29–30
blockhouses: at Boonesborough, 5, 137; described, 137; at Harrod's Fort, 137; at Lexington, 27, 109; at Logan's Fort replica, 267; at McClelland's, 137, 240; at Old Fort Harrod State Park replica, 264; watchtowers, 127
bluegrass. See *Poa pratensis*
Blue Grass Grotto (Lexington), chapter of National Speleological Society, x
Bluegrass Land and Life (Wharton and Barbour), and savanna woodland hypothesis
Blue Grass Park (Scott County), *176*; Ansel (enslaved person), trainer for, 169; described, 165–66; 168–69, 170, 314n17; Georgetown, boundary with, 156–57, 187, 195; Grinstead, acquires records of, 176; Herndon tract of, 165, *167*; homeplace tract, conveyances of, 177; homeplace tract, subdivided, 177; homeplace tract and Commons, *167*; hypothetical layout of, 166–69, *167*; as Keene Richards's home, 165–69, 171, 172, 173–75; postwar operations of, 174–75, 176; praise for, 165–66, 168, 174; race meeting at, 168; race track of, 165, 169; racing stables of, 168–69; Richards, expanded by, 165; Ross tract of, 165, *167*, 168; Royal Spring and, 166, 169; Rucker addition and, 210; Frank Sherritt, manager of, 168; Thoroughbred breeding and, 165, *167*, 168, 169, 174, 176; Troye, conveyed to, 172; Troye's studio on, 168; Union troops encamped at, 170; yearling sale at, 176
Bluegrass region: geomorphic subregions, 76; drainage, 79
Bluegrass Water Supply Commission: Georgetown, member of, 232; Kentucky American Water Co. and, 232
Blue Licks: battle of, 9, 143, 264, 392n26; as landmark in frontier, 111; mineral concentration of waters, 108; prehistoric animals and, 103. *See also*

Battle of Blue Licks; Blue Licks, Lower; Blue Licks, Upper; Blue Licks Battlefield State Park
Blue Licks, Lower, 29; Battle of Blue Licks and, 9, 143, 264, 392n26; Buffalo Path (Alanant-o-wamiowee) and, 29, 107, 125, 140; Indian attack near, 140; McClelland journey and, 125. *See also* Battle of Blue Licks; Blue Licks Battlefield State Park
Blue Licks, Upper, Warrior's Path and, 105
Blue Licks Battlefield State Park, established, 264. *See* Battle of Blue Licks
Blue Ridge Mountains, 38, 41, 47, 49; settlements in, 40
Board of Council, Georgetown: and ordinance against boring wells around Royal Spring, 194; and ordinance against street obstructions, 192–93; and Royal Spring water rights dispute, 191–93, 194; trustees replaced by, 184; utility rates and regulation by, 185
Boggs, Samuel, deposition of, 110
Bonasa umbellus (ruffed grouse), 74
Boone, Daniel (DB): as American hero, 68, 115; appeal of frontier to, 36, 99; biography in Filson's *Kentucke*, 68, 70; birth bicentennial of, 264; Bluegrass, first view of, *65*–66; Bluegrass, searches unsuccessfully for, 64; Squire Boone, brother of, 64–66; Boonesborough, establishes, 5, 51; Boone's Station of, 133, 264, 269; Braddock's expedition and, 63; Cumberland Gap, travels through, 3, 51, *52*, 65; on decline in deer populations, 100; Dunmore's War, service in, 123; endorses Filson's *Kentucke*, 70; John Findlay, befriends, 63; Richard Henderson and, 49, 50; inspired by Findlay's tales of Bluegrass, 63, 64; historic sites associated with, 264; home of, visited by Findlay, 64; home of, Yadkin valley, 64, 66; Kentucky, explores with Findlay and others, 3, 62, 64–66; Kentucky legislature, petitions, 66; memorial sites proposed for, 264; Missouri, moves to, 66; paradisiacal myth and, 66, 71;sent to warn Kentucky surveyors, 120, 122; Felix Walker and, 67; Wilderness Trail blazed by, 50–51, *52*, 67, 95
Boone, Nathan (son of DB), on seasonal migrations of bison, 104
Boone, Squire (brother of DB), explores Kentucky with Daniel, 64–66
Boone County (Kentucky), and Maysville Road, 30
Boonesborough: abandoned, 264; archaeology of, 133; cabins of, 134, 135; as early settlement, xv, 5, 7, 264; established, 51; John Floyd resides at, 77, 127; fortifications of, 5, 130, 137; gates of, 137; Henderson arrives at, 51; as Henderson's capital, 5, 49, 51, *52*, 127; hunters at, 109; inhabitants described, 96; Kentucky River and, 127, 264; land court at, 55; location, *8*; as public fort, 10, 137; as refuge, 10, 127, 142; Royal Proclamation of 1763, violation of, 53; stockade gates of, 137; Levi Todd and, 108; Wilderness Trail and, 27, 51, *52*, 105–6. *See also* Fort Boonesborough; Fort Boonesborough State Park
Boone's Station (Fayette County): archaeology of, 133; Daniel Boone and, 264, 269; given to David's Fork Baptist Church, 269; as state park, 269, 326n31
Botetourt County, Virginia, 140; Fincastle County created from, 35; Andrew Lewis, home of, 302n24; William Preston and, 115
boundary trees, *88–89*; of Royal Spring survey, 90–91
Bourbon County (Kentucky): bourbon history and, 153; division of, 152–53; Inner Bluegrass, included in, 75;

landless households in 1792, 57; "Old Bourbon," refers to larger region, 153; Paris, county seat of, *8* (map), 11; Jacob Spears as bourbon inventor in, 153

bourbon whiskey: Bourbon 30 blenders of, 271; Bourbon County and, 152–53; Bourbon–Scott rivalry concerning, 153; charred oak barrels and, 153; Commonwealth Distillers of, 270; Elijah Craig as inventor of, 149, 151–52, 270–71; Elijah Craig brand of, 270, *272*; federal definition of, 153; Heaven Hill Distillery of, 270; Jacob Spears as inventor of, 153; J. Mattingly brand of, 271, *272*; Maker's Mark brand of, 271; name, origin of, 152–53; Royal Spring Branch Distillery of, 270–71

Boyle County (Kentucky): Constitution Square State Park given to, 269; Danville, county seat of, *8* (map), 11; Inner Bluegrass, included in, 75

Braddock, Edward: and Fort Duquesne, expedition against, 43, 63–64; killed in ambush, 64. *See also* Braddock's expedition

Braddock's expedition (1755): against Fort Duquesne, 43, 63–64; ambushed, 64; Daniel Boone and, 63–64; Braddock killed, 64; George Croghan and, 63; departs Fort Cumberland, 63; John Findlay and, 63–64; Christopher Gist and, 63; as military disaster, 43, 64; Thomas Walker and, 63; George Washington and, 63

Bradford, David, stepson of and assistant to Alexander Elgin, 308n10

Bradford, John: *Gazette* printed on Craig's paper, 151; has house for sale, 114; has land with spring for sale, 114; on printing paper, scarcity of, 151; as publisher of *Kentucky Gazette*, 114, 151

Bradley, Katherine, Big Spring DAR and, 141

Bragg, Braxton, and Confederate invasion of Kentucky, 170

Branta canadensis (Canada goose), hunted by Thomas Walker party, 93

Brashear's Creek, land of Stephen Trigg on, 143

Braun, Lucy, on Bluegrass vegetation, 81

break-in-bulk: in river transport, 14; Ohio River at Louisville, 28

Breckinridge, John C.: Battle of Stones River and, 171; escapes Kentucky, 169–70; planned march into Kentucky, 171

Breckinridge, Mary C., 171

bridge over Royal Spring Branch: constructed, 157–58, *158*, development north of, proposed, 245, 252, 255; TAP grant for repairs to, 307n6

Bristow, Louis L., as Georgetown attorney, 102

Brooking Park (Georgetown), Festival of the Horse in, 157

Brown, John, Sr., on Kentucky as paradise, 67

Brushy Mountains, North Carolina, Daniel Boone, regional home of, 64

Bryant, William S.: Mary Wharton and, 83; savanna woodland hypothesis and, 83

Bryan Station Road (Lexington), and Buffalo Path (Alanant-o-wamiowee), 108

Bryant's Station, Fayette County: Daniel Boone, association with, 264; Buffalo Path (Alanant-o-wamiowee) and, 108; Craig family and, 146; descriptions of, contemporary, 130; fortifications of, 7; land court at, 55; siege of, 146; spring as water supply, *112*; vegetation of, 86

Buckeye. See *Aesculus* sp.

buffalo. *See* bison

Buffalo Path (Alanant-o-wamiowee): Bryant's Station and, 107; Georgetown and, 107; Great

Crossings and, 94, 106; Lexington and, 107; Lower Blue Licks and, 107, 125; Mays Lick and, 107, 125; McClelland journey and, 125; Royal Spring and, 125; in Scott County, 94, 106–7, 125; James Smith on, 107; Stamping Ground and, 94, 106; trail system through northeastern Kentucky, 106–7; Townsend Creek and, 125
Buffalo Springs, Lincoln County, 125–26
buffalo traces. *See* bison; trails
Buford's Gap, Virginia, 41
Bullitt's Lick, 143; as frontier landmark, 111; on old Wilderness Trail, 106; salt works at, 303n32; settlement at, 108; waters of, mineral concentration, 108
Burdett, Frederick, purchases William Hayden, 150
Burdett, Rebecca Cave, leases William Hayden to Elijah Craig, 150
Burgess, Neva Summers: John B. Rogers Producing Co. and, 239; Pageant of Kentucky's Historical Past, directs, 239; Pageant of Scott County History, directs, 239
Burgin, Kentucky, 180
Busbey, Hamilton: editor of *Turf, Field and Farm*, 177
Byrd, Phil, student of John Thrailkill, *222*

Cabin Creek (Lewis County), McClelland journey and, 125
cabins: at Boonesborough, 5, 135; chimneys in, 135, *136*; crowding in, 139; fortification of, 4, 7, 135; James Harrod's, 120, 122; at Harrod's Town, 4; as land improvements, 6–7, 53, 57, 109; Milton Leach's, 247–48, *249*; Jesse Lewis's, 248; at Lexington, 27; log construction methods, 134; at McClelland's Station, 125, 134–35, James Moore's, 143, 144; at Logan's Fort, 267; at Old Fort Harrod State Park, 264–65; replicas of, 264–65, 267; at Royal Spring Park, 247–48, *249*, size of, 134; at St. Asaph's, 5, 126; John Todd's, 108; types, 134, *136*
Campbell, Alexander, 203
Campbell, Julian: on Elkhorn vegetation, presettlement, 88–90; on honey locust (*Gleditsia triacanthos*), 90; on natural meadows, 87; on oaks, prevalence of, 90; on savanna woodland hypothesis, critical of, 83–84, 86; wild cane and, *92*, 295n28
Campbell County (Kentucky), and Maysville Road, 30
Canada, dominated by French, 38
Canada goose. See *Branta canadensis*
cane, wild. See *Arundinaria gigantea*
Cane Run (Mercer County), residence of Stephen Trigg, 143
Cane Run Creek (Scott County), 80; cane on, 91, *92*; course of, 91; dry channel of, 222; research on, 221–23; as source for Royal Spring, 220, 222; swallets of, 221–22, *223*, *224*; as tributary of North Elkhorn, 91, 220; watershed of, *224* (map)
Canis sp. (wolves), 94; decline in numbers, 100; fear of, 98; as threat to livestock, 100
carbonate rocks, x, 16, 75, *78*. *See also* limestone bedrock
Cardinal Valley (Lexington), vii, viii
Cardome Renaissance Center, Legacy Trail and, 263
Carpinus caroliniana (hornbeam, ironwood), 90
Carya sp. (hickory), 86, 88, 90, 91, 122; *Carya cordiformis* (bitternut), 89; Fort Ancient sites and, 85
Catawba Indians, 4
Cavalier, Robert, the Sieur de la Salle. *See* la Salle, Robert Cavalier, the Sieur de
caves: definition of, 78; development of, x; of Inner Bluegrass, vii, 80; as karst feature, xiv, *78*; and karst flow systems, 78; William Lindsay's cave spring, 110; Mammoth Cave, xi; xiv; Mundy's Landing Cave, 80; as

natural refrigerators, xi; prehistoric explorations in Kentucky, xi; prehistoric mineral mining, xi; Preston's Spring Cave, vii, 127, *128*; of region surrounding Bluegrass, xi, 80; Royal Spring, submerged conduit, 80, 226; Russell Cave, 88, *222*; saltpeter mined from, xi; Slack's Cave, 80–81; Vulcan Quarry Cave, 225–26, *226*, *227*
cave spring (Fayette County), improvement made for William Lindsay, 110
Celtis occidentalis (hackberry, hoopwood), 87, 88, 90
central place theory: Bluegrass, central place hierarchy of, 26–27; Walter Christaller and, 25; described, 25–26; Georgetown and, 26–27; Leslie King and, 25; Lexington and, 26; August Lösch and, 25
Central Thompson-Houston Electric Company, suit against Georgetown Electric Light, Heat and Power Co., 182
Cervus canadensis (elk), 74; abundance of, 94; decline in numbers, 99; hunted by Daniel Boone, 66; hunted by Thomas Walker party, 93
Chambersburg, Pennsylvania, 124
Chapman, Robert and Ginger, donate cabin to Royal Spring Park, 248
Chapman, Thomas, 27–28, describes Lexington, 27–28
Chapman, William T., describes Blue Grass Park and Royal Spring, 170
Cherokee Indians: Blue Ridge, southern passage blocked by, 38; at Chillicothe council, 99; declare war on settlements, 129; and early descriptions of Kentucky, 61; homeland of, 61; Kentucky, habitation of, 61; and Kentucky land sale to Henderson, 49–50; as most numerous eastern tribe, 61; outmigration to southern region, 61; trade and, 61
cherry, black. See *Prunus serotina*
Chickasaw Indians, outmigration to southern region, 4
Chillicothe, Ohio, Indian council of 1782, 99
chimneys and hearths, cabin, 135, *136*
Chiswell, Margaret, 124. *See also* McClelland, Margaret
cholera: in 1832–1833, 19, 20, 199–200, 201–3, 206; in 1848–1854, 19, 20, 199, 200, 203–4, *205*, 206; in 1866, 19, 199, 206; in 1872–1873, 19, 20, 199, 206; Bluegrass, first appearance (1832), 201; Bluegrass, supposed immunity from, 199, 201; in Bourbon County, 206; filth and miasmatic theories of, 201, 203–4; in Garrard County, 206; in Georgetown, 199, 201–4, *205*; global incidence, modern, 317n13; global pandemics, 19; in Kentucky, 19, 20, 22, 199–204, *205*, 206; limestone waters theory of, 200–201, 316n5; London epidemic of, 19–20; in Louisville, 206; in Mercer County, 206; mortality of, 199, 213; Nashville, occurrence in, 200–201; Ohio Valley, spread in, 199, 202, 203, 206; pathogen responsible for, 19, 20, 199; sanitary measures against, 203–4; John Snow, research on; 19–20; symptoms of, 199, 211; transmission of, 199, 206; as waterborne disease, 18, 20, 200, 201, 206, 213
cholera, in Georgetown, 199; in 1833, 201–3; in 1849, 203–4, *205*, 206; citizens flee from, 203; mortality of (1833), 202; mortality of (1849), 206; William L. Richards, death from, 163; sanitary precautions against, 204; severity of, 199; William L. Sutton and, 204, *205*
cholera, in Lexington: in 1832, 201; in 1833, 202; in 1849, 204; in 1872–1873, 20–21; citizens flee from, 204; in Lunatic Asylum, 204; mortality of, 202, 204

Christaller, Walter, and central place theory, 25
Christian, Anna, on travel conditions, 98
Christian, Israel, Elkhorn survey of, 93
Christian, Samuel, Elkhorn survey of, 93
Cincinnati, Ohio, 29; as central place, 26; growth of, 28; Mayors Institute for City Design workshop in, 261; population in 1850, 28; as regional metropolitan area, 266; road from Georgetown to, 29, 30; and University of Cincinnati, 262, 263; water supply of, 200
Cincinnati Arch, Bluegrass geologic structure and, 75
cities: infrastructure development, 234; public health and sanitation, 234–35; public spaces, creation of, 235–36; services provided by, 235; townsite consciousness, 235; urban landscape of, 235
Civil War, Kentucky, 11, 241; Battle of Perryville, 170; Battle of Richmond, 170; John C. Breckinridge and, 169–70; Confederate forces, invasion by, 169, 170; Confederate forces abandon, 170; Kentucky adopts Union side, 169; Lexington occupied by Confederates, 170; neutrality adopted, 169; in Scott County pageant, 241
Clark, George Rogers: and Henry Hamilton, capture of, 105; and Gabriel Jones, gunpowder for settlements, 139–40, 302n24; and Louisville, site of, 28; Charles Scott and, 67; Virginia, petitions for new county, 140
Clark, Thomas D., on pioneer reports of Kentucky, 67–68
Clark County (Kentucky): Eskippakithiki Indian village and, 62, 105; John Findlay and, 62; Inner Bluegrass, included in, 75; Strode's Station in, 7; Winchester, county seat of, *8* (map), 11
Clay, Cassius Marcellus, White Hall home of, 269
Clear's Station (Jefferson County), Indian ambush at, 143, 303n32
climate of Kentucky: best in North America, alleged, 71; seasonal variations of, 98; winter of 1780, severity of, 97–98
Clinch River Valley: residence of William Russell, 120; as staging ground for Kentucky settlement, 40; war preparations in, 122
Clinkenbeard, William, condemns wasteful hunting practices, 100
Closson, Lynda W., and Logan's Fort replica, 267
clover. See *Trifolium* sp.
Coastal Plain, 14, 15
Cobbs, John: Royal Spring tract, purchase from Trigg, 143; Royal Spring tract, sells to Craig, 144; suit against Trigg heirs, 144, 146–47, 303n33
Coffman, Anne Payne, *238*; Ann Payne Coffman Day and, *238*; Civic League and, 237; co-author of historical pageant, 240; and park movement, 237; presents history of Georgetown, 239; proposes historical pageant, 239
Coleman, David L.: as Old Fort Harrod State Park manager, 265; on park's cultural and economic benefits, 265
Coleman, J. Winston, on condition of roads, 29
College Street, obstructed by street railway, 191, 192
Collins, Josiah: Boonesborough, describes inhabitants of, 96; on drinking from spring, 109; Lexington, helps establish, 109
Collins, Richard: on Elijah Craig and "first" industries, 149, 305n8; on Craig's paper mill, 151
Columbia, South Carolina, as Fall Line city, 14

Commons (Georgetown), 156, *176*; cleaning of, 214, 236; as community activity space, 157, 158, 255; ice plant built on, 188; industrial degradation of, 34, 234, 236, *243*; landscaping of, 237; Everett Marshall, leveled by, 237; park movement for, 236–37, 241–44; size of, 157; water works built on, 181. *See also* Royal Spring Branch; Royal Spring Park
Commonwealth Distillers (Louisville), and Elijah Craig bourbon brand, 270
Confederate States of America, 172; actions and military forces of, 12, 76, 168, 169–71
Constitution Square (Danville), state park given to Boyle County, 269
Contrecœur, Claude-Pierre Pécaudy de, and conquest of Ohio Company fort, 42
Cook, Abraham C.: on typhoid in Georgetown, 213; water treatment system, urges, 216
Corporation for National and Community Service. *See* AmeriCorps
Cove Mountain, Pennsylvania, as home of William McConnell, 124
COVID-19, financial impact of, 269
Covington, Kentucky: Ohio River bison ford near, 106; as an endpoint of the Buffalo Path (Alanant-o-wamiowee), 106
Craig, Elijah (EC), 67; academy, establishes, 149; bourbon whiskey and, 149, 151–13, 270–71; business ventures of, 147–54; congregation, dissatisfied with, 149; Craig, Parker and Co., 151; criticized for commercialism, 148; William Hayden, employed by, 150; daughter Lucy, 155; daughter Lydia, 149; death of, 154, 166, 306n14; estate of, 155; "first" industries, alleged, 149, 151–52, 305n8; fulling mill of, 149–50, 151, 157, 305n8; Georgetown established by, 73, 100, 188, 269, 271, 273; Georgetown industrial development and, 31, 153–54; grist mill of, 157, 231; house of, 165, 166, 175; house of, residence of Pitts, 155; house of, residence of Richards, 166; imprisoned for preaching, 145; Kentucky, immigrates to, 37, 145, 146; legacy of, 154; McConnell's Run Church, founds, 149; mills and mill dams of, 29, 149–52, 157; paper mill of, 149, 151, 157, 208; retains right to use spring, 156; ropewalk of, 149, 150, 151; sculpture of, *152*, 270; son John, 155; statue of, proposed bronze, 270; will of, 155
Craig, Elijah (nephew of EC), 146; commands Bryant's Station, 146
Craig, John (son of EC), as executor of Elijah's will, 155
Craig, Joseph (brother of EC): immigrates to Kentucky, 145; imprisoned for preaching, 145; ordained Baptist minister, 145
Craig, Lewis (brother of EC): Baptist minister, ordained as, 145; and Kentucky, Baptist church in, 73; Kentucky, compares Heaven to, 67; Kentucky, immigrates to, 72; imprisoned for preaching, 145; South Elkhorn, settlement at, 146; Traveling Church and, 145; Upper Spotsylvania Church (Virginia), pastor of, 145
Craig, Polly Hawkins, and McClelland's Station, 237
Cramer, Frederick A., water works proposal of, 180
Cramer and Laws, city water works proposal of, 180. *See also* Cramer, Frederick A.; Laws, Robert J.
Creek Indians, Blue Ridge, passage southward blocked by, 38
Cresswell, Nicholas, on bison and salt licks, 103
Croghan, George: Braddock's expedition and, 63; on buffalo trail to Blue Licks, 106; established trading posts, 62

Cullen, John, Royal Spring Branch wall, 157, 307n5
cultural heritage tourism: defined, 263–64; significance of, 264
Cumberland County, Pennsylvania, original home of McClelland family, 123
Cumberland Gap: Moses Austin, used by, 58; Daniel Boone and, 3, 50–51, *52*, 94–95; Confederate forces, used by, 170, 171; as gateway into Kentucky, 3, 6, 40, 41, 43, 46, 64, 103, 104; described, 41; development as a wind gap, 286n8; James Harrod, used by, 5; Henderson's purchase of, 50; known to early explorers, 41; long hunters and, 3; Felix Walker, used by, 94–95; Thomas Walker, used by, 41
Cumberland Mountain: described, 104; gaps in, 64, 104. *See also* Cumberland Gap; Pennington Gap
Cumberland River: Ballinger's tavern on, 58; flows through Pine Mountain Gap, 104, 286n8; Thomas Walker, explorations by, 41
Cumberland Saddle, Bluegrass geologic structure and, 75
Currens, James C.: Royal Spring system, studied by, 226–27; Vulcan Quarry Cave, explored by, 225
Cynthiana (Harrison County), 125; as county seat, *9* (map), 11

Dandridge, Bartholomew, land survey on North Elkhorn for, 90
Danville (Boyle County), 106; Constitution Square in, 269; as county seat, *9* (map), 11
Daughters of the American Revolution. *See* Big Spring Chapter, DAR
Davenport, Edwin Rush (ER): water works constructed by, 311n3; water works proposal of, 180. *See also* Davenport, John H. B.
Davenport, John H. B. (brother of ER), represents Edwin Rush Davenport, 180, 311n3. *See also* Davenport, Edwin Rush
David's Fork Baptist Church, Boone's Station State Park given to, 269
Davidson, Ursula: bur oaks and, 83; savanna woodland hypothesis and, 83; Mary Wharton and, 83
Davis, James, manages ropewalk at Frankfort, 150
Davis, S. M., pond of, as water source, 179
deer, whitetail. See *Odocoileus virginianus*
Delaplain (Scott County), and central place theory, 26
Delaware Indians, 117; outmigration to Ohio, 4; Treaty of Stanwix and, 4
Dick's River: Buffalo Springs and, 125; named, 126, 301n6; paper mill on, 151. *See also* Dix River
Dinwiddie, Robert, governor of Virginia, 40
Discovery, Settlement and Present State of Kentucke (Filson), 68, 70–71; accuracy of, 70; bison and salt licks, 103; on bison ford of Kentucky River, 106; Daniel Boone biography in, 68, 70; cane lands on map, 91; endorsements of, 70; immigration to Kentucky, influence on, 68, 72; Willard R. Jillson's analysis of, 70; map of region, 68, 71, 87, 91; plagiarized, 72; popularity in America, 72; reprinted in Imlay's *Topographical Description*, 72; as self-serving work, 70; significance, John Walton on, 68; sources, 70; western paradise, promotion of myth by, 68, 70–71, 72
disease: filth and miasmatic theories of, 18, 113, 199, 201, 203, 282n27; germ theory of, 20, 198, 200, 201, 206, 213, 218; speculation on origins of, 18, 113. *See also* diseases, waterborne
diseases, waterborne: in cities, 18; evidence for, 19–20, 201, 206; Kentucky, epidemics of, 19, 20, 21, 22, 163, 199–206, 210, 211–15, 317n14;

Kentucky Board of Health and, 206; pandemics involving, 20; pathogens of, 16, 19, 199, 210, 317n14; sanitation and, 19, 113, 206–7, 218. *See also* cholera; pathogens; typhoid
Dix River, 79, 146. *See also* Dick's River
Doddridge, Joseph, on decline of wildlife, 99
Drake, Daniel: on cholera, 200; on clearing forests for agriculture, 99
Drake, Joseph: guides John Floyd, 126, 127; Benjamin Logan and, 126; naming of Dick's River and, 126, 301n6
Draper, Lyman C.: Georgetown, visit to, 131; forts, sketches of, *111*, 133; as historian, 130; John McClelland, notes on gravesite, 141; McClelland's Station, notes and sketches on, *126*, 131; pioneer accounts collected by, 131; Royal Spring, described by, 131, 273; travels of, 131
Drennon's Lick, Buffalo Path (Alanant-o-wamiowee) and, 106
drought, Georgetown, 194; of 1897, 188, 189; of 1899, 193–94; of 1930, 21; of 1966, 231; of 1988, 231; cane and, 92; Georgetown water supply and, 22, 188, 189, 192, 193–94, 230; ice company and, 23, 192, 194; natural vegetation and, 90; Palmer Drought Severity Index and, 314n13; Royal Spring and, 231; Vulcan quarry and, 225; water rationing and, 194, 231
Dry Ridge Road (Georgetown Road), built to Cincinnati, 29
Dry Run (Scott County), 201
Duke, Basil, Scott County, describes topography of, 76
Dunmore, Lord. *See* Murray, John
Dunmore's War: Battle of Point Pleasant, 122; Daniel Boone and, 123; James Harrod and, 123; Simon Kenton and, 123; land grants to veterans of, 48; Robert Patterson and, 123; preparations for, 120
Dunwiddie, James, land with spring for sale, 114
Dyes, groundwater tracing using, xiii

Eastern Kentucky University, White Hall State Park given to, 269
Easton, Augustus, Elkhorn Association, invited by, 146
Eastwood, James F.: Royal Spring, groundwater tracing of, 210; Royal Spring, water quality analysis of, 210
Eberhardt, Frederick W.: co-author of historical pageant, 240; Georgetown Baptist Church, pastor of, 240
Eden shale region: defined, 76; soils of, 76
Elgin, Alexander ("Elly"): David Bradford, assistant to, 160; Elly Alley named for, 160; home of, 160; John, mule of, 160; water hauler, 159–60, 308n10
Elijah Craig brand bourbon, 270, *272*
elk, 74; hunted by Daniel Boone, 66. See *Cervus canadensis*
Elkhorn Association of Baptist Churches: Craig, Easton and Garrard, invited by, 146; at Lewis Craig's settlement, 146
Elkhorn Creek (main), 108; branches of, 21, 79–80; discovered and named, 80; followed by explorers, 80; John Floyd and, 80, 118; Forks of Elkhorn and, 80; Kentucky River, as tributary of, 80; Leestown settlement and, 7; Town Branch of, 21; watershed of, 79. *See also* Elkhorn Creek, North; Elkhorn Creek, South
Elkhorn Creek, North: baptisms in, 159; cane on, 91, 93; Cane Run and, 220, *224* (map); course of, 80; dams on, 29, 31, 231; John Floyd and, 80, 88–91, 120–22; Great Crossings of (trail), 106; Royal Spring and, 78, 80, 88, 91, 120–22, 125, 147, 157; Shipp's Station and, 87; vegetation of, presettlement, 88–91

Elkhorn Creek, South: course of, 80; springs on, 80; Steele's Run tributary of, 110
Elkhorn region: described by Thomas Hanson, 66; explored by David Perry, 123; vegetation of, 87
Ellis, William, and Traveling Church, 145
elm. See *Ulmus* sp.
Elymus sp. (rye), 81; as component of savanna woodland, 83
Eskippakithiki (Clark County): abandoned, 63, 105; John Findlay's trading post at, 62; French and Indian War and, 63; French trading post at, 63; as Indian Old Fields, 105; as Shawnee village, 62–63; Upper Howards Creek and, 63

Fagus grandifolia (American beech), 86
Fall Line: cities of, 14, 281n17; colonial settlement and, 14, Falls of the Ohio, compared to, 28
Falls of the Ohio (Louisville): Daniel Boone and, 66; Fall Line, compared to, 28; John Findlay and, 63; John Floyd and, 118; Christopher Gist and, 41; old Wilderness Trail, endpoint of, 106; Charles Scott and, 67
Farrar, Asa, on clearing forests for roads, 86
Farrow, Thornton, Josiah Collins, travels with, 109
Fayette County (Kentucky), 11; Boone's Station in, 133, 264, 269; Bryant's Station in, 7, 55, 86, 107, 130, 133, 137, 146, 264; Cane Run in, 91, *92*, 220, *223*, *224*; division of, 152; Elkhorn Creek watershed and, 79–80; Gist traverses, 41–42; horse sales in, 257; Indian conflicts in, 27; Inner Bluegrass, included in, 75; karst research in, xiii, 221–27; Kentucky Horse Park in, *2*, *82*, *84*, *223*, 225, 226, 256, 257, 258, 259, 260, 263; Lexington, county seat of, *8* (map), 11; McConnell Springs and, ix, 15, 225, 251, 266; Preston's Cave Spring in, vii, 127, *128*, 301n9; Royal Spring recharge area in, xiv, 219–20, 223, *224*–27, 228; Russell Cave in, 88, *222*; Thoroughbred farms in, 256; water supply protection program and, 218, 228; Woodford County created from, 152
Federal Highway Administration, jail conversion, provides grant for, 254
Feeback, Julian, donates log cabin for Royal Spring Park, 247–48
Ferguson, Franklin, death from typhoid, 213
Festival of the Horse (Georgetown), *258*; attendance at, 257, 260; Chamber of Commerce and, 257; Kentucky Horse Park supports, 257
Fidelity Trust and Safety Vault Company, suit against Georgetown Electric Light, Heat and Power Co., 182, 193
Filson, John, *69*; death of, 72; *Discovery, Settlement and Present State of Kentucke* by, 68, 70–71; land acquisitions in Kentucky, 70–71; subsequent obscurity and rediscovery, 72; as surveyor, 68; as teacher, 68
Fincastle County, Virginia: created, 35, 115; first settlers, 35; partitioned and eliminated, 127, 140
Findlay, John: attacked by Ottawa Indians, 63; Braddock's expedition and, 63; George Croghan and, 62; describes Bluegrass to Daniel Boone, 63; establishes trading post at Eskippakithiki, 62; explores Kentucky with Daniel Boone, 62, *65*; friendship with Daniel Boone, 62, 63; name, spelling of, 290n5; paradisical myth, role in, 62
Fitch, John: Georgetown Chamber of Commerce, president of, 257; on Festival of the Horse, 257
Fitzmaurice, Karen, explores Vulcan Quarry Cave, 225

Flat Lick, Kentucky: described by Henry Hamilton, 105; junction of Warriors' Path and Wilderness Trail, 105–6; mineral springs of, 104–5
Fleming, Colonel William: on Fort Harrod, water supply of, 113; land commissioner, 55; on severe winter of 1780, 97–98
Floyd, Charles, (brother of JF), ambushed by Indians, 143
Floyd, John (JF), *116*; Bluegrass region, explored by, 118; Dunmore's War, service in, 123; Elkhorn Creek (main) surveys, 118; Fincastle County, deputy surveyor of, 115, 127; Indian danger, warns of, 130; joins expedition against Shawnee, 122; Kentucky, first trip to (1774), 115–22, 299n8; killed by Indians, 143, 303n32; on land acquisition system, abuses of, 53, 54; Benjamin Logan and, 126; John McClelland, confronts, 127; McClelland family, sympathy for, 127–28; McClelland's Station and, 53; Francis McConnell and, 127; William Nash and, 90; North Elkhorn Creek surveys, 88–91, *89*, 93, 120; Ohio River surveys by, 117, 118; as pioneer, 72; Powell's Valley camp of, 127; William Preston, communications with, 127, 128, 129–30; William Preston, employer of, 115; William Preston, informs of Tories settled on Elkhorn, 127; Preston's Cave Spring and, vii, 127, *128*; residence at Boonesborough, 77, 127; residence at Floyd's Station, 143; Royal Spring, claimed by, 1, 77, 88, 120, 239, 299n8; Royal Spring tract, sold to Cobbs, 143; Royal Spring tract, sold to McClelland, 128, 269; Royal Spring tract, traded to Trigg, 143, 303n31; second trip to Kentucky (1775), 122, 125–27; squatters, disturbed by reports of, 127, 269; St. Asaph's, founding of, 126; surveying, method of, 117; will of, probated, 143
Floyd, Robert, (brother of JF), ambushed by Indians, 143
Floyd's Spring (Royal Spring): Buffalo Path (Alanant-o-wamiowee) and, 125; John McClelland, familiar with, 125; McClelland unaware of Floyd's claim to, 125; named, 101, 120; squatters at, 127. *See also* Royal Spring
Floyd's Station (Jefferson County), residence of John Floyd, 143
Forbes, John: builds Forbes Road, 43, 124; captures Fort Duquesne, 43
Forbes Road: connects eastern colonies to Ohio Valley, 43; home of William McConnell on, 124; *See also* Forbes, John
forests of central Kentucky: David Barrow on, 86; Lucy Braun on, 81; Julian Campbell on, 86, 88–90; canopy openings, 86, 87; canopy trees, 90; cleared for agriculture, 98–99, 138; composition, 86; 88–90; destruction of, 98; of Elkhorn region, 87; fear of, 98; Asa Farrar on, 86; Samuel Matthews on, 86; André Michaux on, 86; soil fertility and, 86; woodlands, compared to, 81, 83. *See also* savanna woodland; vegetation
Forks of Elkhorn, 80, 90
Forks of the Ohio River: Braddock's expedition to, 43; described, 42; fortified, 42–43; strategic importance, 42, 43; western settlement, as launch point for, 42, 43. *See also* Braddock's expedition; Fort Duquesne; Forbes, John; Fort Pitt
Fort Boonesborough, 108; abandoned, 264; archaeology of, 133, 301n16; as collection point for immigrants, 139; descriptions of, contemporary, 130; as early settlement, xv, 7; established, 5, 50; fortifications of, 5, 7, 130; gates of, 137; as public fort, 6, 10, 137, 139; as refuge, 10, 127, 142; size of, 7; spring

as water supply, *112*. *See also* Boonesborough
Fort Boonesborough State Park: established, 264; replica fort at, 264
Fort Ancient culture, 85
Fort Cumberland, Maryland, launch point for Braddock's expedition, 63
Fort Duquesne, Pennsylvania: Braddock expedition against, 43, 63–64; captured and destroyed, 43; established, 42
Fort Harrod, Kentucky. *See* Harrod's Fort
forts and fortifications. *See* blockhouses; public forts; stations; stockades
Fort Pitt, Pennsylvania: established, 43; Forks of the Ohio and, 43; launch point for immigrants, 43, 46; secures access to Ohio Valley, 43
France: Allegheny River, fortifications, 42, 43; Forks of the Ohio, attack at, 42; Great Lakes, control of, 38; Ohio Valley, claims to, 37, 42, 43; trading posts of, 62, 63; western explorations of, 37, 40, 286n5. *See also* French and Indian War
Frankfort (Franklin County): and central place theory, 26; as county seat, *9* (map), 11; Division of Water in, 11; Elkhorn Creek and, 80; establishment, 124; pipeline to Georgetown from, 33, 232; population of, 11, 13; roads to, 29; ropewalk in, 150; state capital, becomes, 29
Franklin County, Kentucky: Elkhorn Creek watershed and, 79–80; Frankfort, county seat of, *8* (map), 11; Gist, traversed by, 41; Inner Bluegrass, included in, 75; McAfee land survey in, 93; pioneer settlements sparse in, 10; vegetation of, presettlement, 93
Franklin County, Pennsylvania: Chambersburg and, 124; Cumberland County, formerly, 123; Elizabeth Lindsay, home of, 124; McClellands, home of, 123
Fraxinus quadrangulata (blue ash): Bluegrass, common in, 81; livestock shade, left standing for, 90; savanna woodland, component of, 83
Fraxinus sp. (ash), 86, 87, 88, 90, 91, 121, 122
Fredericksburg, Virginia, and Traveling Church, 145
French and Indian War (1754–1763): Braddock's expedition, 43, 63–64; British territorial gains from, 43; effect on land speculators, 49; expense of, 44; Forbes's expedition and, 43, 124; Fort Duquesne and, 43; Fort Pitt and, 43; French defeats, 43; initial conflicts, 42–43; land grants to veterans of, 48; Native American migrations and, 4, 61, 63; new taxes on colonies following, 46; Seven Years' War and, 43; Treaty of Paris (1763) and, 43; widows and disabled men from, 36
French Lick, Indiana, and bison trail, 106
Friends of McConnell Springs: Founders' Day, sponsored by, 251; and McConnell Springs Park, 251
frontier settlement model: described, 9–10; Kentucky settlement and, 10; stages of settlement, 10

Gaines, Bill, on waterfowl in Royal Spring branch, 157
gaps. *See* mountain gaps
Garden of Eden, Kentucky as, 62, 68, 71, 72. *See also* western paradise, myth of
Garnet, John, explores Slack's Cave, 80
Garrard, James, Elkhorn Association, invited by, 146
Garrard County (Kentucky): cholera at, 206; Inner Bluegrass, included in, 75; Lancaster, county seat of, *8* (map), 11; William Miller's station in, 298n18
Geismar, Ryan: Royal Spring Park design challenge and, 262; University of Cincinnati, faculty of, 262

George III, King: Royal Proclamation of 1763 and, 35, 43, 44, 49; Virginia's 1609 charter revoked by, 38; western settlement ban and, 35

Georgetown (Scott County): agricultural economy of, 33; as bedroom community, 230; bicentennial community, designated as, 323n4; Bluegrass Water Supply Commission and, 232; Board of Council of, 184, 185, 209, 213, 214–15, 217, 231, 246; Board of Health of, 209, 214, 218; boundaries of, 156–57, 162, 187, 195, 314n17; Buffalo Path (Alanant-o-wamiowee) and, 106; cane and, 92; cholera at, 201–4, *205*; and central place theory, 26; Chamber of Commerce of, 257; city dump, purchase of, 215; commerce and trade of, 32, 285n51; Commons of, 34, 156, 157, 158, *176*, 181, 188, 214, 236–37, 241–44; comprehensive plans for, 245, 252, 263; as county seat, *9* (map), 11; as early settlement, xv; Equine Expo of, 258, 260; established, xii, 11, 147; factors promoting growth, 1, 29; fires and fire protection, 161–62, *161*, 178–79, 181; first courthouse of, 162; Frankfort, pipeline from, 232; growth stimulated by Toyota, 13, 27, 33, 230, 231, 252; historical pageant of, 239–41; as home of Keene Richards, 163, 166, 168, 170, 172, 174, 175; industry in, early, 31–32; jail, old city, 245, 252–55; Kentucky Utilities property and, 130, 243, 246–*47*, 266, 267, *268*; land surveys near, 88–91, *89*; as Lebanon town, 147, 149, 155; Legacy Trail in, 263; McClelland's fort replica and, 243, 245, 246–47, 266, 267, *268*; McClelland's Station and, xv, 147, 254, 265; metropolitan areas, proximity to, 266; John Hunt Morgan and, 168; named, 147; North Elkhorn and, 80; Ohio River, proposed pipeline from, 233; patriotism in, 244; plat of (1824), *148*, 156; population, historic, 147, 213; population, present-day, 1, 33, 233; population growth, 1, 11–12, *12* (map), 27, 33, 233; Public Square of, 161; public wells and cisterns of, 161; recession of 2008, effect on, 255; reservoir plan for, 231, 232, 233; roads, early, 29–31; Royal Spring and growth of, 25; Royal Spring water rights contested by, 188–97; sanitary sewers in, 18, 209, 214, 217; sanitation in, 113, 198–99, 204, 207, 235; tourism and, 245, 257–60; trustees of, 113, 156, 157, 161, 162, 178, 179, 180–81, 182, 184, 188, 204, 207; typhoid in, 219, 212–14; vegetation of, presettlement, 88–93; Water Company, dispute with, 23–25, 188–97; water hauling in, 159–61, *179*; water rationing, in, 194, 231; water supply of, xii, xiv, xv, 1, 13, 22, 23–25, 33, 114, 159, 161, 178–86, *183*, 187–97, 200, 228–30; water supply planning, 33–34, 231, 232–33; water supply protection program of, 228–30; water treatment system and, 215–18; welcome center for, 255; World Equestrian Games and, 257–60. *See also* cholera, in Georgetown; Georgetown Board of Council; Royal Spring; Georgetown trustees

Georgetown Baptist Church, pastor of, 240

Georgetown Board of Council: Commons, orders cleaned, 215; on city dump site, purchase of, 215; dam, purchases, 231; McClelland fort replica, supports, 246; reservoir, purchase of land for, 231; on Royal Spring sources of contamination, 209, 214–15; sewer connections, ordered by, 215; on typhoid in city, 213; utility rates, established by, 185; on water treatment, 215, 217; on water works, 184

Georgetown Chamber of Commerce, 257
Georgetown Civic League: Ann Payne Coffman and, 237; educational and sanitary reforms by, 237; park movement and, 237; succeeded by Woman's Club, 244
Georgetown College: Giddings Hall at, 240; Hinton athletic field at, 240; historical pageant, site of, 239–41
Georgetown Electric Light, Heat and Power Company: incorporated, 181; indebtedness, 182; sold at public auction, 182; suits filed against, 182, 193. *See also* Nichols and Patterson
Georgetown Electric Railway Company, 184
Georgetown Equine Expo: economic failure of, 260; World Equestrian Games and, 258, 260
Georgetown Hotel, destroyed by fire, 178
Georgetown Ice Company, 195, 196; dispute with city, 188–91, *190*, 193; established, 182; land granted to, 188, 190–91; location, 182, *183*; rates, 182; Royal Spring and, 182, 187, 188–89, *190*, 191, 192, 193–94, 196, 107; Water Supply Co. acquires, 184, 189. *See also* Royal Spring Ice Company
Georgetown Jaycees, and McClelland's fort replica, 242–43
Georgetown Junior Woman's Club, and Royal Spring Park, 244
Georgetown Municipal Water and Sewer Service: expansions and upgrades to, 185–*86;* facilities and treatment plant of, *186*, 252, *261*, *268* (map); population served, 231, 233; Harold B. Prather, former chair of, 248; relocated, 185; relocation, suggested for future, 266; Royal Spring, divers explore for, 224; treatment capacity of, 231; warehouse of, *243*; water volume pumped by, 231
Georgetown Renaissance, Inc., grant for old jail renovation, 254
Georgetown/Scott County 2017 Comprehensive Plan: Legacy Trail alternative routes, described in, 263; Planning School report recommendations included in, 263; Royal Spring Park accessibility addressed by, 263
Georgetown/Scott County Regional Airport: improvements to, 258; and World Equestrian Games, 258
Georgetown/Scott County Tourism Commission: Georgetown Equine Expo and, 258; John Simpson, former director of, 260; welcome center for, 255; World Equestrian Games and, 258
Georgetown Street Railway Company: established, 182; Georgetown Ice Co. and, 182; Alice P. Montgomery sells land to, 187, 195; Royal Spring and, 187; Royal Spring Ice Co., buys land from, 187–88; Water Supply Co., acquires, 184. *See also* Georgetown Electric Railway Company
Georgetown Times: on Elly Elgin, 160; fire destroys office of, 179, on Royal Spring, source of waters, 219; on water rationing, 194; on water treatment systems, 216; water works contract published by, 181
Georgetown trustees: Board of Council replaces, 184; city boundaries and, 156; Commons, orders cleaned, 237; fire suppression orders issued by, 162, 178–79; ice company and, 182, 188; land grants by, 188; powers conveyed by legislature to, 162; prohibit sale of produce, 204, 206; public wells and cisterns and, 161; Royal Spring Branch wall and, 157, 207; sanitary orders and, 113, 198–99, 207, 315n1; William L. Sutton and, 204; water works and, 180–81, 188
Georgetown Water, Gas, Electric Light and Power Company: established, 185; Georgetown gas company

acquired by, 185; Lexington Utilities, acquires, 185; presidents of, 185; water treatment system and, 216–18
Georgia, Cherokee in, 61
Gerhard, William P., on Royal Spring contamination sources, 215
Gerhard, William W., distinguishes between typhoid and typhus, 211
Gilbert's Creek, founding of church at, 146
Girty, Simon, condemns environmental despoilation by settlers, 99
Gist, Christopher: Braddock's expedition and, 63; Inner Bluegrass region, traverses, 41–42; journal of, 41, 61; Kentucky, description by, 40, 42, 62; Kentucky, explorations of, 40, 41, 72; Kentucky River and, 41, 42; Ohio Company and, 40, 41, 61; oral dissemination of report, 61; Yadkin River Valley home of, 41, 42
Gist's Fork, land of Stephen Trigg on, 143
Gleditsia triacanthos (honey locust), 88, 90, 91, 121, 122; and Native Americans, 90
Glencoe (Thoroughbred horse), 166; burial site of, 166, 168; offspring presented to Morgan, 171
Goebel, William (governor): assassinated, 253; old city jail and conspirators, 253
Gouzie, Douglas R.: and John Thrailkill, 230; Royal Spring, flow travel times estimated by, 230
Graham, Douglas R.: and James C. Currens, 225; and Karen Fitzmaurice, 225; Royal Spring master conduit, explores, 224–25, *227*; Royal Spring master conduit, geophysical studies by, 224–25; Vulcan Quarry Cave, discovered by, 225, *226*. *See also* Vulcan Quarry Cave
Grant, John (brother of SG), Grant County and, 305n8
Grant, Lydia (wife of SG; née Craig; daughter of Elijah), marriage, 149
Grant, Moses (brother of SG), killed by Indians, 149
Grant, Samuel (SG), 305n8; Georgetown fulling mill of, 149, 150; Grant County and, 305n8; killed by Indians, 149; married Lydia Craig, 149
Grant, Squire (brother of SG), Grant County and, 305n8
Grant County (Kentucky): Grant brothers and, 305n8; name, origin of, 305n8
Grant's Station (Bourbon County), archaeology of, 133
granular aquifers, 15, 24; defined, 16; drinking water and, 16; pollutants and, 16
Graves, Harvey C.: executor for William B. Keene, 174–75; Keene Richards, indebted to, 174–75; obtains Troye's interest in Blue Grass Park, 175
Graves, John, on vegetation at Great Crossings, 93
Graves, John B.: buys and sells Blue Grass Park, 177; deed reference to Royal Spring, 195
Great Appalachian Valley. *See* Great Valley
Great Britain: claims Ohio Valley, 37; colonial governors of, 42, 47, 51, 54, 120; expansion of American territory, 43; French and Indian War and, 43; Revolutionary War and, 4, 9, 10, 36, 37, 46, 48, 53, 54, 55, 101, 127, 130, 141, 245, 251; Royal Proclamation of 1763 and, 35, 44–46, *45*; tax collectors of, 44; taxes imposed on colonies by, 46; Treaty of Paris and, *39*, 43; Treaty of Stanwix and, 4, 118; units of land measurement in, 118; war debts of, 44; western settlement prohibited by, 35, 44–46, *45*. *See also* French and Indian War; Revolutionary War
Great Crossing(s), Kentucky, 80, 91, 92; Buffalo Path (Alanant-o-wamiowee) and, 94, 106; and central place theory,

26; road built to, 29; vegetation of, presettlement, 92, 93
Great Crossings Church: John N. Bradley on, 146; Elijah Craig, pastor of, 146, 149; Samuel H. Ford on, 146; splits, 149
Great Indian Warpath (Athawominee): described, 40; Great Wagon Road and, 40; trail system down the Great Valley, 40, 105–6; Warriors' Path, western branch of, 105
Great Lakes: French and Indian War and, 43; Indian tribes of, 4; St. Lawrence River route to, 38
Great Recession of 2008: housing industry collapse and, 255; and Kentucky Department of Parks, reduced budget from, 267; and Royal Spring, reduced budget from, 255; and World Equestrian Games, reduced visitors from, 260
Great Salt Lick Creek, 105. *See* Licking River
Great Valley: described, 38, 40; gaps and access to, 38, 104; Great Wagon Road in, 40; Indian trading facilitated by, 40, 61; opened to settlement, 40; traversed by Daniel Boone, 65
Great Wagon Road: described, 40; Wilderness Road branch of, 40. *See also* Great Indian Warpath
Green, Ben (husband of NG), 161
Green, Nellie (NG): house of, 161; as washerwoman, 161
Greenfield Plantation, Virginia, home of William Preston, 115
Green River, 53; last bison sighting, 100
Greenup County, Kentucky, 41
Grinstead, James A.: Blue Grass Park purchase by, 175; Blue Grass Park records acquired by, 176–77; as co-owner of Grinstead and Bradley, 176; sells Blue Grass Park to Shelby, 177; Walnut Hills Farm of, 176–77
Grinstead and Bradley (Lexington bank): James Grinstead and, 176; Keene Richards indebted to, 174; Keene Richards sued by, 175
Groundwater: aquifer types, 15, 16, 23; contamination of, 15, 16–17, 198, 201; database, state, xiv; in karst flow systems, x, 16, 77–78, 80, 198; Kentucky monitoring network of, xiv; laws concerning, 23–24; legal definition, 24; as preferred source, 15; protection zones, 218, 227–28, 229–30; purity, perception of, 15, 218; in underground lakes, belief in, 15, 219; springs, x, xi–xii, 6, 7, 14, 78, 102–3, 108–11, *112*, 113–14, 219; and waterborne disease, 18, 19–20, 22, 199–206, 210, 211–15, 317n14; water quality of, 16; in well fields, 14–15. *See also* granular aquifers; groundwater tracing; karst; karst aquifers; Royal Spring; springs
groundwater tracing: dyes used in, 221; history of, 221; qualitative/quantitative methods in, 221; of Royal Spring recharge area, 215–16, 220, 221–23, 318n29
grouse, ruffed. See *Bonasa umbellus*
Grover, Horace M. (brother of JG), Water Supply Co., stockholder in, 184
Grover, Jefferson "Jeff" D. (JG): Blue Grass Park, buys and sells, 177, 187; Alice P. Montgomery, sister of, 177, 187; Royal Spring, leases water rights, 181; Water Supply Co., stockholder in, 184
gunpowder: mission to obtain, 139–40, 142; recovered by Clark and Kenton, 142; shortage of, 139; Three Islands, concealed at, 140
Guthrie, Ben, on cane at Georgetown, 92

hackberry. See *Celtis occidentalis*
Hamilton, Henry, describes Flat Lick, 105
Hammond's Creek (Anderson County), John Cobbs, land on, 143

Hanson, Thomas: Elkhorn region, praised by, 66, 118, 120; Floyd's expedition, chronicled by, 115; Patrick Henry land survey, described by, 90; Royal Spring, described by, 121; on vegetation, presettlement, 90–91
Hardin County Water District, 14
Harrison County (Kentucky), 41, 125; Cynthiana, county seat of, *8* (map), 11; Inner Bluegrass, included in, 75; Ruddle's Station in, 7
Harrod, James: cabin of, 120, 122; and Dunmore's War, service in, 123; Filson's *Kentucke*, endorses, 70; establishes Harrod's Town/Fort, 4–5, 117; Transylvania Colony, angered by, 51
Harrodsburg (Mercer County), xii; as county seat, *9* (map), 11; land court at, 55; surveyor's office, 55
Harrod's Creek (Kentucky), 143
Harrod's Fort (Kentucky), xv, 139, 140; built, 5, 117, 264; descriptions of, contemporary, 130, 133; as early settlement, xv, 7, 53, 264; fortifications of, 5, 130, 137; Graham Springs Park at, 239; as immigrant collection point, 139; and McClelland's Station refugees, 142; Pageant of Kentucky's Historic Past at, 239; as public fort, 6, 10, 132, 137, 139; as refuge, 10, 127, 142; Royal Proclamation of 1763, violation of, 53; site of, 4, 239; size of, 7, 132, 266; stockade gates of, 137; water supply of, 265. *See also* Old Fort Harrod State Park
Harrod's Town (Kentucky): abandoned, 5; 117, 122; established, 4, 117; John Floyd arrives at, 122; site of, 4; town plan, 4. *See also* Harrod's Fort; Harrodsburg
Hart County (Kentucky), and last free-roaming bison, 100
Hauss, David J.: bid to supply water, 185; Georgetown Water, Gas, Electric Light and Power Co., established by, 185; Robert W. Nelson and, 185
Hawkins, Don (council member), Elijah Craig, statue of, 269–70
Hawkins, John, as executor of Elijah's will, 155
Hayden, William (formerly enslaved person): autobiography of, 150; Craig's ropewalk, employed in, 150; Frankfort ropewalk, employed in, 150; Lexington ropewalk, employed in, 150
Heaven Hill Distillery (Bardstown): asserts Craig as "father of bourbon," 270; and Elijah Craig bourbon brand, 270, *272*
Henderson, Gwynn: on number of settlers, 9; on tree species, presettlement, 85
Henderson, Richard: actions condemned, 51; assembly, holds, 51; Boone, sends to establish Boonesborough, 50–51, *52*; Boone, sends to scout Kentucky, 49; and Boonesborough, 5, 50–51, *52*, 53, 127; game, condemns destruction of, 99, 100; home in North Carolina, 49; solicits settlers, 49; Transylvania, compensated for loss of, 53; Transylvania Colony established by, 49–52, *50*, 129; Transylvania Company formed by, 49, 129; negotiates with Cherokee to purchase land, 49–50, 54, 67
Henry, Patrick: governor of Virginia, 140; and gunpowder for settlements, 140; North Elkhorn, land survey of, 90, 93
Herndon, Lunceford, property purchased by Richards, 165
Hickman Creek (Fayette County), reservoir on, 21
hickory. See *Carya* sp.
Hill, William, and Kentucky, explores with Boone, 64
Hinkston's Station: abandoned, 130, 140; founded by John Hinkston, 301n12; location of, 125

Hinton (settler), killed by Indians, 109
Historic sites in Kentucky: Blue Licks Battlefield, 264; Boone's Station, 264; Bryant's Station, 264; Fort Boonesborough, 264; National Register sites, 264; Old Fort Harrod, 264. *See also* National Register of Historic Places; *and specific listings*
Hockhocking River, Indian attack near, 139
Hofstra, Warren, on land engrossment in Virginia, 48
hog peanut (pea vine). See *Amphicarpaea bracteata*
Holston River Valley, as staging ground for Kentucky settlement, 40
honey locust. See *Gleditsia triacanthos*
hoopwood. See *Celtis occidentalis*
horse farms, 84; Blue Grass Park, 165–66, *167*, 168–69, 170, 171, 172, 174–*76*; Kentucky, Thoroughbred farms in, 256; Walnut Hills Farm, 176–77
horses: Arabian, cross-breeding with Thoroughbred, 165, 174; Arabians of Queen Isabella, 163, 165; Bettie West (Thoroughbred), 169; *Blood Horse* journal on, 256; Bluegrass, as Horse Capital, 256; Blue Grass Park and, 166, *167*, 168–69, 174, 176–77; Kentucky, first stock in, 124; genome sequenced, 256; Glencoe (Thoroughbred), 166, 171; Gluck Equine Research Center, 256; Jockey Club, in Lexington, 256; Kentucky, horses in, 256; Kentucky, Thoroughbreds in, 256; Knight of St. George (Thoroughbred), 168; Mokhladi (Arabian), *164*; and John Hunt Morgan, 171; Peytona (Thoroughbred), 167; racing of, 257, 308n2; in Scott County, 257; Standardbred, 257; and Thoroughbred breeding, 166, *167*, 169; *Thoroughbred Times* on, 256
Hudson, John C., frontier settlement model, 9
Hudson, William: killed in attack, 267; remains discovered at Logan's Fort, 267
Hudson River, as gateway to west, 38
Hunleigh, Will T., and Royal Spring, *160*
Hutchins, Thomas: on Great Salt Lick Creek, 105; map of trans-Appalachian region, 91

ice ages, Pleistocene, effects on regional drainage, 79
Imlay, Gilbert, *Topographical Description of the Western Territory of North America*, 72
Indiana, natural meadows of, 87
Indiana Territory, 149
Indian trails. *See* trails
Inner Bluegrass Karst Region, xiii, 1, 16, 77, *78*, 221, *222*
Inner Bluegrass region: abundance of game animals in, 74; agricultural productivity of, 67, 74, 76; area of, 74; bedrock of, 75–76; Daniel Boone explores, *65*–66; cane land of, 91; caves in, 80–81; central place theory and, 25, 26; characteristics of, 4, 27, 29, 74, 75, 77–78; community growth in, 26–27; community water supplies in, 20, 21–22; counties of, 75; county seats of, *8*, 11; created landscape, 84; as cultural region, 75; defined, 74–75; Jessamine Dome, 75; drainage, 79; John Findlay, describes to Boone, 63; as focus of early settlement, 3, 27, 46, 53, 60, 62, 66–68, 72–73, 94, 109; frontier settlement model for, 9–10; Christopher Gist traverses, 41; historical and structural geology, 75–76; as Horse Capital, 256; industry, early, of, 31; as karst region, 1, 16, 77, *78*, 79, 80; landless residents of, 57–58; Lexington as primary city of, 18, 27, 28, 29; map of, *8*; Nashville Basin, similar to, 3, 75; natural resources, 74; paradise, perceived as, 53, 60, 62, 66–68; pioneer stations in,

8, 10–11; potential, perceived, 94; public forts in, 6, *8*; sinkholes as waste dumps in, 17; soil fertility of, 53, 67, 74, 76, 77, 81; springs of, 74, 101–3; Thoroughbred industry in, 76, 256; topography of, 1, 74, 76–77; vegetation, presettlement, 81–93, 293n16; water, perceived scarcity by pioneers, 78–79, 108; watercourses of, 74, 79–80; wild game of, 66, 74
International Equestrian Festival (Lexington), economic failure of, 260
International Museum of the Horse, at Kentucky Horse Park, 256
Iroquois Indians: Kentucky, early descriptions by, 61; land purchases from, 4, 38, 40, 118; treaties with, 4, 38, 40, 118
ironwood. See *Carpinus caroliniana*
Ironworks Pike, as John Floyd's baseline, 88

Jackson, Charles T., limestone waters theory of cholera and, 200–201
Jackson, James P.: Georgetown gas company, sold by; 185; Georgetown Water, Gas, Electric Light and Power Co., president of, 185
jail, old city, *254*; abandoned, 253; arts center, converted to, 254; described, 253; fundraising for, 254; and Goebel assassination conspirators, 253; history of, 252–53; jailor's house, 253, *254*; renamed Scott County Arts and Cultural Welcome Center, 254; renovation of, 245, 255; Scott County Arts Consortium, Inc., and, 254; welcome center, converted to, 255
Jakle, John A., on salt licks and bison, 104
January, Peter, Sr., William Hayden employed in ropewalk of, 150
Jaycees. *See* Georgetown Jaycees
Jay's Treaty (1794), 9
Jefferson, Thomas, *Notes on the State of Virginia*, 70
Jessamine County (Kentucky), 67; Inner Bluegrass, included in, 75; landless households in 1792, 57; Nicholasville, county seat of, *8* (map), 11
Jessamine Dome, Bluegrass geologic structure and, 75–76
Jesse Lewis cabin: Robert and Ginger Chapman and, 248; Jesse Lewis builds, 248; Royal Spring Park, donated to, 248. *See also* Royal Spring Park
Jillson, Willard R., Filson's *Kentucke*, review by, 70
J. Mattingly Bourbon: and Jeff Mattingly, 271; and Bourbon 30 blenders, 271
Jockey Club, offices in Lexington and New York, 256
John B. Rogers Producing Company. *See* Burgess, Neva Summers
Johnson, President Andrew, pardons Keene Richards, 172
Johnson, Harry V., on contamination of Royal Spring, 214
Johnson, Joe E. (former mayor of Georgetown): on building replica fort, 243; on condition of Royal Spring Park, 242
Johnson, John T., on cholera at Georgetown, 203
Johnson, Robert, assignee of Patrick Henry's Elkhorn land, 93
Johnson, Robert and Jemima, settlement of, 146
Johnson's Mill, 147
Jones, John Gabriel: and George Rogers Clark, gunpowder for settlements, 139–40, 302n24; and Clark, petitions Virginia for new county, 140; killed by Indians, 140–41; McClelland's Station, resident of, 139; William Preston and, 139
Juglans sp. (walnut), 86, 87, 89, 91, 122; *Juglans cinerea* (white walnut), 89; *Juglans nigra* (black walnut), 86, 89, 90

Kanawha River, West Virginia, 25, 115
karst: bedrock fractures and, 77; carbonic acid and bedrock dissolution, 77; caves in, 78; defined, 16; distinctive landforms, viii, 16, 77; distribution in Kentucky, 16, 77, *78*; formation of, 16, 77–78; fracture systems and, 80; groundwater percolation, 77; human influence upon, x; of Inner Bluegrass Karst Region, 1, 16, 77, *78*, 79, 80; karst flow systems, 16, 77–78, 198, 201, 209; landscape evolution and, x; limited surface drainage of, 78; sinkholes and sinking stream in, x, xi, xiv, 16, 77, *78*, 80; springs and, 16, 78; urban, x–xi; *See also* Inner Bluegrass Karst Region; karst aquifers
karst aquifers, 16; groundwater tracing of, 210; pollution and, 16–17, 198, 201
Keene, Alexander C. (son of WK): as Georgetown physician, 163; Kentucky property of, 165; Louisiana, moves to, 165
Keene, Hannah (wife of WK), 163
Keene, William B. (WK): Alexander, son of, 163; death of, 165; Eleanora, daughter of, 163; as Georgetown physician, 163; Alexander Keene Richards, grandson of, 163; Royal Spring tract, purchase of, 156, 163, 306n1
Kelly, James Y.: on Royal Spring ownership, 187, 188, 191, 192; on Royal Spring potential contamination sources, 209–10, 214; Royal Spring water rights dispute and, 191, 192; on water hauling, 159
Kennedy, Mary C., on caves and prehistoric Kentuckians, xi
Kenton, Simon: Dunmore's War, service in, 123; as frontier hero, 115; McClelland's Station, helps fortify, 130; Robert Patterson, encounter with, 125; John Williams and, 125
Kentucky: agriculture in, 36, 98–99, 138; bison in, 100, 103–4; canelands in, 91; cholera epidemics in, 19, 20, 199, 203, 206; cities of, largest, 14; Civil War in, 169–71; climate of, 97; community festivals, 257; COVID-19 and, 269; defenses, frontier, 5–6, 9; descriptions of, first, 60–61; distillers in, xii; explorers, early, 40–42, 61, 64–66; Filson's *Kentucke*, 68, 69–72, 91; forest clearing in, 98–99; game animals in, 66, 93–94, 95, 99–100; gateways into, 38, *39*, 40; geology, historical and structural, 75–76; groundwater monitoring network of, xiv; heads of households in 1792, 57; historical pageant of, 239; horses in, 256; immigrants by 1800, 60; immigrant expectations, 58, 60, 67–68, 72, 94, 95, 97; Indian raids on, 4, 7–8, 129; industries, "first," 149–53; karst regions of, 16, *18* (map); Kentucky County created, 127, 140; Kentucky State Medical Society of, *205*; land courts in, 55, 110; land laws and claims in, 47–48, 54–57, 109–10; land speculators in, 11, 37, 45–46, 47, 48–53, *50*, 56, 57–58, 61–62, 72, 109, 129; livestock, first in, 124; macadamized roads in, 30–31; Native American inhabitants of, 3, 62–63; Native American outmigration from, 3–4, 62; as paradisical land, 67–68, 71, 72; population of, settlement era, 94; prehistoric people of, xi, 3; salt licks in, 103, 104, 107–8; settlement, phases of, 10–11; settlement ban on, 44–46; settlement of, barriers to, 37–38; settlement of, motives for, 72; settlement pattern of, xii, 102; settlement period of, 3, 10–11; settlements, early, 3–4; slavery, myth of mild form in, 241; springs in, 102–3; statehood of, 152; state parks of, 264–65, 267, 268; Toyota locates in, 33, 231; trails used by pioneers in, 102, 103, 104–7, *107* (map); vacated by settlers, 142; vital statistics law, first

in, *205*; Water Supply Protection Program in, 227, 229; World Equestrian Games in, 256, 257–60
Kentucky, settlement of: Appalachian Mountains and, 37; barriers to, 36, 37–38, 43; British policies concerning, 35, 37, 44, *45*, 46; Cumberland Gap and, 3, 6, 40, 43, 46, 60, 104; as defensive network, 6; Filson's *Kentucke* and, 68, 71, 72; gateways to region, 38, *39* (map), 40, 43, 60, 104; Inner Bluegrass focus of, 3, 27, 46, 60, 94; land laws concerning, 46–49, 54–56; model of, 9–10; Native Americans, resistance to, 4, 5, 37; Ohio River route into, 42, 46, 60; paradisical myth and, 66–68, 71; period of, 3; speculators and, 40–42, 45–46, 49–53, *50*, 56, 57, 58, 61–62; stages in, 10
Kentucky American Water Company: Bluegrass Water Supply Commission and, 232; Georgetown water company, offer to purchase, 231; Toyota water supply and, 33, 231; water plant, builds new, 232
Kentucky Baptist Education Society: Craig's paper mill site and, 208; mill site sold to Lair, 208
Kentucky Bicentennial Commission, grant to Big Royal Spring, Inc. from, 246
Kentucky Board of Health, report on waterborne disease, 206
Kentucky County, Virginia: created, 53, 127, 140; county surveyor of, 55
Kentucky Division of Water, xiii–xiv; Water Supply Programs and, 229
Kentucky Gazette (Lexington), 32, 153; on Craig building paper mill, 151; Craig's eulogy in, 154; Craig's mill, mentioned, 149; printed on Craig's paper, 151; real estate advertisements in, 113–14; on scarcity of paper, 151
Kentucky General Assembly: act establishing Georgetown boundaries, 156, 195; authorizes turnpike construction, 30
Kentucky Geological Survey, karst research by, 225–26
Kentucky Groundwater Monitoring Network, xiv
Kentucky Heritage Council, jail conversion, provides grant for, 254
Kentucky Horse Park, *82*; description of, 256; geophysical studies at, 226–27; International Museum of the Horse at, 256; Legacy Trail and, 263; location, *2* (map), 256; National Horse Center at, 256; Royal Spring karst system and, 226–27; visitors to, annual, 256; woodland pasture on, *84*; World Equestrian Games, as venue for, 256, 257, 258, 259, 260; World Equestrian Games, revenues from, 259
Kentucky Land Office, 88
Kentucky Parks System: Boone's Station State Park, 269; budget reduction of, 267, 269; Constitution Square State Park, 269; elimination of park sites, 259; Fort Boonesborough State Park, 264; and historic sites, 269; Old Fort Harrod State Park, 264; site maintenance neglected, 257; White Hall State Park, 269; William Whitley House State Park, 269
Kentucky River, 41, 63, 67, 86, 93, 95, 109, 118, 220; antiquity of, 79; bison ford of, at Leestown, 93, 94, 106, 124, 125, 129; Boonesborough on, 5, 127, 264; course of, 79; Elkhorn Creek and, 79; incision of gorge, 79; Kentucky as entry into, 6; Lexington and, 28; Licking River, divide with, 29; McClelland party travels up, 124–25; McClelland's Station isolated by, 9, 130; mouth of, 117; North Fork of, 42; Ohio River and, 79; Teays River and, 79; Transylvania Colony, as boundary of, 50, 51, 129; Thomas Walker discovers, 41; as water supply, 21, 220, 231, 232

Kentucky State Board of Health, report on water quality and health, 206
Kentucky Supreme Court, awards Royal Spring tract to Cobbs, 144
Kentucky Utilities: Georgetown, property of, 130; Georgetown, sells water works to, 185; Lexington Utilities, absorbed by, 185; McClelland's fort replica and substation of, 243, 246–*47*; Tom Prather on substation relocation, 246–47
Kickert, Conrad: Royal Spring Park design challenge and, 262; University of Cincinnati, faculty of, 262
King, Leslie, and central place theory, 25
Knight of St. George (Thoroughbred horse), 168
Knob Lick (Boyle County), on old Wilderness Trail, 106
Koch, Robert, and germ theory of disease, 20

la Salle, Robert Cavalier, the Sieur de: French claim to Ohio Valley and, 37; Ohio River discovered by, 37
Lair, Abraham K.: as city trustee, 208; dam, dispute with city over, 196, 208–9; death of, 209; mill and mill dam of, 208–9
Lake Erie, 42
Lake Ontario, 38
Lalemant, Hierosme, fantastical description of Kentucky, 61
Lancaster (Garrard County), xii, 146; as county seat, *9* (map), 11
land: certificates for, 55, 57, 109; claims, competitive nature of, 110; claims, conflicting, 56, 110; claims, settlement and preemption, 55, 288n33; colonial government grants for, 47; commissioners and courts for, 55, 56, 110; criteria for choosing, 6, 110–11; Crown grants of, 47, 55; fraudulent claims to, 53, 55, 57; headrights for, 47, 55; and "land jobbers," 57; and landless households, 57, 58; laws regarding, 6–7, 47; litigation over, 110; military warrants for, 47, 48, 55; model of frontier settlement and, 10; prices, inflation of, 57; speculators and, 11, 37, 40–42, 45–46, 47, 48–53, *50*, 56, 57–58, 61–62, 72, 109, 129; surveyor for Kentucky County, 55; title, requirements for, 6–7, 47, 53, 55, 109, 138; treasury rights for, 47, 55; treasury warrants for, 47, 55, 56. *See also* land laws of Virginia; land speculators; land surveys
land laws of Virginia: 1705 (headright grants), 47, 54; 1776 (grants to persons in residence), 54; 1777 (settlements), 54; 1779 (recognition of colonial grants; settlement and preemption rights; land commissioners), 54–55; 1779 (establishment of land office), 55–56
land speculators: absentee, 52, 47, 57; exploitation of system by, 11, 37, 46–47, 48, 56; French and Indian War, effect on, 49; Richard Henderson and, 5, 49–53, *50*, 129; land concentrated into hands of, 55, 57, 58; "land jobbers" and, 57; and landless households, 57–58; Loyal Company and, 40–41, 49, 61–62, 72; Ohio Company and, 41–42, 49, 61–62, 72; in Piedmont and Shenandoah Valley, 48–49; Royal Proclamation of 1763, effect on, 45–46, 49; settlers disadvantaged by, 11, 37, 46–47; treasury warrants encourage, 56
land surveys: of Boonesborough town lots, 5; boundary trees, 87–88, *89*, 90, 109, 117; circumferentor, use of, 117, *119*; conflicting, 56, 110; earliest Kentucky, 10, 35, 41, 72, 109; John Floyd's Elkhorn surveys, 88, *89*, 90–91, 93; of Georgetown town lots, 147, *148*, 156–57; Gunter's chain, 118; legal requirements, 6, 47, 55–56, 109; metes and bounds method, 109,

117–18; of Royal Spring, 1–2, 53, 88, 91, 121–22, 125; surveyor for Kentucky County, 55; on treasury warrants, 56; units of measurement, 117–18
Lapham, Increase A., limestone waters theory of cholera and, 200
Laportea canadensis (wood nettle), 91
Laurentia, ancestral North America, 75
Lawrenceburg (Anderson County), as county seat, *9* (map), 11
Laws, Robert J., 180. *See also* Cramer and Laws
Lea, John, limestone waters theory of cholera and, 201
Leach, Milton, cabin of, 248; as formerly enslaved person, 248. *See also* Milton Leach cabin
Lebanon (Georgetown), 149, 155, 156; named, 147; renamed Georgetown, 147
Lee, Willis, killed at Leestown, 129
Leestown, Kentucky: attacked by Indians, 7, 129; bison ford of Kentucky River at, 93, 94, 106, 124, 129; Buffalo Path (Alanant-o-wamiowee) and, 106; McClelland journey, 124, 125; McClelland party, as rendezvous for, 125
Legacy Trail: construction initiated, 263; Georgetown/Scott County, proposed alternate routes of, 263; Horse Park and, 263; Lexington and, 263
Legge, William, Richard Henderson and, 51
Lemons Mill Road, 93
Levisa Fork, Kentucky, Boone explores region in 1767, 64
Lewis, Andrew: Battle of Point Pleasant and, 122; John Floyd and, 122; Richfield, estate of, 302n24
Lewis, Jesse, cabin of, 248. *See also* Jesse Lewis cabin
Lewis, John A., blames Royal Spring for typhoid outbreak, 213–14
Lewis County (Kentucky): Cabin Creek and, 125; Salt Lick Creek and, 124, 125; Vanceburg and, 124
Lexington (Fayette County): bicentennial of, ix; *Blood Horse*, office in, 256; Buffalo Path (Alanant-o-wamiowee) and, 106–7; as central place, 26; Central Rock quarry in, 225; cholera at, 20, 21, 199–200, 201–2, 204; Confederate occupation of, 170; as county seat, *9* (map), 11; as cultural center, 28; economic dominance of, 28, 29; and Elkhorn Creek, North and South, 79; founding of, viii, ix; 109; and Georgetown, 230; growth, factors in, 27, 218; industry of, early, 27–28, 31; International Equestrian Festival of, 260; Kentucky American Water Co. of, 33, 231–33; *Kentucky Gazette* published in, 32, 114; Kentucky Horse Park and, 256; Kentucky River and, 21, 28; Legacy Trail and, 263; Lexington-Fayette Urban County Government (LFUCG) of, 228, 230; Lexington Utilities Co. of, 185; McConnell Springs in, ix, viii–ix, 15; McConnell Springs Park in, 251, 266; naming of, viii, ix, 251; Pepper Distillery in, xii; pioneer defenses, 27; population of, historic, 26, 28, 202; population of, present day, 26; public spring of, 21, 113; road network of, 29, 30; ropewalk in, 150; Royal Spring and, 218, 219, 220, 223, 228, 229, *230*; Sayre Bank of, 175; Scruggs and Hammond firm in, 245; sewer construction in, 18; and Thoroughbred industry, 256; *Thoroughbred Times*, former office in, 256; Town Branch in, 21, 28; trustees of, 21, 113; turnpike built to Georgetown, 30; turnpike built to Maysville, 30; vegetation of, presettlement, 83, 86; water supply of, 15, 18, 20–21, *112*, 179, 200, 283n31; Wilderness Road and, 27; World Equestrian Games and, 256, 259, 260

Lexington-Fayette Urban County Government (LFUCG), and Royal Spring Water Supply Protection Program, 228, 230
Lexington Utilities Company: Georgetown Water, Gas, Electric Light and Power Co., purchased by, 185; Kentucky Utilities, absorbed by, 185
Licking River, 125; bison ford of, 106; divide with Kentucky River, 29; Great Salt Lick Creek, early name for, 105; Hinkston's Station on, 125, 130; McClelland journey and, 125
licks: animals attracted to, 102, 103, 104–5; Cresswell on, 103; Filson on, 103; mineral concentration of, 107–8; origin of name, 103; Rafinesque on, 107; salt production and, 107; seawater, compared to, 107; source of saline waters of, 107–8; trails, influenced by location of, 102; type, clay licks, 107; type, paint licks, 107; type, salt licks, 29, 94, 103, 104–5, 106, 107–8, 124, 125, 303n32, 305n8; type, sulfur licks, 107
limestone bedrock: cholera and, 200–201; distribution in Kentucky, 16; and karst, x, 16, 77–*78*, 201; origin, 75; and soil fertility, 74, 81; soil formation, role in, 74; spring water and, vii, xii, 1, 16
Limestone Creek, Kentucky: Buffalo Path (Alanant-o-wamiowee), endpoint of, 106, 107; as entry point to Bluegrass, 60; Maysville and, 60, 107. *See also* Limestone Landing
Limestone Landing (Kentucky): bison trail from, 27, 107; as entry point to Bluegrass, 27, 60; Ohio river landing at, 27; as port, 152, 153; renamed Maysville, 27, 152
Lincoln County, Kentucky, 5, 127; and Logan's Fort replica, 267
Lincoln County Fiscal Court, William Whitley House State Park given to, 269
Lindsay, Elizabeth, marries Robert Patterson, 124
Lindsay, Henry, at Cave Spring, 110
Lindsay, William, land surveyed for, 110
Line, Edmund, land commissioner, 55
linear cities, 25
Liriodendron tulipifera (yellow poplar, tulip poplar), 86, 89
Lister, Joseph, and germ theory of disease, 20
Logan, Benjamin: accompanies John Floyd, 126; builds Logan's Fort, 5; Joseph Drake and, 126
Logan, Chief (Mingo Indians), family of, slaughtered, 120
Logan, John, and Elijah Craig, partner in fulling mill, 305n8
Logan's Fort, Kentucky: archaeology of, 267; built, 5; as early settlement, xv; human remains discovered at, 267; land court at, 55, 110; as public fort, 6; replica of, 267; as refuge, 126–27, 142 *See also* St. Asaph's
long hunters: Cumberland Gap, familiar with, 41; defined, 3; frontier, appeal to, 36; Henderson, hires to explore Kentucky, 49; Joseph Drake as, 126
Lösch, August, and central place theory, 25
Louisa Company. *See* Transylvania Company
Louisburg, fortress of (Nova Scotia), captured by British, 43
Louisiana, territory acquired by Britain, 43
Louisville, Kentucky: as central place, 26; cholera at, 199, 206; Commonwealth Distillers in, 270; Elijah Craig bourbon distilled at, 270; established, 11, 28; Falls of the Ohio at, 28, 41, 118; possible water source for Georgetown, 233; Heaven Hill Distillery in, *272*; historic population,

28; land court at, 55; as metropolitan area, 266; steamboat traffic and, 28; water supply of, 14, 233
Lower Blue Licks, Kentucky. *See* Blue Licks, Lower
Lower Shawnee Town, 105
Lowry, Abraham Scott (ASL, husband of SL and father of Sarah McClelland), 124
Lowry, John (son of ASL and SL, brother of Sarah McClelland), 124; comes to McClelland's Station, 125
Lowry, Sarah (SL, wife of ASL and mother of Sarah McClelland), 124
Lowry, Stephen (son of ASL and SL, brother of Sarah McClelland): livestock, brings first into Kentucky, 124; McClelland settlement expedition, joins, 123
Loyal Company of Virginia: land grant in Kentucky of, 40, 49; Royal Proclamation of 1763 and, 46, 49; Thomas Walker and, 40–41, 61–62; western settlement promoted by, 61–62

Mackay-Smith, Alexander, biographer of Edward Troye, 172
Maker's Mark bourbon, and Samuels family, 271
Mallon, Mary ("Typhoid Mary"): accounts of, published, 317n21; as typhoid carrier, 211
Mammoth Cave, xi
Mammoth Cave National Park, xiv
Mann's Lick (Jefferson County), on old Wilderness Trail, 106
Marshall, Everett, Georgetown Commons graded by, 237
Marshall, Humphrey, on vegetation of Elkhorn region, 87
Martin, Josiah, condemns Transylvania Colony, 51
Martin's Station (Virginia), Daniel Boone and, 65
Mason County (Kentucky), 99; created, 152; landless households in 1792, 57; Mays Lick in, 125; Stone Lick in, 125
Matson, George C., and Royal Spring groundwater tracing, 215–16, 220, 318n29
Matthew, Samuel, on vegetation at Bryant's Station, 86
Mattingly, Jeff: and Bourbon 30 blenders, 271; and J. Mattingly bourbon, 271; and Samuels family, 271
Maxwell H. Gluck Equine Research Center (Lexington), sequences horse genome, 256
Mayors Institute for City Design: described, 325n26; and National Endowment for the Arts, 261; Tom Prather attends workshop, 261; Royal Spring Park design challenge and, 261–62; and US Council of Mayors, 261. *See also* Royal Spring Park design challenge
Mays Lick (Mason County): Buffalo Path (Alanant-o-wamiowee) and, 106, 125; Drake farm near, 99; McClelland journey and, 125
Maysville (Kentucky): Buffalo Path (Alanant-o-wamiowee), endpoint near, 106, 107; cholera at, 199; established, 27; Limestone, former name for, 27, 106, 152; Limestone Creek and, 60, 107; and Mays Lick, 96, 125; Maysville Road and, 27, 28, 30; as port city, 152–53
Maysville Road, 27, 29; described, 29–30; turnpike built to Lexington, 30
McAfee, James (brother of RM): Elkhorn Creek, discovers, 80; surveys land for RM, 93
McAfee, Robert (RM): Elkhorn Creek, discovers and names, 80; land surveyed for, 93
McBride, Kim: on stations on sloping ground, 131; and Stephen McBride, on archaeology of Logan's Fort, 267

McClelland, Abraham (brother of JM): Kentucky, journey to settle in, 123–25
McClelland, Abraham (son of JM and SM), 128
McClelland, Alexander (brother of JM): Kentucky, early explorations by, 123; Kentucky, journey to settle in, 123–25
McClelland, Benjamin (brother of JM), McClelland's Station, comes to, 125
McClelland, James (son of JM and SM), 129
McClelland, John (JM), 138; children of, 128–29, 301n10; visited by Floyd, 127–28; Floyd's Spring, familiar with, 125; Floyd's Spring, unaware of previous claim to, 125; genealogy of, 300n2; gravesite location, 141–42, 302n27; Kentucky, early explorations by, 123; Kentucky, journey to settle in, 123–25; killed in attack, 3, 9, 128, 141, 142, 237, 267; and Lexington, naming of, 251; McClelland's Station, founder of, 35, 100; Royal Spring tract, not conveyed to him, 142; Royal Spring tract, purchases, 128
McClelland, John (son of JM and SM), 129
McClelland, John Robert (JRM, father of JM), 124
McClelland, Margaret (née Chiswell; wife of JRM, mother of JM), 124
McClelland, Margaret "Peggy" (daughter of JM and SM), 128–29
McClelland, Mary Ann "Polly (daughter of JM and SM), 129
McClelland, Sarah (SM, née Lowry; wife of JM): children of, 128–29; Kentucky, journey to settle in, 123–25; remarries, 129
McClelland, Sarah Louise (née Sterrett; mother of JM), 124
McClelland settlement expedition: divides into two groups, 124; Kentucky, journey to, 123–25; Leestown, reunites at, 125; livestock, brings first into Kentucky, 124; Pittsburgh, departs from, 124; Royal Spring, arrives at, 125
McClelland's Spring, 101. *See also* Royal Spring
McClelland's Station, *133*; abandoned, 3, 9, 11, 142, 271; archaeological potential of, 130; attacked by Indians, 9, 131, 141–42, 237, 267; cabin chimneys, 135, *136*; cabins, number of, 134, 135; characteristics of, 131–39; Polly Hawkins Craig and, 237; crowded conditions at, 139; defensive improvements of, 130, *133*, 135, 137–38; dismantled, 131; Lyman C. Draper and, *126*; Draper's notes on, 131–32; Draper's sketches of, 131–32; as early settlement, xv, 10, 57, 72; established, 2–3, 7, 35, 125, 245; exposed location of, 9; facade of, built for pageant, *240*; John Floyd and, 53–54; gates of, 135, 137; internal layout, 132–35, *133*, 137; land clearing for, 138; livestock and, 124, 139; location of, *126*, 131, 147, *268*; McClelland house at, 125, 130, 134, 135; population of, 132, 134; as refuge, 139; replica of, 243, 246–47, 266, 267, *268*; residents relocate to Harrod's Fort, 142; Revolutionary War dead monument and, 141, 237; Royal Proclamation of 1763, violation of, 35, 53; Royal Spring and, 2–3, 7, 35, 100, 125, *126*, 131–32; size and orientation, *126*, 131–32, 134, 135; enslaved people at, 139; stockade of, 135–36; stockade gates of, 137; vegetation of, 88, *126*; watchtowers at, 127. *See also* McClelland, John; McClelland's Station replica
McClelland's Station replica, *268*; construction materials for, 243; continued interest in, 246–47; dropped from planning, 246–47; fundraising for, 246; Georgetown Jaycees and, 242–43; grants for, 246;

Kentucky Utilities substation and, 243, 246, 266; obstacles for, 243, 246
McConnell, Andrew (cousin to WM): Kentucky, early explorations by, 123; journeys with McClellands, 123–25
McConnell, Francis, Jr. (cousin to WM): journeys with McClellands, 123–25; Kentucky, early explorations by, 123; Preston's Cave Spring tract, squatting on, 127, 301n9
McConnell, Francis, Sr. (brother to WM), journeys with McClellands, 123–25
McConnell, William (WM): Kentucky, early explorations by, 123, 251; journeys with McClellands, 123–25; livestock, brings first into Kentucky, 124; Pennsylvania home of, 124; McClelland's Station and, 125, 251, 300n5; and naming of Lexington, 251
McConnellsburg, Pennsylvania, 124
McConnell's Run Church, founded by Elijah Craig, 149
McConnell Springs, viii–x, xii, 283n31; and Lexington, naming of, viii, ix, 251; Lexington, proposed as water supply for, 15–16; size exaggerated, 279–80n5; threatened by development, 251. *See also* McConnell Springs Park
McConnell Springs Park (Lexington): establishment of, 251, 279n2; Founders' Day at, 251; Friends of McConnell Springs and, 251; land donated, 251; tourism potential, 266; James R. Rebmann and, 251
McCracken, Cyrus, killed at Leestown, 129
McCracken, John, McClelland's Station, comes to, 125
McEwan, Ryan: and Brian McCarthy, tree growth rates post settlement, 85; savanna woodland hypothesis and, 85
McGary's Station (Mercer County), 109; archaeology of, 133
McGregor, Gaille, on behavior of settlers, 97
McMullen, Samuel, on abandonment of McClelland's Station, 142
McRae, Roderick, and Royal Spring, 120
Meade, David, on corn production in Bluegrass, 67
meadows, natural (grasslands, prairie), 81, 87, 93, 94
Meleagris gallopavo (wild turkey), 74; abundance of, 94, 95; decline in numbers, 99; hunted by Walker party, 93; killed by cold weather, 97
Mercer County (Kentucky), 4, 109; Harrodsburg, county seat of, *8* (map), 11; Inner Bluegrass, included in, 75
Mercersburg, Pennsylvania, McClelland family and, 123
Meredith, Samuel, Elkhorn survey of, 93
Miami Indians, outmigration to Ohio, 4
Michaux, André: on decline in bison, 100; observations on forest cover, 86
Middle Trace, McClelland journey and, 125
military crest, defensive advantage of, 131
Miller, William, station of, 298n18
Milton Leach cabin: Milton Leach, built by, 248; restoration of, 248, *249*; Royal Spring Park, donated to, 248. *See also* Royal Spring Park
Mingo Indians, Treaty of Stanwix and, 118
Minorsville (Scott County), and central place theory, 26
Mississippi River: and cholera, 203, 204; discovered, 286n5; explored, 37, 286n5; France, basin claimed for, 37, 43; "Indian Reserve," basin as, 44; prairie on eastern margin, 104; William L. Richards, plantation on, 202
Missouri, settled by Kentucky immigrants, 9–10
Mohawk River. *See* Mohawk Valley
Mohawk Valley, as gateway to the west, 38, 43

Mokhladi (Arabian horse), *164*
Monongahela River: and Braddock's expedition, 64; Ohio River formed by confluence of Allegheny with, 42
Montgomery, Alice P. (AM; wife of HM): Blue Grass Park, purchased by, 177, 187; Jefferson D. Grover, brother of, 177, 187; homeplace tract, subdivided by, 177; Royal Spring, house overlooking, 177; Royal Spring, referenced in deed of, 195; Street Railway Co., sells land to, 187
Montgomery, Henry P. (HM): First National Bank, president of, 177; Georgetown Electric Light, Heat and Power Co., purchase of by, 182; Royal Spring, house overlooking, 177; Royal Spring water rights dispute and, 191, 192, 193; Water Supply Co., president of, 182, 192
Montgomery County, Virginia (Kentucky country), created, 127
Montreal (Canada), French defeat at, 43
Moore, Arthur K., on destruction of forests and game, 99
Moore, James F., and death of John Floyd, 143
Morehead State University, Gary O'Dell and, xiii
Morgan, John Hunt: Bluegrass region, described by, 76; cavalry raid into Kentucky by, 170; Georgetown and, 170; gifted horse by Keene Richards, 171
Morgan, Ralph (pioneer), 108
Morton, Richard L., on speculators, 49
Morus sp. (mulberry), 90
mountain gaps: Cumberland and Pine Mountain, alignment of, 104; discussion of, 286n8; of Eastern Kentucky borderland, 104; water gaps, 38, 104, 286n8; wind gaps, 41, 286n8. *See also specific gaps*
Mud Lick (Bath County): Olympian Springs, known as, 105; and Warriors' Path, 105
mulberry. See *Morus* sp.
Mull, Donald S., on Cane Run and Royal Spring, 220
Mundy's Landing Cave (Woodford County), longest in Bluegrass, 80
Murray, John (Lord Dunmore): as colonial governor of Virginia, 51, 54, 120; Dunmore's War and, 48, 122, 123; and Andrew Lewis, 302n24; Transylvania Colony, condemns, 51; Virginia House of Burgesses, dissolves, 54; war with Indians, warns of, 120, 122; Williamsburg, flees from, 54
Myers, Jacob, paper mill, 151

Nash, William, Royal Spring and, 90, 120
Nashville, cholera at, 200–201
Nashville Basin: early settlement of, 3; eroded from dome structure, 292n3; similarity to Inner Bluegrass, 75–76, 200–201. *See also* Nashville Dome
Nashville Dome: Bluegrass geologic structure and, 75; eroded to Nashville Basin, 293n3. *See also* Nashville Basin
National Horse Center, at Kentucky Horse Park, 256
National Register of Historic Places: Kentucky listings, 264; Royal Spring listed on, 245
National Speleological Society, x
National Trust for Historic Preservation, cultural heritage tourism, defined by, 263–64. *See also* cultural heritage tourism
Native Americans: ambushes at springs, 109; conflicts with settlers, 4, 5, 7, 9, 46, 109, 118, 120, 122, 129, 130, 139, 140–42, 143, 149; controlled burns by, 83, 85, 104; forest destruction, reaction to, 99; Kentucky, cessation of hostilities in, 9, 106; Kentucky, importance to, 4; Kentucky, as inhabitants of, 3; Kentucky, outmigration from, 3–4, 61;

retaliatory actions against, 9; salt production by, 108; threat of, perceived, 3, 5, 10, 31, 43, 44, 46, 60, 95, 117, 129–30, 135; town, Eskippakithiki (Kentucky), 62–63, 105; town, Lower Shawnee Town (Ohio), 105; trails used by, 86, 102, 104; Treaty of Lancaster with, 38; Treaty of Logstown with, 38; Treaty of Stanwix with, 4; western migration hindered by, 37, 38. *See also* French and Indian War; *and tribal listings*
natural flow, principle of. *See* water rights
Nelson, Mary W. (wife of RW): Georgetown Water, Gas, Electric Light and Power Co., president of, 185; Lexington Utilities, sells company to, 185
Nelson, Robert W. (RW): death of, 185; David J. Hauss and, 185; Georgetown Water, Gas, Electric Light and Power Co., established by, 185, 193; Water Supply Co. purchased by, 184, 193
New Orleans, steamboat traffic and, 28
Newport (Kentucky): cholera in, 206; Robert W. Nelson, home of, 184, 185
New River (Virginia/West Virginia), 115
Newtown Pike: bridge over North Elkhorn, 93; Shipp's Station and, 87
Nicholas County (Kentucky), 41
Nicholasville (Jessamine County): central place theory and, 26; as county seat, *9* (map), 11; water supply of, 220
Nichols, John, 180, 193. *See also* Nichols and Patterson
Nichols and Patterson: electrical power, expansion into by, 181; Georgetown Electric Light, Heat and Power Co., incorporate as, 181; indebtedness of, 182; land grant from city, 181, 188; litigation by, 194; right to use Royal Spring of, 181; water rates of, 181; water works, contract of, 180–81; water works, site of, 181 *See also* Georgetown Electric Light, Heat and Power Company; Nichols, John; Patterson, Henry C.
nonpoint source pollution, 16
North Carolina: Cherokee in, 61; Cumberland Gap and, 43; General Assembly of, 51
Notes on the State of Virginia (Jefferson), 70
Nourse, James, on absence of flowing streams, 79; on meadowlands, 93

oak. See *Quercus* sp.
Oakley, Eve: Arts in the Park, initiated by, 252; and Elijah Craig, statues of, 269–70
O'Brien, Michael J., and frontier settlement model, 9, 10
O'Dell, Gary A., vii–x, xii–xiv; Division of Water, employed by, xiii; groundwater tracing by, 319n4; and McConnell Springs, viii–ix; and Morehead State University, xiii; National Speleological Society, joins, x; on pace measurements, 131–32; Preston's Cave Spring and, vii; Royal Spring and, xiii; rural water supply, research by, 111; student of John Thrailkill, xiii, *222*
Odocoileus virginianus (whitetail deer), 74; abundance of, 94; decline in numbers, 99–100; Floyd and Reid, hunted by, 77; hunted by Daniel Boone, 66; hunted by Walker party, 93
Ohio: Battle of Fallen Timbers in, 9; Cincinnati Arch and, 75; John Filson disappears in, 72; French claims to, 42; Christopher Gist's travels through, 41; Indian relocation to, 4; Indian withdrawal from, 9; natural meadows of, 87; Ohio Country, known as, 41; settlement of, 41, 46
Ohio Company: Christopher Gist and, 40, 41; land grant of, 41, 46, 49; Royal Proclamation of 1763 and, 46, 49; trading post at Forks of the Ohio, 42;

William Trent and, 42; western settlement promoted by, 61–62
Ohio River: cholera, spread along, 203, 206; commerce and, 31; contaminants in, 15; de Blainville's journey down, 37; discovery of, 37; Falls of the Ohio on, 28, 41, 63, 66, 67, 105, 118; fords of, 106; Forks of the Ohio, 42–43, formed by confluence of rivers, 42; French claim to region and, 37; glacial origin of, 79; Henderson compensatory grant, as boundary of, 53; Indian raids across, 5, 129; Kentucky river, tributary of, 79; landing places into Kentucky of, 6, 27, 60, 103, 106, 152; McClelland party journey down, 124; pioneer retaliatory raids across, 9; river cities of, 11, 14–15, 25, 27, 28, 41, 106, 107, 117, 118, 125, 140, 152, 199, 206; as route to western frontier, 43, 46, 53, 60, 106; steamboat traffic on, 28; Three Islands in, 140; trails from, 105, 106, 125, 140; Transylvania colony, as boundary of, 50; water supply and, 14, 20, 233
Ohio Valley: access to, 5, 37, 42, 43, 60, 105; bison in, 104, *107*; British claims to, 37–38; cholera in, 203; first explorations of, 40–42; French claims to, 37, 42; Native American claims to, 4, 38; Treaties of Lancaster and Logstown and, 38
Old Fort Harrod State Park: advantages over Royal Spring Park, 265; David Coleman, manager of, 265; cultural/economic benefits of, 265; established, 264; grounds of, 265; Pioneer Memorial State Park, original name of, 264; replica fort at, 264–65, 266; revenues, annual, 265;Royal Spring Park, similar context to, 264; visitors, annual, 265
Olympian Springs. *See* Mud Lick
O'Malley, Nancy: on McClelland's Station, population of, 132; on roads, importance of, 31; on settlement phases, 10; on station crowding, 139
Orangeburg (Kentucky), formerly called Stone Lick, 125
Osler, William, and United States typhoid statistics (1909), 210
Ottawa Indians: attack on John Findlay, 63; Battle of Fallen Timbers and, 9
Outer Bluegrass region: explored by Daniel Boone, 66; defined, 76; soils of, 76

Pacini, Filippo, observes cholera bacteria, 20
Pageant of Scott County History: Big Spring DAR, sponsor of, 239; Neva Summers Burgess, director of, 239; Anne Payne Coffman, proposed by; 239; costumer for, 240; description of, 241; Georgetown College, held at, 239–41; Georgetown Woman's Club, sponsor of, 239; McClelland's Station facade built for, *240*; music for, 241; participation in, 240; racial bias of, 241; script writers of, 240
Paper mill, Craig's: leased by Stedman, 151; paper used by *Kentucky Gazette*, 151; producing paper, 151
paradisical myth. *See* western paradise, myth of; Inner Bluegrass region
Paris (Bourbon County): and central place theory, 26; as county seat, *9* (map), 11
Parker, Alexander and James, partners with Elijah Craig, 151
Parker, Harold, and McClelland's fort replica, 243
Parkersburg (West Virginia), Indian attack near, 139
Pasteur, Louis, and germ theory of disease, 20
pathogens, waterborne, 16; bacterial, 18; protozoan, 18; viral, 18. *See also* cholera; typhoid; diseases, waterborne
Patterson, Henry C., 180. *See also* Nichols and Patterson

Patterson, Robert: on biographical documentation, 299n1; Clark expedition to Illinois, joins, 142; Dunmore's War, service in, 123; gunpowder, effort to secure, 139; home in Pennsylvania, 124; injured in attack, 139; Lexington, established by, 251; Elizabeth Lindsay, marriage to, 124; livestock, brings first into Kentucky, 124; McClelland family, acquaintance with, 124; McClelland settlement expedition, joins, 123; McClelland's Station, finds deserted, 142; McClelland's Station, helps fortify, 130, 137; outfitted by father, 124; recovers from wounds, 142
Paylor, Randall L.: Royal Spring, basin delineation by, 223; Royal Spring, flow travel time estimates by, 230
Payne, William: Blue Grass Park, homeplace tract, buys and sells, 177; dividing wall in branch and, 207
pea vine (hog peanut). See *Amphicarpaea bracteata*
Pendleton County (Kentucky), and Maysville Road, 30
Pennington Gap, 104
Pepper Distillery (Lexington), xii
Perry, David: journeys with McClellands, 123–25; livestock, brings first into Kentucky, 124; surveys in Elkhorn region, 123
Perry, Susan, 161
Peter, Robert, on Royal Spring, source of, 210
Peterson, Jon, defines townsite consciousness, 235
Peytona (Thoroughbred horse), burial site of, 166, 168
Piedmont, 14; as eastern border to Blue Ridge Mountains, 38; region of North Carolina, 49; region of Virginia, 47
Pilot Knob, Kentucky, Boone views Bluegrass from summit, *65*–66
Pine Mountain (Kentucky-Virginia-Tennessee): described, 104; Pine Mountain Gap in, 104, 286n8; Pineville and, 104; Pound Gap in, 42
Pineville (Kentucky), and Pine Mountain Gap, 104
Pioneer life: Daniel Drake on, 96; effect on men, 96–97; effect on women, 96; fear of Indian attack, 3, 95–96; food shortages, 3; isolation and loneliness, 3, 96; lawless behavior, 97; loss of friends and family, 96; poverty of settlers, 96; primitive conditions of, 96. *See also* settlers
Pioneer Memorial State Park, now Old Fort Harrod State Park, 264
Pitts, Josiah: builds wall and springhouse, 156, 306n2; death of, 155; as executor of Elijah's will, 155; financial ruin of, 155; married Lucy Craig, 155; as merchant and tavern-keeper, 155; 155; and Royal Spring property, forced sale of, 156; Royal Spring property, purchased by, 156
Pitts, Lucy (née Craig; daughter of Elijah), married to Josiah Pitts, 155
Pittsburgh (Pennsylvania): and Fort Pitt, 46; French and Indian war and, 124; and gunpowder mission, 139, 140; launch point into Ohio Valley, 46, 123, 124, 300n1; McClelland party and, 124; Patterson recovers from wounds at, 142
Pleakenstalver, John (pioneer), 108
Pluggy, Chief. *See* Pluk-kemeh-notee
Pluk-kemeh-notee ("Chief Pluggy"): alleged burial site, 142, 303n28; attacks McClelland's Station, 141, 237; killed during attack, 141
Poa pratensis (bluegrass), 81, 93
point source pollution, 16
Pollack, David, on number of settlers, 9
pollution. *See* water pollution
Pompey (enslaved person): home of, 166; Keene Richards and, 166
poplar, yellow (tulip poplar). See *Liriodendron tulipifera*

Pound Gap (Virginia-Kentucky), 42; as passage through Pine Mountain, 42
Powell River Valley, Tennessee, 5; John Floyd camps in, 127; as staging ground for Kentucky settlement, 40; Wilderness Road and, 127
Powers, Caleb, co-conspirator in Goebel assassination, 253
Prather, Asa P. (grandfather of TP): arranges city purchase of water company, 248; mayor, four terms, 248
Prather, Harold B. (father of TP), former chair of Georgetown Municipal Water and Sewer, 248
Prather, Tom (TP), *250*; council member, former, 248; Kentucky American Water Co., views on, 231, 233; on Kentucky Utilities substation relocation, 246–47; mayoral vacancy (1986), filled by, 231, 248; and Royal Spring Branch, renovation of, 251–52; Royal Spring Park, support for, 248, 260; terms served, 248, 260; on water resources and community identity, 251
Preston, William: arranges to warn Kentucky surveyors, 120; John Brown, Jr. and, 67; Cave Spring tract, vii; John Floyd, communications with, 127, 128, 129–30; John Floyd, employed as surveyor, 115; Greenfield Plantation and, 115; Smithfield Plantation and, 115; sends Floyd to Kentucky, 115, 122
Preston's Cave Spring, *128*; Floyd surveys for William Preston, vii, *128*; Francis McConnell and, 127; rumor of squatters at, 127
prior appropriation, principle of. *See* water rights
Proclamation of 1763. *See* Royal Proclamation of 1763
Prunus serotina (black cherry), 87, 89
Pryor, Virgil, and McClelland's fort replica, 243
public forts, 6, 7, 10, 57; abandoned, 114; as administrative centers, 6; of Bluegrass, 6, *8* (map), 10; as collection points for immigrants, 6, 139; defensive network, part of, 9; fortifications of, 137; Indian attacks on, 9; as refuges, 6, 9, 10, 126–27; social friction in, 139; as staging points, 6; stations, compared to, 7. *See also individual forts*
public water systems: advent of, Kentucky, 22, 114, 179; and combined sewers, 17–18; of Georgetown, xv, 23, 178, 179–82, *183*, 184–*86*, 188–94, 196–97, 209, 215–18, 224, 230–33; of Lexington, 21; sources used by, 22, 33, 114. *See also* Georgetown Municipal Water and Sewer Service; Kentucky American Water Company

Quebec (Canada), French defeat at, 43
Quercus alba (white oak), 86, 89
Quercus falcata (Spanish oak, southern red oak), 89
Quercus macrocarpa (bur oak), 86; as component of savanna woodland, 83; dendrochronology and, 85; growth rate of, factors affecting, 85; habitat of, 85; in present-day woodland pastures, 81, *82*, 87, 90; seedling establishment of, 85; seedlings intolerant of shade, 83, 85
Quercus muehlenbergii (Chinquapin oak): as component of savanna woodland, 83; in present-day woodland pastures, 90
Quercus shumardii (Shumard oak), 89; as component of savanna woodland, 83; in present-day woodland pastures, 90
Quercus sp., 86, 87, 90; left to provide livestock shade, 90
Quercus velutina (black oak), 89
Quinlan, James, chief geologist, Mammoth Cave Park, xiv

Radcliff (Kentucky), water supply of, 14
Rafinesque, Constantine, on classification of licks, 107
Raitz, Karl, 31; on roads, importance of, 31; on symbolic landscapes, 84–85
Ranck, George W.: death of, viii; and McConnell Springs, viii, ix
Ray, Joseph A., and groundwater tracing, xiv
Rebmann, James R., and establishment of McConnell Springs Park, ix, 251. *See also* McConnell Springs Park
Red River, 79
Reid, Nathan, Jr., on father's memories of Kentucky, 77
Reid, Nathan, Sr.: on fertility of Bluegrass, 77; John Floyd and, 77, 94; on future potential of Bluegrass, 94
Republican Spring (Royal Spring): dispute with city over, 192–93; Georgetown boundaries and, 157, 195; on Georgetown plat, 156; Royal Spring, as designation for, 102; sanitary regulations and, 198–99. *See also* Big Spring; Royal Spring
reservoirs, water supply: of Lexington, 21; planned for Scott County, 231, 232, 233
Revolutionary War, 36, 48, 101, 130; and Battle of Blue Licks, 9, 143, 264, 302n26; and Battle of Lexington, viii, 251; contributing factors, 46; and Daughters of the American Revolution, 141, 237; Indian raids and, 4; land grants to veterans of, 48; Kentucky, settlement during, 9, 10, 46; McClelland's Station and, 245; Scott County war dead from, 237; Tories migrate west during, 127; Virginia war debts, 55; western settlement, barriers removed by, 37; western settlement prior to, 53
Richards, Alexander Keene (son of WR and ER): *164*; Arabian horses, breeding by, 165, 174, 308n2; bankruptcy of, 174; Bethany College, attends, 163; Blue Grass Park and, 165–69, 171, 172, 173–75; character of, 177; Confederate army, service in, 168–71; Craig house, residence of, 166, 175; death of, 176; Edward Troye and, 168, 172 *173*, 174, 175; expatriate in England, 171; financially ruined by war, 172; grand tour of Europe and Middle East, 163, 165; granted pardon, 172; Herndon tract, acquires, 165; indebtedness of, 174–75; inherits land, 165; John C. Breckinridge and, 169–71, 175; John Hunt Morgan and, 171; lifestyle of, 165; Mary Breckinridge and, 171; mortgages property, 174–75; racing and, 168, 169, 174; race track and stables, built by, 165; returns to America postwar, 172; Ross tract, acquires, 165; Royal Spring and, 195, 196, 202; people enslaved by, 166, 169, 171; suits filed against, 175; as Thoroughbred breeder, 165, *167*, 168, 169, 174, 176–77, 257, 308n2; Transylvania Plantation and, 165, 169, 171, 172, 174; Troye, contract with, 175; withdraws from war, 171
Richards, Eleanora (ER; née Keene; wife of WR): daughter of William B. Keene, 163; death of, 163; marries William L. Richards, 163
Richards, William L. (WR): death of, 163, 202–3; as Georgetown physician, 163; marries Eleanora Keene, 163
Richmond (Madison County), 171; battle near, 170; and central place theory, 26; as county seat, *9* (map), 11
Richmond, Virginia, on Fall Line, 14
richweed (white snakeroot). See *Ageratina altissima*
riparian doctrine. *See* water rights
roads, early Bluegrass, 29–31; macadamized, 30, 285n46; turnpike construction in Bluegrass, 30–31
Roanoke Gap, 40

Robison, Brandon, on fraudulent land claims, 57
Rockcastle County (Kentucky), and Wilderness Trail, 106
Rockcastle River, and Daniel Boone, 65
Rodman, William B.: on groundwater quality, 207; on sanitation and disease, 206–7, 213; on typhoid, waterborne, 213
Ross, Webb, property purchased by Keene Richards, 165
Royal Proclamation of 1763, 44–46, *45* (map); anger generated by, 45–46; boundary adjusted, 46; effect on land speculators, 46, 49; Indian Reserve created by, 44; land grants forbidden by, 44; unenforceable, 46; western settlement banned by, 35, 44
Royal Spring, xv, 115, 146, *176*, *190*, *243*; on 1824 Georgetown plat, *148*, 156; aesthetic appeal of, 1, 157, 170, 234, 236; alternate names for, 101–2; art depicting, 34, *160*; Cane Run and, 220; cholera and, 203; as city park, 34, 101; contamination, potential sources of, 209–10, 213–14, 215, 218, 229–30; contamination of, 219–20, 228–29, 232; contamination of, measures against, 208, 209–10; conveyed to Trigg heirs, 143; Elijah Craig, land sold to, 144, 147; discovery, 1, 77, 80, 90, 120–21; described, 121, 170, 131, 273, 314n17; dispute over water rights to, 22–25, 188–97, *190*; discharge volume of, 189, 193, 224, 230; explored by divers, 224; fertility of site, 11; fire engines, supplied by, 178; Floyd's survey of, 121–22; Georgetown Ice Co. and, 187; Georgetown Street Railway and, 187; groundwater tracing of, xiii, 215–16, 220, 221–23, 225–26, 228; insufficient for future demand, 233; insufficient to supply Toyota, 33, 230–31; karst flow system, potential length of, 81; karst flow system, travel times, 230; Kentucky Utilities substation and, 243, 246–*47*; known to John McClelland, 125; largest in central Kentucky, 266; location, 101, 152; master conduit of, 224–27; McClelland's Station and, 2–3, 7, 35, 100, 125, 130, 131, 132, 137, 138; mills and mill dams on, 31, 101; monument at, 141, 237; named by John McClelland, 125; National Register of Historic Places listing, 245; North Elkhorn Creek and, 78, 157; ownership, question of, 187–97; recreation and, 158; recharge area, delineation of, xiv, 203, 215–16, 220–27, 228; recharge area of, speculation on, 209–10, 214, 215, 218, 219, 220; sanitary regulations and, 198–99; stewardship of, 34; tourism and, 248; type of spring, 78; typhoid and, 213–14, 215; unfamiliar to new residents, 252; vegetation around, presettlement, 87–91; Vulcan Quarry Cave and, 224–25; water hauling from, 159–61, *179*; water intake pipes in, 188–90, 191, 192–93, 196, 197; water quality of, 198, 210, 213–14, 226–27; water rationing from, 194, 231; as water supply, xiv, xv, 1, 2, 11, 22–23, 25, 33, 101–2, 114, 122, 156, 159–61, 170, 179–82, *179*, *183*, *186*, 184–98, 199, 201, 203, 207–8, 210, 213–17, 219, 227–31, 232, *240*, 251; water supply protection program of, 218, 227–30, *229*; water treatment of, 215–18; water works and, 180–81. *See also* Georgetown Water, Gas, Electric Light and Power Company; Royal Spring Park; Royal Spring Water Supply Protection Program; Water Supply Company of Georgetown
Royal Spring Branch, 29, 120, 151, 327n32; baptisms and, 159; bridge over, 157–58, *158*, 245, 307n6; dams and mills on, 31, 101, 149–50, 151–52, 157, 208–9, 234, 245;

Georgetown, boundary with, 22–23, *148*, 156–57, 188, 195; as green space, 234, 245, 248; industrial degradation of, 34, 234, *243*, 248; livestock use of, 156, 207; north of bridge, 245, 252, 255; recreation on, 158; renovation of, 251–52; springhouse in, 156, 207, 306n2; wall dividing, 156, 157, 207, 306n2, 314n17; wall lining east bank of, 157, 307n5; waterfowl in, 157. *See also* Commons

Royal Spring Branch Distillery: David Adams and, 270–71; established, 270–71; Jeff Mattingly, sold to, 271; renamed Bourbon 30, 271

Royal Spring Ice Company: dispute with city, 194, 196–97; established, 184; Royal Spring, drills well above, 194; warehouse of, *183*. *See also* Georgetown Ice Company

Royal Spring Park, *261*; accessibility issues, 261–62, 263; acreage of, 327n32; Arts in the Park and, 252; Big Royal Spring, Inc. and, 245–46; Ann Bolton Bevins and, 245–46; budget cuts to, 255, 260; city comprehensive plan recommends, 245, 252; Elijah Craig, statues in, *152*, 269–70; early movement for, 236–37, 241–44; economic potential of, 263; established, 101, 245–46; expansion north of bridge, 245, 252, 255, 261; festivals in, *253*; as green space, 248, 252; Jesse Lewis log cabin at, 248; map of, *268*; Mayors Institute design challenge for, 261–62; McClelland's fort replica and, 243, 245, 246–47, 266, 267, *268*; McConnell Springs Park, compared to, 266; Milton Leach cabin at, 247–48, *249*; Tom Prather, support for, 248, *250*; Scott County Historical Society and, 245; Scruggs and Hammond, feasibility study for, 245, 252, 255; shelter built for, 259; Thomas K. Shuff and, 245; spring as attraction for, 265; state park, potential as, 267, 269; tourism potential, 266; University of Cincinnati recommendations for, 262–63; World Equestrian Games and, 259. *See also* Royal Spring Park design challenge

Royal Spring Park design challenge: challenge presented by Tom Prather, 261; citizen involvement, 262; development, author's recommendations for, 266–67; Georgetown, visited by design team for, 262; Mayors Institute for City Design workshop and, 261; recommendations incorporated in comprehensive plan, 263; Royal Spring Park accessibility issues, 262; Royal Spring Park and Main Street, focus of, 262. *See also* Georgetown/Scott County 2017 Comprehensive Plan

Royal Spring Water Supply Protection Program: objectives of, 228; multi-jurisdictional approach, 228; as pilot program, 228; signage of, *229*

Royle Spring (Lexington), viii

Rucker addition (subdivision): and Blue Grass Park, 210; contamination, potential source of, 210; groundwater tracing from, 210; sinkholes in, 210

Ruddles Station (Harrison County), 7

Russell, William: sends warning to Kentucky surveyors, 120; Tories settled on his land, 127

Russell Cave (Fayette County), 88, *222*

Russell County (Virginia), 120

Rutherford County (North Carolina), 67

rye. See *Elymus* sp.

Sadieville (Scott County): and central place theory, 26; population, 26

Safe Drinking Water Act, and Water Supply Protection programs, 227–28

Salt Lick (Bath County), and Warriors' Path, 105

Salt Lick Creek (Lewis County): McClelland journey and, 124, 125; site of Vanceburg, 124
saltpeter, mined from caves, xi
Salt River, 118, 143; cane lands on, 4; salt licks on, 106
Samuels family: and Jeff Mattingly, 271; and Maker's Mark bourbon, 271
Sanders, Lewis, on "first" industries, 305n8
Sanitation, water supply: cholera and, 203–4, 317n13; at Fort Harrod, 113; at Lexington, 113; measures taken for, 19, 113, 198–99, 214–18, 236; at Royal Spring, 113; sanitary movement and, 18, 235
savanna woodland, 90; bison and, 83; as component of local ecologies, 87; as created landscape, 84, *84*, 86, 90; critiqued by Campbell, 83–84, 86; Ursula Davidson and, 83; dendrochronology and, 85; as dominant vegetation, presettlement, 81, *82*, 83; as ecological myth, 81, *82*; evidence contradicting, 85–87; hypothesis of, 83; Native Americans and, 83; present-day, 83, *84*, 86, 90; prominent tree species of, 83; promoted by Bryant and Wharton, 83; promoted by Wharton and Barbour, 83; Raitz and Van Dommelen and, 84–85; as romantic stereotype, 84; as widely accepted ecological interpretation, 81
Sayre Bank (Lexington): Keene Richards, indebted to, 175; Keene Richards sued by, 175; purchases Blue Grass Park at auction, 175, 177; sells Blue Grass Park to Grinstead, 175, 177
Schu, Sandy, and Elijah Craig, sculpture of, 152, 270
Scioto River, Ohio, and Lower Shawnee Town, 105
Scioto Valley, Ohio, Shawnee of, 63
Scott, Abram, Georgetown blacksmith, 248
Scott, Charles: and Battle of Fallen Timbers, 9; George Rogers Clark and, 67; on rapid growth of corn in Kentucky, 67
Scott, Patrick, and Charles Scott recollections, 67
Scott County, Kentucky, xiv, 1, *2* (map), 7, 110; agricultural economy of, 32; Arts and Cultural Welcome Center of, 254–55; Arts Consortium, Inc., of, 254; Black population of, 241; Bicentennial Commission of, 246; and bourbon, invention of, 153; Buffalo Path (Alanant-o-wamiowee) and, 106; Cane Run in, 91, *224*; cholera in, 201; Circuit Court of, 156, 192, 195–96, 209, 217; Confederacy, support for, 12, 170; created, 57, 147, 152; Detention Center of, 253; Elkhorn Creek in, 79–80; Fiscal Court of, 232, 246, 254, 321n21; Georgetown, county seat of, *2* (map), *8* (map), 11; growth rate, 233; Inner Bluegrass, included in, 75, 77; karst research in, xiii, 221–23; historical pageant in, 239–41; Historical Society of, 245; horse sales in, 257; horses, number of, 257; landless households in 1792, 57; Legacy Trail in, 263; McClelland's Station in, 7; John Hunt Morgan and, 170; population of, 233; racetracks in, 257; reservoir planned for, 231, 232, 233; Revolutionary War dead of, 141; road to Cincinnati, 30; salt lick in, 94, 106; Slack's Cave in, 80; slavery in, 32, 241; springs in, 102–3; tavern, first in, 155; tourism and, 259, 260; Toyota in, *2*, 33; traversed by Gist, 41; typhoid in, 212; water supply of, 230–33; Woman's Club of, 239, 241
Scott County Arts and Cultural Welcome Center: discontinued in 2020, 255; and old jail conversion, 254. *See also* Georgetown/Scott County Tourism Commission

Scott County Arts Consortium, Inc., and old jail conversion, 254
Scott County Bicentennial Commission, McClelland fort replica, supports, 246
Scott County Circuit Court: *A. K. Lair v. City of Georgetown and Georgetown Water Company*, 196, 209; and boundaries of Georgetown, 156; *City of Georgetown v. Georgetown Water, Gas, Electric and Power Company*, 217; *City of Georgetown v. Water Supply Company*, 195–96; *Water Supply Company v. City of Georgetown*, 193
Scott County Detention Center, replaces old city jail, 254
Scott County Fiscal Court: jail conversion, provides grant for, 254; McClelland fort replica, supports, 246; and reservoir site, proposed, 232, 321n21
Scott County Historical Society: Royal Spring Park and, 245; Thomas K. Shuff, president of, 245
Scott County Woman's Club: as Civic League, 244; and historical pageant, 239; and Royal Spring Park, 241, 242, 244
Scruggs and Hammond, Inc., and Royal Spring Park, 245
Sendlein, Lyle V.: karst research program of, 221; succeeds John Thrailkill, 221
settlements: abandonment of, 3, 9, 11, 114, 142; archaeological studies of, 133; central place theory and, 25; construction of, 134–35, *136*, 137; crowding in, 139; defenses of, 5–6, 9, 130, 131, 137–38; of eastern colonies, 13–14; as forts and stations, 6–7; gunpowder, shortage in, 139, 140, 142; of Inner Bluegrass, 3, *8* (map), 10; Inner Bluegrass, peripheral to, 3; Kentucky, earliest in, xv, 4–5, 7, 10; of Nashville Basin, 3; on rivers, 13–14; salt supply of, xii, 108; site and situational factors in, 6, 13, 25, 102, 111; springs and pattern of, xii, 2, 102, 108, 110–11; in violation of British policy, 35, 44–46, 53; water supply of, 6, 7, 20, 111. *See also individual forts and stations*
settlers: abandoned settlements, 3, 9, 11, 114, 142; behavior of, 97–99, 98; hardships endured by, 3, 95–98; increasing numbers of, 9, 35, 46, 53, 109, 129; Indian warfare and, 4, 5, 7, 9, 46, 97, 109, 118, 120, 122, 129, 130, 139, 140–42, 143, 149; Inner Bluegrass, focus on, 3, 27, 53, 60; land claiming activities, xii, 6–7, 35, 56, 109–11, 117–18, 138–39; land clearing by, 98–99, 138; landless households, 57; land loss to gentry, 97; lawless behavior, 97; majority in Bluegrass region, 57; motivations of, 35, 36–37, 72–73, 95; orientation on arrival, 6; poverty of, 96; resentment of later arrivals, 97; residing in public forts, 3, 5–6, 9, 10–11, 27, 57, 96, 111, 138, 139; residing in stations, 7, 9, 10–11, 96, 111, 130, 134, 135, *136*, 137, 138, 139; routes taken by, 60, 103, 104–7, 108; Scotch-Irish ancestry of, 97; slaughter of wildlife by, 99–100; springs, importance to, 102, 108–9, 110–11; women and children, scarcity of, 128. *See also* land
Seven Years' War, 43, 44. *See also* French and Indian War
sewage disposal: development of sewers for, 17; environmental degradation by, 17; Georgetown, construction of sewers for, 18; Lexington, construction of sewers for, 18; privies and cesspools for, 17
sewage treatment, 18
Shawnee Indians: attack on Patterson camp, 139; Battle of Fallen Timbers and, 9; Battle of Point Pleasant and, 49, 122; captives of Iroquois, 61; at Chillicothe council, 99; Dunmore's War and, 48, 122, 123; early descriptions of Kentucky from, 61;

Eskippakithiki village and, 62–63; French and Indian War and, 61; habitation of Kentucky, 61; Iroquois, conflicts with, 61; Lower Shawnee Town of, 105; raids on settlements by, 4, 5, 129; relocation north of Ohio River, 3–4, 61, 63; threat of war with, 117, 122, 129; Treaty of Logstown and, 38; Treaty of Stanwix and, 4, 118
Shawnee Run (Mercer County), 109
Shelby, John T., buys and sells Blue Grass Park, 177
Shenandoah Valley; settlements in, 47; and Treaty of Lancaster, 38
Sherritt, Frank: hosts race meeting, 168; manager of Blue Grass Park, 168
Shipp, Laban, and Shipp's Station, 87
Shipp, Mary "Polly," on vegetation of Scott County, 87
Shipp's Station, 87
Shuff, Thomas K.: president of Historical Society, 245; proposes Royal Spring Park, 245
Simpson, John, former director of tourism commission, 260
Sinclair, Abner H. (former mayor of Georgetown), and Royal Spring water rights dispute, 192
sinkholes: groundwater contamination and, 17; groundwater tracing and, xiii; karst systems and, x, xi, xiv, 16, 77, *78*, 80; Lexington ordinance concerning, 251; Royal Spring, connections to, 203, 209, 210, 214, 215–16, 219, 220, 230; urban development and, xi; waste disposal, used for, xi, 17, 251
situational factors in urban growth and development: defined, 13; central place theory and, 25–26; role of water as, 13–14
Slack's Cave, Scott County: historical account, 80–81; parallels Royal Spring system, 80
slavery/enslaved people: Ansel, 169; in eastern colonies, 35; in Georgetown, pioneer era, 11; Christopher Gist, companion of, 41; headright grants and, 47; historical pageant, reference to, 241; in Kentucky, 1777, 142; Kentucky, myth of mild form of, 241; at McClelland's Station, 139; Milton Leach, 248; Pompey, 166; Scott County, in economy, 32; Scott County, percent of population, 241; at Transylvania Plantation (Louisiana), 169, 172, 174; on Wilderness Trail with Boone, *52*; William Hayden, 150
Smith, Blake, on risk of Indian attack, 95
Smith, Edmund Kirby, and Confederate invasion of Kentucky, 170
Smith, James, 107
Smithfield Plantation (Virginia): John Floyd returns to, 122; home of William Preston, 115, 118
Snow, John: on cholera as waterborne disease, 19–20; and germ theory of disease, 20
South Carolina, Cherokee in, 61
Spain, cedes Florida to Britain, 43
Spangler, Lawrence E.: Gary O'Dell, field assistant of, xiii, 223; Royal Spring, basin delineation by, 223; Royal Spring and Cane Run, studies, xiii, 222–23; student of John Thrailkill, *222*
speculators. *See* land speculators
Spencer, John H. and Burlilla B., criticize Elijah Craig, 148
Spears, Jacob, alleged inventor of bourbon, 153
Spirit of the Times (newspaper), ownership and name changes, 309n5
Spotsylvania County (Virginia): Traveling Church and, 145
springs: Kentucky, abundance of, 102–3; artesian springs, 78; base level springs, 78; source in underground lakes, belief, 15, 219; gravity springs, 78; Indian ambushes at, 109; in karst flow systems, 77–78; Kentucky settlement, influence on, xii, 102, 108; as landmarks in frontier, xi–xii, 102, 108,

109, 111; manufacturing, use in, xii; mineral springs, xii, 102; modifications to, 103, 114; in mythology, xi; pioneer terms for types of, 110; perched springs, 77, 78; proximity to forts, 111, *112*, 298n18; purity, perception of, 15, 102, 218; real estate advertising and, 113; salt production, use in, xii; sanitation and, 111, *112*; types, 78; as water supplies, x, 6, 7, 14, 102, 111, *112*, 113, 114; whiskey production, use in, xii. *See also* licks; *and specific springs*
St. Asaph's, 7; established, 5, 126; land court at, 55, Benjamin Logan and, 126; 110; Stanford and, 126. *See also* Logan's Fort
St. Lawrence River, as gateway to west, 38, 43
Stamp Act (1765), 46
Stamping Ground (Scott County): bison trails and, 94, 106; and central place theory, 26; population, 26
Stanford, Kentucky: and Logan's Fort replica, 267; and St. Asaph's, 5, 126. *See also* Logan's Fort; St. Asaph's
stations, 57; abandoned, 3, 9, 11, 114, 130, 142; crowded conditions, 139; defensive network, part of, 9; defined, 7; kinship ties of residents, 139; as landmarks, 111; locations, *8*; phases in establishment, 10; public forts, differences from, 7, 137; as refuges, 138, 139; size, 7; sloping ground and, 131; springs and, 111; temporary occupancy, 139. *See also individual stations*
Stedman, Ebenezer: on cholera at Georgetown, 202; on Craig's fulling mill, 149–50; Craig's paper mill, leased by, 151; on paper manufacture, 151; Royal Spring, on appearance of, 157
Steffee (person in Georgetown), death from cholera, 202
Steele, Andrew, settlement certificate, 110
Steele's Run (Fayette County), 110
Sterrett, James, 125
Sterrett, Sarah, 124. *See* Lowry, Sarah
stinging nettle. See *Urtica dioica*
Stockades: blockhouses in, 137; construction of, 135, 137; corner cabins and, 135; gates in, 137; portholes for sharpshooters in, 137; watchtowers on, 137
Stone Lick (Mason County), McClelland journey and, 125
Stoner, Michael, sent to warn Kentucky surveyors, 120, 122
Strode's Station (Clark County), 7
Sugar Act (1764), 46
sugar maple. See *Acer saccharum*
Susquehanna Gap, Great Wagon Road and, 40
Sutton, William L., *205*; cholera, directs preparations for, 204, *205*; and first vital statistics law, *205*; Georgetown trustees, chair of, 204; and Kentucky State Medical Society, *205*; on typhoid, epidemic of 1840s, 212; on typhoid, transmission of, 212; on typhoid, treatise by, *205*, 212
Sycamore Shoals (Tennessee): Henderson negotiates with Cherokee, 50; Watauga River and, 50
Szwirschina, Mary, costumer for historical pageant, 240

Taconic Orogeny, Bluegrass geologic structure and, 75
Taylor, Hancock, Elkhorn Creek, discovers, 80
Taylor, John: criticizes Elijah Craig, 148; on journey of Traveling Church, 145–46
Taylor, Samuel, attorney for John Cobbs, 147
Teays River: Kentucky River and, 79; as precursor to Ohio River, 79
Tennessee: Cherokee in, 61; Cincinnati Arch in, 75; Cumberland Gap and, 43; Nashville Basin/Dome, 3, 75,

292n3; settlements in northeast, 40; staging ground for Kentucky settlement, 40, 43
Teute, Fredrika, on landless households in Kentucky, 57
Thomas, Elizabeth, on John McClelland gravesite, 302n27
Thomasson, John C., on typhoid outbreak in Georgetown, 213
Thompson, James and John, death from cholera, 201
Thoroughbred horse. *See* horses
Thrailkill, John: and Douglas R, Gouzie, 230; graduate students directed by, 221–23; karst research program of, xiii, 221, *222*; retirement of, 221; Royal Spring, flow travel time estimation by, 230; succeeded by Lyle Sendlein, 221
Tidewater, region of Virginia, 47
Tingle-Sames, Karen (former mayor), and Royal Spring Park, 255
Todd, John (JT): attacked by Indians, 140; gunpowder and, 140; killed at Blue Licks, 302n26; Lexington defenses and, 27; McClelland's Station, helps fortify, 130; Todd's Spring and cabin of, 108
Todd, Levi (brother of JT), 294n21, 302n26; describes attack on McClelland's Station, 88; endorses Filson's *Kentucke*, 70; on water scarcity in Bluegrass, 108
Todd, Robert (brother of JT), 294n21; wounded at McClelland's station, 141, 294n21
Topographical Description of the Western Territory of North America (Imlay), 72
Toulmin, Harry, on growth of corn in Bluegrass, 67
Tourism: cultural heritage, 244, 245, 263–64, 266; festivals, local, 257–58, *258*, 260; in Georgetown/Scott County, 254–55, 255, 257–60, 267; Kentucky, impact of, 264; Kentucky Horse Park and, 256, 257, 258, 259, 260; leisure travel defined, 326n30; Old Fort Harrod State Park and, 264; Royal Spring and, 244, 245, 266, 267; World Equestrian Games and, 257–60. *See also* cultural heritage tourism
Town Branch (Lexington), Ater Spring on, viii; cholera and, 201; flow of, 28; as middle fork of Elkhorn, 21; Royle Spring on, viii; springs on, 21
Town Creek (Harrodsburg), Harrod's Fort and, 265
Townsend Creek: Buffalo Path (Alanant-o-Wamiowee) and, 125; McClelland journey and, 125
Townshend Acts (1767), 46
Toyota Motor Manufacturing of Kentucky: employment, 33, 231; and Georgetown, economic development of, *12*, 13, 27, 33, 230–31, 252; and Georgetown, established at, 33, 230; and Georgetown, population growth of, 13, 27, 33, 231, 252; incentives package offered to, 231; Kentucky American Water Co. supplies, 33, 231; location of, *2* (map); water requirements of, 231
traces. *See* trails
trading posts: British compared to French, 62; George Croghan and, 62; at Eskippakithiki, 62; John Findlay and, 62
trails: Buffalo Path (Alanant-o-wamiowee), 106–7; buffalo traces, known as, 103; created by bison, 4, 27, 29, 41, 86, 90, 94, 103–8, 125, 140, 141, 146, 304n3; Great Indian Warpath (Athawominee), 40, 105; improved to roads, 27; and Leestown ford, 93, 94, 106, 124, 125, 129; map of, *107*; Middle Trace, 125; to Royal Spring, 94; Warriors' Path, 104–5; Wilderness Trail, 27, *52*, 58, 95, 104, 106. *See also* bison; roads
Transylvania Colony (Kentucky) 49–53, *50* (map), 54; boundaries, 50;

condemned, 51; established, 5, 50; Richard Henderson and, 49–53, 67, 127, 129; House of Delegates of, 51; land titles and, 129; purchase voided by Virginia, 53, 140; secondary speculators and, 52; validity of prior land claims, 52; validity of purchase challenged, 51–52; viewed as a feudal estate, 51; violates colonial laws, 51; violates Royal Proclamation of 1763, 51. *See also* Transylvania Company; Henderson, Richard

Transylvania Company: Louisa Company and, 49; Richard Henderson and, 49–53

Transylvania Plantation (Louisiana): confiscated during war, 172; cotton cultivation on, 174, 175; Keene Richards and, 165, 169, 171, 172, 174, 175; enslaved people on, 169, 172

Traveling Church: Elijah, Lewis, and Joseph Craig and, 145; William Ellis and, 145; Gilberts Creek Church, founded by, 146; Great Crossings Church, founded by, 146; John Taylor describes journey, 145–46; Upper Spotsylvania Church (Virginia), former, 145; Wilderness Road followed by, 146

Treaty of Fort Stanwix (1768), and Indian land cession, 4, 118

Treaty of Greenville (1795), 9

Treaty of Lancaster (1744): differing interpretations of, 38; modified by Treaty of Logstown, 38

Treaty of Logstown, (1752): disputed by Shawnee and Cherokee, 38; Kentucky ceded to Virginia, 38

Treaty of Paris (1763): provisions of, *39*, 43–44

Trent, William: and fort at Forks of the Ohio, 42; and Ohio Company, 42

Trifolium sp. (clover), 81, 87, 91, 93, 95; buffalo (*Trifolium reflexum*), 91; as component of savanna woodland, 83; running (*Trifolium stoloniferum*), 91; white (*Trifolium repens*), 91

Trigg, Stephen: John Cobbs sues heirs of, 144, 146–47, 303n33; killed at Blue Licks, 143; as land commissioner, 55, 143; residence near Harrod's Fort, 143; Royal Spring property exchange with Floyd, 143, 303n31; Royal Spring tract, sells to John Cobbs, 143

Troester, Joseph W.: Royal Spring, basin delineation by, 221–22; Royal Spring and Cane Run, studies, 222; student of John Thrailkill, 221

Troye, Edward, *173*; biographer of, 172; as British subject, 172; connives with Richards to avoid property loss, 172, 175; conveys interest in Blue Grass Park, 175; cosigns notes for Richards, 174; death and burial of, 175; friendship with Richards, 168, 172, *173*, 174; as livestock artist, 168, 175; Middle East, trip to, 168; painting of Mokhladi by, *164*; studio of, 164, 168

Turf, Field and Farm: Hamilton Busbey, editor of, 177; eulogizes Keene Richards, 177; praises Keene Richards's racing stock, 174

turkey. See *Meleagris gallopavo*

Typhoid: carriers of, asymptomatic, 211; diagnosis of, 211; in Georgetown, 210; global incidence, modern, 317n21; misidentified as typhus, 211; pathogens responsible for, 210; symptoms of, 211–12; transmission of, 210–11; Typhoid Mary (Mary Mallon) and, 211, 317n21; United States (1909), endemic in, 210; United States (1909), prevalence, morbidity, and mortality of, 210, 212, 213; as waterborne disease, 18

Typhoid in Georgetown: 1840s outbreak, 212; 1908 outbreak, 210, 213–14, 218; Franklin Ferguson, death from, 213; prevalence, morbidity, and mortality

(1908), 213; Royal Spring, attributed to, 213–14
Typhus, 211

Ulmus sp. (elm), 86, 88, 90, 91, 122
University of Cincinnati, School of Planning: College of Design, Architecture, Art and Planning, unit of, 262; faculty of, 262; Mayors Institute for City Design (2015), hosted by, 261; recommendations for Georgetown, 263
University of Kentucky: student research of, xiii, 83, 221–26, *222*, 227, 228; Maxwell H. Gluck Equine Research Center of, 256
Upper Howard's Creek (Clark County), site of Eskippakithiki village, 63
Ursus americanus (black bear), 74; hunted by Daniel Boone, 66; decline in numbers, 99; fear of, 98; hunted by Walker party, 93; as threat to livestock, 100
Urtica dioica (stinging nettle), 91
US Council of Mayors, Royal Spring Park design challenge and, 261

Vanceburg, Kentucky, region of: Christopher Gist arrives at, 41; McClelland party arrives at, 124; Salt Lick Creek and, 124
Van Dommelen, Dorn, on symbolic landscapes, 84–85
Varney, Everette, former mayor of Georgetown, 260
vegetation: Lucy Braun on, 81; Julian Campbell on, 83–84, 86, 87, 88–90; forests compared to woodlands, 81, 83; edge habitats, 91, 92; of Elkhorn region, 87, 88–90; meadows/grasslands, 81, 87, 93, 94; pioneer accounts of, 83, 85; presettlement, 81–93; of southern Scott County, 87; understory, 83; woodlands, defined, 81–82. *See also* savanna woodland; *and individual species*
Versailles (Woodford County), xii; and central place theory, 26; as county seat, *9* (map), 11
Vincennes (Indiana): bison ford of Wabash River at, 106; George Rogers Clark and, 105
Virginia, 43; boundaries by 1609 royal charter, 37–38; Cherokee in, 61; conflict with France, 42; Cumberland Gap and, 43; currency depreciation of, 56; declares independence from Britain, 64; fortifies the Forks of the Ohio, 42; General Assembly of, 47, 54, 140; governor Robert Dinwiddie of, 42; House of Burgesses of, 54; land laws of, 6–7, 47, 54–56; Piedmont region of, 47; population expansion of, 47; Revolutionary War debts, 55; Tidewater region of, 47; Shenandoah Valley of, 38, 47; Virginia Conventions, 53–54
Virginia Land Commission: certificates issued by, 55, 57, 109–10; and claims, conflicting and fraudulent, 56; commissioners in Kentucky of, 55, 97, 143; established, 55, 110; land courts of, 55
Vulcan Materials Company: quarry operations of, 225; Royal Spring conduits, intercepted by, 225; Vulcan Quarry Cave, breaks into, 225, *226*
Vulcan Quarry Cave: description of, 225; entrance of, 225, *226*; Doug Graham discovers, 225; Royal Spring, groundwater trace from, 225–26; Royal Spring master conduit and, 225–26

Wabash River, Indiana, bison ford at Vincennes, 106
Walker, Felix: on Bluegrass region, 67, 95; present at Henderson's purchase, 67; helps blaze Wilderness Trail, 67, 95
Walker, Thomas, 65; Braddock's expedition and, 63; and Cumberland

Gap, 41, 65; journal of, 41, 61; Kentucky, description of, 40; Kentucky, explorations of, 40–41, 72; Loyal Company and, 40; oral dissemination of report, 62; on wild game, 93
walnut. See *Juglans* sp.
Walnut Hill Farm, bur oak on, *82*
Walton, H. B., limestone waters theory of cholera and, 200
Walton, John, Filson, biographer of, 68
Warriors' Path: route described, 105–6; branch of Great Indian Warpath (Athawominee), 105
Washington, George: Braddock's expedition and, 63; demands French abandon Ohio Valley forts, 42; Christopher Gist and, 42
Washington County, Virginia (Kentucky country), created, 127
Watauga River, Tennessee: Henderson negotiates with Cherokee at, 50, 67. *See also* Sycamore Shoals
water: and location of early American settlements, 13; and location of Kentucky cities, 14; as site and situational factor, 13
water gaps: access to Great Appalachian Valley by, 38; defined, development of, 286n8
water pollution: by cesspools and privies, 17; by chemical pollutants, 218, 220, 228–29; cities and, 17–18; in karst, 16–17, 198, 201, 203; of Ohio River, 15; and pathogenic disease, 18, 20, 206–7, 212, 218; point sources of, 16; nonpoint sources of, 16–17; of Royal Spring, 203, 207–8, 209–10, 213–16, 217, 220, 227, 228–30, 232; Safe Drinking Water Act and, 227; sewers and, 17–18; Water Supply Protection programs and, 227–30, *229*; water treatment of, 215, 216–18, 229. *See also* diseases, waterborne
water rights: in English common law, 23; Georgetown, dispute with water company over, 188–97; in groundwater, 23–24; litigation concerning, 193, 194–97; principle of natural flow, 23; principle of prior appropriation, 23; riparian doctrine, 23, 24, 188; Royal Spring and, 23, 24–25
Water Street: A-1 Auto Parts store on, 270; Blue Grass Park gate on, 166; Bourbon 30 blenders on, 271; ice company buildings on, *183*; Kentucky Utilities property on, 130, 185, 243, 246, 247, *247*, 266, 267, *268*; North Water Street development, 245, 255, 261, 252, 262; old jail on, 252–55; Royal Spring Branch Distillery on, 270–71; town Commons on, 157; washerwomen of, 160–61; water plant on, 185, *183*, 188
water supply: effects of population growth on source type, 20–22; Lexington's historic evolution of, 20–21; public systems, 179; rainwater collection for, 21, 22, 114; reservoirs used for, 21, 22, 114, 179; sanitation and, 111, *112*, 113; springs as source of, 20, 111, *112*, 113–14; wells used for, 21, 22, 114. *See also specific communities*
Water Supply Company of Georgetown: completes electric plant, 184; dispute with city, 23, 24–25; 188–97, *190*; Georgetown Electric Railway Co. established by, 184; Georgetown Ice Co., acquired by, 184, 189; incorporated, 182, 184; Henry P. Montgomery, president of, 182, 184; purchase by city, proposed, 184; purchased by Robert W. Nelson, 184; Royal Spring and, 188–97, *190*; Royal Spring Ice Co., established by, 184; sold at auction, 184; stockholders of, 184; Street Railway Co., acquired by, 184
Water Supply Protection programs: of Calvert City, 228; of Elizabethtown,

228; of Georgetown, 228–30; Kentucky Division of Water and, 229; authorized by Safe Drinking Water Act, 227–28. *See also* Royal Spring Water Supply Protection Program
water works, Georgetown: constructed for, 161, 198; Nichols and Patterson, contract for, 180–81; proposals for, 179–80; water rates, 181. *See also* Georgetown Water, Gas, Electric Light and Power Company; Nichols and Patterson; Water Supply Company of Georgetown
Watson, Patty Jo, on prehistoric cave explorers, xi
Waugh, Alexander, and Royal Spring tract, 299n8
Wayne, Anthony, and Battle of Fallen Timbers, 9
Wellhead Protection Programs. *See* Water Supply Protection programs
western paradise, myth of: Daniel Boone and, 62, 66; John Brown Sr. and, 66; Lewis Craig and, 66; John Findlay and, 62; ideal climate of, 61, 97; religious roots of, 68; reports on Bluegrass alluding to, 3, 66–67; Felix Walker and, 66
Wharton, Mary E.: *Bluegrass Land and Life*, 83; William S. Bryant and, 83; critiqued by Campbell, 83; Ursula Davidson and, 83; savanna woodland hypothesis and, 83
White, Charles, killed at McClelland's Station, 141
White Hall State Park: Cassius Marcellus Clay and, 269; given to Eastern Kentucky University, 269
white snakeroot (richweed). See *Ageratina altissima*
Wigglesworth, Michael, and fear of American forests, 98
Wilderness Trail (Boone's), 27, 127; new route blazed by Daniel Boone, 50–51, *52*, 95, 105–6; Felix Walker and, 95. *See also* Wilderness Road; Wilderness Trail (old)
Wilderness Trail (old): and bison traces, 106; continues into Indiana, 106; as Indian trail, 40, 105–6; route of, 106. *See also* Wilderness Trail (Boone's)
Wilderness Road (Kentucky), 98, 106, 146; Great Valley, separate from road of, 286n8; immigrants on, 58; Powell's Valley and, 127. *See also* Wilderness Trail
Wilderness Road (Virginia–Tennessee): branch of Great Wagon Road, 40; located in Great Appalachian Valley, 286n8
Wildlife: birds of prey, 100; decline of, 99–100; efforts to eliminate non-game species, 100; game animals, abundance of, 66, 74, 93, 94, 95; non-game species, 94, 98, 100; slaughtered by settlers, 99. *See also individual species*
Williams, John: Simon Kenton and, 125; Robert Patterson, encounter with, 125
Williamsburg, Virginia, 67
William White House State Park, given to Lincoln County Fiscal Court, 269
wind gaps, 41, 286n8
Wilson, Joseph, marries Sarah McClelland, 129
Wilson Spring: exaggerated size, 279–80n5; Lexington, proposed as water supply for, 15–16; Pepper Distillery and, xii. *See also* McConnell Springs
Winchester (Clark County): and central place theory, 26; as county seat, *9* (map), 11
Wolf Run Creek (Lexington), vii
wolves. See *Canis* sp.
Woman's Club. *See* Scott County Woman's Club
Woodford County (Kentucky), 10, 41, 79, 93; created from Fayette, 152;

Elkhorn Creek watershed and, 79–80; Inner Bluegrass, included in, 75; landless households in 1792, 57; Mundy's Landing Cave in, 80; Versailles, county seat of, *8* (map), 11
woodland pastures. *See* savanna woodland
woodlands, 87; compared to forests, 81, 83; factors perpetuating, 90. *See also* savanna woodland
wood nettle. See *Laportea canadensis*
Wooley, Carolyn M., and McConnell Spring, ix
World Equestrian Games: attendance, actual, 260; attendance, expected, 256; economic impact of, 257, 259–60; and Georgetown/Scott County, 257–60; Kentucky Horse Park, venue for, 256, 257, 258, 259, 260; recession, impact on, 260; and visitor origins, 260
Worthington, Edward, wounded at McClelland's Station, 141
Wyandot Indians, 9; at Chillicothe council, 99; attack McClelland's Station, 141–42
Wymore, Martin, 21

Yadkin River Valley (North Carolina), Christopher Gist and, 42; Richard Henderson and, 49
Yarnell, Lundsford P., on cholera at Lexington, 201
York River, Lord Dunmore and, 54
Youtsey, Henry, co-conspirator in Goebel assassination, 253